Palgrave Studies in European Union Politics

Following on the sustained success of the acclaimed *European Union Series*, which essentially publishes research-based textbooks, *Palgrave Studies in European Union Politics* publishes cutting edge research-driven monographs.

The remit of the series is broadly defined, both in terms of subject and academic discipline. All topics of significance concerning the nature and operation of the European Union potentially fall within the scope of the series. The series is multidisciplinary to reflect the growing importance of the EU as a political, economic and social phenomenon. We will welcome submissions from the areas of political studies, international relations, political economy, public and social policy, economics, law and sociology.

Submissions should be sent to Amy Lankester-Owen, Politics Publisher, 'a.lankester-owen@palgrave.com'.

Titles include:

Ian Bache and Andrew Jordan (*editors*)
THE EUROPEANIZATION OF BRITISH POLITICS

Richard Balme and Brian Bridges (*editors*)
EUROPE–ASIA RELATIONS
Building Multilateralisms

Derek Beach and Colette Mazzucelli (*editors*)
LEADERSHIP IN THE BIG BANGS OF EUROPEAN INTEGRATION

Milena Büchs
NEW GOVERNANCE IN EUROPEAN SOCIAL POLICY
The Open Method of Coordination

Dario Castiglione, Justus Schönlau, Chris Longman, Emanuela Lombardo, Nieves Pérez-Solórzano Borragán and Mirim Aziz
CONSTITUTIONAL POLITICS IN THE EUROPEAN UNION
The Convention Moment and its Aftermath

Morten Egeberg (*editor*)
MULTILEVEL UNION ADMINISTRATION
The Transformation of Executive Politics in Europe

Kevin Featherstone and Dimitris Papadimitriou
THE LIMITS OF EUROPEANIZATION
Reform Capacity and Policy Conflict in Greece

Stefan Gänzle and Allen G. Sens (*editors*)
THE CHANGING POLITICS OF EUROPEAN SECURITY
Europe Alone?

Isabelle Garzon
REFORMING THE COMMON AGRICULTURAL POLICY
History of a Paradigm Change

Palgrave Studies in European Union Politics
Series Standing Order ISBN 978–1–4039–9511–7 (hardback)
ISBN 978–1–4039–9512–4 (paperback)

You can receive future titles in this series as they are published by placing a standing order. Please contact your bookseller or, in case of difficulty, write to us at the address below with your name and address, the title of the series and one of the ISBNs quoted above.

Customer Services Department, Macmillan Distribution Ltd, Houndmills, Basingstoke, Hampshire RG21 6XS, England

---

The Protection of Minorities in the Wider Europe

Edited by

Marc Weller

Denika Blacklock

and

Katherine Nobbs

Published under the auspices of the
European Centre for Minority
Issues, Flensburg, Germany, and the Centre for
International Constitutional Studies at the
University of Cambridge

Editorial matter and selection © Marc Weller, Denika Blacklock and
Katherine Nobbs 2008

Individual chapters © contributors 2008

First published 2008 by
PALGRAVE MACMILLAN

Palgrave Macmillan in the UK is an imprint of Macmillan Publishers
Limited, registered in England, company number 785998, of Houndmills,
Basingstoke, Hampshire RG21 6XS.

Palgrave Macmillan in the US is a division of St Martin's Press LLC,
175 Fifth Avenue, New York, NY 10010.

Palgrave Macmillan is the global academic imprint of the above companies
and has companies and representatives throughout the world.

Palgrave® and Macmillan® are registered trademarks in the United States,
the United Kingdom, Europe and other countries.

ISBN-13: 978–0–230–00129–9
ISBN-10: 0–230–00129–7

This book is printed on paper suitable for recycling and made from
fully managed and sustained forest sources. Logging, pulping and
manufacturing processes are expected to conform to the
environmental regulations of the country of origin.

A catalogue record for this book is available from the British Library.

Library of Congress Cataloging-in-Publication Data
The protection of minorities in the wider Europe / [edited by] Marc
    Weller.
        p. cm. — (Palgrave studies in European Union politics)
    Includes index.
    ISBN 978–0–230–00129–9 (alk. paper)
    1. Minorities—Government policy—Europe. 2. Minorities—Legal
    status, laws, etc.—Europe. I. Weller, M. (Marc)
    JV7590.P77 2008
    323.14—dc22

                                                                2008027565

10   9   8   7   6   5   4   3   2   1
17   16   15   14   13   12   11   10   09   08

Printed and bound in Great Britain by
CPI Antony Rowe, Chippenham and Eastbourne

Contents

**Part III   Minority–Majority Relations in Practice
in an Enlarged EU**

Notes on the Contributors

Denika Blacklock is Programme Analyst with the United Nations Development Programme in Kosovo. She holds a degree in International Conflict Analysis from the University of Kent, Canterbury. Previously, she worked with the European Centre for Minority Issues and the Slovak Institute for International Studies. Her technical and academic work to date has focused on the situation of minorities in transitional and post-conflict countries, with a special interest in institutional reform. Born and raised in Canada, she currently resides in Kosovo.

Martin Brusis is Research Fellow at the Centre for Applied Policy Research, Ludwig-Maximilian University Munich. From 1992 to 1994 he was Research Assistant in a project on 'Institutionalization of Democratic Structures in Post-socialist Societies' at the Institute of Eastern European Affairs, FU Berlin. Currently, the focus of his work is on minority issues in Central and Eastern Europe and on the integration of Central and Eastern European countries into the European Union.

Krzysztof Drzewicki is Senior Legal Adviser to the OSCE High Commissioner on National Minorities. He holds an LLD in International Public Law, and served as Professor of the University of Gdańsk, Poland (on leave since 1997). He has written more than 90 scholarly contributions on the international protection of human rights and international humanitarian law.

Hans-Joachim Heintze is Senior Researcher and Associate at the Institute for International Law of Peace and Armed Conflict at the Ruhr-Universität Bochum and President of the International Association for the Study of the World Refugee Problem (AWR). He has taught and lectured on humanitarian, human rights and international law around the world, and is the author of many specialized contributions on minority rights.

Rainer Hofmann is Professor of International Law at the Johann Wolfgang Goethe University, Frankfurt am Main, Germany, and Director of the Walther-Schücking-Institute for International Law at the University of Kiel, Germany. He is also the former President of the Advisory Committee of the Council of Europe Framework Convention for the Protection of National Minorities; a Member of the Board of the European Centre for Minority Issues, Flensburg, Germany; and a Member of the Academic Advisory Board on International Law to the German Foreign Ministry. He has published extensively in the field of human and minority rights.

Will Kymlicka is currently Canada Research Chair in Political Philosophy at Queen's University in Canada, and a visiting Professor in the Nationalism Studies programme at the Central European University in Budapest. His works have been translated into 30 languages. Since 2004 he has served as President of the American Society for Political and Legal Philosophy.

Tove H. Malloy is Senior Researcher at the Institute for Minority Rights at the European Academy in Bolzen/Bolzano. She is an expert in political system design, and wrote her PhD thesis on human and minority rights in Europe. Previously, she taught part of the European Masters Degree in Human Rights and Democratization in Venice. She is also an experienced diplomatic practitioner.

Katherine Nobbs is Research Associate and Publications Coordinator at the European Centre for Minority Issues in Flensburg, Germany. She holds an MPhil in International Relations from the University of Cambridge, a BA in Politics from the University of Nottingham and a Graduate Diploma in Law from the College of Law, Bloomsbury.

Annemarie Peen Rodt is Research Associate and a doctoral candidate at Nottingham University, specializing in EU Common Foreign and Security Policy towards conflict prevention in the Western Balkans and the South Caucasus. She has worked for the High Representative of the International Community in Peace Implementation in Bosnia-Herzegovina, in the Political Section of the Royal Danish Embassy in Sarajevo and with the European Commission Framework Six Project on Human and Minority Rights in the Life Cycles of Ethnic Conflicts.

Wojciech Sadurski is Professor of Legal Philosophy in the Faculty of Law at the University of Sydney (currently on leave of absence), and Professor of Legal Theory in the Department of Law at the European University Institute in Florence (since September 1999). His research interests include: the philosophy of law, especially moral dimensions of law; theories of rights; freedom of expression; constitutional theory and comparative constitutionalism, notably post-communist constitutional law and constitutional theory; and constitutional aspects of enlargement of the EU.

Nathalie Tocci is Marie Curie Fellow at the Robert Schuman Centre for Advanced Studies, European University Institute, Florence. She holds a PhD in International Relations from the London School of Economics. Her primary research expertise is on the enlargement of the EU, Turkey, Cyprus–EU relations and relations with the Caucasus.

Gabriel von Toggenburg is a Senior Researcher at the European Academy of Bolzano/Bozen responsible for European integration and European Community Law and former PhD researcher at the European University Institute,

Florence. He currently heads the project PECEDE (Platform for an Enriching Culturally and Ethnically Diverse Europe) which focuses *inter alia* on the relationship between EU/EC law and minority protection.

Marc Weller is Director of the European Centre for Minority Issues in Flensburg, Germany. His writings mainly focus on conflict management, issues of international law and minority rights. He has acted as a legal adviser to several governments and organizations, and has been a member of international peace processes. Dr Weller is a Reader in International Law at the University of Cambridge, and a Fellow of the Lauterpacht Research Centre for International Law and Hughes Hall. He is also the Director of the Carnegie Project on Resolving Self-determination Disputes through Complex Power-sharing, and of the Cambridge Rockefeller Project on Restoring an International Consensus of the Rules Governing the Use of Force.

Stefan Wolff is Professor of Political Science at the University of Nottingham, UK, and Senior Non-resident Research Associate at the European Centre for Minority Issues. He holds an MPhil in Political Theory from Magdalene College, Cambridge, and a PhD in Political Science from the London School of Economics. He has written extensively on ethnic conflict and conflict resolution. Published works include *Ethnic Conflict: A Global Perspective*, and the conflict prevention handbook *Power Sharing, Self-governance and Participation in Public Life*. He is also the founding editor of the journal *Ethnopolitics*.

Preface

This book asks whether we are moving towards an integrated system of legal provision for minorities in Europe. This development, while hesitant, is made necessary by the significant number of new members of the European Union. Many of these have a keen interest in seeing minority issues addressed. On the other hand, minority issues remain controversial and suspect to a number of traditional EU member states. It is therefore far from certain how the EU and other institutions in Europe will develop in this respect.

The book considers the evolution of minority governance in Europe, before turning to the mechanisms and institutions available for this purpose. Finally, it addresses minority–majority relations in practice in an enlarged Union, investigating the particular answers that have been found by the recent accession states to the challenges posed by ethnic diversity.

This project originated in discussions held with many of the authors during a conference in Berlin. Further contributions were commissioned in the wake of those discussions in order to present a comprehensive picture of the issues that arise when considering the architecture for minority policies of the future. We are grateful to the original authors, and to those who have joined us in this venture subsequent to our initial discussions.

In addition to the authors, our gratitude extends to those at the European Centre for Minority Issues who supported this project over a significant period. These include Colleen French, Adriana Nikolova, Heu Yee Leung, Janina Dill, Vladislav Michalcik, Stephanie Rehm and, especially, Katherine Nobbs. In addition, Matthew Ward has done a tremendous job in managing the copy-editing process.

We also want to express our gratitude to Amy Lankester-Owen and Gemma D'Arcy Hughes of Palgrave Macmillan Publishers who managed the publications process with a great deal of patience and professionalism.

Flensburg Marc Weller

Introduction: The Outlook for the Protection of Minorities in the Wider Europe

Marc Weller

Europe often considers itself the global champion of the legal provision for minorities. After all, the Council of Europe has generated the world's only legally binding treaties on minority rights in general and on language rights in particular. Compliance with minority rights has been imposed as one of the conditions for entry into the EU of the states of Central and Eastern Europe. Furthermore the Organization for Security and Cooperation in Europe (OSCE) has even created an institution to address issues concerning minorities, the High Commissioner on National Minorities (HCNM). Moreover, the EU seeks to promote the position of minorities in its external relations, especially in its near abroad, in states adjoining the newly expanded EU boundaries.

While this may strike one as an impressive balance sheet relating to EU involvement in minority issues, the reality of the situation is very different. Thus far, no coherent policy on minorities has developed within the EU. Minority issues remain intensely controversial. Four out of the present EU members have not ratified the Council of Europe Framework Convention for the Protection of National Minorities (FCNM), with no less than thirteen remaining outside the ambit of the European Charter for Regional and Minority Languages.[1] This is due to the fact that a small number of states either deny the relevance of the issue or adopt a very restrictive approach to it. France, for instance, has long maintained that it is a state of equal citizens, thereby rendering minority provisions superfluous. Greece has limited the application of minority rights to a distant historical context. Even states that have signed and ratified the Convention have, at times, attempted to limit artificially its scope of application to certain minority groups designated by them. Hence, there was a significant dispute involving the Council of Europe FCNM Advisory Committee and Denmark relating to the possible application of the Convention to members of the Sinti and Roma communities. Other states, in particular in Central and Eastern Europe, tend simply to deny the existence of certain groups for complex historical and political reasons. Hence, no minority protection can be accorded to them. Germany and a number of other states are keen to ensure that the legal framework applicable to minorities

1

is applied to only 'autochtonous' or indigenous groups. This would exclude more recently arrived, often sizeable migrant communities who have settled permanently in EU states.

Some of the more recent EU members are plagued by other concerns. In addition to wishing to exclude the one or other specific group from the definition of minorities, there is the question of substantive entitlements. There is a fear that minority representative groups might deploy the rights granted to them in order to mount a destabilizing political campaign against the central state. This might lead to demands for territorial autonomy, or perhaps even secession, it is sometimes feared.

The EU is a creature of consensus politics. Hence, the position of the Union as an institution on certain issues is disproportionately affected by the concerns of the one or the other of its member states. Given the variety of issues that trouble individual states, this means that the EU indeed may not be best placed to address the issue. Thus far, minority issues have had to be tackled in a fractionated way, almost by stealth. Hence, while the Union has addressed discrimination and social inclusion, cultural diversity, 'lesser-used languages', Roma issues, and several other issues of relevance to minorities, it has been unable to commit itself to initiatives on minorities as such.

This situation did not change with the debate about the Treaty establishing a Constitution for Europe. The drafters managed to include – after much discussion and at the last moment – only a vague reference to minorities among its guiding values. The Charter of Fundamental Rights, which survived the renegotiation process following the failure of the Constitution, does not add anything new. Membership of a national minority is mentioned only as a ground for prohibited discrimination. In this way, the Charter does not really progress beyond the provision for minorities attained at the universal level already in 1966 in the International Covenant on Civil and Political Rights (ICCPR), namely Article 27. That venerable provision originally reflected a very conservative, negative perception of non-discrimination – a view that has long since been overcome in the implementation practice of the ICCPR Human Rights Committee. Modern practice focuses not only on anti-discrimination but also on the obligation of states to create conditions whereby members of minorities can exercise full and effective equality both in law and in fact.

Hesitation in relation to minority issues is of course not only the preserve of the EU. The Council of Europe Framework Convention was drafted as exactly that: a framework. While the provisions of the Convention are legally binding, the states party to it are given a wide margin of appreciation in implementing the commitments that are, in themselves, rather general. With respect to the Language Charter, states have even greater freedom to pick and choose which of the obligations they wish to accept. This approach reflects very much the sense of uncertainty and danger that appears to grip some European governments when engaging with minorities in terms of legal provision. Accordingly, neither of the two treaties was included within the jurisdiction of the European Court of Human Rights. The provisions contained in the Conventions therefore are not directly justiciable at the European level. Thus, the powerful European Court of Human Rights has only been able to address minority issues in an incidental way. Instead of opting for access to a human rights court, each convention was equipped with its own Advisory or Expert Committee to engage states party in a softer form of implementation dialogue.

There is little else to make up for this gap. The innovative Office of the OSCE High Commissioner on National Minorities is restricted in its mandate. Rather than watching over rule-of-law-based implementation, the High Commissioner's mandate is focused on quiet diplomacy as a means of conflict prevention.

It was, of course, the security dimension that led to the development of standards and mechanisms on minorities in Europe in the first instance. While the ethnopolitical conflicts of the immediate post-Cold War years in Europe triggered a strong interest in this area, and a comparatively rapid reaction, this background also created some of the problems we are facing now. Considering minority issues as security problems stigmatizes minorities or states facing difficult ethnic issues. Minorities are seen as the 'problem' that needs addressing if threats to the stability of existing states or their boundaries are to be avoided. Moreover, this approach has led to a claim of double standards. As a price for admittance to the European Club, the states of Central and Eastern Europe claim that they had to accept solutions that would have been unacceptable for many Western European states.

The question is, what happens now, after the initial process of accession is almost complete? Already, several of the newly admitted states are requesting the Union to direct its attention to minority issues. To them, minority issues are not an alien problem affecting states external to the Union. These are internal issues and problems that need to be engaged within the Union. Consider the dispute between Hungary and neighbouring states about the treatment of ethnic Hungarians living abroad. This problem was addressed through the OSCE HCNM. Now, with all the parties to that dispute having joined the EU, the underlying problems brought out into the open in this instance will need to be addressed as a matter of EU internal policy.

In this environment, it will not remain possible for long to pretend that minority issues cannot, or should not, be addressed as minority issues. Consequently, this book seeks to investigate the prospects for the further development of standards, policies and mechanisms that will address minority issues in the future, now that a very major step in the process of EU enlargement has been completed. This question is relevant, as it is undeniable that the Union will now need to address the minority dimension head-on. However, the institutional set-up for this purpose remains haphazard. As the Union has not been able to include minority issues in its foundational instruments in a sufficiently broad way, there is no firm legal basis for engaging with this problem, either now or in the future. Instead, it is likely that the Union will continue to address minority problems indirectly, through its policies on social exclusion, employment, culture, and so on. Over time, this may consolidate into a minority policy in its own right. The newly established EU Fundamental Rights Agency is likely to help consolidate this trend.

In the meantime, however, the Council of Europe will retain its pre-eminence in relation to minority issues within the wider Europe, including the EU area. While the European Court on Human Rights will most likely make some inroads into this area, much of this development will continue to be driven by the Expert or Advisory Committees attached to the two Council of Europe conventions on minorities and by the Council's political bodies. The Parliamentary Assembly, where minorities have gained direct representation in some instances, will continue to press for such action.

When considering the institutional furniture on minority issues in the enlarged EU area, a further question arises. What will be the role of the HCNM? In the past, this institution mainly has addressed minority issues outside the EU, in the East or Centre of Europe. But now, much of that area is part of the EU. The HCNM will need therefore to intrude into the EU area, if it wishes to continue tackling many of the unresolved problems there. Moreover, there will be pressure on the HCNM to address its geographic imbalance by also addressing minority issues and problems in Western Europe.

In addition to these institutional questions, there remains the question of legal standards. The FCNM and the Language Charter are seen by many as somewhat imperfect documents that ought to be reviewed and enhanced. In this way, one might overcome the 'framework' character of the legal commitments made, and the dining *à la carte* approach of the Language Charter. However, at present, there seems little appetite for a major revision of the legal framework among the governments of Europe, including the EU members. There certainly seems little prospect for a EU legal instrument on minorities at present. Nevertheless, there has emerged at least a discussion about having the EU join the relevant Council of Europe legal standards, which might in turn have a bearing on minority issues.

Overall, therefore, there is a whole host of issues that now arise in relation to minority issues in the wider Europe. In order to help address these, this book is organized into three main sections. First, we consider some conceptual aspects of the development of minority rights discourse in Europe. Second, we examine the institutional arrangements covering minority issues in Europe. Finally, we consider aspects of the implementation practice of this institutional design and architecture.

In the first section, Will Kymlicka asks whether there ever existed a consensus in Europe on standards relating to minorities. While he finds that autonomy solutions have often been adopted in Western Europe, the granting of cultural rights appears to have been emphasized in the East. However, many minority groups did not see the latter approach as sufficient. Instead of granting autonomy, recent emphasis has been placed on political participation mechanisms. However, the author considers it unlikely that these will provide a minimum standard of provision for minorities in the future.

Hans-Joachim Heintze addresses a further important conceptual issue in framing provision for minorities for the future. This concerns the long-running debate relating to individual and collective rights. Generally speaking, states have been quite hesitant in relation to the latter, and, as a consequence, most international instruments speak of 'persons belonging to minorities' instead of 'minorities'.

Tove Malloy considers a different kind of collective dimension when she broaches the need to address the ever-increasing diversity of identities in the post-accessions environment. She considers it necessary to enhance the policies directed at sub-national, regional entities seeking to express their cultural identity. This includes even possible integration among them, by way of 'fourth level politics'.

After the principal conceptual debates relating to minority provision in Europe, the book then turns to the newly emerging institutional architecture. First, Gabriel von Toggenburg offers a very comprehensive assessment of the prospects for action within the framework of the EU. While the now defunct Constitution, which may in this respect be carried over into the more modest Reform Treaty, has been much criticized, he notes that one could not realistically have expected much more on minority issues than it delivered. Instead, he emphasizes the need to develop a cooperative relationship with the Council of Europe in relation to the development of new initiatives in this area.

Nevertheless, the EU has already managed to offer some significant innovations, in particular with respect to recent and current attempts to help manage or transform inter-ethnic conflicts in its external policy. This aspect is examined by Stefan Wolff and Annemarie Peen Rodt, in their chapter on the EU and its burgeoning policy of conflict prevention. After the initial disaster of the EU's early involvement in Bosnia and Herzegovina, significant credibility was gained when the Union addressed, jointly with the US, the situation in Macedonia, and then re-engaged in a more impressive way with Bosnia and Herzegovina. At present, however, EU unity is once again strained in relation to the status of Kosovo, though greater EU involvement in the area is likely in the end to lead to its assumption of a the lead role foreseen for it there.

Krysztof Drzewicki considers EU enlargement in relation to the mandate and functions of the OSCE High Commissioner on National Minorities. The High Commissioner's Office has not only been serving within the OSCE context, but it has also performed important functions for the EU, for instance, the evaluation of accession states' compliance with the Copenhagen criterion relating to minorities. Moreover, the Office played a significant role in helping to stabilize relations among the states of Central and Eastern Europe during the pre-accession period. The author assesses how this role will continue with respect to both the external and internal policies of the Union.

Traditionally, the Council of Europe has played the lead role in relation to minority issues in Europe. The Council has generated the two legally binding instruments in this area. Moreover, it has developed these significantly through the work of the treaty monitoring bodies attached to them. In addition to standards and their implementation, the Council has also generated a significant number of projects and activities on diversity in the wider Europe. Nevertheless, the debate over the Constitution, and the accession of a large number of states to the EU, has given rise to questions about the future role of the Council of Europe. Accordingly, some have argued, the EU should start to cover minority issues. As already noted above, however, this is not realistic. Moreover, the Council of Europe, with its powerful Court of Human Rights, enjoys decades of experience and credibility on human rights issues. Accordingly, Rainer Hofmann, in his chapter on the future role of the Council, rightly foresees that it will remain the principal point of reference on minority issues. If anything, it would be necessary to strengthen the Council in this respect, for instance by transforming the Framework Convention into a Protocol to the European Convention on Human Rights in order to make it justiciable before the Court.

Having considered the principal institutional mechanisms covering minority issues, the book then turns in its final section to the accession process itself and its impact on the minority policies of the relevant states. Wojciech Sadurski asks why it is that most accession states were so reluctant to engage with minority issues, doing so only at the prodding of international agencies, and often at the minimum level required. He considers the constitutional design in Central and Eastern Europe, the different articulations of minority rights in the respective states and the role performed by their constitutional courts in pronouncing upon them. The author questions whether the effects of conditionality can be preserved far into the post-accession period, especially if the Union does not genuinely universalize minority rights among its entire membership.

Martin Brusis picks up this theme, considering political power-sharing mechanisms that have emerged in several Central or Eastern European states, in his view, as a consequence of the need to meet EU accession criteria. In these instances, the emphasis on conflict prevention in the OSCE and EU approach resulted in consociationalist power-sharing solutions that might not otherwise have proven attractive to the majority parties.

Finally, the section concludes with a special study of the interrelationship between minority issues as they concern Greece, Cyprus and Turkey. Greece may count itself as an established member of the EU, Cyprus is a recent, and still problematic, accession state, and Turkey hopes to consolidate its candidacy.

Based on this review, what prediction may one offer when considering minority provisions in the wider Europe? It is certainly clear that minority issues will play an ever-greater role, even within the EU context, given that the Union is increasingly addressing diversity issues such as language policy and exclusion of certain groups from economic and social opportunities. There are also opportunities to coordinate to even greater effect the efforts of existing institutions, including the European Commission, the Council of Europe and the Office of the OSCE High Commissioner. This relates both to EU internal issues, and to the work relating to the remaining accession states and those just outside of the membership region. Whether there will be major reforms and advances on standards remains to be seen in the mid-term. There certainly would be room for an advanced minority rights treaty that is justiciable before the European Court of Human Rights. Finally, minority issues will retain their relevance fully, or even gain in relevance, with respect to the remaining candidates, and the longer-term aspirants. For the latter group, human and minority rights considerations will be equally as decisive as the *aquis* proper when their capacity for membership is at issue.

Note

1. In the case of the FCNM, of the current 27 member states of the European Union, Belgium, France, Greece and Luxembourg have failed to ratify; in the case of the ECRML, those outside its remit are Belgium, Bulgaria, Estonia, France, Greece, Ireland, Italy, Latvia, Lithuania, Malta, Poland, Portugal and Romania.

Part I

The Evolution of Minority Governance in Europe

1

The Evolving Basis of European Norms of Minority Rights: Rights to Culture, Participation and Autonomy

Will Kymlicka

Since 1989, we have witnessed a remarkable trend towards the internationalization of minority rights issues in the European context. There are now a wide range of international institutions – including the Organization for Security and Cooperation in Europe (OSCE), the Council of Europe (CoE), the EU and NATO – actively involved in decision-making about state–minority relations. These institutions formulate standards on how states should treat their minorities, monitor whether states are living up to these standards and make recommendations about how to improve state–minority relations. They also offer a wide range of rewards for countries that comply with these international standards and recommendations, and impose penalties on those that fail to do so. Whist these norms are, in principle, intended to apply to all European countries, West and East, the focus of these organizations to date has fallen almost exclusively on the post-communist states of Central and Eastern Europe.

The precise details of how these various international organizations operate – their standards, monitoring functions, reporting procedures and enforcement mechanisms – have been described elsewhere.[1] Moreover, although many of these institutions are still relatively new, there have been some attempts to evaluate the effectiveness of particular mechanisms in protecting minorities and in preventing or reducing ethnic violence in post-communist Europe.[2]

This chapter steps back and asks more general questions about the trend of internationalizing minority rights. This very project implies that there are such things as 'international norms' (or at least 'European standards') regarding the rights of national minorities.[3] In reality, however, there are important disagreements over the rights of national minorities, both within the Western democracies and between Western and Eastern Europe. In particular, there are deep disagreements about whether national minorities have a right to territorial autonomy or self-government.

Given these disagreements, European organizations have tried to avoid appealing to such a right when formulating their international norms.

Instead, they have relied heavily on two other, less controversial, ideas: (i) the right to enjoy one's culture, and (ii) the right to effective participation. European organizations have hoped that, if these two rights are respected, there will be no need for, and thus no demand for, more controversial ideas of autonomy and self-government.

Despite this, the following chapter will attempt to demonstrate that the idea of self-government, while contested and resisted, cannot be easily avoided. It often re-enters the debate through the back door, albeit in *ad hoc* ways. The result, it is suggested, is a number of confusions, ambiguities and moral inconsistencies in the application of international norms to post-communist Europe. These ambiguities have their short-term use in deferring or papering over difficult issues, but it is argued that the long-term prospects for the peaceful and democratic accommodation of minority nationalisms in post-communist Europe require a rethinking of the nature and function of the international norms of minority rights.

The internationalization of minority rights in post-communist Europe

As communism collapsed in Central and Eastern Europe in 1989, a number of violent ethnic conflicts broke out. In retrospect, these conflicts were confined for the most part to the Caucasus and the Balkans, but this was not clear at the time. In the early 1990s, many commentators feared that ethnic tensions would spiral out of control in wide swathes of post-communist Europe. For example, predictions of civil war between the Slovak majority and Hungarian minority in Slovakia, or between the Estonian majority and Russian minority in Estonia were not uncommon. Overly optimistic predictions about the rapid replacement of communism with liberal democracy were supplanted with overly pessimistic predictions about the replacement of communism with ethnic war.

Faced with these potentially dire trends, Western democracies in the early 1990s felt they had to do something. Thus they decided, in effect, to 'internationalize' the treatment of national minorities in post-communist Europe. They declared, in the words of the OSCE in 1990, that the status and treatment of national minorities 'are matters of legitimate international concern, and consequently do not constitute exclusively an internal affair of the respective State'.[4]

The international community often makes pious declarations of its concern for the rights and well-being of peoples around the world, without ever really intending to do much about it. However, in this case, the West backed up its words with actions. The most important and tangible action in this regard was the decision by the EU and NATO in December 1991 to make minority rights one of the four criteria that candidate countries had to meet in order to become members of these organizations. Since most post-communist countries viewed membership in the EU and NATO as pivotal to their future prosperity and security, any 'recommendations' that the West might make regarding minority rights were taken very seriously. As a result, minority rights moved to the centre of post-communist political life, a core component of the process of 'rejoining Europe'.

Having decided in 1990–1991 that the treatment of minorities in post-communist Europe was a matter of legitimate international concern, the next step was to create institutional mechanisms that could monitor how post-communist countries were treating their minorities. Since 1991, therefore, various international bodies have been created with the mandate of monitoring the treatment of minorities and of recommending changes needed to live up to European standards of minority rights. A crucial step here was the formation of the Office of the High Commission on National Minorities of the OSCE High Commission on National Minorities in 1993, linked to OSCE mission offices in several post-communist countries. Another important step occurred at the CoE, which set up a number of advisory bodies and reporting mechanisms as part of its Framework Convention for the Protection of National Minorities (FCNM) in 1995. The EU and NATO did not themselves create new monitoring bodies specifically focused on minority rights[5] but they have made clear that they support the work of the OSCE HCNM and the CoE and expect candidate countries to cooperate with them as a condition of accession.

In short, Western states have made a serious commitment to internationalizing minority rights, embedding that commitment not only in formal declarations but also in a dense web of European institutions. It is interesting to consider how and why this commitment emerged. After all, the EU showed very little interest in the question of minority rights prior to 1989, and deliberately avoided including any reference to minority rights in its own internal principles. Nor did Western countries traditionally show much interest in protecting minorities elsewhere around the world. On the contrary, Western states often propped up governments in Africa, Asia or Latin America that were known to oppress their minorities, even to the point of selling military equipment with the knowledge that it would be used against minority groups (for example, selling arms to Indonesia to suppress minorities in Aceh and East Timor, or to Guatemala to suppress the Maya). So, why did the West suddenly become a champion of minorities in post-communist Europe?

There are a number of possible reasons for this. One factor was the humanitarian concern to end the suffering of minorities who faced persecution, mob violence and ethnic cleansing. However, humanitarian concern is rarely enough, on its own, to mobilize Western governments. A more self-interested reason was the belief that escalating ethnic violence would generate large-scale refugee movements into Western Europe, as indeed was the case in Kosovo and in Bosnia and Herzegovina. In addition, ethnic civil wars often create pockets of lawlessness that become havens for the smuggling of arms and drugs or for other forms of criminality and extremism.

Another reason, more diffuse, was the sense in the West that the ability of post-communist countries to manage their ethnic diversity was a test of their overall political maturity, and hence of their readiness to 'rejoin Europe'. As the General Secretary of the CoE put it, respect for minorities is a fundamental measure of a country's 'moral progress'.[6] The ability of a country to get its deficit down to under 3 per cent of its GDP (another of the accession criteria) may be important from an economic point of view but it does not tell us much about whether the country will 'fit' into European traditions and institutions.[7]

In short, for a complex mixture of humanitarian, self-interested and ideological reasons, minority rights have become 'internationalized' in Europe. Acceptance of international monitoring and enforcement of these norms have become a test of a country's readiness for European integration. Meeting international norms of minority rights is seen as proof that a country has left behind its 'ancient ethnic hatreds' and 'tribal nationalisms' and is able to join a 'modern' liberal and cosmopolitan Europe.

Defining European minority rights norms

Between 1990 and 1993, therefore, a rapid consensus developed among all the major Western organizations: that the treatment of national minorities by post-communist countries should be a matter of international concern and that there should be international mechanisms to monitor a country's compliance with international norms of minority rights.

However, there was one glaring problem with this approach: namely, that it presupposed 'international norms' or 'European standards' of minority rights. In reality, there were no such standards. There were no formal declarations or conventions enumerating the rights of national minorities. Indeed, the terms 'minority rights' or 'rights of national minorities' were largely unknown in the West.

Western countries differ greatly in how they talk about issues of accommodating diversity. For example, some countries (notably, France, Greece and Turkey) simply deny that they have 'minorities'.[8] Other countries acknowledge that they have 'minorities', but differ about what sorts of groups this term applies to. In some countries (the United Kingdom, for example), the term 'minorities' generally refers to post-war migrant groups, typically from the Caribbean or South Asia, but not to the historic Welsh or Scottish groups. In other Western countries (as in most of post-communist Europe), it is the opposite: 'minorities' typically refers to historic groups (like the Slovenes in Austria) but not to post-war migrants (like the Turks in Austria), who are described instead as 'foreigners'.

So the term 'minority' has different connotations across the West. In any event, in none of these countries was there widespread reference to general principles about 'the rights of national minorities'. To illustrate, debates about Scots in the UK, or about Catalans in Spain, or about Slovenes in Austria, were not phrased in the form:

- all national minorities have a right to X;
- Scots/Catalans/Slovenes are a national minority;
- therefore Scots/Catalans/Slovenes have a right to X.

Claims of particular national groups are not deduced from some broader principle or theory about what 'national minorities', as a category, have 'rights' to. Instead, the rights of particular groups are debated in terms of historic settlements, built up over time, by which various accommodations have been reached between different communities.

In fact, the term 'national minority' had no legal status or meaning in any Western country prior to the adoption of the Framework Convention in 1995. No legislation in any Western country specified which groups were 'national minorities', and which rights flowed from having that status. No Western country had an 'Office of National Minorities', or a 'Law on National Minorities'.

In short, there was no Western discourse of 'the rights of national minorities' prior to 1990, either within particular countries or across Europe as a whole. If you asked citizens or elites in Western Europe what 'the rights of national minorities' were, you would probably get a blank stare. Thus, the decision to internationalize state–minority relations through the articulation of 'European standards of the rights of national minorities' was, in a sense, a remarkable decision. It is not surprising that Western governments wanted to 'do something' about ethnic conflict in post-communist Europe but it is surprising that they chose do so in an idiom or vocabulary that was essentially foreign to the Western experience. As Chandler notes, Western countries were determined to develop European standards as a way of monitoring post-communist countries but they 'had no conception of how to apply such policies in relation to their own minorities'.[9]

How, then, were these international norms constructed? Observers with a long memory recalled that this question had been tackled earlier, in the last major period of imperial breakdowns after World War I, resulting in the 'minority protection scheme' of the League of Nations. A mini-industry has arisen examining that older scheme and trying to learn lessons from its successes and failures for contemporary European debates.[10]

Nevertheless, the minority protection scheme of the League of Nations was particularistic, not generalized. It involved multilateral treaties guaranteeing particular rights for particular minorities in particular (defeated) countries, while leaving many other minorities unprotected. It did not attempt to articulate general standards or international norms that all national minorities would be able to claim. Indeed, that was one reason why the idea of minority rights fell out of favour and largely disappeared from the post-war international law context, replaced with a new focus on 'human rights'.

However, the idea of minority rights did not disappear entirely from international law. It retained a foothold in some of the human rights declarations at the United Nations. In fact, there were two quite different UN provisions that could be seen as laying a foundation for international norms on the rights of national minorities. The first provision, dating back to the Charter of the United Nations and reaffirmed in Article 1 of the 1966 International Covenant on Civil and Political Rights (ICCPR), states that all 'peoples' have a right to 'self-determination' by which they can 'freely determine their political status'. The second provision, found in Article 27 of the same Covenant, states that 'members of minorities' have the right to 'enjoy their own culture... in community with other members of their group'.[11]

These two provisions have been part of international law since at least 1966 and have been invoked by minorities around the world. Neither of them, however, is adequate for the context of national minorities in post-communist Europe. To oversimplify, we might say that, for most national minorities, Article 1 (as traditionally understood) is too strong, and Article 27 (as traditionally understood) is too weak. Most national minorities need to be accommodated somewhere in between and recent developments in Europe regarding minority rights are precisely an attempt to codify certain standards in between Articles 1 and 27.

The right to self-determination in Article 1 is too strong, for it has been interpreted traditionally to include the right to form one's own state. Precisely for this reason, its scope has been drastically restricted in international law. It has been limited by what is called the 'salt-water thesis'. The only 'peoples' who have a right to independence are those subject to colonization from overseas; national minorities within a territorially contiguous state do not have a right to independence. Hence, internal minorities are not defined as separate 'peoples' with their own right of self-determination, even if they have been subject to similar processes of territorial conquest and colonization as overseas colonies.

For those national minorities denied recognition as 'peoples' under Article 1, the only other option was to appeal to Article 27 ICCPR. But this Article is too weak, for 'the right to enjoy one's culture' has traditionally been understood to include only negative rights of non-interference, rather than positive rights to assistance, funding, autonomy or official language status. In effect, it simply reaffirms that members of national minorities must be free to exercise their standard rights of freedom of speech, freedom of association, freedom of assembly and freedom of conscience.

Needless to say, there is a vast spectrum between Article 1 rights to an independent state and Article 27 rights to freedom of cultural expression and association. Indeed, almost all of the conflicts relating to national minorities in post-communist Europe are about this middle area, including: the right to use a minority language in court or local administration; the funding of minority schools, universities and media; the extent of local or regional autonomy; the guaranteeing of political representation for minorities; the prohibition on settlement policies designed to swamp minorities in their historic homelands with settlers from the dominant group, and so on. These issues are an important source of ethnic conflict and political instability in post-communist Europe. Yet international law, until recently, has had virtually nothing to say about any of them.

As a result, national minorities have been vulnerable to serious injustice. Article 27 has helped protect certain civil rights relating to cultural expression but it has not stopped states from rescinding funding for minority-language schools, abolishing traditional forms of local autonomy, or encouraging settlers to swamp minority homelands. None of these policies, which can be catastrophic for national minorities, violate the rights to cultural expression and association protected in Article 27.[12]

For these and other reasons, it is widely recognized that we need a new conception of the rights of national minorities that can fill in the gap between Articles 1 and 27. We need a conception that accords national minorities substantive rights and protections (unlike Article 27) but that works within the framework of larger states (unlike Article 1). This was the task facing European organizations when developing 'European standards of minority rights'.

While there was a broad consensus that these standards should fill in the space between Articles 1 and 27, there was disagreement about where to start. An oversimplification would be to say that some actors wanted to start with Article 1's right to self-determination but to weaken it so as to render it consistent with the territorial integrity of states. This leads us in the direction of various models of 'internal self-determination'. Other actors wanted to start with Article 27's right to enjoy one's culture and strengthen it to provide substantive protections. To date, neither option has proven adequate. In the next two sections, this chapter will examine the respective problems posed by each.

The right to internal self-determination

Not surprisingly, most minority elites preferred to start with a (weakened) form of a right to self-determination. Throughout the early 1990s, many intellectuals and political organizations representing national minorities pushed for recognition of a right to internal self-determination, typically through some form of territorial autonomy (hereafter TA). For a brief period from 1990 to 1993, there was some indication that this campaign might be successful. For example, the very first statement by a European organization on minority rights after the collapse of communism – the initial 1990 Conference on Security and Cooperation in Europe (CSCE) Copenhagen Declaration – went out of its way to endorse territorial autonomy (Article 35):

> The participating States note the efforts undertaken to protect and create conditions for the promotion of the ethnic, cultural, linguistic and religious identity of certain national minorities by establishing, as one of the possible means to achieve these aims, appropriate local or autonomous administrations corresponding to the specific historical and territorial circumstances of such minorities and in accordance with the policies of the State concerned.[13]

This paragraph does not recognize a 'right' to TA but recommends it as a good way of accommodating national minorities.

An even stronger endorsement of TA came in 1993, in Recommendation 1201 of the Parliamentary Assembly of the CoE (PACE). It contains a clause (Article 11) stating that:

> in the regions where they are a majority, the persons belonging to a national minority shall have the right to have at their disposal appropriate local or autonomous authorities or to have a special status, matching this specific historical and territorial situation and in accordance with the domestic legislation of the State.[14]

Unlike the OSCE Copenhagen Declaration, this Recommendation recognizes TA as a 'right'. Of course, parliamentary recommendations are just that: recommendations, not legally binding documents. Still, this shows that in the early 1990s there was movement in the direction of endorsing a general principle that justice required some effective mechanism or other for sharing power between a majority and national minorities, specifically mentioning TA as one such mechanism.

Many national minority organizations in post-communist Europe viewed the passage of Recommendation 1201 as a great victory. Ethnic Hungarian organizations, in particular, viewed it as evidence that Europe would support their claims for TA in Slovakia, Romania and Serbia. They assumed this Recommendation would play a central role in the CoE's FCNM, which was being drafted at that time, and that complying with this Recommendation would be required for candidate countries to join the EU.

This expectation was bolstered by the fact that internal self-determination for national minorities had clearly become the general trend within the West itself. The practice of territorial autonomy for sizeable, territorially concentrated national minorities was virtually universal in the West. Indeed, one of the most striking developments in ethnic relations in Western democracies over the past century has been the trend towards creating political sub-units in which national minorities form a local majority and in which their language is recognized as an official language, at least within their self-governing region and perhaps throughout the country as a whole. At the beginning of the twentieth century, only Switzerland and Canada had adopted this combination of territorial autonomy and official language status for sub-state national groups. Since then, however, virtually all Western democracies containing sizeable sub-state nationalist movements have moved in this direction. The list includes: the adoption of autonomy for the Swedish-speaking Aaland Islands in Finland after World War I; autonomy for South Tyrol in Italy and for Puerto Rico in the United States after World War II; and federal autonomy for Catalonia and the Basque Country in Spain in the 1970s, for Flanders in Belgium in the 1980s and, most recently, for Scotland and Wales in the 1990s.

If we restrict our focus to sizeable and territorially-concentrated national minorities, this trend is now essentially universal in the West. All groups over 250,000 that have demonstrated a desire for TA now have it in the West, as well as many smaller groups (such as the German minority in Belgium).[15] The largest group that has mobilized for autonomy without success is the Corsican population in France (175,000 people). However, even here, legislation was adopted recently to accord autonomy to Corsica and it was only a ruling of the Constitutional Court that prevented its implementation. Thus, it can be assumed that France, too, will soon jump on the bandwagon.

Moreover, while the shift to territorial autonomy was originally controversial in each of the countries that adopted it, it has quickly become a deeply entrenched part of political life in these countries. It is inconceivable that Spain or Belgium or Canada, for example, could revert to a unitary and monolingual state. Nor is anyone campaigning for such a reversal. Indeed, no Western democracy that has adopted territorial autonomy and official bilingualism has reversed this decision. This is evidence that such a model for accommodating sizeable/concentrated national minorities has been very successful in terms of liberal-democratic values of peace, prosperity, individual rights and democracy.[16]

In short, if there were a 'European standard' for dealing with mobilized national minorities, some form of internal autonomy would appear to be it. This is the model Western democracies use today to deal with the phenomenon of sub-state nationalist groups, and national minorities in post-communist Europe had reason to hope that it would be established as a norm for their countries as well.

Of course, the fact that internal autonomy has become the norm in practice in the West does not mean that it can be codified into a general norm in international law. As noted earlier, these Western practices were not debated in terms of general principles of 'the rights of national minorities', and it is not clear how a norm of internal self-determination could be formulated in a generalized way. However, it is worth noting that this very issue was being debated in a closely related context of international law: namely, the rights of indigenous peoples. The UN Declaration on the Rights of Indigenous Peoples 2007 has several articles affirming the principle of internal self-determination, including:

Article 3: Indigenous peoples have the right to self-determination. By virtue of that right, they freely determine their political status and freely pursue their economic, social and cultural development.

Article 4: Indigenous peoples, in exercising their right to self-determination, have the right to autonomy or self-government in matters relating to their internal and local affairs, as well as ways and means for financing their autonomous functions.

Article 14: Indigenous peoples have the right to establish and control their educational systems and institutions providing education in their own languages, in a manner appropriate to their cultural methods of teaching and learning.

Article 26: Indigenous peoples have the right to own, use, develop and control the lands, territories and resources that they possess by reason of traditional ownership or other traditional occupation or use, as well as those which they have otherwise acquired.

Article 34: Indigenous peoples have the right to promote, develop and maintain their institutional structures and their distinctive customs, spirituality, traditions, procedures, practices and, in the cases where they exist, juridical systems or customs, in accordance with international human rights standards.[17]

This declaration has been binding in international law since 2007.[18] The basic idea that indigenous peoples have a right to internal self-determination is now widely endorsed throughout the international community, however, and this is reflected in other recent international declarations on indigenous rights, including those by the Organization of American States and the International Labour Organization.

This shows that there is no inherent reason why international law cannot accept the idea of internal self-determination. Of course, the status of national minorities in post-communist Europe is not identical to that of indigenous peoples in the Americas or Asia. Nevertheless, there are some important similarities in both history and aspiration, and many of the standard arguments for recognizing a right of internal self-determination for indigenous peoples apply to national minorities as well.[19]

National minorities in post-communist states reasonably could hope that some form of internal self-government would be codified as part of the 'European standards' for the treatment of national minorities. This approach is, in fact, the norm within Western Europe today, which has been recognized as a valid principle in international law with respect to indigenous peoples and has been endorsed in important statements by European organizations, including the OSCE in 1990 and PACE in 1993.

However, as it turns out, the latter's Recommendation 1201 constituted the high water mark of support for TA within European organizations. Since then, there has been a distinct movement away from it. The Framework Convention, adopted just two years after Recommendation 1201, avoided any reference to TA. Not only is TA not recognized as a 'right', it is not even mentioned as a recommended practice. Nor does it appear in any subsequent declaration or recommendation of European organizations, such as the series of Hague, Oslo and Lund Recommendations adopted by the OSCE from 1996 to 1999.[20] Moreover, the European Commission for Democracy through Law has ruled that national minorities do not have rights of self-determination.[21] For all intents and purposes, ideas of internal self-determination have disappeared from the debate about 'European standards' on minority rights.

There are a number of reasons for this. For one thing, the idea of autonomy faced intense opposition from post-communist states. They feared that recognizing any idea of internal self-determination or minority autonomy would be destabilizing. Governments worried that granting TA to some groups would lead to problems of both 'escalation' and 'proliferation'.[22] The former fear is that groups granted internal self-determination would then escalate their demands into full-blown secession; the latter fear is that if internal self-determination is offered to one highly vocal or mobilized group, other groups, previously quiescent, might emerge and demand their own autonomy.

Of course, the same two fears of escalation and proliferation were present in the West, as well, and yet Western states have nonetheless proceeded with internal autonomy. Fears of escalation and proliferation have turned out to be exaggerated, at least in the Western context.[23] However, these fears are exacerbated in many post-communist countries by the fact that national minorities often share a common ethnic or national identity with a neighbouring state, which they may therefore view as their 'kin-state' or 'mother country' (for example, ethnic Hungarian minorities in Slovakia *vis-à-vis* Hungary, or ethnic Russian minorities in the Baltics *vis-à-vis* Russia). In such cases, the fear of escalation is not so much that minorities will become secessionist but rather that they will become irredentist – that is, that they could serve as a fifth column, supporting efforts by their neighbouring kin-state to take over part or all of the country.[24] More generally, the very idea of recognizing minorities as 'nations within', possessed of their own inherent rights to self-government, challenges the ideology of most post-communist states. These states aspire to be seen as unified nation-states, premised on a singular conception of popular sovereignty, rather than as unions or federations of two or more peoples.[25]

For a variety of reasons, then, claims to internal self-determination have been bitterly resisted in post-communist Europe. As the HCNM has noted, claims to TA meet 'maximal resistance' on the part of states in the region. Any attempt by Western organizations to push such models through would therefore require maximum pressure and would make relations between East and West much more combative and costly. Hence, in the HCNM's judgment, it is more 'pragmatic' to focus on more modest forms of minority rights.[26]

Moreover, there was also strong opposition to the idea of entrenching a right to TA for minorities *in the West* and to the idea that there would be international monitoring of Western states' treatment of their minorities. As we have seen, France, Greece and Turkey traditionally have opposed the very idea of the existence of national minorities. Even those Western countries that accept the principle of self-government do not necessarily want their laws and policies regarding national minorities to be subject to international monitoring. This is true, for example, of Switzerland and the United States.[27] The treatment of national minorities in various Western countries remains a politically sensitive topic and many countries do not want their minority–majority settlements, often the result of long and painful negotiation processes, reopened by international monitoring agencies. In short, while they were willing to insist that post-communist states be monitored for their treatment of minorities, they did not want their own treatment of minorities examined in the same way.

Given these obstacles, it is not surprising that efforts to codify a right to autonomy or internal self-determination for national minorities have failed.

The right to enjoy one's culture

As support for recognizing a right to internal self-determination has dwindled, the obvious alternative has been to build instead on the principle underlying Article 27 of the ICCPR – namely, the 'right to enjoy one's culture'. In many ways, the provisions of the 1995 CoE FCNM and of the 1996–1999 OSCE Recommendations can be understood in this way. They start from a right to enjoy one's culture but seek to strengthen it, so as to entail certain positive rights and protections.[28] These positive rights include, for example, public funding of minority elementary schools and of minority media or the right to spell one's surname in accordance with one's own language. In contexts where minorities form a local majority, these rights also might include the right to bilingual street signs and the right to submit documents to public authorities in the minority language. All of these are said to enable the members of minorities to 'enjoy their own culture, to profess and practise their own religion, or to use their own language'.

While stronger than the original Article 27, this approach is still relatively weak in the rights it accords to national minorities. In particular, it provides no recognition of rights to self-government and no guarantees of official language status. Nor does it guarantee that minorities can pursue higher-level education or professional accomplishment in their own language.

More generally, there is nothing in the FCNM or OSCE Recommendations that challenges the desire of post-communist states to be unitary nation-states with a single official language. States can respect these standards fully and yet centralize power in such a way that all decisions are made in forums controlled by a dominant national group. They can also organize higher education, professional accreditation and political offices so that members of minorities must either assimilate linguistically in order to achieve professional success and political power or migrate to their kin-state. (This is often referred to as the 'decapitation' of minority groups: forcing potential elites from minority communities to leave their community to achieve higher education or professional success.) In short, these norms do not preclude state policies aimed at the disempowerment and decapitation of minorities.

From the perspective of minorities and of many commentators, therefore, these documents smack of 'paternalism and tokenism'.[29] In contrast, most post-communist states are relieved about the general direction these norms are taking. They have expressed much less resistance to the 1995 FCNM and the 1996–1999 OSCE Recommendations than to earlier documents endorsing TA. Post-communist states grumble about the double standards in the way these norms are applied but they do not contest their basic validity.[30] In this sense, the decision to base European standards on an updated version of the Article 27 right to enjoy one's culture has indeed proven more 'pragmatic'.

In another sense, however, this approach has proven quite ineffective. Recall that the original point of developing these norms was to deal with violent ethnic conflicts in post-communist Europe, such as in Kosovo, Bosnia and Herzegovina, Croatia, the Former Yugoslav Republic of Macedonia (hereinafter referred to as Macedonia), Georgia, Azerbaijan, Moldova and Chechnya. None of these conflicts revolved around Article 27-type rights to enjoy one's culture. The violation of such rights was not the cause of violent conflict and respect for such rights would not resolve the conflicts. The same is true about the other major cases where European organizations feared potential violence, such as the Hungarian minorities in Romania and Slovakia, or the Russian minority in Ukraine.

In all of these cases, the issues in dispute are not covered by the FCNM or the OSCE Recommendations. These are conflicts involving large, territorially concentrated groups who have manifested the capacity and the aspiration to govern themselves and to administer their own public institutions in their own language, and who typically have possessed some form of self-government and official language status in the past. They have mobilized for territorial autonomy, official language status, minority-language universities and consociational power-sharing. None of these groups would be satisfied with the meagre rights guaranteed by the FCNM and the OSCE Recommendations.

The fact that these national minorities are not satisfied with these provisions is sometimes taken as evidence of the illiberalism of their political culture or the radicalism of their leadership. It is worth noting, however, that no sizeable politically mobilized national minority in the West would be satisfied either. No one can seriously suppose that national minorities in Catalonia, Flanders, Quebec, Bern, South Tyrol, the Aaland Islands or Puerto Rico would be satisfied simply with minority elementary schools but not mother-tongue universities, or bilingual street signs but not official language status, or local administration but not regional autonomy.

This is not to say that there are no contexts in post-communist Europe where current FCNM or OSCE norms would provide a realistic basis for state–minority relations. They may work well in those countries which are essentially ethnically homogenous – that is, where the dominant group forms 90–95 per cent of the population – and where the remaining ethnic groups are small, dispersed and already on the road to assimilation. This is the situation, for instance, in the Czech Republic, Slovenia and Hungary. None of the minorities in these countries are, in fact, capable of exercising regional autonomy or of sustaining a high degree of institutional completeness (for example, of sustaining their own universities) and most already show high levels of linguistic assimilation. For these groups, the FCNM/OSCE norms provide all that they could ask for. They allow such small and half-assimilated minorities to negotiate their integration into the dominant society with a certain amount of dignity and security. It allows them to 'die with their boots on'.[31] Similarly, the FCNM/OSCE norms are likely be satisfactory to small, dispersed and partly assimilated minorities in other post-communist countries, such as the Vlach in Macedonia, or the Armenians in Romania.

The problem, of course, is that these minorities were not (and are not) the ones involved in serious ethnic conflict. The problem of ethnic violence and potentially destabilizing ethnic conflict in post-communist Europe is almost exclusively confined to groups that are capable of exercising self-government and of sustaining their own public institutions, and which therefore battle with the state for control over public institutions.[32] For these groups, the FCNM and OSCE norms are largely irrelevant.

In the end, therefore, the new European standards are not especially pragmatic. If the goal is to deal effectively with the problem of potentially destabilizing ethnic conflict, then we need norms that actually address the source of these conflicts. Any norms that start from an Article 27-style 'right to enjoy one's culture' are unlikely to do so.[33]

A retreat from minority rights?

It seems, therefore, that neither of the two approaches to building European standards of minority rights – whether based on a right to self-determination or a right to enjoy culture – has succeeded in developing meaningful and effective international norms. Even though self-determination is being interpreted in a weakened form compared to its original formulation in Article 1 ICCPR, it is still too strong for many countries to accept. Even though the right to enjoy one's culture is being interpreted in a strengthened form compared to its original formulation in Article 27 ICCPR, it is still too weak to actually resolve the sources of ethnic conflict.

If neither of these options is feasible and effective, what are the alternatives? One option would be to abandon the idea of developing European norms on minority rights. After all, the EU and NATO survived and flourished for many years without paying any attention to minority rights.[34] Why not reconsider the decision to make minority rights one of the foundational values of the European order?

Indeed, one could argue that the original decision in the early 1990s to develop such norms was based on a mistaken prediction about the likelihood that ethnic conflict would spiral out of control. It has since become clear that ethnic violence is a localized phenomenon in post-communist Europe and that the prospects for violence in countries like Slovakia or Estonia are virtually nil for the foreseeable future. So, perhaps it is unnecessary to monitor whether these countries are treating their minorities in accordance with (so-called) European norms.

Although it is clear that Western observers may not like some of the policies that these countries would adopt if left to their own devices, it is unlikely that they would lead to violence and instability. Some of these countries might experiment with heavy-handed assimilationist policies but, if so, these would almost certainly fail and, in the end, a domestic consensus would emerge along more liberal lines. This is what happened in the West and there is no reason to assume it would not or could not happen in the East. Moreover, liberal policies are more likely to be perceived as legitimate and, consequently, to be stable, if they emerge from these sorts of domestic processes, rather than being imposed from without.

For these reasons, some commentators have suggested that we stop pressuring post-communist countries to comply with international norms on minority rights.[35] This would not necessarily preclude all forms of Western intervention. As noted earlier, ethnic conflicts can undermine regional peace and stability. Violence, massive refugee flows and arms smuggling can spill over into neighbouring countries and destabilize entire regions. The international community has a right to protect itself against such potentially destabilizing ethnic conflicts in post-communist Europe.

However, insofar as *security* is the real motivation for Western intervention, then presumably state–minority relations should be monitored not for their compliance with international norms but for their potential threats to regional peace and security. Monitoring should aim to identify those cases in which the status and treatment of minorities might lead to these sorts of spillover effects.

Indeed, European organizations have been engaged in this sort of security monitoring. In addition to the monitoring of compliance with international norms, European organizations have also been engaged in a parallel process of monitoring countries for their potential threats to regional security. This parallel process has been organized primarily through the OSCE, including the office of the HCNM. Moreover, the HCNM's mandate is explicitly defined as part of the OSCE's 'security' basket and his or her task is to provide early warning of potential threats to security and to make recommendations that would defuse these threats.[36] Behind the OSCE, of course, lies NATO, with its security mandate and its power to intervene militarily if necessary, as seen in Bosnia and Herzegovina and in Kosovo.

In short, there exist two parallel processes of 'internationalizing' state–minority relations: one process monitors post-communist states for their compliance with general norms of minority rights (that we can call the 'legal rights track'); while a second monitors post-communist states for their potential threats to regional stability (the 'security track').[37]

The existence of this parallel security track means that, even if compliance with international norms were no longer monitored, Western states could still intervene on the basis of considerations of regional security in circumstances where spillover risks were identified. In fact, this security track has always been more important than the legal rights track in determining actual intervention in post-communist states. The most important and well-known cases of Western intervention on minority issues in post-communist states have worked through the security track. These interventions have been based on calculations about how to restore security, not on how to uphold universal norms such as the FCNM.

Consider the way Western organizations have intervened in the major cases of ethnic violence in post-communist Europe: Moldova, Georgia, Azerbaijan, Kosovo, Bosnia and Herzegovina, and Macedonia, for example. In each of these cases, Western organizations have pushed post-communist states to go far beyond the requirements of the FCNM. They have pushed states to accept either some form of territorial autonomy (in Moldova, Georgia, Azerbaijan and Kosovo) and/or some form of consociational power-sharing and official language status (as in Macedonia and Bosnia and Herzegovina).

In short, where Western organizations really have faced destabilizing ethnic conflict, they have recognized immediately that the FCNM is of little use in resolving the actual conflicts and that some form of power-sharing is required. The precise form of power-sharing is determined by a range of contextual factors, not least the actual military balance of power among the contending factions. Since the motivation for Western intervention is the protection of regional security, it is necessary that the recommendations of the West be based on an accurate assessment of the actual threat potential raised by the various actors.

Since the security track has done much of the real work in enabling and guiding Western policies towards post-communist Europe, why do we need the legal rights track? If, as I have argued, there is no feasible way to ground effective international norms of minority rights on either a right to self-determination or a right to enjoy culture, why not just give up on the idea of a legal rights track, while preserving the capacity to intervene in post-communist Europe based on considerations of security?

There may be some leaders of Western organizations who regret having established the legal rights track in 1990 and who might wish now to retreat from it. However, as mentioned earlier, ideas of minority rights have become institutionalized at several different levels in Europe and would be difficult, if not impossible, to dislodge.

Moreover, the security track may not work without an underlying legal rights track. On its own, the security track has a perverse tendency to reward state intransigence and minority belligerence. It gives the state an incentive to invent or exaggerate rumours of kin-state manipulation of the minority, so as to reinforce its claim that the minority is disloyal and that extending minority rights would jeopardize the security of the state. It also gives the minority an incentive to threaten violence or seize to simply power, since this is the only way its grievances will reach the attention of the international organizations monitoring security threats. Merely being unjustly ignored is not enough to get Western attention within the security track, unless it is backed up with a credible threat to destabilize governments and regions.[38]

For example, consider the OSCE's approach to TA. As mentioned above, after its initial recommendation of TA in 1990, the OSCE shifted towards discouraging TA and has even counselled various minorities to give up their autonomy claims, including the Hungarians in Slovakia. However, the OSCE has supported autonomy in several other countries, including: Ukraine (for Crimea), Moldova (for Gagauzia and Transdniestria), Georgia (for Abkhazia and South Ossetia), Azerbaijan (for Nagorno-Karabakh) and Serbia (for Kosovo). What explains this variation? The OSCE says that the latter cases are 'exceptional' or 'atypical'[39] but, as far as the evidence shows, the only way in which they are exceptional is that minorities seized power illegally and extra-constitutionally, without the consent of the state.[40] Where minorities have seized power in this way, the state can revoke autonomy only by sending in the army and starting a civil war. For obvious reasons, the OSCE discourages this military option and recommends instead that states negotiate autonomy with the minority and accept some form of federalism or consociationalism that provides after-the-fact legal recognition of the reality on the ground. Hence, the HCNM recommended that it would be dangerous for Ukraine to try to abolish the autonomy that Russians in Crimea (illegally) established.[41]

In contrast, wherever a minority has pursued TA through peaceful and democratic means, within the rule of law, the OSCE has opposed it on the grounds that it would increase tensions. According to the HCNM, given the pervasive fears in post-communist Europe about minority disloyalty and secession, any talk of creating new TA arrangements is bound to increase tensions, particularly if the minority claiming TA borders on a kin-state. This has led the HCNM to recommend that Hungarians in Slovakia not push for TA, given Slovak fears about irredentism.[42]

In short, the security approach rewards intransigence on the part of both sides. If minorities seize power, the OSCE rewards them by putting pressure on the state to accept an 'exceptional' form of autonomy; if the majority refuses to even discuss autonomy proposals from a peaceful and law-abiding minority, the OSCE rewards *it* by putting pressure on minorities to be more 'pragmatic'. This is perverse from the point of view of justice but it seems to be the inevitable logic of the security-based approach. From a security perspective, it may indeed be correct that granting TA to a law-abiding minority increases tensions, while supporting TA after being seized by a belligerent minority decreases tensions.

However, insofar as this is the logic of the security approach, it has the paradoxical effect of undermining security. Long-term security requires that both states and minorities moderate their claims, accept democratic negotiations and seek fair accommodations. In short, long-term security requires that state–minority relations be guided by some conception of justice and rights and not just by power politics. This, of course, is what the legal rights track was supposed to promote and why it must supplement the security track.

The right to effective participation

It would seem that the international community is caught in a bind. European organizations have made an irreversible commitment to developing international legal norms regarding national minorities. However, existing attempts to develop such norms have been either too strong (if based on norms of self-determination) or too weak (if based on a right to enjoy one's culture). Is there some third approach that can fill the gap between Articles 1 and 27, and can provide a more principled guide for regulating the sort of claims that actually underlie the serious cases of ethnic conflict in post-communist Europe?

One option that seems to be gaining strength is the invocation of the principle that the members of national minorities have a right to 'effective participation' in public affairs, particularly in relation to matters affecting them. This idea of 'effective participation' is present in the original 1990 Copenhagen Declaration. Indeed, it was on the basis of this principle that the Declaration recommended TA. Minority autonomy was advocated as a good vehicle for achieving effective participation. More recent declarations have dropped the reference to internal autonomy but retain the commitment to effective participation.[43] Indeed, references to effective participation are becoming more prominent. For example, it is the central topic of the most recent set of OSCE Recommendations (the Lund Recommendations on Effective Participation of National Minorities, adopted in 1999).

This idea of a right to effective participation is attractive for a number of reasons. For one thing, it sounds admirably democratic. Moreover, it avoids the tokenism of a right to 'enjoy one's culture'. It recognizes that minorities want not only to speak their language or profess their religion in private life but also to participate as equals in public life. A right to effective participation recognizes this political dimension of minority aspirations, while avoiding the 'dangerous' and 'radical' ideas of national self-determination.[44]

The main reason why effective participation has become so popular, however, is that it is vague, subject to multiple and conflicting interpretations and, as such, can be endorsed by people with very different conceptions of state–minority relations. In this sense, the apparent consensus on the importance of effective participation hides – or postpones – deep disagreements as to what this actually means.

By the most minimal reading, the right to effective participation means simply that the members of national minorities should not face discrimination in the exercise of their standard political rights to vote, to engage in advocacy and to run for office. This minimalist reading has been invoked to push Estonia and Latvia to grant citizenship to ethnic Russians in their respective countries, and to enable them to vote and to run for office even if they lack full fluency in the titular language.

By a more robust reading, effective participation requires, not just that members of minorities can vote or run for office, but that they actually achieve some degree of *representation* in the legislature. This may not require that minorities be represented precisely in proportion to their share of the overall population, but serious under-representation would be viewed as a concern. This reading is invoked to prohibit attempts by states to gerrymander the boundaries of electoral districts so as to make it more difficult to elect minority representatives. It can also be invoked to prohibit attempts by states to revise the threshold needed for minority political parties to gain seats in proportional representation electoral systems.

In Poland, for example, the German minority regularly elects deputies to parliament because it is exempted from the usual 5 per cent threshold rule. A similar policy benefits the Danish minority party in Germany. In contrast, Greece raised its electoral threshold precisely to prevent the possibility of Turkish MPs being elected.[45] This sort of manipulation might well be prohibited in the future.

Nevertheless, neither of these two readings – focusing on the non-discriminatory exercise of political rights and equitable representation – really gets to the heart of the problem in most cases of serious ethnic conflict. Even when minorities are able to participate without discrimination, and even when they are represented in rough proportion to their population, they may still be permanent losers in the democratic process. This is particularly true in contexts where the dominant group views the minority as potentially disloyal and so votes as a bloc against any policies that empower minorities (consider the near-universal opposition within Slovakia to autonomy for the Hungarian-dominated regions or the opposition within Macedonia to recognizing Albanian as an official language). In these contexts, it may not matter whether minorities exercise their vote or elect MPs in accordance with their numbers, for they will still be outvoted by members of the dominant group. The eventual decision will be the same whether minorities participate through voting or not.

Taken literally, the term 'effective participation' would seem to preclude this situation of national minorities being permanent political minorities. After all, 'effective' participation implies that participation should have an effect – in other words, that participation changes the outcome. The only way to ensure that participation by minorities is effective in this sense is to adopt counter-majoritarian rules that require some form of power-sharing. This may take the form of internal autonomy or of consociational guarantees of a coalition government.

We can call this the maximalist reading of a 'right to effective participation', that is, one that requires counter-majoritarian forms of federal or consociational power-sharing. This is obviously the interpretation that many minority organizations endorse. However, it is strongly resisted by most states, East and West, for precisely the same reason that earlier references to internal self-determination were resisted (fears of escalation, proliferation and irredentism). Having successfully blocked the move to codify a right to internal autonomy, states are not going to accept an interpretation of effective participation that provides a back door for autonomy. Agreement on a right to effective participation was possible precisely because it was seen as an alternative to, not a vehicle for, minority self-government. The prevailing interpretation of effective participation is likely, therefore, to remain focused at the level of non-discrimination and equitable representation, that is, at a level which does not address the actual sources of ethnic conflict.

There is one potential exception to this generalization. European organizations may adopt a maximalist interpretation of effective participation *where forms of power-sharing already exist*. It is widely recognized that attempts by states to abolish pre-existing forms of minority autonomy are a recipe for disaster (for example, Kosovo, Nagorno-Karabakh and South Ossetia). European organizations would like therefore to find a basis in international law to prevent states from revoking pre-existing forms of minority autonomy. The norm of effective participation is a plausible candidate: attempts to revoke pre-existing autonomy regimes can be seen as a deliberate attempt to disempower minorities, and hence a denial of their right to effective participation.

This idea that effective participation protects pre-existing forms of autonomy and power-sharing has been developed by some commentators[46] and has implicitly been invoked by the OSCE itself when justifying its recommendations for TA and consociationalism in countries like Georgia and Moldova. As mentioned earlier, these power-sharing recommendations emerged out of the 'security track', rather than from any reading of international legal norms, but Western organizations have been keen to show that these recommendations were not just a case of rewarding belligerent minorities and that there is a normative basis for their recommendations. The claim that abolishing pre-existing forms of power-sharing erodes effective participation provides a principled basis for their recommendations.

The difficulty, of course, is to explain why it is only *pre-existing* forms of TA that protect effective participation. If TA is needed to ensure the effective participation of Abkhazians in Georgia or Armenians in Azerbaijan, why is it not also needed for Hungarians in Slovakia or Albanians in Macedonia? If abolishing pre-existing autonomy disempowers minorities, why are there no minorities whose claims to autonomy were never accepted also disempowered? (Conversely, if power-sharing institutions are not needed to ensure the effective participation of the Hungarians in Slovakia, why are they needed for Armenians in Nagorno-Karabakh or Russians in Crimea?)

There seems to be no principled basis for privileging those minorities that happen to have acquired or seized autonomy at some point in the past. The differential treatment of claims to autonomy can only be explained as a concession to *Realpolitik*. From a prudent point of view, it is simply much more dangerous to take away pre-existing autonomies from minorities who have fought in the past to acquire it than to refuse to grant new autonomies to minorities who have not shown the willingness to use violence in their pursuit of autonomy.

In short, interpretations of 'effective participation' that privilege pre-existing autonomy suffer from the same flaw as the security track: that is, they reward belligerent minorities while penalizing peaceful and law-abiding minorities. Like the security track, the 'effective participation' approach, as interpreted by some, is calibrated to match the threat potential of the contending parties. Those minorities with a capacity and willingness to destabilize governments and regions can acquire serious forms of power-sharing in the name of effective participation; those minorities who have renounced threats of violence do not.

This suggests that the effective participation approach may end up replicating, rather than resolving, the problems we identified with the other approaches. If effective participation is interpreted maximally, to entail power-sharing, then it is too strong to be acceptable to states and will be rejected for the same reason as the internal self-determination approach. If effective interpretation is interpreted minimally, to cover only non-discrimination and equitable representation, then it is too weak to resolve serious cases of ethnic conflict and will be ineffective for the same reasons that the right to culture approach was ineffective. If we examine how the idea of effective participation actually has been invoked in cases of conflict, we will see that, like the security track, it is based on power politics and not on general principles.

We can make the same point another way. When we talk about effective participation, we need to ask 'participation in what'? From the point of view of most post-communist states, the members of national minorities should be able to participate effectively in the institutions of a unitary nation-state with a single official language. From the point of view of many minority organizations, the members of national minorities should be able to participate effectively in the institutions of a multilingual, multination federal state. These different conceptions of the nature of the state generate different conceptions of what is required for effective participation within the state. Commentators sometimes write as if the principle of effective participation can be invoked to resolve these conflicts over the nature of the state but, in fact, we need to resolve first the question of the nature of the state before we can even apply the principle of effective participation. To date, that basic conflict over the nature of the state has been resolved in post-communist Europe by force, not principles. Where minorities have seized autonomy, effective participation has been interpreted as supporting federal and/or consociational power-sharing within a multilingual, multination state. Where minorities have not used force, effective participation has been interpreted as requiring only non-discriminatory participation and equitable representation within a unitary, monolingual state.

Notwithstanding these limitations, it seems clear that European organizations now view the idea of effective participation as the most promising avenue for the ongoing development of international norms on minority rights. We are almost certain to see new – and perhaps more successful – interpretations emerging in the future. For example, some commentators have suggested that the Advisory Committee, which monitors compliance with the FCNM, can and should adopt a norm of 'progressive implementation', which would expect and require countries to fulfil progressively stronger interpretations of the various FCNM provisions. What counts as adequately fulfilling the FCNM's norms regarding language rights or effective participation today will not be sufficient five years from now. Each time a state submits a report to the Committee it will be asked: 'what have you done for minorities *lately*?' The idea is not simply to prevent countries from regressing (the non-retrogression clause mentioned previously) but also to raise the bar continuously in terms of what is required to meet the FCNM norms.[47]

There is no doubt that the Advisory Committee has done some innovative thinking along these lines, aided by the fact that it is composed of independent experts rather than state representatives.[48] If this analysis is correct, however, there are likely to be limits on the extent to which the independent experts on the Advisory Committee will be able to ratchet up the requirements of the FCNM. In particular, there are doubts as to whether official language status or TA will come to be seen as requirements of the FCNM, except where minorities have shown a willingness and capacity to undermine stability and security. At the end of the day, the Advisory Committee is only advisory: its recommendations must be approved by states. It is anticipated that any attempt to raise the bar to include TA and official language status will be rejected by states for the same reason that previous attempts to codify such rights have failed.

Conclusion

This chapter has argued that attempts to develop international norms of minority rights in Europe since 1990 have run into a series of dilemmas. Appeals to a right to internal self-determination have proven too controversial, appeals to a right to enjoy one's culture have proven too weak and appeals to a right to effective participation have proven too vague to address any of the conflicts in post-communist Europe that generated the call for the 'internationalization' of minority issues in the first place.

This is not necessarily a bad thing. As noted earlier, the initial impulse to develop these norms was an unduly pessimistic view about the likelihood of ethnic violence in post-communist Europe. If violence is unlikely, then why not let states come to their own settlements on ethnic issues, at their own speed? After all, it took Western countries many decades to work out their current accommodations with national minorities and, arguably, the success of these accommodations is due to the fact that they were the result of gradual domestic negotiations, rather than imposition through external pressure.

However, it is often forgotten that international pressure did play an important and beneficial role in several Western cases. For example, the autonomy arrangement for the Aaland Islands was an externally determined solution under the League of Nations which has worked very well. Germany's accession to NATO in 1955 was conditional on its working out a reciprocal minority rights agreement with Denmark, an agreement which is now seen as a model of how kin-states can work constructively through bilateral relations to help minorities in neighbouring states. There was strong international pressure on Italy to accord autonomy to South Tyrol in 1972, which today is seen as an exemplar of successful accommodation. In all of these cases, a certain degree of international pressure was needed to initiate settlements,[49] although they have become domestically self-sustaining and, indeed, have often been enhanced or expanded as a result of domestic procedures.[50]

It would be inaccurate therefore to suggest that Western states have 'naturally' or inevitably gravitated towards fair accommodation of national minorities without international pressure. In fact, some combination of international pressure and/or domestic violence was present at one point or another in most Western cases of autonomy.[51] Given this history, it seems naïve to assume that countries in Central and Eastern Europe will move inevitably and peacefully towards significant minority rights through their own domestic democratic processes. As in the West, some extra-parliamentary push – whether it is international pressure and/or domestic violence – may be needed for post-communist countries seriously to consider federal or consociational power-sharing. However, the goal of any instance of international pressure should be to start a process that becomes domestically self-sustaining (and, ideally, domestically self-improving).

In that sense, perhaps the international community should limit its role in post-communist Europe to ensuring that there is the minimum level of respect for human rights and political freedom needed to create a democratic space for states and minorities to work out their own accommodations slowly. The increasing prominence of the idea of 'effective participation' may reflect the belief that Western intervention should be aimed at creating the conditions for post-communist societies to work out their own account of minority rights through peaceful and democratic deliberations, rather than seeking to impose some canonical set of internationally defined minority rights.

This may be the direction we are headed in – and perhaps this is the most that reasonably we can expect. Attempts to formulate general principles of international law to resolve deep conflicts over autonomy, power-sharing and language rights may simply be unrealistic.[52] Over time, we might hope and expect that post-communist countries will follow the Western trend towards multilingual, multinational states but it is unnecessary – and perhaps counter-productive – to try to jump-start this process through the codification and imposition of international norms of substantive minority rights.

However, if this is indeed the direction we are headed in, it is important that the minimal standards being demanded of post-communist states be presented precisely as *minimum* standards. A serious problem confronting society at the moment is that many actors view the FCNM and other international norms, not as a minimum floor from which minority rights should be domestically negotiated, but rather as a maximal ceiling beyond which minorities must not seek to go.

There is, in fact, a concerted effort by most post-communist states to present the FCNM and OSCE Recommendations as defining the outside limits of legitimate minority mobilization. Any minority leader or organization that asks for something beyond what these documents provide is immediately labelled a 'radical'. These minimal international standards are not being treated as the preconditions needed to negotiate the forms of power-sharing and self-government appropriate to each state democratically but are viewed instead as eliminating the need to adopt – or even to debate – forms of power-sharing and self-government. When minority organizations raise questions about substantive minority rights, post-communist states respond: 'we meet all international standards', as if that forecloses the question of how states should treat their minorities. The claim that 'we meet all international standards' has, in fact, become a mantra among post-communist states, taking the place of any substantive debate about how to address minority claims regarding powers, rights and status.

Sadly, it seems that the international community is often complicit in this effort to treat international norms as a maximum ceiling, rather than as a minimal floor, and to stigmatize minority leaders who dare to ask for the sorts of substantive minority rights enjoyed by most sizeable national minorities in the West.[53] If it proves impossible to codify substantive minority rights in international law, we must at least be clear that the meagre provisions currently codified in European instruments are the starting-point for democratic debate, not the end-point.

Notes

1. G. Pentassuglia, 'The EU and the Protection of Minorities: The Case of Eastern Europe'. *European Journal of International Law* 12(1) (2001): 3–38; G. Pentassuglia, *Minorities in International Law* (Strasbourg: Council of Europe, 2003); Minority Rights Group, *The Framework Convention for the Protection of National Minorities: A Guide* (London: Minority Rights Group International, 1999).

2. See, for example, J. Cohen, *Conflict Prevention Instruments in the Organization for Security and Cooperation in Europe* (The Hague: Netherlands Institute of International Relations, 1998); R. Zaagman, *Conflict Prevention in the Baltic States: The OSCE High Commissioner on National Minorities in Estonia, Latvia and Lithuania*, ECMI Monograph No. 1 (Flensburg: European Centre for Minority Issues, 1999); J. Packer, 'The OSCE and International Guarantees of Local Self-government', *European Commission for Democracy through Law: Local Self-Government, Territorial Integrity and Protection of Minorities*. (Strasbourg: Council of Europe, 1996), 250–72; J. Packer, 'Making International Law Matter in Preventing Ethnic Conflicts', *New York University Journal of International Law and Politics* 32(3) (2000): 715–24; K. Gal, *Bilateral Agreements in Central and Eastern Europe: A New Inter-State Framework for Minority Protection*, Working Paper No. 4 (Flensburg: European Centre for Minority Issues, 1999); and G. Alfredsson and D. Turk, 'International Mechanisms for the Monitoring and Protection of Minority Rights: Their Advantages, Disadvantages and Interrelationships', in A. Bloed (ed.), *Monitoring Human Rights in Europe: Comparing International Procedures and Mechanisms* (Norwell, MA: Kluwer, 1993), 169–86.

3. By 'national minorities', I mean groups living on (what they view to be) their historic homeland but whose homeland (or part of it) has been incorporated into a larger state in which they form a minority. This includes both trans-border minorities, i.e. national groups that form the majority in one state but whose historic homeland extends across what is now an international boundary, so that some members of the group are on the 'wrong' side of the border from their 'kin-state' (e.g. ethnic Hungarians in Romania and Slovakia). It also includes stateless nations, i.e. groups that think of themselves as 'nations' but do not control any state and whose historic homeland is incorporated into a larger country (e.g.

Scots) or divided between two or more countries (e.g. Basques). Some commentators would also include indigenous peoples, like the Saami, into this category, since they also share the characteristic of having their historic homeland incorporated into a larger state. However, most commentators distinguish indigenous peoples from national minorities, partly on the grounds that indigenous peoples have not traditionally understood themselves as 'nations', or engaged in the project of 'nation-building'. I will return to these definitional issues below.

4. Organization for Security and Cooperation in Europe (OSCE), Consolidated Summary of the Implementation Meeting on Human Dimension Issues' 12–28 November 1997.

5. The EU did set up the European Monitoring Centre on Racism and Xenophobia in 1997 but it has focused primarily on immigrant groups rather than national minorities, and on member states in the West rather than on post-communist Europe.

6. A. Burgess, 'Critical Reflections on the Return of National Minority Rights to East/West European Affairs', in K. Cordell (ed.), *Ethnicity and Democratisation in the New Europe* (London: Routledge, 1999), 49–60.

7. The case of Greece was perhaps a warning here. Greece has the formal trappings of a liberal-democracy with a market economy and would seem therefore to be a good fit for the EU. Yet, in fact, most Western European countries are exasperated by the way Greece's often xenophobic and illiberal political culture has jeopardized various EU projects and no one in the EU wanted to admit a dozen countries that would act in the same way. Greece's poor record on minority rights is often seen as a symbol or indicator of its overall political culture.

8. R. Brett, 'The Human Dimension of the CSCE and the CSCE Response to Minorities', in M.R. Lucas (ed.), *The CSCE in the 1990s: Constructing European Security and Cooperation* (Baden-Baden: Nomos Verlagsgesellschaft, 1993), 143–60. For a detailed discussion of the way various countries try to deny the existence of minorities, see Greek Helsinki Monitor, 'Statement at the OSCE on (Partly or Fully) Unrecognized Minorities in Albania, Bulgaria, France, Greece, Macedonia, Slovenia and Turkey', MINELRES 24 October 2000, <http://www.minelres.lv>

9. D. Chandler, 'The OSCE and the Internationalisation of National Minority Rights', in K. Cordell (ed.), *Ethnicity and Democratisation in the New Europe* (London: Routledge, 1999), 61–76, at 66.

10. M. Cornwall, 'Minority Rights and Wrongs in Eastern Europe in the Twentieth Century', *The Historian* 50 (1996): 16–20; A. Sharp, 'The Genie That Would Not Go Back Into the Bottle: National Self-Determination and the Legacy of the First World War and the Peace Settlement', in S. Dunn and T.G. Fraser (eds), *Europe and Ethnicity: The First World War and Contemporary Ethnic Conflict* (London: Routledge, 1996); M. Burns, 'Disturbed Spirits: Minority Rights and the New World Orders, 1919 and the 1990s', in S.F. Wells and P. Bailey-Smith (eds), *New European Orders: 1919 and 1991* (Washington, DC: Woodrow Wilson Center Press, 1996); M. Kovacs, 'Standards of Self-determination and Standards of Minority Rights in the Post-communist Era: A Historical Perspective', *Nations and Nationalism* 9(3) (2003): 433–50.

11. ICCPR Article 1: 'All peoples have the right of self-determination. By virtue of that right they freely determine their political status and freely pursue their economic, social and cultural development.' Article 27: 'In those States in which ethnic, religious or linguistic minorities exist, persons belonging to such minorities shall not be denied the right, in community with the other members of their group, to

enjoy their own culture, to profess and practise their own religion, or to use their own language'.

12. For a more detailed elaboration of the way that traditional human rights principles fail to protect national minorities from grave injustice, see W. Kymlicka, *Politics in the Vernacular: Nationalism, Multiculturalism and Citizenship* (Oxford: Oxford University Press, 2001). The Helsinki CSCE Decisions stated that states 'will refrain from resettling and condemn all attempts, by the threat or use of force, to resettle persons with the aim of changing the ethnic composition of areas within their territories' ('Helsinki Document 1992: The Challenges of Change', Helsinki Decisions VI: 23 and 27 [Helsinki: CSCE, 1992]). However, prohibitions on resettling people (i.e. ethnic cleansing) do not preclude deliberate state settlement policies (i.e. providing financial incentives such as free land or lower taxes) to people who move into a minority's homeland.

13. Conference on Security and Cooperation in Europe (CSCE), 'Document of the Copenhagen Meeting of the Conference on the Human Dimension of the CSCE' (Copenhagen, 1990).

14. Council of Europe Parliamentary Assembly (PACE), Recommendation 1201 (1993) on an additional protocol on the rights of national minorities to the European Convention on Human Rights (Strasbourg, 1993).

15. The focus here is on groups that demonstrate a desire for TA, as reflected, for example, in consistently high levels of support for politicians or political parties that campaign for TA. These can be labelled 'mobilized' national minorities, since their members have demonstrated consistent support for typically nationalist goals of autonomy and official language rights. The emergence of such mobilized national minorities is, of course, the result of political contestation. National minorities do not enter the world with a fully formed nationalist consciousness; they are constructed by ethnic entrepreneurs and ethnic elites who seek to persuade enough of their members that it makes sense to mobilize politically as a national minority for national goals. There are cases where these attempts to generate a nationalist consciousness among the members of a minority have failed. One clear case in Western Europe is the Frisians in the Netherlands. From a historical viewpoint, they have as much claim to be a distinct 'nation' as any other ethno-national group in Europe. Yet attempts by Frisian elites to persuade people of Frisian descent or people living in historic Friesland that they should support nationalist political objectives have repeatedly failed. This is fully acceptable from a liberal point of view. National minorities may have a right to claim territorial autonomy but they certainly have no duty to do so. Whether or not a national minority claims territorial autonomy should be determined by the wishes of the majority of its members, as shaped and expressed through free democratic debate and contestation. In this sense, European states deal with those groups that have demonstrated a desire for territorial autonomy, i.e. in which nationalist political leaders have succeeded in a free and democratic debate in gaining the support of a majority of the members of the group. That is not to assume that such nationalist constructions will (or should) succeed. Their success has to be explained, not simply taken as a given, just as the failure of the nationalists in Friesland has to be explained, rather than taken as somehow normal or natural. The purpose of this chapter is not to explain the success or failure of particular acts of nationalist construction but rather to explore how states should respond to the cases of successful mobilization, in which the members of national minority groups have shown consistently high levels of support for nationalist objectives. It is these cases that are the 'problem'

to which European organizations are seeking a solution through the adoption of international norms of minority rights.

16. For a more detailed defence of this claim, see W. Kymlicka, 'Canadian Multiculturalism in Historical and Comparative Perspective'. *Constitutional Forum* 13(1) (2003): 1–8.

17. Declaration on the Rights of Indigenous Peoples, adopted by the UN General Assembly, 2 October 2007, Resolution 61/295.

18. S.J. Anaya, *Indigenous Peoples in International Law* (New York: Oxford University Press, 1996).

19. Indeed, the most influential discussion of the international law on indigenous rights accepts that other national groups should also be able to claim rights to internal self-determination. See Anaya, *Indigenous Peoples, supra* note 18. For a discussion of the similarities and differences between indigenous peoples and national minorities, see Kymlicka, *Politics in the Vernacular supra* note 12. It is worth noting that organizations representing one national minority in Eastern Europe – namely, the Crimean Tatars – have explicitly defined themselves as an 'indigenous people' for the purposes of international law.

20. Hague Recommendations on Education Rights of National Minorities (1996); Oslo Recommendations on Linguistic Rights of National Minorities (1998); Lund Recommendations on Effective Participation of National Minorities (1999).

21. European Commission for Democracy through Law, *Opinion of the Venice Commission on the Interpretation of Article 11 of the Draft Protocol to the European Convention on Human Rights appended to Recommendation 1201* (Strasbourg: Council of Europe, 1996).

22. C. Offe, '"Homogeneity" and Constitutional Democracy: Coping with Identity Conflicts with Group Rights', *Journal of Political Philosophy* 6(2) (1998): 113–41; and C. Offe, 'Political Liberalism, Group Rights and the Politics of Fear and Trust', *Studies in East European Thought* 53(3) (2001): 167–82.

23. I discuss and criticize Offe's claim that escalation and proliferation are inherent dangers of TA in W. Kymlicka, 'The Impact of Group Rights on Fear and Trust: A Response to Offe', *Hagar: International Social Science Review* 3(1) (2002): 19–36.

24. This is one of the factors that contributes to the general 'securitization' of state–minority relations in post-communist Europe, as discussed in W. Kymlicka, 'Justice and Security in the Accommodation of Minority Nationalism', in Alain Dieckhoff (ed.), *The Politics of Belonging: Nationalism, Liberalism and Pluralism* (New York: Lexington, 2004), 127–54. It is interesting to note that even when national minorities in the West are linked by ethnicity to a neighbouring state, they do not today raise fears of disloyalty or security. The French in Switzerland or Belgium are not seen as a fifth column for France; the Flemish are not seen as a fifth column for the Netherlands. Even the Germans in Belgium, who have historically collaborated with Germany's aggression against Belgium, are no longer viewed that way. This is testament to the extraordinary success of the EU and NATO in 'desecuritizing' ethnic relations in Western Europe.

25. This is particularly true of those countries, like Romania or Turkey, influenced by the French Jacobin tradition.

26. M. van der Stoel, *Peace and Stability through Human and Minority Rights: Speeches by the OSCE High Commissioner on National Minorities* (Baden-Baden: Nomos Verlagsgesellschaft, 1999), at 111.

27. Chandler, 'The OSCE and the Internationalisation', *supra* note 9; S. Ford, 'OSCE National Minority Rights in the United States: The Limits of Conflict Resolution', *Suffolk Transnational Law Review* 23(1) (1999): 1–55, at 49.

28. A similar approach was already under way at the United Nations. The 1992 UN Declaration on the Rights of Persons Belonging to National or Ethnic, Religious and Linguistic Minorities was similarly an attempt to expand and strengthen Article 27.

29. S. Wheatley, 'Minority Rights and Political Accommodation in the "New" Europe', *European Law Review* 22 (Suppl) (1997): HRC63–HRC81, at 40. For example, these norms often allow minorities to submit documents to public authorities in their language but do not require that they receive an answer in their own language.

30. Post-communist countries believe they are much more closely monitored for compliance with these norms than Western countries like France or Greece, and that they are criticized for engaging in practices that go unnoticed in the West. See Cohen, *Conflict Prevention Instruments, supra* note 2; and S. Ratner, 'Does International Law Matter in Preventing Ethnic Conflicts?', *New York University Journal of International Law and Politics* 32(3) (2000): 591–698.

31. This phrase is taken from Druviete, although she was describing the attitude of the Soviet Union to minority languages. See I. Druviete, 'Linguistic Human Rights in the Baltic States', *International Journal of the Sociology of Language* 127 (1997): 161–85.

32. One exception to this generalization is the Roma. Some commentators speculate that issues relating to the Roma could become sources of violence and instability, even though the Roma have not shown an interest in territorial autonomy or in creating their own separate public institutions. European organizations are therefore devoting much time and effort to examining state policies towards the Roma. However, the current FCNM/OSCE norms were not intended to deal with the situation of the Roma. Indeed, the OSCE has recently recommended the adoption of a separate Romani Rights Charter.

33. There is no conceptual or philosophical reason why a right to enjoy one's culture cannot be interpreted in such a robust way as to support claims to territorial autonomy or official language status. Indeed, this is precisely what various 'liberal nationalist' political theorists have done in their writings. The idea of a right to culture is invoked by writers like Yael Tamir and Joseph Raz as the basis for their defence of a right to national self-determination. See Y. Tamir, *Liberal Nationalism* (Princeton: Princeton University Press, 1993); and A. Margalit and J. Raz, 'National Self-determination', *Journal of Philosophy* 87(9) (1990): 439–61. Politically speaking, there is no chance that such a 'nationalist' reading of a right to culture will be adopted in international law. As we have seen, the whole idea underlying the Article 27 right to enjoy one's culture was to provide an alternative to the Article 1 right of national self-determination.

34. Recall that, prior to 1989, the EU tacitly allowed Greece to persecute its minorities and NATO allowed Turkey to persecute its minorities. See J. Batt and J. Amato, 'Minority Rights and EU Enlargement to the East', EUI, RSC Policy Paper No. 98/5 (1998).

35. When Western governments were deciding whether to intervene in Kosovo, an American columnist famously said: 'give war a chance'. War is bad, he said, but it is important for both sides to learn the hard way that they cannot defeat the other and so accept the need to sit down and negotiate a compromise. A more modest version of the same idea is defended by Adam Burgess. He says we should 'give assimilation a chance'. See Burgess, 'Critical Reflections', *supra* note 6. Assimilationist policies in post-communist Europe might be unpleasant and might fail, but it is important for states (and dominant groups) to learn the limits of their

capacities and the strength of minority resistance, thus accepting the necessity of coming to some settlement with their minorities.

36. M. Estébanez, 'The High Commissioner on National Minorities: Development of the Mandate', in M. Bothe *et al.* (eds), *The OSCE in the Maintenance of Peace and Security* (The Hague: Kluwer, 1997), 123–65; and van der Stoel, *Peace and Stability*, *supra* note 26.

37. For a more detailed discussion of these two tracks, see W. Kymlicka and M. Opalski (eds), *Can Liberal Pluralism Be Exported? Western Political Theory and Ethnic Relations in Eastern Europe* (Oxford: Oxford University Press, 2001).

38. 'Minorities should not be confronted with the situation that the international community will only respond to their concerns if there is a conflict. Such an approach could easily backfire and generate more conflicts than it resolves. An objective, impartial and non-selective approach to minorities, involving the application of minority standards across the board, must therefore remain a crucial part.' (Alfredsson and Turk, 'International Mechanisms', *supra* note 2: 169–86, at 176–77.) See also Chandler, 'The OSCE and the Internationalisation', *supra* note 9.

39. Zaagman, *Conflict Prevention in the Baltic, supra* note 2: 253 n. 84; L. Thio, 'Developing a "Peace and Security" Approach towards Minorities' Problems', *International and Comparative Law Quarterly* 52 (2003): 115–50, at 132.

40. In all of these cases, except Crimea, the minority seized power through an armed uprising. In the case of Crimea, the Ukrainian state barely existed on Crimean territory and so the Russians did not have to take up arms to overthrow the existing state structure. They simply held an (illegal) referendum on autonomy and then started governing themselves.

41. van der Stoel, *Peace and Stability*, *supra* note 26: at 26.

42. *Ibid.*: at 25.

43. 'The participating States will respect the right of persons belonging to national minorities to effective participation in public affairs, including participation in the affairs relating to the protection and promotion of the identity of such minorities' (OSCE Copenhagen Declaration 1990, Article 35). 'The Parties shall create the conditions necessary for the effective participation of persons belonging to national minorities in cultural, social and economic life and in public affairs, in particular those affecting them' (FCNM 1995, Article 15).

44. W. Kemp, 'Profiting from Instability: Crime, Corruption and Inter-Ethnic Conflict', in V.-Y. Ghebali and D. Warner (eds), *New Security Threats and Challenges within the OSCE Region* (Geneva: IUHEI, 2003), 49–73.

45. Minority Rights Group, *The Framework Convention, supra* note 1.

46. Verstichel argues that the Advisory Committee examining conformity with the FCNM has implicitly adopted a non-retrogression clause regarding autonomy. A. Verstichel, 'Elaborating a Catalogue of Best Practices of Effective Participation of National Minorities: Review of the Opinions of the Advisory Committee Regarding Article 15 of the Council of Europe Framework Convention for the Protection of National Minorities', in ECMI, *European Yearbook of Minority Issues 2* (Flensburg, ECMI, 2002/3). Similarly, Lewis-Anthony argues that the jurisprudence regarding Article 3 of the First Protocol of the European Charter of Human Rights can be extrapolated to protect existing forms of autonomy. S. Lewis-Anthony, 'Autonomy and the Council of Europe – With Special Reference to the Application of Article 3 of the First Protocol of the European Convention on Human Rights', in M. Suksi (ed.), *Autonomy: Applications and Implications* (The Hague/London/Boston: Kluwer Law International, 1998), 317–42. At a more

philosophical level, Allen Buchanan argues that there should be international protections for existing forms of TA, but denies that there should be norms supporting claims for TA by groups that do not yet have it. A. Buchanan, *Justice, Democracy and Self-determination: Moral Foundations for International Law* (Oxford: Oxford University Press, 2004).

47. For optimistic views along these lines, see Verstichel, 'Elaborating a Catalogue', *supra* note 46; and M. Weller, 'Filling the Frame: 5th Anniversary of the Entry into Force of the Framework Convention for the Protection of National Minorities', *Conference Report*, Strasbourg: Council of Europe. 30–31 October 2003.

48. R. Hofmann, 'Protecting the Rights of National Minorities in Europe: First Experiences with the Council of Europe Framework Convention for the Protection of National Minorities', *German Yearbook of International Law* 44 (2002): 237–69.

49. Conversely, several commentators argue that some of the more intractable conflicts in the West, such as Northern Ireland and Cyprus, cannot be resolved by purely domestic procedures and negotiations, and that the international community needs to play a more active role. See the essays in M. Keating and J. McGarry (eds), *Minority Nationalism and the Changing International Order* (Oxford: Oxford University Press, 2001).

50. For a discussion of some of the factors that have helped make these settlements domestically self-sustaining and self-enhancing, see Kymlicka, 'Canadian Multiculturalism', *supra* note 16.

51. The role of violence is obvious in Northern Ireland, the Basque Country, Cyprus and Corsica, but there were also low-level acts of violence in Quebec and South Tyrol (e.g. bombings of state property like mailboxes or energy pylons). The knowledge that some members of the minority were willing to resort to violence undoubtedly concentrated the mind of the state. As Deets puts it, 'Across Europe, autonomy came out of specific historical and political contexts, and it is far easier to discuss the political calculations and the desire to quell bombing campaigns that went into autonomy decisions than it is to point to a clear acceptance of principles of justice for minorities'. See S. Deets, 'Liberal Pluralism: Does the West Have Any to Export?', *Journal on Ethnopolitics and Minority Issues in Europe* 4 (2002).

52. However, the case of indigenous peoples shows what can be achieved on these issues through international law where there is a political commitment to do so.

53. Or so I argue in Kymlicka and Opalski, *Can Liberal Pluralism be Exported?*, *supra* note 37.

2
Collective Rights in the Context of EU Accession*

Hans-Joachim Heintze

The issue of collective rights for minorities has been discussed for years. There are many different questions involved. In the context of EU accession, the discussion has focused primarily on the underlying tension in the concept of minority protection stemming from the classical view that states may oppose entitlements which might call into question their sovereignty or territorial integrity. Minority rights, as part of human rights, challenge this assumption. On the one hand, there is a need to reassure governments that the granting of rights to minorities does not undermine these principles. On the other hand, it is necessary also to ensure that persons belonging to minorities are able to maintain their identity and enjoy their rights as members of a minority group.

This balancing act is performed through the doctrine of minority rights as part of human rights. The European instruments of the Council of Europe (CoE) and the Organization for Security and Cooperation in Europe (OSCE) follow this traditional and recognized approach. However, during the EU accession process, it was clear that some candidate states considered minority rights as collective rights. Formulations referring to group rights were used by the Slovene and Latvian legislation, and were even more consistently used in Hungarian legislation in 1993. The Hungarian law speaks of 'community rights' and contains sections on cultural cultivation of identity, the right of association and freedom of media, cross-border minority contacts and political participation.[1] Though Hungary has been considered by European bodies as a 'leading example' in the field of minority protection,[2] its collective approach was viewed by some experts as discriminatory and, therefore, sharply rejected.[3] Other experts argue that general reluctance to give legal shape to group rights for minorities may be due to the fact that there is no means to enforce such rights judicially.[4]

---

*The article is an extended version of a commentary first published in M. Weller (ed.), *The Rights of Minorities: A Commentary on the European Framework Convention for the Protection of National Minorities* (Oxford: Oxford University Press, 2005), 85.

Minority issues in Europe

The protection of minorities via the collective rights contained in international conventions became an issue after World War I, when the Treaty of Versailles imposed the creation of new states and changed the geography of Europe considerably.[5] There is no doubt that these border shifts had a dramatic effect on the populations of some countries. For example, the Hungarians were split among Slovakia, Romania, Ukraine and Serbia.[6]

Inevitably, this division of peoples led to instability in the post-war order. The victorious powers, quickly acknowledging the existence of that instability, deemed it necessary to offer these newly created minorities adequate protection from acts of revenge carried out by the newly created majorities. The need to prevent the emergence of secessionist demands prompted the victors to establish a number of protection mechanisms for minority groups under the umbrella of the League of Nations.[7] However, this international system failed due to the lack of universal acceptance of its rules – a fact that was visible particularly in regard to the protection of minorities, as only the states bound by the post-World War I peace treaties were obliged to respect minority regulations, while the great powers of that time were not bound by these norms. For example, the Polish proposal for a global convention on the protection of minorities in 1934 was rejected by France, the United Kingdom, Italy and Belgium. Moreover, the whole system lost credibility after Nazi Germany misused the idea of minority protection for its expansion.

Since the topic of minority protection had been exploited systematically for hostile purposes, the post-World War II community of states was very reluctant to grant rights to minorities through their express inclusion in the emerging catalogue of human rights. Instead, while adopting the United Nations Charter, the states focused on the protection of individual human rights, arguing that these would also protect persons belonging to minorities. The same approach was pursued during the codification of the International Covenant on Civil and Political Rights (ICCPR), adopted in 1966 by the UN General Assembly. It must be stressed that Article 27 of the ICCPR contained (and contains still) the only universal legally binding norm on minority protection, thereby introducing minority protection firmly into the body of human rights.[8]

Since the end of the Cold War, Europe has witnessed unexpected and bloody explosions of nationalism in its former communist countries. Several parts of Eastern and Southeastern Europe have been devastated by ethnic and religious conflict, during which hundreds of thousands of persons belonging to minorities were killed, severely injured or became victims of 'ethnic cleansing'. The European populace, shocked by these events, demanded that international organizations develop new mechanisms of minority protection, in addition to improving those already in existence. However, there were no proposals to establish mechanisms for the collective protection of minorities.

The first European body to react to this challenge was the Conference for Security and Cooperation in Europe (CSCE), later renamed the Organization for Security and Cooperation in Europe (OSCE). By 1990, all European countries had become CSCE members, having accepted the Copenhagen Document, the first politically binding document to contain a detailed set of commitments towards minorities. It must be added that this document clearly combined minority protection with obligations concerning the rule of law and democratic constitutions. Hence, the CSCE/OSCE broke new ground in the field of minority rights.

Recognizing this, other European actors in the field, including the CoE Commission for Democracy through Law (ECDL), proposed that the CSCE promulgate a legally binding treaty on this topic at the beginning of the 1990s.[9] The outcome of this process was the 1996 Framework Convention for the Protection of National Minorities (FCNM) of the Council of Europe. The EU planned to use the CoE criteria as a common standard of achievement and, since the EU had (and still has) insufficient means to ensure member states' compliance with the minority rights commitments undertaken during the accession process,[10] the Framework Convention presented a very useful compliance mechanism.

Discussions on collective rights in the Council of Europe

During the elaboration of the CoE's FCNM, the issue of collective minority rights was discussed. The first draft by the ECDL greatly influenced the Parliamentary Assembly because it opted for the same approach as in its Recommendation 1201, which was intended for adoption as a Protocol to the European Convention on Human Rights and Fundamental Freedoms (ECHR). In fact, the Preamble of the Protocol refers to the general obligation to protect the rights of national minorities and Article 1 of the same Protocol provides a rather ambiguous definition of the concept of minority in that the expression 'national minority' is said to refer to a group of persons in a state who:

(a) reside on the territory of that state and are citizens thereof;
(b) maintain long-standing, firm and lasting ties with that state;
(c) display distinctive ethnic, cultural, religious or linguistic characteristics;
(d) are sufficiently representative, although smaller in number than the rest of the population of that state or of a region of that state; and
(e) are motivated by a common concern to preserve that which constitutes their common identity, including their culture, their traditions, their religion or their language.[11]

However, Recommendation 1201, along with the proposed Protocol, was rejected in 1993 at the Vienna Summit of the CoE. It appeared that the codification of collective minority rights in the European context still faced tremendous resistance, largely because the concept and nature of minority protection remained vague. Nonetheless, at the Vienna Summit Meeting of the CoE, on 7 October 1993, the delegates decided to work out a new instrument on the protection of national minorities, resulting in the FCNM, which was opened for signature in 1995.

On 4 November 1993 the Committee of Ministers established an Ad Hoc Committee for the Protection of National Minorities (CAHMIN), composed of experts in the field of minority rights. The terms of reference of CAHMIN reflected the Vienna Decisions of the Summit of the CoE states, which meant that the instrument under consideration was not connected to the European human rights protection mechanisms. CAHMIN started work in late January 1994. The first product, the preliminary draft opening provisions, contained certain principles of the Framework Convention. The working paper prepared by the Secretariat was based on the ECDL Draft. Article 1 reads:

> The international protection of the rights of national minorities, as well as the rights of persons belonging to those minorities, as guaranteed by the present Convention, is a fundamental component of the international protection of human rights, and as such falls within the scope of international co-operation.[12]

The approach of CAHMIN differed from the traditional approaches because it referred to the 'rights of the minority', that is, to collective rights. All previous documents had dealt with the protection of the rights of individuals belonging to a minority group. The difference is striking when compared with the revised Federal Union of European Nationalities (FUEN) Draft for an Additional Protocol to the ECHR of 1994, which advocates individual rights only.[13]

It is surprising that no further discussion on the question of collective rights for minorities followed from this paper. Instead CAHMIN debates focused on the relationship between minority rights and human rights. The Committee's Italian expert argued that confirming that 'the protection of national minorities ... forms an integral part of the international protection of human rights' did not correctly reflect the Vienna Declaration, which envisioned a document devoted to the protection of minorities, independent and distinct from the international instruments on the legal protection of human rights. However, the intervention of the Italian expert was unsuccessful and finally CAHMIN stressed that the 'main purpose of Article 1' was to specify that the protection of national minorities is integral to the protection of human rights.

The importance of this formulation lies in the fact that minority protection does not fall within the exclusive competence of states. With regard to the collective aspect of this article, which contradicts the individualistic human rights approach, CAHMIN underlined that, without providing any explanation, the wording made it clear that no collective rights of national minorities were envisaged. This approach cannot be considered satisfactory from the point of legal theory; it is, however, a common approach, as has been shown by other CoE documents. The same tactic of mixing collective and individual rights was also used by the Parliamentary Assembly of the CoE in its Recommendation 1492 (2001), stressing 'the importance of effectively protecting the rights of minorities in Europe. It considers that adequate protection for persons belonging to national minorities and their communities is an integral part of the protection of human rights'.[14]

The European approach: collective versus individual rights?

The FCNM contains no definition of the notion of 'national minority' because it was impossible to agree upon one. Former attempts to forge a definition, such as Recommendation 1201, had been rejected by state parties, leading to the 1993 ECDL conclusion that the definition of minorities '[was] a delicate problem and one solution might be not to include a specific definition in the text but to rely on the usual meaning of the word'.[15] CAHMIN followed that recommendation: paragraph 12 of the explanatory report to the FCNM called for 'a pragmatic approach'.

The term 'national minorities' consists of two explanatory elements: the noun 'minorities' and the adjective 'national'. The circumstances of groups considered to be 'minorities' differ greatly from one state to another, and it is therefore difficult to create a definition that encompasses all categories of minorities. The most controversial points are the minimum size of the minority group and the need for a subjective feeling of solidarity. The situation became even more complicated when some states – such as France and Turkey – denied the existence of minorities in the name of national unity. Such states fear that the existence of a commonly agreed definition of a minority supports the regional claims and secessionist movements which they have long resisted.[16] It is symptomatic that both countries made reservations to Article 27 of the ICCPR to the effect that this article was not applicable. The fear of secessionist movements largely explains the reluctance of many states to reach a consensus on the general definition of the term 'minority'.

Due to the lack of a general definition, international instruments have confined their scope of applicability to certain types of minorities, for example, ethnic, linguistic or religious minorities. An excellent illustration of this approach is provided by Article 27 of the ICCPR, which enumerates several categories of minorities. These categories can be identified easily, at least in those countries that do not deny the existence of minorities or that recognize minority groups on their territory. The UN Declaration on the Rights of Persons Belonging to National or Ethnic, Religious and Linguistic Minorities adds 'national minorities' to the beneficiaries (ethnic, religious or linguistic minorities) mentioned in Article 27 of the ICCPR.[17] According to the Commentary of the UN Working Group on Minorities, this does not mean that the overall scope of application is extended beyond the groups already listed in Article 27. The Commentary states: 'there is hardly any national minority, however defined, that is not also an ethnic or linguistic minority'.[18] Therefore an overlap is unavoidable. The Working Group on Minorities rejects the idea that because minorities can be categorized into four groups their rights have a somewhat different content and strength.

The FCNM confines its realm of applicability to 'national' minorities. This apparently narrows the class of beneficiaries of the rights granted in comparison with the ICCPR. However, the expression 'national minority' is used less widely because it is rather ambiguous in the European context. In France, for example, it refers to citizenship, where all citizens of the state belong to the French nation. This understanding is consistent with the 1997 European Convention on Nationality, which defines 'nationality' as 'the legal bond between a person and a state and does not indicate the person's ethnic origin'.[19] By contrast, the German concept of a national minority follows the idea of a linguistic and cultural community and is not necessarily related to citizenship. According to this approach, a national minority must be connected to a larger nation already represented by a state, forming a so-called kin-state.

This second conceptual framework forms the basis of the mandate of the OSCE High Commissioner on National Minorities (HCNM). Indeed, the HCNM has a mandate to investigate minority rights issues that have only an inter-state dimension. The OSCE has affirmed that kin-states have a legitimate interest in the situation of minorities sharing the same ethnic origin outside their borders.[20] This means that the HCNM is precluded from dealing with minorities living within a single state.

Despite this formal distinction, the HCNM has declared on several occasions: 'I know a minority when I see one'.[21] This highlights two distinctions: (1) a minority is a group with linguistic, ethnic or cultural characteristics distinct from the majority; and (2) it is a group which not only seeks to maintain its identity but also tries to give stronger expression to that identity.[22] The HCNM's observation reflects the overlap between the protection of ethnic, cultural, linguistic and religious minorities, on the one hand, and national minorities on the other. This is also true of the FCNM. In practice, international minority rights aim to protect all those 'who would be in a position of disadvantage and vulnerability *vis-à-vis* the exercise of democratic power which, in each specific situation, is a function of the constitutional order'.[23] Therefore, the terms used by states, such as 'national minorities', 'nationalities' or 'communities' are without adverse effect, as the right to protection for all groups should be guaranteed regardless of definition. Minority rights law applies to any person belonging to a national, ethnic, linguistic or religious group in a non-dominant position in the state in which they live.

Despite the absence of a clear general definition of a national minority, it is possible to find some elements of a definition in other provisions of the FCNM. The Preamble states that a pluralist and genuinely democratic society should not only respect the ethnic, cultural, linguistic and religious identity of each person belonging to a national minority, but should also create the appropriate conditions necessary to express, preserve and develop that identity. Moreover, Article 6 FCNM refers to ethnic, cultural, linguistic and religious identities. It is clear that these are the central criteria that need to be taken into account when defining a minority. Consequently, one can safely conclude 'that we are not too far away from the definition' contained in Recommendation 1201.[24] Alfredsson argues that the necessary elements of the definition are known and largely accepted:[25] many state parties explicitly share this view. Though this definition is not part of the FCNM, it has been raised to the status of a legal obligation by its inclusion in friendship and good neighbourliness treaties drawn up between various member states of the CoE.[26] These treaty obligations might eventually acquire the status of regional customary law,[27] a perspective shared by the Advisory Committee.[28]

The FCNM Explanatory Report highlights that Article 1 refers to the protection of national minorities and of the rights and freedoms of persons belonging to those minorities. This distinction and the difference in wording make it clear that it does not envisage protection of the collective rights of national minorities. Legal literature has criticized the FCNM for relying exclusively on individual rights to the detriment of group rights. Because of this bias, discriminatory patterns are likely to persist.[29]

However, the apparent reason for rejecting the idea of collective rights is that many states fear secessionist demands. In order to overcome these fears, the FCNM acknowledged that the protection of a national minority group could be achieved through the protection of the rights of individuals belonging to that group. The authors of the FCNM chose to concentrate on this point as they had already underscored, in the Explanatory Report to the Convention, that the implementation of the principles set out in the FCNM would be effected through national legislation. However, this 'does not imply the recognition of collective rights'.[30] Another reason for this approach might be liberal fears that according collective rights to persons belonging to national minorities provoked could endanger the primacy of individual rights.[31] Consequently, the FCNM followed the universally recognized individualistic human rights approach typical of all instruments dealing with minority issues: it signalled that the individual *per se* – and not the minority group – was considered to be the rights-holder.

This departure point, however, has not solved consistent problems emerging from the group character of minorities. Many persons belonging to national minorities advocate the protection of their collective identity, the most important element of that identity being the right to organize themselves as a group. To this end, they demand the right to use their language, to practise their culture, to influence the content of the education of their children and to participate in the political decisions that affect them.[32] The FCNM tries to resolve the latent contradiction in Article 3(2) by allowing persons belonging to national minorities to exercise their minority rights 'in community with others'. Thus, it recognizes that persons belonging to national minorities cannot avail themselves of the rights listed in the FCNM without the participation of others belonging to the same group. As such, there is undoubtedly a collective dimension encapsulated in Article 1.

The dominance of the human rights approach

The rights of persons belonging to minorities are an aspect of human rights. The decision to embed minority rights in the human rights framework constitutes the major difference between the League of Nations' approach and that of 'modern' minority rights. However, it seems that the latter did create some problems in the post-communist EU accession states.[33] Minority rights overlap with human rights and, hence, are applicable to persons belonging to minorities. The basic human rights principles of non-discrimination, equality and participation in the process of self-determination are particularly relevant to minorities.[34]

Nonetheless, one notes that the inclusion of minority rights in the human rights system generates problems, notably concerning the relationship between non-discrimination and affirmative action. In order to reconcile both approaches, the norm of non-discrimination needs to be interpreted in a more sensitive way, especially when issues of culture and identity are at stake. This is especially true when considering the relationship between individual and collective rights, where the traditional human rights approach – that collective rights should not undermine individual rights – may not apply to situations of minority rights. To better support the integration of minority rights into the body of human rights, one should speak of human rights as including the rights of persons belonging to minorities.[35]

The drafters of the FCNM, like the accession states, appeared less interested in the theoretical aspect of integrating minority rights into the human rights system, having chosen instead to focus on the fate of national minorities as an international concern. However, one could argue that leaving state parties to determine who is to benefit from such a human rights convention runs contrary to this understanding. Therefore, state parties do not enjoy full interpretive licence over the term 'national minority'. Accordingly, a majority of state parties did not declare any beneficiaries of this clause upon ratification.

In principle, in the absence of a definition of 'national minority', the protection offered by the FCNM also applies to non-kin-state minorities. This approach is consistent with the application of Article 27 of the ICCPR.[36]

In reality, however, this is a secondary issue since minorities must display a certain stability in their existence. That said, the contribution of individual human rights to minority protection is more important against the background of prohibition of special discriminatory measures designed to protect and promote the identity of a minority. Nevertheless, the question arises whether citizenship is one of the criteria for identifying beneficiaries. In the European context, this criterion has been referred to several times in both the CoE European Charter for Regional and Minority Languages and in Recommendation 1201 of the Parliamentary Assembly, for instance. One must also take into consideration the considerable number of declarations by state parties linking the term 'national minority' to citizenship. Similarly, the criterion of firm and long-standing ties to the state in which a minority group lives sustains the connection between the minority and citizenship.

With an understanding of minority rights as an integral part of human rights, the Advisory Committee requested information on the state parties' participation in, and cooperation with, international organizations, including the identification of relevant international human rights instruments to which they were party.[37] All state reports provided lists of state participation and cooperation, which resulted in the Advisory Committee noting that the states had ratified a wide range of relevant international instruments. It concluded therefore that: '[o]n the basis of the information currently at its disposal, the Advisory Committee considers that implementation of this article does not give rise to any further observations'.[38]

None of the states that are party to the FCNM have offered any further information regarding the implementation of relevant international human rights instruments concerning minorities. This may be a consequence of the FCNM's contradictory approach. Although minority rights form 'an integral part of the international protection of human rights', the rights mentioned in the FCNM are not justiciable. This shortcoming pinpoints one of the main criticisms of the FCNM: that modern human rights instruments must include national legal remedies and international complaint procedures as a general standard.

In light of this weakness, the role of the implementing bodies established by the ECHR has to be taken into consideration. However, these organs have reiterated that the ECHR does not provide an explicit guarantee of minority rights and that 'the protection of individual members of such a minority is limited to the right not to be discriminated in the enjoyment of the Convention rights on the grounds of their belonging to the minority (Article 14 of the Convention)'.[39] This means that the Strasbourg bodies protect minority groups under Article 14 of the ECHR, in combination with the other substantial rights enshrined in the ECHR.[40]

In reality, states enjoy a wide margin of appreciation under the ECHR, which is not conducive to the idea of minority protection. Furthermore, the group dimension of an individual complaint is not taken into consideration. In *Beard v. UK*, the European Court of Human Rights (ECtHR) observed that:

> [T]here may be said to be an emerging international consensus amongst the Contracting States of the Council of Europe recognising the special needs of minorities and an obligation to protect their security, identity and lifestyle (... in particular the Framework Convention for the Protection of Minorities), not only for the purpose of safeguarding the interests of the minorities themselves but to preserve a cultural diversity of value to the whole community.[41]

Yet, the Court regretted having to come to the conclusion that the consensus was not sufficiently concrete and that it was not possible to derive any guidance from any particular situation.[42]

Conclusion

The accession process has, without doubt, contributed to the peaceful transformation of former socialist countries. Part of this transformation is the acceptance of the individual human rights of persons belonging to minorities. Following the end of the authoritarian system of one-party rule in the socialist countries, minority conflicts, which had been smouldering unseen for decades, erupted suddenly. Now the transitional phase between the greatly weakened statehood of the post-communist countries and the establishment of democratic orders has come to an end, with the acceptance of the FCNM conception of minority rights constituting a valuable part of that phase. Now it falls to the EU member states as a whole to contribute to an overarching implementation of the FCNM that reflects the common standard of achievement in Europe. The objective is to overcome double standards among the European countries.[43]

In relation to the accession states, their recent history and, in particular, their experience in using individual human rights in addition to collective minority rights as a means of overcoming ethnic tension suggest that they would be amply qualified to set the course for addressing the current problems of minority rights protection in Europe.

Notes

1. See G. Brunner, *Nationality Problems and Minority Conflicts in Eastern Europe* (Gütersloh: Bertelsmann Foundation Publishers, 1996).
2. OSCE High Commissioner on National Minorities, Address given in Budapest, 7 May 2001 <http://www.osce.org/documents/hcnm/2001/05/479_en.pdf>

3. See S. Riedel, 'Minderheitenpolitik in der EU-Erweiterungsperspektive', *SWP-Studies* 24: section 24 (2001).
4. See Brunner, *Nationality Problems, supra* note 1.
5. See S. Bartsch, *Minderheitenschutz in der internationalen Politik* (Opladen: Westdeutscher Verlag, 1995).
6. Z.G. Pataki, 'Overview of Proposals for Minority Self-Governments of Hungarian Minorities in Central Europe', in K. Gal (ed.), *Minority Governance in Europe* (Budapest: Open Society Institute, 2002), 245.
7. J. Rehman, *The Weaknesses in the International Protection of Minority Rights* (The Hague: Kluwer Law, 2000).
8. M. Nowak, *UN Covenant on Civil and Political Rights: CCPR Commentary* (Kehl: Engel, 1993).
9. G. Gilbert, 'Minority Rights under the Council of Europe', in P. Cumper and S. Wheatley (eds), *Minority Rights in a 'New' Europe* (The Hague: Nijhoff, 1999), 62.
10. Open Society Institute (ed.), *Monitoring the EU Accession Process: Minority Protection Volume II* (Budapest: Open Society Institute, 2002).
11. Council of Europe Parliamentary Assembly (PACE), Recommendation 1201 on an Additional Protocol on the Rights of National Minorities to the European Convention on Human Rights.
    Article 1 (1993).
12. Ad Hoc Committee for the Protection of the National Minorities (CAHMIN) (1994). Report of the 1st Meeting. CAHMIN/GR (94).
13. Federal Union of European Nationalities (FUEN), 'Fundamental Rights of Persons belonging to Ethnic Groups in Europe', Draft for an Additional Protocol to the ECHR (1994).
14. PACE, Recommendation 1492 on the rights of national minorities (2001).
15. European Commission for Democracy through Law (ECDL), 'Explanatory Report to the Proposal for a European Convention for the Protection of National Minorities' (1993), CDL-MIN (93) 7.
16. F. Benoit-Rohmer, *The Minority Question in Europe, Texts and Commentary* (Strasbourg: Council of Europe, 1996).
17. UN Declaration on the Rights of Persons Belonging to National or Ethnic, Religious and Linguistic Minorities (1992), UNGA Res A/47/135.
18. A. Eide, 'Final Text of the Commentary to the Declaration on the Rights of Persons Belonging to National or Ethnic, Religious and Linguistic Minorities' (1998), UN Doc. E/CN.4/Sub.2/AC.5/2001/2.
19. Council of Europe (CoE) European Convention on Nationality, ETS 166, Article 1 (1997).
20. L.A. Thio, 'Developing a "Peace and Security" Approach towards Minorities' Problems', *International and Comparative Law Quarterly* 52(1) (2003): 115–50.
21. See W. Kemp (ed.), *Quiet Diplomacy in Action: The OSCE High Commissioner on National Minorities* (The Hague: Kluwer Law, 2001).
22. M. van der Stoel, *Peace and Stability through Human and Minority Rights* (Baden-Baden: Nomos Verlagsgesellschaft, 1999), at 45.
23. OSCE High Commissioner on National Minorities, 'Note on the Possible Use of Terminology in the Process of Incorporating Into Domestic Law International Standards for the Protection of Minorities' (2003), at 3.
24. H. Klebes, 'The Council of Europe's Framework Convention for the Protection of National Minorities', *Human Rights Law Journal* 16(1–3) (1995): 92–8, at 93.
25. G. Alfredsson, 'A Frame with an Incomplete Painting: Comparison of the Framework Convention for the Protection of National Minorities with International

Standards and Monitoring Procedures', *International Journal of Minority and Group Rights* 7(4) (2000): 291–304. He mentions: objective characteristics, self-identification and long association (one or two generations) with the country or territory concerned.

26. H.J. Heintze, 'Bilateral Agreements and their Role in Settling Ethnic Conflicts', in U. Schneckner and S. Wolff (eds), *Managing and Settling Ethnic Conflicts* (London: C. Hurst, 2004).

27. PACE Recommendation 1492 (2001), *supra* note 14.

28. Advisory Committee on the Framework Convention for the Protection of National Minorities, *Opinion of the Advisory Committee on PACE Recommendation 1492 on the rights of national minorities* (2001), Paragraph 4.

29. See W. Bergem, 'Culture, Identity and Distinction: Ethnic Minorities between Scylla and Charybdis', in S. Wolff (ed.), *German Minorities in Europe* (New York: Berghahn, 2000).

30. CAHMIN, *Explanatory Report to the Framework Convention for the Protection of National Minorities* (1995), CAHMIN H(1995) 010, Paragraph 13.

31. W. Kymlicka, *Multicultural Citizenship* (Oxford: Oxford University Press, 1995).

32. A. Eide, 'Minorities in a Decentralized Environment', UN Working Group on Minorities, Background Paper for the International Conference on Human Rights, 2–4 September 1998.

33. See K. Cordell, 'Poland's German Minority', in S. Wolff (ed.), *German Minorities*, *supra* note 29.

34. G. Pentassuglia, 'On the Models of Minority Rights Supervision in Europe and How They Affect a Changing Concept of Sovereignty', in ECMI, *European Yearbook of Minority Issues* (Flensburg: ECMI, 2001/2002), 1.

35. A. Rönquist, 'The Council of Europe and National Minorities', *Helsinki Monitor* 6(1) (1995): 38–44.

36. UN Human Rights Committee (HRC), General Comment 15/27, UN Doc. CCPR/C/21/Rev.1, Paragraph 7.

37. Advisory Committee on the FCNM, 'Outline for Reports to be Submitted Pursuant to Article 25, Paragraph 1 of the Framework Convention for the Protection of National Minorities' (1998), ACFC/INF(1998)001.

38. *Ibid.*

39. European Commission on Human Rights (HCommHR), *X v. Austria*, Appl. No 8142/78. 10.10.1979.

40. G. Gilbert, 'The Legal Protection Accorded to Minority Groups in Europe', in *Netherlands Yearbook of International Law* 23 (1992): 67–104.

41. EcommHR, *Beard v. United Kingdom*, 24882/94. 18.01.2001.

42. Similar arguments to the ECtHR include: *Chapman v. United Kingdom*, Appl No. 27238/95. 18.01.2001; *Jane Smith v. UK*, Appl. No. 25154/94. 18.01.2001; *Coster v. United Kingdom*, Appl. No. 24876/94. 18.01.2001; and *Lee v. United Kingdom*, Appl. No. 25289/94. 18.01.2001.

43. H.J. Heintze, 'Human Rights and Political Interests – Is there a Double Standard?', in IFSH (ed.), *OSCE Yearbook 2001* (Baden-Baden: Nomos, (2002).

3
Forging Territorial Cohesion in Diversity: Are National Minorities Promoting Fourth-Level Integration?

Tove H. Malloy

> Regions matter politically, as they constitute a meeting place and an arena for negotiation of functional and territorial systems of action, in economics, society and politics. They provide, in many instances, a basis for identity, especially where they possess their own language, and a culture of strong historical traditions. Regions may provide a framework for political mobilization, and they are emerging as a system of government. Finally, they are in many cases constituting themselves as actors in state and European arenas, where a development coalition has been able to formulate a regional interest and its own project. (Michael Keating)[1]

Introduction

Ensuring the territorial cohesion of the European Union (EU) is perhaps one of the biggest challenges facing the policy of 'unity in diversity'. While highly contested in the politics of the EU, the significance of unity in this context is its role as the centripetal force that has been promoting integration in Europe for decades. Diversity, on the other hand, while certainly one of the centrifugal forces threatening territorial cohesion, has not been translated into an individual signifier.

While it has long been acknowledged that the EU has both a diversity of member state national and cultural – mainly immigrant – identities, the existence of regionally defined, historic national minority identities has not received equal explicit acknowledgement as an aspect of diversity. Although the Treaty establishing the European Community (TEC) recognizes that the national and regional diversity of the member states must be respected and promoted by the European Community (EC),[2] it remains ambiguous as to the meaning of 'regional' in this context. Moreover, while the 1991 Maastricht Treaty established the Committee of the Regions (CoR),[3] the historic regions exhibiting national minority identities are not recognized as members except in the few instances where a member state appoints representatives of national minority regions.[4] Likewise, economic and social cohesion programmes, such as the Structural Funds, do not explicitly recognize the importance of national minority regions, except in those cases where these may be characterized as underdeveloped and in need of being brought closer to the desired level of prosperity of the EU. More curiously, the goal of territorial cohesion has only recently been explicitly attached to the policy of economic and social cohesion.[5] It would seem, therefore, that the European peace project, which came about to a large extent as a result of more than a century of national minority controversy, is ignoring the lessons of history and, instead, is attempting to forge territorial cohesion based on homogenizing identities and mono-cultural values within member states.

However, culture-blind policies are not conducive to an ethos of 'unity in diversity'. Historic national minority regions have shown signs that they wish to integrate economically and socially on their own terms, retaining the right to maintain their specific national minority identities and cultures. With regard to the 15 pre-May 2004 member states (EU15), the historic regions of Catalonia, Flanders, Scotland and Wallonia, together with the federated units of Germany, have mobilized *vis-à-vis* their governing bodies, to the extent that some now talk about 'third-level politics'.[6] Other less politicized 'regions', such as Brittany and Wales, are in the process of rediscovering their identities.

While they are not mobilizing in Brussels, they have become aware of the political significance of EU funding in promoting their regional and native languages.[7] This is a result largely of programmes adopted by the European Commission under pressure from the European Parliament (EP). In addition to these long-established national minority identities, the May 2004 and January 2007 enlargements of the EU to 27 member states (EU27) has rendered the EU home to a plethora of national minority identities. Although most of these are not constituted as administrative or self-governing regions, some new member states, as well as accession states, have municipalities and geographical regions representing large national minority populations. Thus, the Narva municipality in Estonia is 85.1 per cent Russian, and the Daugavpils municipality and region in Latvia is 84 per cent Russian. Similarly, the population of Northern Cyprus is predominantly Turkish. In Romania, one of the 2007 accession states, two counties in Transylvania (Co-vasna and Harghita) are more than three-quarters Hungarian. Some new member states have deliberately drawn new districts dividing historic national minority regions.[8] In others, such as Cyprus, where the current 'sub-division' of the island is challenging the territorial cohesion policy not only in terms of national identities but also in terms of territorial security, the national minorities of these entities possess distinct identities strongly attached to the territory of specific historic regions and spaces.

Looking to the most recent accession states, the territory of the EU now includes arguably one of the most cohesive national minority 'regions', which exhibits strong national minority identity: namely, the region of

Transylvania, which is home to the largest Hungarian minority outside Hungary.[9] Moreover, the accession of Turkey would present the EU with yet another strong national minority identity: the Kurdish minority. The region of southeast Anatolia, the homeland claimed by the Kurdish minority in Turkey, has been administered with a heavy hand from Ankara since 1987, and it is contended by the Workers Party of Kurdistan (PKK) that the region is colonized and deliberately impoverished to quell rebellion. However, the lack of development and self-administration of southeast Anatolia is likely to be a tool in the hands of the Kurdish freedom movement should Turkey become a member of the EU, and quite possibly during accession negotiations also.[10]

Thus, if these national minorities show particularly strong abilities to mobilize politically, drawing on long-term histories and self-identification as sub-state identities, whether empowered or disempowered, they could become a force for EU policy-makers to contend with following a subsequent round of EU enlargements.

This is not to argue that the EU is unaware that national minorities are a significant part of European heritage and history. Certainly, over the years, the EP has consistently drawn the attention of policy-makers to the fact that national minorities and their cultures deserve legal protection.[11] With the adoption of the European Charter of Fundamental Rights and Freedoms in 2000, discrimination based on membership of a national minority was proscribed. If the successor to the now defunct constitution, the so-called Reform Treaty, is ratified, it is possible that this prohibition will be entrenched within EU law; furthermore, Article 13 of the 1997 Amsterdam Treaty had proscribed discrimination based on ethnic origin. This Article was backed up by a legally binding directive on anti-discrimination in 2000.[12] Article I-3 of the Reform Treaty also expands Article 1 TEC to include 'respect for persons belonging to minorities' within the Union's founding values. While this provision does not constitute a right as such, its ratification would nevertheless mark a major milestone in national minority history in Europe.

This development was the result of pressure from various actors both during the drafting of the Constitution and the subsequent Intergovernmental Conference.[13] The insertion of a reference to respect for persons belonging to minorities was perhaps one of the most significant victories in recent EU politics, as the absence of a policy on minorities has been the focus of much debate over the last decade.[14] However, 'minority' is a broader and more comprehensive concept than 'national minorities', and respect is not synonymous with protection. More importantly, respect is not synonymous with empowerment. For national minorities who are already empowered or who are seeking empowerment at the member state level, encouragement was to be found in the Constitution's expansion of the principle of subsidiarity.

Under pressure from democratic deficit debate, the hitherto slow development of the principle of subsidiarity resulted in the drafters of the Reform Treaty awarding the CoR the right of recourse to the European Court of

Justice (ECJ) on matters relating to the implementation of subsidiarity.[15] Of course, it is important to note that the Treaty is still awaiting signature and ratification. Moreover, much would also depend on how this procedural right were to be implemented in practice. Nevertheless, it did seem that the EU was prepared to acknowledge (although not explicitly) greater co-management to self-governing regions as political players in the emerging horizontal system of multi-level governance envisaged by the Reform Treaty. Of course, the only national minority regions that would benefit from this procedural right awarded by the CoR would be the Belgian minorities.[16] However, the space of national minority politics is neither static nor limited to the few recognized national minority regions. As noted above, EU27 is faced with both established national minority identities in regions that possess considerable economic powers, and with established but often neglected national minority 'regions' that seek to attain greater powers through the economic opportunities offered by the EU's Cohesion Policy.

The horizontal level of EU politics may thus be presented with a number of new challenges in terms of integration. How will national minority regions behave in the new EU25 and beyond? How will they mobilize at the local and member state levels to influence decision-making at the suprastate level? The answers to these questions are significant for the stability of Europe. Will national minorities mobilize across member state borders? This is significant for the future of EU external and foreign politics. Which issues will they mobilize around? This is important for EU internal policy-making and the current division of competences in the EU. Which tools will they implement to influence decision-making? This is significant for the architecture of Europe. Will they lobby directly or will they cooperate with the existing structures of member states? Will they pressure the CoR to redefine and restructure? These are but a few of the issues stemming from the salient question: Europe, whither?

The overarching focus on this chapter will be on the forging of a new level of politics, in competition with the politics of third-level integration in relation to national minority regions, existing and emerging. In addressing this issue, it will seek to elucidate why this is (still) a frontline issue in the forging of a European history of peace, unity and prosperity.[17] To that end, this chapter will begin with a brief description of the phenomenon of third-level integration – its history, its principles and institutions – ('Third-level integration'), and will continue with a section on the EU's Cohesion Policy, which will encompass the issue of territorial cohesion ('EU Cohesion Policy'). Next, attention will be drawn to the issue of defining a national minority 'region' ('Defining national minority "regions"'), and will then turn to a discussion of the phenomenon of 'regions in the making' and the issues that characterize the political mobilization of national minorities in regions that are vying for influence and development support ('National minority "regions" in the making'). The latter entails a discussion of, among other things: districting, aspects of transition, political institutionalization, Europeanization, minority–majority relations, kin-state relations, national minority histories and identities, socio-economic development, internationalization and political mobilization in relation to cohesion policies.

Of course, much of this is beyond the scope of a single chapter, but the aim here is to familiarize the reader with the issues related to the political mobilization of national minority 'regions'. It should be noted at this juncture that the focus is, first and foremost, on the structure of these regions and how and why they mobilize politically, rather than their function *vis-à-vis* Brussels.[18] This notwithstanding, the viability of the structure is best understood in the context of the functions of the space it inhabits; hence, the initial sections on the functions of third-level integration, its principles and institutions, as well as its policy, are necessary. The discussion of the structure of national minority regions will be supported by examples from cases of national minority 'regions' that are new to EU governance and that will, it is argued, pose challenges to the policy of 'unity in diversity' in the EU of 27 member states and beyond.

A discussion of political mobilization necessarily entails an explanation of some of the new tools used by national minority regions at the multilateral level – a level, it is contended, that may be developing into a 'politics of the fourth level' ('Moving towards the "politics of fourth-level integration"'). As these tools include quasi state-like tools, the chapter will conclude by questioning whether acting in accordance with the logic of the centralized state remains feasible when promoting an ethos of 'unity in diversity', especially in an era when national minorities are pushing for a greater role as sub-state actors in Europe ('Conclusions'). If the making of national minority regions is seen as an isolated intra-state phenomenon, the changing fabric, not only of member states, but also of the European mosaic of diverse identities, may pose a serious challenge to the policy of 'unity in diversity'.

Third-level integration

'Third-level integration' is a concept related to the aspects of decentralization and multi-level governance in the EU institutional set-up. In addition, it must be seen in the light of the democratic deficit *problematique* that gained authority in the late 1980s and the subsequent subsidiarity discourse.[19] Decentralization refers both to the function of vertical delegation and/or power-sharing within member states that took place in the 1980s and 1990s, and to the horizontal power-sharing that began in the 1990s as a result of the democratic deficit debate. The latter form of decentralization was largely a result of the erosion of the role of member state parliaments due to the increasing centralization that followed the Single European Act (SEA) of 1986. Not only member states' parliaments, but also the parliaments of federal units that held self-governing powers at the national level, felt sidelined by the forces of integration towards a unified political approach. This led to significant criticism of the hegemonic decision-making process in Brussels and, eventually, to the adoption of the principle of subsidiarity in the 1991 Maastricht Treaty. Today, we speak not of decentralization but of subsidiarity.

Although the normative aspect of the principle of subsidiarity was not immediately legitimized and institutionalized, a system of vertical multi-level governance emerged, largely as a result of the adoption of the principle of subsidiarity, which forced the principle to become normatively accepted and implemented. As it is, national minority regions have a place in only the vertical system.

Views on the character and impact of third-level integration in the EU vary. While some argue that the emergence of a so-called 'new regionalism' will result in a weakening of member state boundaries[20] (and thus perhaps the elimination of the member state level), others argue that the new regionalism in fact means stronger and more politicized regions and thus a buttressing of the three levels.[21] Certainly, there is merit to the argument that, even though Europe is uniting and integrating each time it is enlarged, it is also becoming a larger mosaic of diverse nationalities adding more languages and more regions. In addition, as more states join the EU, some smaller states become *de facto* minorities and thus Europe becomes a territory of minorities.[22] This phenomenon in turn creates national minorities that are eyeing opportunities to manifest their identities more strongly, not only at the member state level, but also at the supra-state level.

Indeed, one might argue that if the twentieth century was the era of consolidating Europe at the member state level to counter the emergence of further major bellicose conflicts, the twenty-first century might be seen as the era where the EU consolidates at the regional level to counter emerging cultural conflicts. Certainly, the EU has seen the need to address the growing democratic deficit resulting from state-level consolidation by expanding its system of governance to include those authorities that are closest to the individual citizen, that is, the local and regional authorities.[23] To avoid having to address a 'culture deficit' in terms of neglected sub-state identities, the EU may therefore wish to pay attention to national minority 'regions' seeking inclusion in the third-level integration process.

The historic road towards third-level integration began with the adoption of the 1986 Single European Act (SEA), which entailed a strengthening of central power that alarmed those regions that had traditionally enjoyed a high level of self-government, such as the German Länder. The increased salience of regions within the then member states, particularly in the federal systems, coincided with the broader political developments of European supranational integration.[24] Specifically, the German Länder felt increasingly threatened in their prerogatives *vis-à-vis* the federal level by the way in which European measures were implemented. The traditional prerogatives of the Länder were being eroded because of EC Directives that made national governments responsible for their implementation. Therefore, the Länder insisted on being represented on the Council of Ministers when this dealt with issues falling within their range of competences. Consequently, they initiated a series of conferences entitled the 'Europe of the Regions', with the aim of putting the question of federal Europe onto the political agenda. Similarly, the Belgian sub-state authorities, created during the period 1988–1993, were keenly in favour of a 'Europe of the Regions'. The Spanish Autonomous Communities, like the German Länder, and the Italian regions also had motives for supporting such a development.[25]

Moreover, the 1988 reform of the Structural Funds marked an important turning point in relations between regions and the EC. Thus, the increasing demands by regions for a formal right to be represented at the EC level, combined with the European Commission's own desire to reinforce regional consultation procedures, prompted the creation in 1988 of the Consultative Council of Regional and Local Authorities,[26] the immediate precursor of the CoR. Being a weak and fragmented body, the Consultative Council revealed itself incapable of putting any pressure on the European institutions.

Pressure for greater access to decision-making for regions continued to increase, especially under the leading role of the German Länder. A Conference of Heads of Governments and Minister-Presidents of the European Regions was set up, with the aim of demanding the insertion of the principle of subsidiarity into the EC Treaty and the creation of a consultative Regional Council. The European Commission strongly supported the idea of a 'Committee of the Regions', which might reduce the perceived democratic deficit and represent a good ally. Eventually, this led the European Council to accept the foundation of the CoR, which was established officially in 1994 by Article 263 of the Maastricht Treaty. Subsequent treaties have fine-tuned the role of the CoR[27] and refined the scope and reach of the subsidiarity principle.

In practice, subsidiarity is the principle that the EU does not take action unless it is deemed more effective than action at the member state level. Thus, it is closely tied to the principles of proportionality and necessity, which require that any action by the EU should not go beyond what is necessary to achieve the objectives of the treaties. Measures have been taken in the Reform Treaty to extend this democratic principle to regional and local authorities.[28]

While the principle of subsidiarity and the related proportionality principle did not become fully operational until the Amsterdam Treaty, the Maastricht Treaty established them as a protection mechanism of last resort for member states that found themselves in a voting minority on a specific issue. Thus, the principle of subsidiarity was meant to regulate the exercise of powers and was seen as a vital democratic tool assuring that the individual member states had a degree of leverage on questions of equal or joint competence. By this reading, the instigation of the subsidiarity principle was one of the stages in European constitutionalism where the politics of integration addressed the supremacy of state sovereignty. However, the bottom line of the subsidiarity principle is to ensure that decisions are taken as closely as possible to the citizen and that constant checks are made as to whether action at the Community level is justified in light of the possibilities available at the member state level.

However, the justiciability of the principle of subsidiarity, which is entrusted to the ECJ, is the object of much debate, in particular, in relation to the issue of feasibility. The Maastricht Treaty did not establish criteria for the sharing of powers and responsibilities among all levels of government. With the Amsterdam Treaty, the principle became increasingly operational and the CoR was included in the bodies that the Commission and the Council could consult.[29] The 2001 Laeken Declaration on the future of the EU raised questions for the Convention drafting the Constitution on issues of democratic governance in relation to the citizens of Europe, and stipulated that the challenge of reform would have to address again the question of competence, including the competences of regions.[30] Although there was not much attention devoted to regions in the Convention, nonetheless there was widespread support for including regions more solidly in the Constitution. Despite the failure of the latter, this support has been carried over into the Reform Treaty which in many instances elevates the CoR's status to that of an advisory body on an equal footing with the Social and Economic Committee,[31] as well as entrusting it with the above-mentioned procedural right to petition the ECJ on matters related to the exercise of the principle of subsidiarity.[32] This would have the effect of empowering considerably a body that began its life in 1994 as little more than a discussion club. Indeed, the eventual ratification of the Reform Treaty would bring the Belgian national minorities a strong legal standing within the EU.

Thus, the principle of subsidiarity could gain direct relevance for national minorities with leverage *vis-à-vis* their member state government. Consequently, it could indirectly empower national minorities active in local and member state government.

The successful elevation of the CoR in the Constitution and, subsequently, the Reform Treaty was the result of hard work by both the CoR and a group of its members with self-government rights. Dissatisfied with the weak powers afforded the CoR in the 1990s, the latter established in 2000 an informal cooperative venture of 20 powerful autonomous regions with legislative powers to lobby the Intergovernmental Conference drafting the Treaty of Nice. United in the Conference of the Presidents of Regions with Legislative Powers (RegLeg), these regions represented around 56 per cent of the EU15 population. While not successful with the Treaty of Nice, RegLeg pressured their state representatives to ensure greater inclusion at the level of regions in the Constitution. Thus, it has been argued that the real leverage in the Convention was not the six representatives of the CoR but the lobbying of RegLeg.[33] This is likely to be true, as RegLeg members have the ability to influence EU politics through their respective parliaments. More-over, some of them represent strong economic forces and are thus able to influence the agendas of their federal parliaments. Contrary to the CoR, Reg-Leg was lobbying for a restructuring of the CoR to reflect the power of the large group of national minority regions with legislative powers. The drafters of the Constitution did not, however, agree to this restructure.

With regard to the Convention, the CoR itself advocated three major changes to its role in the EU decision-making process. First, it requested that its status be elevated to that of EU institution, on a par with the EP, the Council, the Commission, the ECJ and the Court of Auditors. Secondly, it called for greater consultation rights. This request had two components: first, the CoR wanted governing bodies to consult widely with associations of regional and local governments; and, secondly, the CoR wanted to be included in the consultation mechanism with the member states' parliaments. This is the Early Warning System (EWS), whereby member state parliaments, according to the Constitution, would have the right to comment on the European Commission's legislative proposals and to give reasoned opinions if they felt a proposal did not comply with the division of competences as laid out in the principle of subsidiarity. Thirdly, the CoR wanted the right to bring actions to the ECJ. This was a bold step inasmuch as recourse to the ECJ is usually seen as the exception rather than the rule. While these three areas were basically the same as the ones the CoR had sought to be incorporated in the Amsterdam Treaty without success, the pressure of RegLeg may have helped the CoR to increase its own pressure on the drafters of the Constitution. However, in the Working Group on the Principle of Subsidiarity to the Convention, there was wide agreement that rights should be given to the CoR but not to RegLeg.[34]

The CoR consists of members representing regional (regions) and local (municipalities) authorities, which either hold an electoral mandate or are politically accountable to an assembly elected by direct universal suffrage.[35] The members are nominated by member states and appointed by the Council for four-year terms. Each member state has its own selection procedure for members and Belgium currently allocates seats to autonomous self-governing national minority regions. Germany and Austria allocate seats to the Länder and Germany includes representatives from the Länder as observers in its delegation to the European Commission. According to the Maastricht Treaty, the Council and the European Commission are obliged to consult with the CoR in five areas: economic and social cohesion, trans-European infrastructure networks, health, education and culture. The Amsterdam Treaty added a further five areas for consultation: employment policy, social policy, environment, vocational training and transport. Outside these areas, the European Commission, the Council and the EP have the option of consulting the CoR on issues if they see important regional or local implications to a proposal. The CoR can also draw up opinions on its own initiative, which enables it to put issues on the agenda. Its work is organized through six commissions, made up of CoR members and specializing in particular policy areas. The commissions draw up draft opinions on the European Commission's proposals. The draft opinion must be approved at one of five plenary sessions each year before being sent to the European Commission, the Council and the EP. The Bureau is the driving political force behind the CoR. It draws up the political programme at the start of each new term, oversees its implementation and generally coordinates the work of the plenary sessions and the commissions.

This is not to argue that the CoR has found a comfortable place in the system of multi-level governance of the EU. For instance, relations with the Council are not always uncomplicated. The Council, at present, plays an important role in determining both the composition and functioning of the CoR. Despite the existence of a working procedure between the Secretary General of the Council and the CoR to systematize the exchange of information, the Council does not issue reports on the follow-up that was given to the opinions. While this may be indicative of the degree of importance that the member states afford the CoR, it also reveals that future relations between the EU institutions may well become a battleground of identities. Of course, it also shows that third-level integration continues to be constrained by strong powers at the member state level. As regions with or without legislative powers cannot address the EU institutions directly, they must still go through their national parliaments. Where sub-state units have autonomy and perhaps co-governing rights, their political power is considerably stronger at the member state level than at the EU level. The depth of this problem will vary from member state to member state, and the ease with which it can be remedied depends heavily on constitutional arrangements.[36] The ratification of the Reform Treaty would mean the introduction of more democratic tools, and the CoR might become an entity with which the member states would have to contend. Thus, regions are slowly becoming an essential factor in the EU's quest for greater cohesion at all levels.

EU Cohesion Policy

The EU's Cohesion Policy (also known as the regional policy) traces its roots back to 1975 when, partly as a result of the UK's entry to the European Economic Community (EEC),[37] the European Regional Development Fund (ERDF) was established. The concept of economic cohesion was introduced in the Single European Act and resulted in the adoption of policies supported by the Structural Funds. Since the Maastricht Treaty, these have constituted one of the priorities of EU policy. Furthermore, according to Article 158 of the 1997 Amsterdam Treaty, cohesion is a precondition for harmonious development in the EU in order to promote an overall well-balanced growth. This means that the EU should develop and pursue actions leading to the strengthening of its economic and social cohesion, and aimed at reducing disparities between the levels of development of the various regions and the backwardness of the least-favoured regions or islands, including rural areas.

Under the 2000–2006 EU Cohesion Policy, €213 billion (in 1999 prices) (that is, approximately one third of the entire EU budget) was distributed.[38] There are four types of Structural Funds, each of them with its own specific focus,[39] and the budget for the Structural Funds alone amounted to €195 billion in 2000–2006.[40] The Cohesion Fund was established in 1993 as an instrument to provide direct finance for individual projects, with the aim of improving the environment and developing transport networks to member states with a per capita GNP of less than 90 per cent of the Community average (Greece, Spain, Ireland and Portugal). The Cohesion Fund supports projects at the member state level and, as requested by the EP, aims to maintain a 50:50 balance between environment and transport projects. The Cohesion Fund for the period 2000–2006 is €19 billion.[41] At present, the Cohesion Policy has three priority objectives. Objective One – assisting areas whose economic and social development is lagging behind – is accorded fundamental priority. Only areas with a per capita GDP lower than 75 per cent of the Community average are eligible for assistance under this objective. Nearly 70 per cent of all Structural Funds has been put into the achievement of this objective. Activities within the framework of Objective Two concentrate on supporting a thorough economic and social conversion of areas experiencing structural difficulties in industry, agriculture, and so on, while Objective Three stresses modernizing education, training and employment systems.

Since the establishment of the Cohesion Policy, member states have had to negotiate on two levels: on the one hand, at the supra-state level; and, on the other hand, at the regional and local levels. Particularly in classic unitary states, the central level has more or less successfully tried to preserve its role of 'gatekeeper' by channelling contracts through central ministries and constraining the authorities of sub-state governments.

Central governments play an important role on two levels: programming, and the management of the programmes. Programming was an essential element of the 1988, 1993 and 1999 reforms of the Structural Funds. Programming involves the preparation of multi-annual development plans[42] and is undertaken through a partnership-based decision-making process, in several stages, until the measures are taken over by the public or private bodies entrusted with carrying them out.[43] Development and conversion plans are submitted by the member states. Under the new Structural Funds, member states must also appoint a managing authority (at the state, regional or another level) for each programme. The tasks of this authority cover the implementation, correct management and effectiveness of the programme (collection of statistical and financial data, preparation and transmission to the Commission of annual reports, organization of the mid-term evaluation, and so on).

According to the system of districting within member states, there are different methods by which the regions may have access to the funds. In France, for example, the regions have been formally excluded from the process of attracting EU Structural Funds and the prefectures, as representatives of the Ministry of the Interior, have led the negotiations, defining the object of intervention, the zones of eligibility and the inter-regional distribution of the funds.[44] Nevertheless, France has recently adopted a decentralization law, which introduces the possibility for regional councils and other territorial governments to experiment with the management of the 2000–2006 programme.[45] In the same way, the UK's sub-state authorities have had little influence on the EU Cohesion Policy, while the German Länder have had a strong influence, leaving the federal government with little authority.

Thus, although it is clear that the relative power of sub-state authorities on European policy-making varies, the EU has nonetheless enhanced their position in recent years. In new member states, the managing authority for the programme is always the central government, through the ministries related to the programmes. In other cases with a higher degree of self-governing sub-state entities – such as Germany, Italy or Spain – the local/regional governments are designated to play the role of managing authorities.

Since 2000, the EU's Cohesion Policy has undergone a fundamental change as a result of enlargement. The new member states have already benefited from pre-accession funding. The PHARE[46] programme has been funding modernization in the Central and Eastern European states for over ten years. In 1997 and 1999, it was modified to meet the requirements of accession and to prepare the accession states for Structural Funds. It financed a raft of projects, including cross-border cooperation schemes, in areas that would be covered by the Structural Funds. The Pre-Accession Structural Instrument (ISPA) funded transport and environmental schemes in all the Central and European states from early 2000, along the same lines as the Cohesion Fund model designed for the least prosperous EU member states. It provided direct financing for environmental projects to help apply directives that called for heavy investment, and for transport projects directly connected to the 10 pan-European corridors that have been identified in these countries.[47] The Special Accession Programme for Agriculture and Rural Development (SAPARD) was also in operation from 2000, helping applicants prepare for the Common Agricultural Policy (CAP), in particular, for its standards of food quality and consumer and environmental protection.

As the GNP of almost all the new member states was lower than 50 per cent of the Community average, 48 EU regions qualified in 2000 for assistance under Objective One, since their income was lower than 75 per cent of the Community average.[48] As the number of such regions in the EU27 has grown to at least 84, several EU15 beneficiaries stand to lose their right to assistance under Objective One if the current rules of the European regional policy are maintained, because the average GNP is lower in the EU27. This problem is referred to as the 'statistical effect'. The European Commission calculates that as many as 16 regions that have been receiving EU assistance may find themselves in this predicament.

In July 2004, the European Commission adopted a proposal of five new regulations for renewed Structural Funds and instruments. Over the period 2007–2013, these instruments will represent about a third of the EU budget or a total of €307.6 billion.[49] The majority of this amount will be spent in less-developed member states and regions. Almost every region of the new member states will be eligible to receive the Structural Funds. Already, the new member states have received €5.76 billion for rural development during the 2004–2006 period.[50] As Poland is predominantly an agricultural country, it has received nearly half of this aid. These funds are meant to help farms in these states to modernize, restructure and comply with EU production standards.

The management of Structural Funds for the new member states implies far-reaching changes in the practice and operations of all levels of administration to comply with the legal framework of regulations on which structural assistance is based. Considerable effort has already been made in the establishment of an appropriate legal framework and the definition of an administrative breakdown of the territory according to the Nomenclature of Territorial Statistical Units (NUTS)[51] system.[52] Arguably, however, the sheer size of the EU budget being allocated to these regions, and the effects these funds will have on the future life of the populations living in these regions, augurs for the Cohesion Policy area being a highly contested area of politics. The result of such a strong concentration of power is likely to have its impact upon those regions where national minorities who have witnessed disregard and suppression by central governments for years are seeking to develop their economy. Although the Cohesion Policy is primarily seen as a socio-economic tool in the effort to secure territorial cohesion, it is important to keep in mind that the socio-economic sphere of the EU is indeed culturally diverse and culture is usually the driving force behind strong political movements, including at the member state level. Before turning to the question of what makes a 'region', it may be instructive to examine briefly what defines a 'region'.

Defining national minority 'regions'

The word region is used in different ways.[53] Strictly defined, a region connotes physical contiguity. However, proximity is also a characteristic of a region. Thus, when defining a region at the member state level, it is a prerequisite that the territory in question is contiguous and in proximity to the member state. Islands can therefore also constitute regions. This is not to be confused with the region as a grouping of states defined by homogeneity. This can be social homogeneity based on race, religion, language or history but it can also be – and more often is – based on economic homogeneity. Finally, a region of states can be based on political homogeneity, as is the case in the European region, which is now largely defined as a homogenous region in terms of democracy. Regions in most of the EU15 states were defined through an interest-driven process, which was highly particularistic for each member state.[54] In many states, regions either existed organically or became mobilized from the bottom up with a view to creating opportunities for development. There was, therefore, no uniform system of sub-state administration and the drive for rationalization was the primary function. This drive changed after the adoption of the Maastricht Treaty and the subsidiarity principle, after which regions have in fact been 'designed' in order for member states to access greater portions of the Structural Funds.

Regionalism, on the other hand, refers to a set of attitudes, loyalties and ideas that influence the identities of the people inhabiting the region. In a sense, regionalism is to regions what nationalism is to 'nation-states'.[55] At the inter-state level, these visions often result in institutional frameworks based on regional themes, such as security, democratization, or, indeed, integration; at the intra-state level, regionalism may derive its force from geographical themes, but certainly also from cultural identities such as national minority identities.

Hence, the definition of a region is contested.[56] For the purpose of this chapter, a national minority 'region' is a social construction *within* territorial boundaries. The territorial element is fundamental, even if it does not constitute the precise delineation of the region, and the social, economic and political content of regionalism and the identity of the people living in the national minority 'region' vary according to the outcomes of political processes.

Significantly, the region is a social force in addition to being a separate historical and linguistic entity. Regions where national minorities are in the majority have also been termed nations or sub-state nations. This is for the purpose of delineating the contrast with the nation of the majority. In some cases, these may even be seen as co-nations.[57] Co-nations are social groups that are socially cohesive and that represent a strong social force at the political level based on a separate sub-state nationalism.

The prominent example in the EU15 of sub-state nations – or co-nations regionally defined – is the case of Belgium. The Belgian state has been ethnically mixed for centuries, with a Flemish community in the north and a French-speaking Walloon community in the south. The national question in Belgium was initially defined as a language issue, although later it also assumed socio-economic aspects. The Flemings constitute 57.8 per cent of the total population, the Walloons 32.6 per cent, while a small minority of Germans constitute 0.7 per cent. The peculiarity of Belgian federalism is that it uses not only 'regional territory' as the basis of its federal structure, but comprises also a non-territorial element. Thus, there are officially three territorially defined entities, called regions: the Flemish Region (Flanders), the

Walloon Region (Wallonia) and the Brussels Capital Region (Brussels). Furthermore Belgium is divided into three cultural communities: the Flemish community, thus bringing together the Dutch-speakers who live in Flanders and in Brussels; the French community, assembling the French-speakers who live in Wallonia and in Brussels; and a tiny German-speaking community in the east of the country. Each of these regions and cultural communities has its own parliament and executive entrusted with constitutionally assigned powers. Belgium is therefore a plurinational state based on the idea of multilingualism and the coexistence of different ethnic groups enjoying equal rights.

However, the main thrust of the political integration of the EU continues to be linked to territory – the territory of the sovereign member states, that is. Territory defines the political power of the member state.[58] It supports a prevailing view of citizenship, identity, culture and rights, and it legitimizes the use of control. Territory provides the space for social and economic interaction, it sustains human life and from territory springs solidarity. Member states subdivide sovereign territory for economic and democratic purposes, the aim and scope of which differ from member state to member state. Some subdivide on purely economic lines, many subdivide on the basis of geographical definitions, and a few have subdivided along the lines of sub-national identities. Many have employed a combination of these. In those states where subdivision is along the lines of sub-state identities, these identities are often linked to the national identity of a neighbouring kin-state (for example: Alto Adige, Italy; Western Poland; Narva, Estonia; Daugavpils, Latvia; Hungarians in Slovakia; Turks in Cyprus; and the Belgian regions), or to the possession of unique characteristics (for instance, Wales, Scotland, the autonomous Spanish regions and Brittany).

While most member states respect sub-state identities, both new and old member states have created subdivisions that divide – or virtually 'bury' – socially cohesive sub-state national groups administratively (Slovakia and Denmark). In some new member states, sub-state groups are so small that they cannot be defined by subdivision, but might perhaps be dominant in smaller units, such as municipalities (Estonia and Latvia). More importantly, in some accession and candidate states, sub-state identities are strongly attached to territory and kin-state identity (Transylvania, Romania; and Krajina, Croatia). One example is unique in that sub-state identity is in fact formed and redefined in diaspora communities in the EU (southeast Anatolia, Turkey).

During the transition to democracy and in preparation for accession to the EU, the territorial transformation of the new member states was initially a reaction to the weakness of the central state.[59] However, the post-Cold War era also experienced a rise of sub-state nationalisms. These sub-state nationalisms asserted a strong sense of cultural distinctiveness, and some made or implied demands for economic and political self-determination driven by a potentially distinctive logic that draws on strong ties to history and territory and builds on deep collective solidarity, cultural affinity and exclusive membership. Sub-state groups with such potentially strong alter-national identities, different from that of the majority, are usually referred to as ethnic minorities because they may be distinguished from the majority in terms of language, religion and certainly culture and ethnicity. They may more correctly, however, be considered to be national minorities where there is the proximity of a kin-state. In either case, they are driven by a desire for cultural survival, both in terms of culture and language, but also in terms of national sentiments attached to a territory. Most importantly, they represent a sub-state national identity that stands in contrast to the national identity of the majority. Sub-state nationalisms, whether kin-state related or independent, may therefore represent strong social forces, in addition to representing antagonistic cultural forces.

In Central and Eastern European states, the issue of territorial division eventually became influenced by two main factors, both related directly to EU accession. First, the restoration of democracy entailed a strong will to adopt the institutional standards of Western European countries; this included the restoration of local government. A second factor was the influence of the EU and the prospect of membership. The growing importance of the EU's regional policy provided an incentive to establish or reinforce regional institutions as a way of improving compliance with EU requirements, with a view to eventual membership and access to EU Structural Funds.

The sheer variety of systems of subdivision within the EU has been expanded with the inclusion of 10 new member states, even though the enlargement did not involve an influx of federal and regionalized states. However, most new member states have organized primarily as classic unitary or devolving unitary states. While there are differences in the constitutional positions of the local authorities, for example, in their numbers, powers, their capacity to engage in external relations, and their relationship to each other within the system, the general thrust has been to adapt to EU accession conditions. This may also be seen as a result of a strong 'push factor' from the European Commission for a symmetric model that would enable the disbursement of Structural Funds in a more uniform manner.[60] Thus, most of the new member states undertook territorial decentralization reform before becoming members.

In Slovakia, administrative reform in 2001 divided the country into self-governing municipalities, districts and regions (*Kraje*). Originally, the draft proposal recommended that Slovakia be divided into 12 regions, to reduce the fragmentation of the Hungarian minority, but the parliament approved the existing eight-region division for regional government. The main decision-making body in Slovakia is the Regional Council, and direct election to the Regional Council is based on the highest number of votes obtained, with a two-round direct election for the position of chairperson. The Hungarian minority viewed this decision as a tool to eliminate the possibility that any of their representatives could win the election to the post of chairperson.

In Poland, a three-tier local government system was established during the 1990s. The three tiers are municipality (*gmina*), county (*powiat*) and region/voivodship (*wojewodztwo*). Each level is governed by a legislative council and executive boards. Legislative authorities at all three levels are elected directly. The Voivode is an official appointed by the Prime Minister, and he adopts the position of chief of state administration at the voivodship level.[61]

In Estonia, local government consists of two levels: municipalities and regions. At the regional level, the central government is represented by counties, which are unelected bodies. Under the Government of the Republic Act, a county governor is appointed by the central government, following a proposal by the Prime Minister, and in concordance with the regional union of local authorities.

Similarly, Latvia's local government system consists of two levels. The first includes the municipalities, the second the regional governments. According to the law, a local government is an administration that, through elected representation (the council, or the dome), ensures the execution of functions conferred upon it, by legislation, by the Cabinet of Ministers and by local voluntary initiatives. Deputies at the municipal level are elected directly, whereas on district councils they are the chairs of municipal councils.

In Romania, recentralization efforts have been made, even though the new democratic constitution contains provisions on self-governing functional and local units. Local administration comprises a two-tiered system: the local level and the county (*judet*) level. Local councils with legislative power are elected at the municipal level as well as at *judet* level. Prefects appointed by the government head the counties. The law clearly specifies that the referendum is an important means for local councils to deal with special local problems. The Law on Regional Development in Romania has established eight development regions,[62] representing the framework for the elaboration, implementation and evaluation of regional development policy, and for collecting specific statistical data according to the European regulations issued by the Statistical Office of the European Union (EUROSTAT) for the NUTS 2 level of territorial classification. The regions do not, however, have any decision-making power.

It is clear that the heterogeneity in the systems of districting prevents any comparative assessment of the feasibility of empowering national minorities within their historic regions. Many factors determine, not only how a state subdivides its territory, but also how it empowers the subdivisions. National minority regions are naturally, not physically, constructed, although they may be constructed in imagination. However, the forces of market integration, globalization, internationalization and Europeanization, to name but a few, present the EU and its member states' governments with a new context of integration. Moreover, where the EU member states do not address these external forces and their relation to the new context of integration, national minorities may decide to do it independently. Indeed, we noted above that national minority regions in Western Europe have taken the lead in devising separate tools with which to improve their ability to act independently at the international level.

Consequently, the remainder of this chapter will discuss, first, the making of national minority 'regions' not yet constituted as empowered players and, second, the tools at their disposal devised by their brothers in the EU15.

National minority 'regions' in the making

The process of 'making' national minority regions in Europe has followed different paths in Eastern and Western Europe. In Western Europe, some national minority regions survived the decentralization process due to their strong sub-state identities and their histories as semi-independent units. In Eastern Europe, national minority 'regions' were faced with legacies of central distribution on the one hand, and Europeanization and globalization demands on the other. At the same time, political liberalization and democratic procedures created space for regional diversity and local government. Also, as noted, the knowledge and availability of EU funds propelled regions and emerging national minority 'regions' into the arena of European politics.[63] Thus, in this landscape, incentives for national minority 'regions' to mobilize politically for their own social and economic prosperity appear strong.

The making of national minority 'regions' is determined by the availability of a number of factors that facilitate the mobilization force. In fact, the degree of availability may influence the degree to which political mobilization happens. Although the making of national minority 'regions' is actor-oriented and the existence of elites is vital to success,[64] external factors are the facilitators that fuel the engine. The legal framework and the existence of autonomous institutions at the level of the 'region' are another defining aspect of the force of political mobilization. If the legal framework oppresses national minorities seeking self-promotion, it is more likely that the political mobilization force will be aimed at the external and EU levels.

In the new member states in Eastern Europe, in particular, the history of transition plays a major role in how national minorities will act in third-level integration politics. Not only recent history, but also pre-communist and Cold War history, impacts on the way in which national minorities react to the range of opportunities offered by EU membership. If national minority 'regions' with strong identities were subjected to oblivion during the communist era, they are more likely to seek restitution of these identities in the public's mind.

This identity discourse spills over into the strategies that national minorities devise for the socio-economic development of their 'regions'. Drawing on strong identities provides resources for institution-building in the national minority 'region', which in turn strengthens and broadens the regions' ability and opportunity to act and interact politically, both at the international and at the supra-state levels. Thus, to regard the making of national minority 'regions' as an isolated intra-state phenomenon is no longer feasible, and the aspects of Europeanization and internationalization are perhaps the strongest factors in the changing fabric, not only of member states, but also of the European mosaic of diverse identities. A closer look at each of these aspects of making national minority 'regions' reveals diversity, not only of identities, but also of cultures and manners in which these new member state identities may approach third-level integration.

The taming of ethnic nationalism and the dismantling of authoritarianism were the major tasks of democratization in all states in transition. This process was complicated by the weak state syndrome, a hallmark of transition, which discouraged state authorities from sharing power with an equally weak civil society, let alone with different ethnic groups.[65] As this syndrome has motivated the national majority to concentrate all power in its own hands, historical questions are vital to an understanding of national minority political mobilization – or lack thereof – in the subsequent institutional set-up. Dilemmas and paradoxes experienced during the post-communist transition have influenced post-communist state designs, and the existence of national minorities has had implications for reforms and democratic transitions. The legacy of socialism in elite action in terms of oligarchies and opportunity has constrained the shift to modern democratic institutionalism.

The example of Estonia is instructive. Estonia's peaceful secession from the Soviet Union was accompanied by anxiety concerning the creation of a 'pure' Estonian identity. For this reason, when Estonia restored its independence in 1991, Soviet-era settlers and their descendants were denied any automatic right to Estonian citizenship.[66] After the adoption of the Law on Aliens in 1993 by the Estonian Parliament, the ethnic Russian minority felt threatened by the possibility of being expelled. The Law on Aliens stated that non-citizens would have to apply for residence and work permits along with travel documents. Those who did not apply or had their applications rejected could face expulsion from Estonia, being considered to be illegal residents on its territory. In response to this law, the Russians living in Narva and Sillamae prepared for local referenda on the issue of autonomy. The Estonian Government declared the referenda illegal and threatened to use force if necessary to prevent the break-up of Estonia. Russian vigilante groups began to arm themselves and the Russian President warned that he would intervene if necessary to protect the rights of Russian speakers. It was due mainly to the intervention of the OSCE High Commissioner on National Minorities, who met with representatives of the Narva city council and President Meri of Estonia, that the tension between state and national minority was alleviated. The EU enlargement process since 1995 and the Copenhagen criteria have pushed Estonia to improve its legislation on national minorities, especially concerning citizenship and language issues, and the EU continues to voice support for the integration of the Russian-speaking community into the Estonian socio-political institutions.

Transition history is not, however, defined purely by the state of post-communism. In Northern Cyprus, transition history is in the making, as reflected in the recent changes in the enclave's achieved favouritism after the rejection in the Greek South of the referendum on reunification based on the so-called Annan Plan. Moreover, transition history in terms of third-level integration is not merely a new member state phenomenon. In France, recent districting changes have influenced the way the region of Brittany has rediscovered its cultural roots and renewed its interest in functioning as a national minority 'region'. A similar process has taken place in Wales.

While tense minority–majority relations are most often the reason why post-independence institutionalization does not fall out in favour of national minorities, peaceful relations between national minorities and the majority are largely dependent on the degree to which national minorities are ensured a voice in the decision-making process. Systems of group representation vary from member state to member state and the extent to which a state is centralized, decentralized or devolved in terms of power. Although demands for group representation appeal to some of the most basic practices and principles of representative democracy,[67] governments are often strongly opposed to institutionalizing group differences in terms of political representation, holding that this goes against the general tenets of liberal democracy and the individual's right to a voice.

Other aspects of minority–majority tensions are related to cultural rights and freedoms. Discrimination in access to public administration jobs and other employment is often cause for friction, as is the right to education in national minority languages. Legal frameworks also play a vital role in minority–majority relations, especially in regard to a political voice. Problems of second-class citizenship, quiet discrimination, social and economic exclusion, marginalization and invisibility represent the dark side of minority–majority relations and thus impact on the capability of national minority 'regions' to mobilize politically.

Specifically, for post-communist states in transition, political institutionalization has introduced a variety of other dilemmas that have influenced the reluctance to devolve power to sub-state units of national minorities. These included the relation between old and new systems – or the combination thereof – and the path-dependency resulting from this. Depending on the speed with which the old systems adopted economic liberalization and democratization, the post-communist institutionalization process retained degrees of authoritarian policies, to the detriment of national minorities wishing to self-promote their 'regions'. The availability of resources was another factor in the democratization process that resulted in continuity rather than change. Modernization and the resulting spheres of sociological vacuum influenced the way in which national minorities were able to mobilize, especially in those states where a transition from heavy industry resulted in high social costs. Corruption and clientelism also worked to the detriment of national minorities seeking power-sharing, resulting in virtual culture gaps between identities in power and identities without power.

As the legal frameworks and systematization of the access of national minorities to the democratic process were cast during a period of heavy Europeanization, institutionalization also became heavily influenced by European normative standards on human rights and minority rights. This type of Europeanization began with the new democracies in Central and Eastern Europe seeking membership in the Council of Europe and the CSCE/OSCE, which was widely regarded as the path to membership in NATO and the EU, and thus constituted a first step in Europeanization towards the EU. Once memberships had been obtained or promised, and the path towards adopting normative standards had begun, a second step in Europeanization focusing on the institutionalization of post-communism took place. This step focused on defining the new democracies in relation to the traditional Western European concept of market economy with emphasis on the influence of late modern production structures, such as growth, and competitiveness, technology, communication and scientific research.

The latter process is far more fluid, competitive and difficult to map. It has strong links to the EU's Cohesion Policy, as it influences the way in which Europeanization towards the EU informs the political mobilization of national minority 'regions' and the ability of the national minority 'regions' to tap into the funds distributed under this policy. The capacity of national minority 'regions' to mobilize lobbying mechanisms, both at the level of the central member state government and the supra-state level in Brussels, is therefore related to this policy. Thus, European spaces have been created in which national minority regions and aspiring 'regions' interface with each other and with the institutions of the internal market economy.

Kin-state relations are another essential tool in the making of national minority 'regions'. While it may not seem overly important to the former EU12 and EU15 member states – as half a century of integration and peace has mellowed sentiments and redirected sympathies – it has often been good kin-state relations that have contributed to the forging of peace in border regions, as in the case of the Danish–German or the Austrian–Italian border regions. With regard to the EU27, a century of communist hegemony and other totalitarian ideologies restraining national minority identities must be taken into account as this has resulted, not only in suppressed identities, but also suppressed geopolitical strategies. Although geopolitical strategies would seem anathema to EU integration, the sentiments driving such suppressed strategies may not have abated. Certainly, the case of Cyprus is presenting the EU with this type of dilemma.

Another example of this might be the so-called 'Status Law' adopted by the Hungarian Parliament in June 2001 to support Hungarians in neighbouring countries in various ways, financially, and in the areas of education and employment.[68] As this law seeks to establish a legal relationship between the home-state and kin abroad and, in this sense, sets up a 'transnational' or cross-border form of 'citizenship', it could be argued that kin-state relations take on a nineteenth-century character. Unlike the *bilateral* Bonn–Copenhagen Declarations, which initiated a similar type of protection, the Hungarian law was a *unilateral* move disliked by its neighbours. Hungary committed itself to repealing any provision that would not be compatible with EC law before accession to the EU. In the case of the Northern Cyprus–Turkey relationship, matters are even more volatile in that Turkey maintains up to 30,000 troops in Northern Cyprus. The existence of 'foreign' troops on EU territory is thus another matter related to national minority identity for which the EU will have to prepare.

Indeed, the relevance of national minority histories to national minority 'region' mobilization is particularly acute in Europe. National minority existence as a concept and the recognition of national minority membership date back to the 1815 Congress of Vienna[69] and perhaps further still.[70] The existence of national minorities has continued to dominate the agenda of European politics since Vienna, at times more prominently than others.[71] In particular, following each major conflict, the issue has sought resolution and, each time, the histories of national minorities have been replete with resettlements, redefinitions, restructuring and false reassurances. Indeed, during times of major upheavals, national minorities have been thrown into tumultuous periods of uncertainty about belonging. Consequently, the social forces of national minorities have become strengthened in the bonds of suppressed identities that tied them to the territory, rather than to the ever-changing state. National minority identities are thus more likely to forge independent action in an effort to protect against the rule of overlords.

National minority identity is a phenomenon ascribed from membership of the societies to which national minorities belong, namely, family, religion and the nation. As societies establish identities, and identities form the norms and conventions of societies, national minority identities become historically attached to the values of the society to which the national minority belong. Thus, national minority identities become dependent on cultural survival and demonstrate high-level self-preserving energy.[72]

In this process, national minority identities are almost always in tension with the national identity of the majority, and national minority 'region' identities, in particular, include aspects of contrasting identities. As national minority identities are therefore an 'us-versus-them' syndrome involving aspects of 'friend–enemy' and *modus vivendi* theory, the relevance of national minority identities as politically mobilized social capital becomes particularly acute. Social capital refers to features of social organization, such as trust, norms and networks that can improve the efficiency of society by facilitating collective action in terms of, for instance, associational life, local media, political participation and political party formation.[73]

There is a theory of civic capacity, which has seldom been put forward in the context of national minority identity. This is a theory that argues that institutions are constructed by human beings and inhabited by humans self-identifying towards specific but multi-layered social and cultural constructs. As symbolic resources may play an important part in this identity formation, social resources and capital draw on the history and territory of the national minority 'regions' when mobilizing for political power-sharing.

The most prominent case of national minority power-sharing in Europe is Belgium, as noted above. The present redistribution of power between federal and sub-state entities is the result of a long devolution reform under pressure from the Walloon and Flemish nationalistic demands. Reform came in three major waves. First, in 1970, the existence of different territorial and cultural identities and the right to autonomy were constitutionally recognized. Belgium's unitary state structure had resisted ethnic pressure until 1970, when the government declared before parliament that 'the unitary state, its structure and functioning as laid down by law, had become obsolete'.[74] The second wave came in 1980, when the state was regionalized. This reform opted more unambiguously for regionalization. The cultural communities gained new competences, the socio-economic regions were given institutional infrastructures and regional autonomy in general was strengthened. In addition to this, legislative acts of the regional and community councils were given the same legal status as federal laws. The third wave of federalization began in 1989. This constitutional reform stopped short of creating a federal state but opted for a more systematic implementation of the dual federalism ('two worlds') model than that of 1980, albeit with a peculiar twist.

As usual under dual federalism, very few competences were concurrent; most competences were exclusive. This reduced the potential for the federal level to interfere with the regions and communities, and vice versa. However, the second component of dual federalism, according to which the division of powers runs along jurisdictional rather than functional lines, was still weak. The 1993 reform formally characterized Belgium as a federal state and Belgium finally became a federal state *de jure*. A mini-reform in 2001 further deepened federalization. The revisions put in place the several institutions and mechanisms typical of a modern federation: direct election of regional councils; a senate representing constituent units' interests; residual competences vested within constituent units; fiscal federalism (changes in financing mechanisms and more fiscal autonomy); constitutional autonomy for each level over its working rules; international competences and treaty power; and coordination and conflict resolution machinery.[75] One of the principal features of the new Belgian federal system is that there is no hierarchy between the federal level and the sub-state level. Thus, the Belgian political system, after the reform of 1993, can be identified as a cooperative system, where the sub-state entities and the federal government are mutually interdependent.

The far-reaching character of the Belgian reform is visible in the international competences of the Belgian sub-state authorities. With the reform of 1993, the sub-state authorities acquired the right to conclude international agreements in those policy fields in which they possessed exclusive competences, providing they respect two limitations: to act within the confines of their competences and to recognize the general principles of Belgium's foreign policy.

Belgium's three territorial regions and three cultural-linguistic communities enjoy extensive involvement in EU institutions. The coordination of EU policy-making in Belgium is based on a highly institutionalized negotiating system and on an extensive set of informal agreements. This ensures that regions and communities are both directly involved in the formulation of Belgian responses to EU policy, and hold representation in the Council of Ministers. In 1994, a Cooperation Agreement (CA) was concluded between the sub-state governments and the federal state, which set up a system of consultation and coordination among the different Belgian authorities. According to the CA, the Federal Foreign Ministry plays a central, albeit non-preponderant, role in Belgian coordination on Council issues by way of its Directorate for European Affairs.[76] The Directorate organizes meetings where federal and sub-national representatives take part (the Permanent Representative of Belgium to the EU is also present), in order to determine the instructions for Belgian representatives in the EU Council. A crucial element of the system is that the regions and communities can exercise a veto in the determination of Belgium's policy in the Council. According to Article 146 of the Maastricht Treaty, it is possible for Belgium to be represented in the Council by a member of one of its sub-state governments. With regard to the different competences (exclusive federal, exclusive sub-state or shared competences), the CA determines which governmental level is responsible for the issue in the Council. This mechanism obliges both sides (federal and sub-state) to work together if they want to gain something within the EU Council and to achieve their individual and joint interests. While the Belgian model is only a good practice scenario, and none of the member states in the EU is trying to emulate this approach to national minority accommodation and empowerment at third-level integration, let alone at member state integration, it serves as a reminder that devising an ethical system of accommodation takes time but is needed nonetheless, even in the more socially and economically developed and integrated member states.

The functional dynamic of economic restructuring is another powerful force behind national minority mobilization.[77] As new territorial hierarchies and new systems of action seek to escape the control of central governments, local policy-makers seek to maximize the capacity of their territory to compete by emphasizing its human capital and other resources. Through mobilizing local energies in an effort to compete in global economic restructuring and technological change, national minority regions become active political players at the international level, perhaps even before they find a voice at the state level. In this dynamic national minority, regions can additionally draw on strong identities and systems of solidarity and may prove more powerful and successful in developing their societies. Path-dependency – in terms of reinforced institutions, formal as well as informal, cultural and ethnic, through the rationality of actors calculating costs and benefits, and reproducing institutional opportunities while drawing on cultural codes, ideologies and world views – determines the degree of mobilization.[78] Other theoretical frameworks include cultural toolkits in terms of historical and territorial self-identification turned into action. Thus, clientelism can also work to the benefit of national minorities. At the informal level, nostalgic narratives, reference to stories, codes, values and norms can also influence the strength with which political mobilization happens. The making of national minority 'regions' refers therefore to institutional arrangements, social fabric, networks and discourses as well as strategies, social construction, self-identification and collective identification.

As post-communist states went through political transition, national minority mobilization of social capital also became dependent on social and economic changes in terms of both outcomes and opportunities. This resulted in different scenarios concerning the way in which national minority regions sought to influence their future existence, both as political and social actors. For instance, dissatisfaction with the ability of central governments to procure resources and development aid for national minority regions in Western Europe manifested itself in local policy-makers seeking to influence decisions in Brussels otherwise reserved for the supra-state level. Another aspect is the varied level of social and economic development in national minority regions. Some national minority regions are more successful in obtaining funds than other regions. As they liaise, they may create coalitions to lobby for increased funding for the regions. Thus, the interactive process of 'structuration',[79] including the invention of new strategies of interaction and collective action, creates opportunities through existing frameworks, including legal frameworks, as well as inventing new frameworks and using horizontal and vertical alliances of trust-building.

The example of the Hungarian minority in Romania shows how trust and existing frameworks are important factors. Although the economic situation of the Hungarians in Romania is mixed, the Hungarians in Transylvania have gained certain advantages in the private sector, since many of them were familiar with the economic situation and model in Hungary. They are also linked by family and friendship ties with Hungary and benefit from them in business. Consequently, a stratum receptive to entrepreneurship appeared relatively early after the beginning of transition and started to work more efficiently than was the case with the Romanian population. Thus, participation in private business is vital to Romania's Hungarians. This is the sector where Hungarian entrepreneurs face the least institutional barriers and where, both in services and in production, one can easily find very profitable and presently non-supplied sectors. In their endeavours to expand, cooperation with foreign partners is often considered more effective. Of course, foreign cooperation is primarily with Hungarian partners in the motherland. Hungary is one of the largest investors in Romania and the base capital of registered companies is in the three-digit millions. This indicates that there is considerable interest on both sides in developing economic relations. As such, it constitutes a force by which the Hungarians develop their international relations through their kin-state.

Horizontal internationalization of national minority regions happens at different levels and implements varied tools and social capital, and is also focused in terms of mobilizing networks. Networks constitute the new social morphology of our societies and the diffusion of the networking logic substantially modifies the operation and outcomes in the processes of production, experience, power and culture. This is the view that dominant functions and processes in the information age are increasingly organized around networks. While the networking form of social organization has existed in other times and spaces, the new information technology paradigm provides the basis for its pervasive expansion throughout the entire social structure.[80] This network logic or form of organization induces a social determination at a higher level, one that was unknown before. Concerning national minority regions, this is particularly relevant, as the causal power of network flows becomes more important than the specific interests they represent. It becomes vital to be present in a network and not to be excluded from it. Hence, the emergence of the space of a new level of integration.

Moving towards the 'politics of fourth-level integration'

It is debatable how powerful the politics of third-level integration is and, certainly, the importance of national minority regions in this discourse is still low, if not insignificant. The visibility of new national minority 'regions' in the new member states is minimal at this point. The funds that these regions wish to receive from the EU are still by and large accessible only via the intermediary of the capitals of member states. Moreover, the period between the Maastricht and the Amsterdam treaties was largely seen as a 'farewell to the third level', due to the weak powers of the CoR.[81] However, while there was disillusion with the politics of the third level in the mid-1990s, the early part of the twenty-first century has seen a revival. This was evident in connection with the two Intergovernmental Conferences leading up to the Treaty of Nice in 2000, the adoption of the Constitution in 2004 and the Reform Treaty of 2007. It has manifested itself in a number of ways at the horizontal level.

Perhaps the most visible evidence of national minority politics at this possible fourth level is the emergence of national minority transnational party coalitions. These party associations have successfully expanded due to the disaffection of electorates with existing traditional political parties. They are defined as referring to the efforts of geographically concentrated peripheral national minorities that challenge the working order of member states.[82] They have followed the model of socialist parties by developing transnational links and political groups. Indeed, the EP funds programmes to encourage cooperation between parties in Europe for elections and within the EP itself. The European Free Alliance (EFA) is an example of this type of cooperation (with members from the Scottish National Party, Wales and Catalonia), allied with the Greens in the EP. Since its creation in 1981 (signed by six parties), membership in the EFA has increased dramatically to include over twenty parties.

The above-mentioned RegLeg is another strong coalition of 20 powerful EU regions. RegLeg regions have competence in three areas of government: legislative, executive and judiciary. Indeed, a large percentage of the EU population live in RegLeg regions. The aim of RegLeg is to strive for an enhanced role for those regions in the EU. This means increased political and legal status in all domains of EU governance, according to their competences and responsibilities.

Finally, a third example of coalition is the Federal Union of European Nationalities (FUEN). This association represents national minorities, whether territorially defined or not, and pursues the goal of preserving their national identity, language, culture and history. It works towards the neighbourly, peaceful coexistence of majority and minority in one state or region. FUEN supports all state activities aimed at the peaceful reconciliation of interests and democratic minority policy and attempts to persuade European parliaments and governments that part of the peaceful development of Europe involves taking account of the interests that national minorities and ethnic groups are entitled to in preserving their original identity and helping them to preserve their traditional culture.

Another aspect of national minority politics at the fourth level is representation offices established in Brussels. These are considered a mushrooming phenomenon that have emerged in the EU15 realm. As an answer to a perceived lack of information emanating from European institutions, on the one side, and national governments, on the other, regions lobbying within the EU have been seen to invoke two complementary strategies. First, regions have used 'intra-state' strategies to lobby the EU through national institutions. Individually or collectively, regions seek to influence national government positions on EU policy that will be transmitted through the Council and the Committee of Permanent Representatives (COREPER) to the European Commission. Secondly, 'extra-state' strategies, employed by regions to lobby the European Commission directly have resulted in the establishment of a number of regional offices in Brussels.[83] The first such office was established in 1984 by the Birmingham City Council. By 1988, 15 offices had opened; 54 were open by 1993 and 140 by 1995.[84] Although its relevance to the mobilization of national minority 'regions' is unknown and only well-established national minority regions have offices in Brussels, the number of representation offices has reached almost 170, including both regional (151) and local or municipal (17) authorities representations.

Furthermore, some states, such as Germany, Austria and Spain, have a regional representative within the offices of the national Permanent Representations to the EU in Brussels. Their main task is to inform the governments of local and regional authorities and parliaments of all EU policy developments that could affect their exclusive competencies or essential interests. This is aided by their receipt of all EU documents from the Council Secretariat and other EU institutions. Equally important is the task of bringing regional interest or concerns about EU proposals to the attention of their colleagues in the Permanent Representation offices.

In terms of structure, there are different models of regional information offices established in Brussels. This variety reflects the degree of decentralization in the member states on the one hand, and the purposes and activities that the office wants to carry on within the European institutions, on the other. The most common model is to represent the regional/local authority jointly. Another common model is the consortium model, representing local authorities (and sometimes regional development agencies, higher education institutions, and so on) through a pooling of resources. These are small offices with a group of staff that does not represent the individual members of the partnership in particular but, rather, the agency as a whole. There are other variants, including having a development agency representative in a government office or having a university representative in a government office. Finally, there is a third model, which foresees the establishment of a multilevel office for the representation and coordination of both governmental and nongovernmental, public and private interests.

The first model of single regional/local authority offices is used by the German Länder, most of the Italian regions and some Spanish regions. This kind of office represents one single territorial entity and is often considered the direct extension of the region's European strategy and operations. Whether it has to report to the president's office, or the Department/Ministry of European Affairs, Finance or Justice of the region often depends on the level of importance and competence it is given. This, in turn, leads to different sets of working criteria, prestige and, perhaps, political influence. The German Länder established their Regional Information Offices between 1986 and 1992, with the main purpose of boosting their capacity for input into the European decision-making process and of accessing European information flows and policy debates. There are also other reasons for the establishment of Länder offices in Brussels, such as access to the Structural Funds and various other EU funding sources. They constitute an important reciprocal communication channel to the European Commission to receive information as early as possible on European Commission initiatives and priorities that may be of interest to the Länder executives. Secondly, regional offices exercise a more proactive role, in which they seek to feed information into the European Commission at the early stages of policy debate and formulation.

The first model is also used to represent cross-border regional offices. Here, the regional office is composed of sub-state entities from different member states, such as the joint Anglo-French office of the county of Essex and the region of Picardy; the Austrian–Italian EU Liaison Bureau of Tyrol, Alto Adige and Trentino; or the Euroregion Secretariat of Kent, Nord-Pas de Calais and Wallonia. They are often based on former and, hence, close relationships between the entities, a shared tradition and interest, as well as joint participation in European initiatives and programmes. Despite some initial institutional and legal difficulties or misunderstandings within their own federated system, these transnational regional offices are able to provide the know-how, contacts, linguistic ability and experience of internal structures and agendas of at least two member countries. Given these advantages, this model might be regarded as *the* future model for bases in the EU.[85]

A good example of the second model of consortia of regional/local authorities is the regional representation office of Catalonia. The Patronat Català Pro Europa is a public consortium created in 1982 by Catalonia Generalitat and by a joint group of Catalan entities representing economic, financial, cultural, administrative and academic interests. It was first established in the region's capital, Barcelona, in order to prepare and familiarize the Catalan population with Spain's integration into the EU. In 1986, the institution opened a delegation office in Brussels, which supplies information and maintains contacts with the Commission and other Community institutions. Nearly 50 per cent of these are requested by economic, social and professional sectors. The Patronat carries out its tasks mainly in Barcelona (even though the institution also has offices in the provinces of Tarragona, Girona and Lleida, which ensure a bottom-up approach), while the Brussels delegation has been established with the aim of fostering inter-regional cooperation and of maintaining close relations with the Permanent Representation and with the other European institutions. It takes care of organizing, promoting and coordinating activities linked to the Community and other European organizations. Chaired by the President of Catalonia, the Patronat assembles representatives of Catalan universities, savings banks, Chamber of Trade and Industry, local government associations, and the town hall of Barcelona. The body's council is organized in three sections: academic, parliamentarian and socioeconomic, in which entrepreneurial organizations, professional associations and unions participate, including Catalan representatives of Community lobbies and officials in Brussels. The Brussels delegation is composed of 15 members, who deal with European affairs, commercial and cultural promotion, as well as courses and seminars about the EC specifically addressed to economic and professional sectors and the diffusion of the Community's R&D programmes. The office also houses a consulting service aimed at providing information about the impact of the internal market.

An example of the third model is Scotland House in Brussels, created in 1999. Scotland House brings together Scotland Europa, the umbrella organization promoting Scotland's non-governmental and commercial interests in Europe, the Scottish Executive EU Office, the Convention of Scotland Local Authorities (CoSLA), the Highlands and Islands European Partnership and several other offices from both the public and private sectors. A total of 50 full-time staff work in Scotland House for 20 organizations from both the public and private sectors. Although the various organizations work independently, collaboration occurs frequently where priorities overlap. The original feature of the Scotland House model is that it reflects the plurality of Scottish civic, governmental and commercial society. It allows a wide range of Scottish bodies to participate in having their own direct access to information and scope for influence. When Scotland Europa was established in 1992, it was not considered appropriate by the Scottish Executive Office to seek a separate presence in Brussels. Nevertheless, the Scottish Executive Office gave its blessing to the Scottish enterprise-led initiative to set up Scotland Europa. Following the change of government in 1997 and the prospect of devolution, the Scottish Executive Office set up a two-person team in Brussels.

However, the list of regional office models is not exhaustive, in the sense that more forms of representations could be identified and defined. For example, it is not unusual for the regional offices to cooperate in specific fields, establishing *ad hoc* partnership offices. This type of regional office can be described as a partnership of sub-state bodies in the sense that the bodies have come together of their own volition to work together on a range of issues that have a European dimension. They normally do not have any formal or institutionalized role in the governmental structures (e.g. NASC West Ireland EC Liaison and Regio Randstad (NL)).[86] Only a few of the new member states have set up regional or local representation in Brussels so far. Poland has the highest number of regional representation offices (11 regions out of 16 have their regional representation office in Brussels). Slovakia has three regional offices in Brussels, while from Estonia only Tallinn City is represented. Latvia and Cyprus do not have any regional representation offices as yet. Romania's national association of county councils is represented by a separate office, although the link between regions and the decision-making process is also handled by Romania's Representation. Aiming at enhancing the dialogue and cooperation between regional and local authorities in the EU and Romania, a Joint Consultative Committee between representatives of local authorities from Romania and the CoR is envisaged.

Certainly, it is not only the regions of the established EU15 member states that have shown an ability to organize themselves for lobbying; the new and aspiring member states are also preparing for this activity. For the new member states, the desire to access EU funding flows has been, and remains, the driving force behind the establishment of a presence in Brussels. Even though national minority 'regions' in the candidate countries have not established direct regional representations in Brussels, it is likely to be a phenomenon of the near future. While it has been documented that elite players in regional and local authorities of the new member states have been rather more astute at networking with their peers in EU15 states than engaging directly with Brussels,[87] it would seem to be just a matter of time before they put the knowledge achieved through such contacts to work in the competition for funds. Moreover, the ability to network is not altogether different from the networking that national minority regions in the EU15 member states have been practising for some time, the so-called para-diplomacy networking.

The phenomenon of para-diplomacy has emerged as a result of the stronger national minority regions seeking expanded leverage through partnerships. One definition of para-diplomacy holds that it is functionally specific, usually limited to matters of common economic or cultural interest, although in the case of national minority regions it does extend to the promotion of the territory as something more than a mere region and serves to legitimize nationalist aspirations.[88] The concept of para-diplomacy thus refers to external relations of sub-state actors. Such relations can be either coordinated with or complementary to activities at the central state level or pursued in conflict or concurrence with traditional diplomacy. The term 'para-diplomacy' appeared in the literature in the 1960s, with the international involvement of American and Canadian federal states and provinces in the context of globalization.[89] As para-diplomacy concerns all levels of international action (military, cooperation, development, human rights) when regional governments become international actors, the transnational relations of the regions may constitute a challenge to the member state's monopoly over international relations. The objective of para-diplomatic actors is thus to encourage transnational as opposed to international collaboration.

Para-diplomacy means that, although European states remain the principal actors of European integration, they are no longer in a position of monopoly. The bulk of para-diplomatic activity in Europe occurs between regional governments and national minority regions holding self-government (inter-regional or transborder/national relations). The 'Four Motors' of Europe is an example of this type of para-diplomacy with cross-border and inter-regional cooperation (the regions of Baden-Württemberg, Catalonia, Rhônes-Alpes and Lombardia). Traditionally, European states have acted according to the logic of a centralized state when determining which international policies to adopt. However, sub-state actors lobby for a greater role for regions in Europe towards both their state government and European institutions.

National minority regions seek to become international actors in order to obtain resources and support, which they often lack at the internal level. Globalization and European integration have provided a new context for territorial politics and regional restructuring. Regions are no longer confined within their state borders but have become an element in European and international politics.[90] The need for recognition and identity construction of certain regions explains the priority of para-diplomacy for nationalist substate movements. Thus, nationalism is a crucial force behind para-diplomacy. Indeed, the development of para-diplomacy is much stronger in national minority regions where there are strong nationalist movements. While many central governments consider the intrusion of these movements into their exclusive domains of foreign policy as essentially negative, this is arguably a paradigm that has emerged as a result of a more diverse world picture.

However, the phenomenon of para-diplomacy is not universal. It has always been stronger in federal or decentralized structures – where sub-state entities have many political responsibilities – than in centralized states. Thus, Wallonia has one of the most extensive para-diplomatic networks of any national minority region as it has also developed bilateral relations with states around the world. In addition, it is involved in European institutions, has developed relationships with neighbouring regions, and also participates in multilateral forums. The action of para-diplomacy in international relations engenders a division of the international order in the state and sub-state actors, which is perhaps a natural outcome of the heavily statist approach that has dominated twentieth-century international politics.

Conclusions

It would seem that in order to foster an ethos of 'unity in diversity' in the EU, several levels must be allowed to mobilize. This chapter has endeavoured to address the issue of national minority diversity in relation to the strategy of territorial cohesion through social and economic development. Specifically, it is has sought to identify the impact of national minority identities at the horizontal level of EU politics, and to illustrate the new challenges that these pose to the EU in terms of integration. It has questioned how national minority regions will behave in the new EU27 and beyond, and how they will mobilize in terms of structure and influence at the supra-state level. Formerly, national minority regions have had a place in only the vertical system. Yet if the Reform Treaty is ratified, the Belgian regions that are members of the CoR will gain influence in the horizontal system through the CoR's recourse to the ECJ on matters related to subsidiarity. Furthermore, national minority regions that are not members of the CoR might seek to influence the decision-making process in Brussels. This chapter has cautioned that national minority regions – existing as well as emerging 'regions' – may use the politics of third-level integration to further their cause. They may thus become a frontline for the EU to contend with in Europe's future history of peace, unity and prosperity.

EU integration is an historical process that has sought to integrate European states economically, and, more recently, politically, over the last half century. This is a process that is far from finished and that has seen much energy spent on the reconciliation of divergent political and economic systems, as well as diverse national identities. At a time when it was beginning to attain a common identity, at least at the economic level, geopolitical history has suddenly confronted Europe with the inevitable choice of integrating yet another set of politico-economic systems and national identities. However, the post-1989 systems and identities draw on a very different history: a history of suppressed identities and strategies. Moreover, the new national majority identities are far more contested than in Western Europe. The new national majority identities are in many cases revived identities that, in their revival, have come to discover that they are not homogeneous. Indeed, most of them consist of sub-state national identities in addition to national identities in the Westphalian sense. Thus, European integration is faced with not one identity per new member state but several identities per new member state. This is arguably a new social and cultural space to which the EU will have to adapt. When these diverse national minority identities mobilize to develop economically through the influence of the EU decision-making process, the EU may have to revisit its conventional views of national identities and national power.

Sub-state nationalisms, whether kin-state-related or independent, represent strong social forces, as well as antagonistic cultural forces. To avoid having to address a 'culture deficit' in terms of neglected sub-state identities, the EU may have to pay attention to national minority regions seeking inclusion in the third-level integration process. Indeed, European spaces have been created in which national minority regions and aspiring regions interface with each other and with the institutions of the internal market economy. Networks, para-diplomacy and representation offices are the currency of these new spaces, which perhaps may be described as fourth-level politics. As social resources and capital draw on the history and territory of national minority regions to mobilize for economic development, then institutional arrangements, social fabrics, networks and discourses, as well as strategies, social constructions, self-identification and collective identification will become part of the making of national minority regions. Seeing the making of national minority regions as an isolated intra-state phenomenon is thus no longer feasible and Europeanization and internationalization are perhaps the strongest factors in the changing fabric not only of member states, but also of the European mosaic of diverse identities. Where European states have traditionally acted according to the logic of the centralized state, they may now be faced with sub-state actors pushing both their state government and European institutions for a greater role for national minority regions in Europe. If these national minorities show a particularly strong ability to mobilize, it would seem that, whether empowered or not, they may become a force for EU policy-makers to contend with in the new EU27 and beyond.

Notes

1. M. Keating, *The New Regionalism in Western Europe. Territorial Restructuring and Political Change* (Cheltenham: Edward Elgar, 1998), at 185.
2. Treaty Establishing the European Community 1957 (TEC), Article 151, renumbered III-280 in the Treaty establishing a Constitution for Europe.
3. TEC, Article 263, reframed in Article III-386 of the Treaty establishing a Constitution for Europe. See also Protocol 2 of the Constitution for Europe.
4. Belgium currently allocates seats to autonomous self-governing national minority regions.
5. The Treaty establishing a Constitution for Europe establishes territorial cohesion in Article III-220.
6. U. Bullmann, 'The Politics of the Third Level', in C. Jeffery (ed.), *The Regional Dimension of the European Union: Towards a Third Level in Europe?* (London: Frank Cass, 1997).
7. Keating, *The New Regionalism, supra* note 1.
8. In Estonia, the municipality of Narva is 85 per cent Russian while, in Slovakia, the region along the southern border is 20–50 per cent Hungarian.
9. Romania is also home to the largest number of different national minorities. There are currently 19 acknowledged national minorities in Romania.
10. See further, F. Ibrahim, 'The Kurdish National Movement and the Struggle for National Autonomy', in B. Berberoglu (ed.), *The National Question: Nationalism, Ethnic Conflict and Self-Determination in the 20th Century* (Philadelphia: Temple University Press, 1995), 36–60.
11. Resolution on Measures in Favour of Minority Languages and Cultures, *Official Journal of the European Communities*, C68 of 14 March 1983, 103; Resolution on the Languages and Cultures of Regional and Ethnic Minorities in the European Community, *Official Journal of the European Communities*, C318 of 30 November 1987, 160; Resolution on Languages in the Community and the Situation of Catalan, *Official Journal of the European Communities*, C19 of 28 January 1991, 142; Resolution on Linguistic and Cultural Minorities in the European Community, *Official Journal of the European Communities*, C61 of 28 February 1994, 110; Resolution on a Community Charter of Regional Languages and Cultures and on a Charter of Rights of Ethnic Minorities, *Official Journal of the European Communities*, C287 of 9 November 1981, 106; Resolution Adopting the Declaration of Fundamental Rights and Freedoms of 12 April 1989, *Official Journal of the European Communities*, C 120/51 of 16.5.89, Part II at 1.
12. This provision is being implemented through two anti-discrimination directives, namely: Council Directive 2000/43 of 29 June 2000 Implementing the Principle of Equal Treatment between Persons Irrespective of Racial or Ethnic Origin, *Official Journal of the European Communities*, 2000 L 180/22, and Council Directive 2000/750 Action Programme to Combat Discrimination, *Official Journal of the European Communities*, 2000 L 303/23 of 2 December 2000. In the Constitution for Europe, Article 13 TEC will be incorporated as Article III-3 and III-8.

13. See Contribution submitted by P. Balazs and J. Szajer, members of the Convention, and N. MacCormick, P. Eckstein-Kovacs and I. Szent-Ivanyi, alternate members, 'Respect for Minorities and the European Constitutional Structure' (2003), CONV 639/03, CONTRIB 286. 25 March <http://www.hhrf.org/htmh/background/prop_eu.htm>. For the High Commissioner on National Minorities' intervention, see K. Drzewicki, 'A Constitution for Europe: Enshrining Minority Rights. Words Can Make Worlds of Difference', *OSCE Magazine*, 14 March 2005.

14. J. Hughes and G. Sasse, 'Monitoring the Monitors: EU Enlargement Conditionality and Minority Protection in the CEECs', *Journal on Ethnopolitics and Minority Issues in Europe* 1 (2003): 1–37, at 13. See also B. de Witte, 'The Constitutional Resources for an EU Minority Protection Policy', in G.N. Toggenburg (ed.), *Minority Protection and the Enlarged European Union: The Way Forward* (Budapest: OSI/LFI, 2004), 107–25, at 116.

15. Treaty of Lisbon 2007 amending the Treaty on European Union and the Treaty Establishing the European Community (hereinafter, Reform Treaty), Article 8 of the Protocol on the Application of the Principle of Subsidiarity and Proportionality.

16. Belgium currently allocates seats to autonomous self-governing national minority regions (see further below).

17. I would like to thank Lucia Pantella for research assistance.

18. For a good discussion of the function of regions in the current EU governance system, see F. Palermo and A. Santini, 'From NUTS to Constitutional Regions: Addressing EU Regions in the EU Framework', in R. Toniatti *et al.* (eds), *An Ever More Complex Union: The Regional Variable as a Missing Link in the EU Constitution?* (Baden-Baden: Nomos, 2004), 3–26.

19. For a good discussion of this, see M.P. Maduro, 'Europe and the Constitution: What if this is as Good as it Gets?', in J.H.H. Weiler and M. Wind (eds), *Rethinking European Constitutionalism* (Cambridge: Cambridge University Press, 2000).

20. M. Anderson, *Frontiers: Territory and State Formation in the Modern World* (Cambridge: Polity Press, 1996).

21. Keating, *The New Regionalism*, *supra* note 1.

22. M. Keating, *Plurinational Democracy: Stateless Nations in a Post-Sovereignty Era* (Oxford: Oxford University Press, 2002).

23. See also J. Hughes, G. Sasse and C. Gordon, 'The Regional Deficit in Eastward Enlargement of the European Union: Top Down Policies and Bottom Up Reactions', ESRC 'One Europe or Several' Programme Working Papers 29 January 2001 <http://www.one-europe.ac.uk/pdf/w29gordon.pdf>

24. J. Loughlin, 'Representing Regions in Europe: The Committee of the Regions', in Jeffery (ed.), *The Regional Dimension of the European Union*, *supra* note 6.

25. See G. von Toggenburg, ' "Unity in Diversity": Searching for the Regional Dimension in the Context of a Somewhat Constitutional Credo', in Toniatti *et al.* (eds), *An Ever More Complex Union*, *supra* note 18, 27–54.

26. The Consultative Council consisted of 21 members at the local level and 21 at the regional level, proposed by the main organization of local and regional authorities and nominated by the Commission.

27. G. Avolio and A. Santini, 'The Committee of the Regions in the EU Policy-Making Process: Actor or Spectator?', in Toniatti *et al.* (eds), *An Ever More Complex Union*, *supra* note 18, 85–116.

28. Reform Treaty, Article 2 of the Protocol on the Application of the Principle of Subsidiarity and Proportionality, *supra* note 15.

29. Chapter 4 TEC and Protocol 30.
30. See the Declaration on the Future of the European Union, adopted at the European Council at Laeken, December 2001.
31. Reform Treaty, Articles 14, 75, 116(a), 127(iv), 144(a), 147, 214(b), 246.
32. *Treaty establishing a Constitution for Europe*, Article 8 of the Protocol on the Application of the Principle of Subsidiarity and Proportionality.
33. C. Jeffery, 'Regions and the Future of Europe', *EU Reform Spotlight* (2003), 2.
34. Report from the Chairman of Working Group I on the Principle of Subsidiarity, CONV 286/02 of 23 September 2002, at 8.
35. CoR Resolution of 3 June 1999 amended the Maastricht Treaty, CdR 54/99 fin F-D-NL/JKB/CH/JW/vh.
36. See, in general, Toniatti *et al.* (eds), *An Ever More Complex Union, supra* note 18.
37. Prior to adopting the SEA in 1986, the Community was known as the EEC.
38. Council Regulation (EC) No. 1264/1999 of 21 June 1999 amending regulation (EC) No. 1164/94 establishing a Cohesion Fund, *Official Journal of the European Communities*, L 161, 26/06/1999 P. 0057–0061.
39. The European Regional Development Fund (ERDF); the European Social Fund (ESF); the European Agricultural Guidance and Guarantee Fund (EAGGF); and the Financial Instrument for Fisheries Guidance (FIFG).
40. Council Regulation (EC) No. 1260/1999 of 21 June 1999 laying down general provisions on the Structural Funds, *Official Journal of the European Communities*, L 161, 26/06/1999 P. 0001–0042.
41. Council Regulation (EC) No. 1264/1999, *supra* note 38
42. A Development Plan is the analysis prepared by a member state in light of the objectives referred to in Article 1 and the priority needs for attaining those objectives, together with the strategy, action priorities, specific goals and the related indicative financial resources. A Community Support Framework (CSF) is a document approved by the Commission, in agreement with the member state concerned, following appraisal of the Development Plan submitted by the member state. It contains the action strategy and specific objectives.
43. See B. Brunazzo, 'The Partnership Principle in the EU Cohesion Policy and its Environmental Assessment: The Regional Involvement in the French Case', in Toniatti *et al.* (eds), *An Ever More Complex Union, supra* note 18, 201–20.
44. Bullmann, 'The Politics of the Third Level', *supra* note 6.
45. Brunazzo, 'The Partnership Principle', *supra* note 43.
46. The term 'PHARE' – Poland and Hungary Assistance for the Restructuring of the Economy – initially described the international efforts to provide economic support to the emerging Polish and Hungarian democracies. It is now the EU's main financial instrument for accession of the Central and Eastern European countries.
47. The 10 pan-European transport corridors were defined at the second Pan-European Transport Conference in Crete, March 1994 as routes in Central and Eastern Europe that required major investment over the next ten to fifteen years. Additions were made at the third conference in Helsinki in 1997. Therefore, these corridors are sometimes referred to as the 'Crete corridors' or 'Helsinki corridors', regardless of their geographical locations. A tenth corridor was proposed after the end of hostilities between the states of the former Yugoslavia.
48. European Commission (Ecomm), Communication from the Commission to the Council, the European Parliament, the Economic and Social Committee and the Committee of the Regions on the Results of the Programming of the Structural Funds for 2000–2006 (Objective 1), COM(2001) 378, 5 July 2001.

49. Ecomm, Proposal for a Council Regulation Laying Down General Provisions on the European Regional Development Fund, the European Social Fund and the Cohesion Fund, COM(2004)492, final 2004/0163(AVC), 14 July 2004.
50. European Commission Communication from the Commission to the European Parliament and the Council on the Implementation of Commitments Undertaken by the Acceding Countries in the Context of Accession Negotiations on Chapter 21: Regional Policy and Coordination of Structural Instruments, COM(2003) 433 final, 16 July 2003.
51. In order to facilitate the collection, compiling and dissemination of comparable regional statistics, the European Union is introducing a common classification of territorial units for statistical purposes (NUTS) in place of the one established by EUROSTAT. The NUTS classification divides up the economic territory of the member states, including their territory outside regions as such. The latter comprises parts of the economic territory that cannot be assigned to a given region such as air space, territorial waters and the continental shelf, territorial enclaves (embassies, consulates and military bases), or resource deposits located in international waters and exploited by units residing in their territory. The NUTS classification is hierarchical in that it subdivides each member state into three levels: NUTS levels 1, 2 and 3. The second and third levels are subdivisions of the first and second levels respectively. Member states may decide to go further still in terms of hierarchical levels by subdividing NUTS level 3.
52. See Hughes *et al.*, 'The Regional Deficit' *supra* note 23.
53. M. Keating and J. Loughlin (eds), *The Political Economy of Regionalism* (London: Frank Cass, 1996).
54. Hughes *et al.*, 'The Regional Deficit' *supra* note 23.
55. G. Evans and J. Newham, *The Penguin Dictionary of International Relations* (London: Penguin, 1998), at 473–4.
56. Keating, *The New Regionalism, supra* note 1.
57. The Cluj Declaration adopted by the Democratic Alliance of Hungarians in Romania (DAHR) on 25 October 1992. See also T. Malloy, *National Minority Rights in Europe* (Oxford: Oxford University Press, 2005).
58. Keating, *The New Regionalism, supra* note 1.
59. See Hughes *et al.*, 'The Regional Deficit', *supra* note 23.
60. *Ibid.*
61. P. Bajda, M. Syposz and D. Wojakowski, 'Equality in Law, Protection in Fact: Minority Law and Practice in Poland', in A.-M. Biro and P. Kovacs (eds), *Diversity in Action: Local Public Management of Multiethnic Communities in Central and Eastern Europe* (Budapest: Open Society Institute, 2001).
62. Law No. 315/2004.
63. M. Tatur (ed.), *The Making of Regions in Post-Socialist Europe – The Impact of Culture, Economic Structure and Institutions: Case Studies from Poland, Hungary, Romania and Ukraine* (Wiesbaden: VS Verlag Für Sozialwissenschaften, 2004).
64. See, in general, Hughes *et al.*, 'The Regional Deficit', *supra* note 23.
65. P. Järve, 'Introduction', in P. Järve and S. Smooha (eds), *The Fate of Ethnic Democracy in Post-Communist Europe* (Budapest: ECMI/LGI, 2005).
66. D.J. Smith, 'Minority Rights, Multiculturalism and EU Enlargement: the Case of Estonia', *Journal of Ethnopolitics and Minority Issues in Europe* 1 (2003).
67. W. Kymlicka, *Multicultural Citizenship* (Oxford: Oxford University Press, 1995).
68. The law was designed to foster the position of the Hungarian minorities abroad and granted them, on the basis of registration, in Hungary, certain rights and

privileges in the areas of education and culture. One of the law's major provisions allows kin-state Hungarians to work in Hungary for a three-month period each year; it offers financial support for public transportation costs as well as assistance for students in institutions of higher education while they are in Hungary; and it extends assistance to Hungarians abroad who have more than two children in Hungarian-language schools. In exchange the Hungarians beyond the borders have to do little more than establish their credentials as ethnic Magyars.

69. P. Thornberry, *International Law and the Rights of Minorities* (Oxford: Clarendon Press, 1991).
70. G. Gilbert, 'Religio-Nationalist Minorities and the Development of Minority Rights Law', *Review of International Studies* 25 (1999): 389–410.
71. J. Jackson-Preece, *National Minorities and the European Nation-States System* (New York: Oxford University Press, 1998).
72. P. Allott, *Eunomia: New Order for a New World* (Oxford: Oxford University Press, 1990). By the same author see also Allott, *The Health of Nations: Society and Law Beyond the State* (Cambridge: Cambridge University Press, 2002).
73. R. Putnam, *Making Democracy Work: Civic Traditions in Modern Italy* (Princeton: Princeton University Press, 1993).
74. L. Hooghe, 'Belgium: From Regionalism to Federalism', in J. Coakley (ed.), *The Territorial Management of Ethnic Conflict* (London: Frank Cass, 2003), 73–99.
75. *Ibid.*
76. B. Kerremansm and J. Beyers, 'The Belgian Sub-national Entities in the European Union: Second or Third Level Players', in Jeffery (ed.), *The Regional Dimension of the European Union, supra* note 6.
77. Keating, *The New Regionalism, supra* note 1
78. Tatur (ed.), *The Making of Regions, supra* note 63.
79. A. Giddens, *The Constitution of Society: Outline of the Theory of Structuration* (Cambridge: Polity Press, 1984).
80. M. Castells, *The Rise of the Network Society* (Oxford: Blackwell, 2000).
81. C. Jeffery, 'Regional Information Office in Brussels and Multi-Level Governance in the EU: A UK–German Comparison', in Jeffery (ed.), *The Regional Dimension of the European Union, supra* note 6.
82. F. Müller-Rommel, 'Ethnoregionalist Parties in Western Europe: Theoretical Considerations and Framework of Analysis', in L. de Winter and H. Türsan (eds), *Regionalist Parties in Western Europe* (London: Routledge, 1998).
83. P. Lynch, 'Regions and the Convention on the Future of Europe: A Dialogue with the Deaf?', *European Urban and Regional Studies* 11(2) (2004): 170–7.
84. Jeffery (ed.), *Regional Information Office, supra* note 76.
85. A. Heichlinger, *A Regional Representation in Brussels: The Right Idea for Influencing EU Policy-Making?* (Maastricht: EIPA, 1999).
86. *Ibid.*
87. See Hughes *et al.*, 'The Regional Deficit', *supra* note 23.
88. Keating, *The New Regionalism, supra* note 1.
89. P. Soldatos, 'An Explanatory Framework for the Study of Federal States as Foreign-Policy Actors', in H.J. Michelmann and P. Soldatos (eds), *Federalism and International Relations: The Role of Subnational Units* (Oxford: Oxford University Press, 1990), 34–54.
90. Keating, *The New Regionalism, supra* note 1.

Part II

European Mechanisms for the Management of Minority–Majority Relations

4
A Remaining Share or a New Part? The EU's Role *vis-à-vis* Minorities after the Enlargement Decade

Gabriel von Toggenburg

After Europe's E-Day: introducing the post-enlargement era

The process of eastwards enlargement is often regarded as the primordial catalyst moving the protection of minorities onto the EU agenda. However, a comparable conclusion can also be reached with respect to the two other primary international organizations active on European soil: namely, the Council of Europe (CoE) and the Organization for Security and Cooperation in Europe (OSCE). Admittedly, the latter two players have *traditionally* had a clear and outspoken interest in the protection of minorities. Nevertheless, it seems rather obvious that it was only the fall of the 'Iron Curtain' that created the political *momentum* that finally allowed for the adoption and widespread ratification of the two prominent legal instruments, the European Charter for Regional or Minority Languages (Language Charter) and the Framework Convention for the Protection of National Minorities (FCNM) within the CoE. Further, the remarkable establishment of a High Commissioner on National Minorities (HCNM) within the framework of the OSCE is, in the end, the fruit of the *annus mirabilis*, 1989.

However, with regard to the minority-related policies of the last decade, a striking difference can be detected between the CoE and the OSCE, on the one hand, and the EU, on the other, in the sense that the former two organizations raised cheer with their revamped engagement, while the fresh and perhaps unexpected engagement of the EU was met with highly critical remarks, the allegation 'double standards' being the most widespread.[1]

In fact, the EU was behaving as if minority protection were an export product that was not fit for domestic consumption.[2] However, legally speaking, this is not an untenable position. Even politically speaking, it is important not to ignore the fact that complete inaction from the EU would have been much more detrimental. In the end, one has to recognize that the very different approaches of the EU, the CoE and the OSCE to the issue of minority protection are to be explained (and justified) by the very different respective characters of the 'big three'. The OSCE – the interface between the East and the West during the Cold War – has a long history of diplomatic pacification and prevention of political conflicts. The CoE has a long-standing tradition of elaborating standards and codifying them in legally binding instruments of international law. Finally, the EU has become the centre of gravity in Europe, in the sense that the majority of European states found the possibility of becoming a member of this exclusive and welfare-creating club a very attractive one. In the post-Cold War period, the OSCE created with the HCNM an institution that intervened silently but efficiently behind the diplomatic scenes for the protection of minorities. During the enlargement decade, the CoE drafted two prominent, legally binding Conventions. Finally, the EU used its lever of conditionality in order to influence the performance of minority protection in all states applying for EU membership.

The fact that the EU's minority engagement was – in contrast to the engagement of the CoE and the OSCE – more or less limited to its external sphere made 1 May 2004 a potential turning point in the EU's relationship towards minorities. With Europe's big 'E-Day', the former (external) targets of the EU's minority policy have become an integral part of that union and the EU has lost its conditionality leverage. In the literature, the image of an enlarged EU silently fading from the area of minority protection is juxtaposed with one of an enlarged EU embarking on a revamped engagement with its internal minorities.[3]

This chapter attempts to identify the role of the EU *vis-à-vis* (its) minorities after the enlargements of 2004 and 2007. The main question is whether the EU will continue simply to take care of the remainder of the tasks it has set itself so far or whether it will take on a new role by adopting fresh approaches and innovative means. In the former scenario, the EU would continue merely to apply the conditionality policy *vis-à-vis* current and future candidate states. In the latter eventuality, the EU would revamp its conditionality policy in its external relations, strengthen considerably its cooperation with the other two European players in the area of minority protection and foster stronger internal engagement with minorities living on the territory of member states.

Important voices have advocated this second scenario.[4] Already, with the entry into force of the Treaty of Amsterdam and the new Article 13 of the EC Treaty (EC), commentators have identified a tendency towards 'internalization', in the sense that the issue of minority protection has started to move from the external agenda to the internal agenda of the EU.[5] Minority-minded politicians and NGOs active in the field have lobbied for a minority clause to be inserted in the Charter of Fundamental Rights during the first Convention, in the Constitutional Treaty (CE) during the second Convention, and again in relation to the Draft Treaty of Lisbon amending the Treaty on European Union and the Treaty Establishing the European Community (Reform Treaty). This shows that, despite obvious limitations, the role of the EU in the area of minority protection is on the move.[6]

At this point it seems appropriate to ask the following questions: first, how has the EU developed its conditionality policy *vis-à-vis* the Western Balkans ('Third wave of enlargement: applying a fine-tuned conditionality policy'); secondly, what kind of instruments does the EU currently have in the area of minority protection, and what instruments could it have gained through the now derailed Constitution and the Reform Treaty respectively ('The Treaty of Lisbon: waiting for what?'); thirdly, is the EU acquiring new leverage and channels through the increased application of instruments of so-called 'new governance' ('Modes of governance: changing policy preferences?'); fourthly, how has the issue of cooperation between the international organizations mentioned above gained momentum ('The EU, OSCE and CoE: creating an "inter-organizational trialogue"'); and, fifthly, how does the EU fit into an integrated system of minority governance in Europe ('Conclusion: the EU within an integrated system of minority governance')?

Third wave of enlargement: applying a fine-tuned conditionality policy

During recent years, the EU's policy *vis-à-vis* the Western Balkans has not only upheld the Copenhagen criterion of the 'respect for and protection of minorities' but has also applied a revised conditionality policy. This 'second generation' conditionality was established by the Council's conclusions on the application of conditionality in the Western Balkans as of 29 April 1997, and it follows a so-called 'graduated approach'.[7] The conditions to be fulfilled by the third state depend on whether the EU is about to grant autonomous trade preferences, to implement PHARE (originally, the 'Poland and Hungary: Assistance for Restructuring their Economies' programme but now extended to include other accession countries) or to enter into contractual relations. The first level of conditionality does not refer *expressis verbis* to minority protection. The second level of this graduated approach (PHARE) requires the country's 'credible commitment to democratic reforms and progress in compliance with the generally recognised standards of human and minority rights'. At the third level of the graduated approach, conditionality is explicitly described as an 'evolutionary process'.

The start of negotiations is only possible if the country in question fulfils 10 general conditions. These include the '[c]redible offer to and visible implementation of real opportunities for displaced persons (including so-called "internal migrants") and refugees to return to their places of origin, and absence of harassment initiated or tolerated by public authorities'; the '[a]bsence of generally discriminatory treatment and harassment of minorities by public authorities'; and the '[a]bsence of discriminatory treatment and harassment of independent media'. The permission to begin negotiations requires 'a lower level of compliance than the conclusion of the agreements. At each stage, including after the conclusion of agreements, the situation should be monitored and, in accordance with the relevant articles of the agreement, its application could be suspended in case of serious non-compliance'. An annex to this sort of Conditionality-Decalogue provides the EU with '[e]lements for the examination of compliance' with the various criteria. With respect to the protection of minorities, three elements are explicitly listed, namely the '[r]ight to establish and maintain...own educational, cultural and religious institutions, organisations or associations'; '[a]dequate opportunities for...minorities to use their own language before courts and public authorities'; and '[a]dequate protection of refugees and displaced persons returning to areas where they represent an ethnic minority'.

In the framework of the Stabilization and Association Process (SAp) this graduated approach is combined with a country-to-country approach, which provides the flexibility to tailor conditionality to specific situations in different countries. Most of the SAp instruments refer to the described elements of conditionality.[8] This is especially true for the Community Assistance for Reconstruction, Development and Stability in the Balkans (CARDS) regulation.[9] The system of 'European Partnerships' also refers to the CARDS regulation and second-generation conditionality.[10]

When comparing first-generation conditionality (*vis-à-vis* Central and Eastern European countries) with second-generation conditionality (*vis-à-vis* countries of the Western Balkans), one can observe that conditionality has been fine-tuned. Those in favour of minority protection have become much more outspoken. Special emphasis is given to the return of refugees. Moreover, it seems as if the experience of the terrible atrocities that have taken place in the Balkans has contributed to the fact that second-generation conditionality is more exposed, not only from a normative perspective, but also from a political point of view. It is interesting to note, for example, that the Council and the European Council – and hence the representatives of the national governments – have substantially contributed to the development of second-generation conditionality. This might indicate that minority protection is no longer exclusively seen as a condition for *becoming* a member state of the EU but increasingly as an expression of *being* an EU member state. It seems as if the Council and the Heads of State and Government are aligning themselves with the legal position of the European Commission, which regularly holds that minority protection is part of the founding principles of the EU as outlined in Article 6 of the Treaty of European Union (TEU).[11] In fact, the Heads of States and Government declared in 2003 at the EU-Western Balkans Summit that they all share the value of respecting '*minority rights*'.[12] The Council declared in a joint action that the EU is committed to encouraging, in all countries in the Balkans region, the promotion of the values and models on which the EU itself is 'founded', and that among these values is the respect for minorities.[13]

Thus, we can conclude that, after eastwards enlargement, the EU's 'minority momentum' has – with respect to the EU's external sphere – not only been upheld, but also increased and improved. The question remains, however: how far does this translate into the EU's internal sphere?

The Treaty of Lisbon: waiting for what?

The law as it stands

To begin once more with the obvious: according to EU primary law, the EU does not hold an explicit competence in the area of minority protection. Nevertheless, the EU retains remarkable 'constitutional resources', which can be used for the protection of minorities.[14] This functional approach, developed in the literature and in the area of policy consulting, is gaining recognition in EU politics.[15] This can also be seen from the Parliament resolution on minority protection.[16] The 'Moraes Resolution' clearly decouples questions of constitutional development from necessary (and possible) projects of legislation in the area of minority protection.[17] The resolution suggests that various existing provisions in EU primary law – such as Article 13 EC (anti-discrimination policy), Article 49 EC (freedom to provide services), Article 95 EC (harmonization of the Common Market), Article 151 EC (cultural policies), Article 64 EC (cooperation in civil matters), Article 31 EU (judicial cooperation in criminal matters), Article 149 EC (educational policies), Article 137 (employment, social exclusion) and Article 163 EC (research policy) – can be used in order to implement various provisions of the CoE's FCNM within the sphere of the EU.[18] Also the Network of Independent Experts in Fundamental Rights (CFR-CDF), established in 2002, underlines the possibility and necessity of taking minority issues into account when becoming active within the current EU framework. The network refers in this context to, for example, the regulation of television broadcasting or services of general interest.[19]

Apart from these scattered constitutional resources, primary law offers under Article 13 EC a prominent competence base that could be central to protecting minorities in the context of EU law. Article 13 allows the Community to 'take appropriate action to combat discrimination based on sex, racial or ethnic origin, religion or belief, disability, age or sexual orientation'. It is still open to discussion whether and to what degree affirmative actions or even group rights could be based on Article 13. Its wording suggests – especially when compared to those provisions in primary law that deal with sex discrimination – that it takes a rather formal view of equality.[20] Article 13 does not, at first glance, seem to aim for the establishment of *de facto* equality but, rather, to fight discrimination. On the other hand, the fact that it views anti-discrimination as a *process* without defining any result leaves the notion of equality open to interpretation. This shows that Article 13 EC is a double accessory provision: first, it can only be applied 'within the limits of the powers conferred' on the Community; and, secondly, it does not lend itself to a stand-alone interpretation of how far legislative intervention can go in terms of equality. Therefore, it might be appropriate to label Article 13 a sort of 'container provision', since it is, with respect to the definition of equality, not self-sustaining. Its reach depends on the notion of equality applied by the legislator, and it is well known that the European Court of Justice (ECJ) applies a rather individualistic and formal reading of equality. However, this position is not carved in stone, and it will depend on constitutional developments with respect to equality perceptions at the national level.

So far, Article 13 has been used as a basis for Directives,[21] for action programmes,[22] the extension of such programmes to third countries,[23] and a number of 'European years', such as the 'European Year of Equal Opportunities for All'.[24] Of all these measures based on Article 13, the so-called 'Race Directive' has the most far-reaching legal implications for persons belonging to minorities.[25] However, the potential of Article 13 is far from exhausted, as illustrated by the discussion on a specific 'Roma Directive'.[26] It has been argued that Article 13 could even allow for the adoption of an instrument prohibiting the discriminatory application of rules related to nationality in order to prevent certain minorities from being denied access to official documents.[27]

The law as it might become

With the background of this potentially very strong provision, one wonders what the Reform Treaty will do if it enters into force; it was signed by all member states on 13 December 2007 and is currently in the process of ratification. It is, in any case, worth underlining that, with the Constitution and the Reform Treaty, minority-minded groups succeeded for the first time in the history of European integration in integrating the dreaded word 'minorities' into a text of primary EU law. The beginning of the Constitution listed in Article I-2 'the respect for human rights, including the rights of persons belonging to minorities' as one of the founding values of the EU. This amendment, which was agreed upon not in the drafting stage but at the Intergovernmental Conference under the Italian presidency at the end of 2003, remains ambiguous[28] and rather modest. It did not refer explicitly to 'minority rights'[29] or to minority 'groups'.[30] This exact wording has been carried over in Article I-3 of the Reform Treaty, which provides for a new Article I-a EC as follows:

> The Union is founded on the values of respect for human dignity, liberty, democracy, equality, the rule of law and respect for human rights, *including the rights of persons belonging to minorities*.[31]

However, in neither the Constitution nor the Reform Treaty was this provision followed up by a policy provision or competence base.

It is little wonder, therefore, that the provision has been considered a 'foundation on which it would be difficult to build a solid edifice'.[32] The clause does no more than confirm the legal opinion of the European Commission without clarifying what rights which minorities under what circumstances could invoke. This is somehow unsatisfying. The explanations of the Presidium (of the European Convention drafting the earlier provision contained in the Constitution) advocated a very short value provision representing:

> a hard core of values meeting two criteria at once: on the one hand, they must be so fundamental that they lie at the very heart of a peaceful society practising tolerance, justice and solidarity; on the other hand, they must have a clear non-controversial legal basis so that the Member States can discern the obligations resulting therefrom which are subject to sanction.[33]

Whether this second criterion is met by the value of minority protection introduced by the Reform Treaty might be open to doubt. Nevertheless, the new provision in Article I-3 might be seen as another important 'container provision', presenting itself as a base rock upon which a European notion of minority rights could be developed, both through the legislative trialogue between the institutions and through the case law of the ECJ.

If the Reform Treaty enters into force, Articles 21 and 22 of the Charter of Fundamental Rights (CFR), on the principle of non-discrimination and the obligation to respect cultural, religious and linguistic diversity, respectively, will finally become legally binding.[34] Article 21 states that:

> [a]ny discrimination based on any ground such as sex, race, colour, ethnic or social origin, genetic features, language, religion or belief, political or any other opinion, *membership of a national minority*, property, birth, disability, age or sexual orientation shall be prohibited.[35]

As opposed to Article I-13 EC, this provision contains a clear-cut and directly applicable prohibition.[36] The catalogue of prohibited grounds for discrimination in Article 21 is open ('any ground such as') whereas the catalogue of discriminations that the EU may combat with legislative means is closed.[37] Hence the enabling provision in Article 13 EC takes up only 9 of the 17 forbidden grounds listed in the prohibitive provision of Article 21 CFR. Thus, if ratified, the Reform Treaty will lead to the slightly disappointing situation that the EU will hold no competence to combat discriminations on the grounds of language or on the grounds of membership of a national minority despite the fact that discrimination on these grounds would be forbidden by EU law. Furthermore, it is interesting to note that Article 21 speaks of 'national minority', whereas Article I-2 Reform Treaty uses the very general notion of 'minorities'. The use of 'national minority' transforms this notion into a term of EU law that can and will be interpreted by the ECJ. This again might have led to the long-sought (especially in the framework of the CoE) but never commonly agreed definition of what is meant by 'national minority' in Europe.[38]

Article 22 CFR, which obliges the EU to 'respect cultural, religious and linguistic diversity', is interesting because of the discrepancy between its strongly minority-related genesis and its weak legal relevance in this respect. Although the drafting history of the Constitution indicates that the provision was indeed angled towards the protection of minority interests,[39] from a formal perspective it remains a hopelessly vague provision that does not provide for any sort of right, either individual or collective. Although it enshrines a duty for the EU to respect diversity, due to the vagueness of the wording this ultimately boils down to no more than a policy aim.

However, this does not, of course, do away with the fact that Article 22 CFR also comprises, to a certain degree, minorities and their cultures. As has been maintained elsewhere, the constitutionally diverse *acquis* of the EU generally oscillates between *international diversity* (diversity *between* the member states) and *intranational diversity* (diversity *within* the member states) but has a certain preference for the former notion. This will make it rather difficult to hijack the notion of diversity in order to encourage member states to bring their minority policies in line with a supposed European notion of minority-related diversity.[40] Such a notion might develop over the years to come but, in any case, the latter will have to conform to the EU's obligation to respect the identities of the member states. In that sense, the Janus-headed notion of European diversity can be referred to as a self-restricting value.

From a practice-oriented perspective, the most important novelty of the Reform Treaty is probably Article II-18. Herein the EU is obliged to 'combat discrimination based on sex, racial or ethnic origin, religion or belief, disability, age or sexual orientation' when 'defining and implementing the policies and activities' in all the various EU-policy areas.[41] What is at stake here was much more than a mere obligation of the EU to avoid discrimination within its different policy instruments.[42] Rather, the EU, due to the horizontal obligation in Article II-18 Reform Treaty, will have, not only to avoid discrimination, but also actively to combat discrimination in all its policies.[43] Here, again (as with Article 13 EC), the problem arises that discrimination on the basis of language or on the basis of membership of a national minority is excluded. Nevertheless, the EU's new duty to actively combat *semper et ubique* all forms of discrimination based on racial or ethnic origin, religion or belief are of obvious and crucial relevance for Europe's minorities.

Conclusion

From a minority perspective, one can conclude that the Reform Treaty is characterized by a contradiction: while it adopts a strong symbolic pro-minority message, it disappoints in its rather weak policy relevance. If all goes well, however, its ratification will constitute the historic step of introducing the term 'minorities' into EU constitutional law, establishing respect for the 'rights of persons belonging to minorities' as a founding value of the EU and prohibiting any discrimination on the basis of 'membership of a national minority' via the mechanism of legal entrenchment of Article 22 CFR. However, in practical terms, this is merely the confirmation of a growing legal reality and the Reform Treaty fails to make provisions for any stand-alone policy instruments or clarifications that would put these legal principles into daily practice.[44] It remains important, therefore, to continue to look for alternative channels for minority protection within the EU system.

Modes of governance: changing policy preferences?

Mainstreaming, impact assessment and open method of coordination

It would appear timely to check to what degree the new forms of governance are of relevance for the protection of minorities. This is especially true in our context, since these forms of governance are unique to the EU and can therefore contribute to a convincing division of labour between the three international players. In the following section, we shall focus on the elements of mainstreaming, the assessment of impacts and the 'Open Method of Coordination'.

To date, the concept of mainstreaming has been used mainly in the context of gender equality. However, there is nothing that would prevent the application of the mainstreaming concept to all other grounds of discrimination covered under Article 13 EC.[45] So far, minorities have profited from mainstreaming activities mainly in the framework of the fight against racism. The EU action plan against racism foresaw that the fight against racism and discrimination should be integrated into all areas of activity that lend themselves to this.[46] These areas include, in particular, employment, the European Structural Funds, education, training and youth programmes, public procurement policy, research activities, external relations, information work, and cultural and sports initiatives.

Applying the concept of mainstreaming means that the fight against discrimination, if not the establishment of effective equality, is viewed as a cross-cutting and integral part of all public intervention. Applying the technique of mainstreaming to the area of minority protection would mean that minority interests have to play a relevant role in the formulation and implementation of all EU policies. In order to ensure efficient mainstreaming, all actors – from the legislators, through the Commission's various units and down to the national civil servant – have to apply a minority perspective. However, once again, this requires adequate sensibility and sound competence that are currently lacking, at least on this scale.

Another potential weakness of the concept of mainstreaming is that its scope, procedures and methods remain undefined. An important point that should be clarified in this respect is, for example, whether and to what degree mainstreaming should be open to a bottom-up approach, that is, to the participation of citizens and NGOs specialized in the field. All of these questions, which have not been defined at a normative level, might gain in relevance under the perspective of the Reform Treaty, which, as mentioned above, would put the EU under a legal obligation to mainstream in all areas currently mentioned in Article 13 EC. Moreover, the EU's new impetus in the area of assessing impacts implies first a formalization of the mainstreaming approach.

Impact assessment is meant to produce better law-making. After the Treaty of Amsterdam entered into force, it was mainly the area of environment where Impact Assessments (IAs) were applied. In 2002, the Commission fused these various IAs into a new form and extended them to the social sector. These so-called Extended Impact Assessments (EIA) apply to all regulatory proposals, such as directives and regulations, but also to other proposals, such as white papers, expenditure programmes and negotiating guidelines for international agreements that have an economic, social or environmental impact.[47] There have been doubts as to whether the social sector would be overruled by interests of the economic and environmental sectors when it comes to assessing the relative impact on these three areas.[48] However, recent developments show that the Commission also wants to place specific emphasis on the impact of the rights as they are enshrined in the Charter of Fundamental Rights. This seems to be of special relevance for the relative standing of the social sector in the framework of the EIAs.

The Commission decided in March 2001 to check all of its proposals against the provisions of the Charter, despite the fact that the latter was not yet legally binding. In April 2005 this approach was strengthened further.[49] Human rights-sensitive proposals have to refer to the Charter in their explanatory memorandum.[50] More importantly, every IA now has to take fundamental rights into account. The Commission did not establish a fourth sector of potential impacts – next to the categories of economic, social and environmental impacts – but decided to treat fundamental rights as a cross-cutting issue that must be checked within the other three sectors of potential impacts.[51] Here, it might be worth recalling that Article 21 of the Charter forbids any discrimination on the basis of membership of a national minority and that Article 22 of the Charter has been read by the CFR-CDF as an obligation to protect minorities. Against this background, it is tempting to detect here a development that looks at minority protection as a cross-cutting issue aim spanning all EU policies. It is therefore worthwhile to examine the new impact assessment guidelines in this context.

According to the new guidelines, as of 15 June 2005, every EIA has to check nine subgroups of potential social impacts of a legislative proposal. One subgroup of potential effects has the heading 'Social inclusion and protection of particular groups'. Under this subheading, the Commission has to control the proposal's potential impact according to the following criteria:

> Does the option affect access to the labour market or transitions into/out of the labour market?
> Does it lead directly or indirectly to greater in/equality?
> Does it affect equal access to services and goods?
> Does it affect access to placement services or to services of general economic interest?
> Does the option make the public better informed about a particular issue?
> Does the option affect specific groups of individuals, firms, localities, the most vulnerable, the most at risk of poverty, more than others?
> Does the option significantly affect third-country nationals, children, women, disabled people, the unemployed, the elderly, political parties or civic organisations, churches, religious and non-confessional organisations, or ethnic, linguistic and religious minorities, asylum seekers?

Another subgroup of potential social effects is headed 'Equality of treatment and opportunities, non-discrimination'. Under this subheading the Commission has to take a close look at the following questions:

> Does the option affect equal treatment and equal opportunities for all?
> Does the option affect gender equality?
> Does the option entail any different treatment of groups or individuals directly on grounds of e.g. gender, race, colour, ethnic or social origin, genetic features, language, religion or belief, political or any other opinion, membership of a national minority, property, birth, disability, age or sexual orientation? Or could it lead to indirect discrimination?[52]

From this, one might conclude that the fact that minority interests figure in the frame of the EIAs as potential *social* impacts leads to a concentration on economic and social issues. In fact, from the above questions it is not conceivable so far that the mainstreaming of Articles 21 and 22 of the Charter is meant specifically to enhance the *cultural*, let alone the *political*, dimension of minority issues.

Whereas mainstreaming and impact assessments are two ways of developing and implementing policies either at the national or European levels, another form of modern European governance, namely the Open Method of Coordination (OMC), is by definition a link between the European and the national level of governance in the form of a permanent dialogue. OMC is generally seen as a means of spreading best practices among the member states and of thereby achieving greater convergence towards the main EU goals. As such, it is designed to help member states to develop their own policies progressively. This is done by providing fixing guidelines, combined with specific timetables for achieving the goals that they set in the short, medium and long terms; establishing, where appropriate, quantitative and qualitative indicators and benchmarks as a means of comparing best practices; and translating these European guidelines into national and regional policies by setting specific targets and adopting measures, taking into account national and regional differences. The performance of the states is then periodically monitored through a system of national reports and European evaluations. All this together is supposed to induce mutual learning processes.[53]

In fact, the OMC allows for a great degree of flexibility. However, this form of governance can hardly be considered to be governance by legal rules. Consequently, it might engender scepticism on the part of member states, should they look upon the OMC as an instrument allowing the EU to encroach on policy domains that have traditionally been reserved to them. Moreover, the OMC might also give rise to doubts on the part of the EU, if the latter fears that it is being used as a method of escaping traditional hard law solutions at the EU level by recourse to watered-down engagement.[54] Proposals to 'constitutionalize' the OMC in the Constitution failed;[55] hence, it will remain an exercise that takes place in an unregulated space.

However, despite these caveats, the OMC is an attractive tool that might reconcile the ambitions of the EU to coordinate and inspire diverging national policies with the preoccupation of individual member states with preserving their national autonomy and preventing the EU from encroaching on policy areas that are considered, politically speaking, 'sensitive'. Consequently, it is plausible to look at the OMC as a *modus* for member states to expose their treasured and highly divergent approaches to minority protection to a multilateral policy-shaping process. In fact, minorities play a crucial role in three areas where OMC applies: namely, employment policy, social policy and migration policy.

Minorities and the European Employment Strategy

In the framework of the European Employment Strategy (EES), every member state has drawn up a National Reform Programme (until 2005, National Action Plan), which describes how the Employment Guidelines (which are proposed by the Commission and approved by the Council) are put into practice at the national level. They present the progress achieved in the member state over the previous 12 months and the measures planned for the coming 12 months and, as such, are both reporting and planning documents.

Between 1998 and 2004, the Employment Guidelines were adopted on an annual basis. From 2005 onwards, they are set for a three-year period.[56]

From 1999 onwards, the Guidelines have expressly referred to minorities.[57] The policy performance of the member states is assessed on an annual basis in the progress reports, which are adopted by the Council together with the Commission (Joint Employment Report). The latter contain country-specific information, as well as a comparison and synthesis of developments in the area of employment from a European point of view. With regard to minorities, the reports state that the 'lack of comparable data describing the scale or nature of the needs of disabled people and ethnic minorities is a serious handicap for assessing policies addressed to these groups'.[58] Moreover, the reports complain about the fact that the term 'ethnic minorities' has been interpreted in the various National Action Plans in a different way, which leads to a lack of comparability between them.[59]

The Joint Employment Report of 2004 states that the majority of member states implement measures to support the integration of migrants and ethnic minorities, such as literacy programmes, language courses, diversity plans to increase recruitment of migrants, training and vocational guidance, and so on. However, only a very few set numeric national targets for improving the labour market position of non-EU nationals or ethnic minorities.[60] The Commission calls upon all the member states to pay greater attention to 'minorities who have the citizenship of the Member State of residence' and to determine whether they face additional barriers in accessing the labour market.[61] The 2005 Joint Employment Report says that the 'potential of migrants and disadvantaged people, such as minorities and the disabled, is still insufficiently recognized and exclusion from the labour market remains an issue'. The report recognizes that some member states have developed strategies to increase labour participation of all underrepresented groups in the labour market and that specific policies for the integration of migrants and minorities are being developed 'with a focus on assimilation and access to the labour market, including language training, literacy programmes or vocational guidance'. However, the report then goes on to say that the 'burden . . . is often placed on individuals to adapt. The Roma or migrants, for example, often seem to be portrayed as responsible for their own situation.'[62]

In conclusion, one might say that the Employment Strategy not only helps to throw light on the special problems that minorities and migrants face, but initiates a transnational way of thinking that compares various policy approaches to the overall problem of enhancing the living standards of minorities. However, it also becomes quite clear from the reports mentioned that the minority issue is, in this context, not focused on as a cultural phenomenon or a question of political participation, but as an issue of inclusion in the employment market. Consequently, belonging to an ethnic minority is seen primarily as a 'particular risk factor' that enhances exclusion.[63]

Minorities and the 'Process of Social Inclusion'

The same can be said for the 'Process of Social Inclusion'. The European Council of Lisbon (March 2000) agreed on the need to take decisive steps in order to help eradicate poverty by 2010. This policy area also applies to the OMC. The European Council agreed in Nice (December 2000) on four main aims, and confirmed that one of them is to help 'the most vulnerable'. The first round of National Action Plans for Social Inclusion in 2001 demonstrated the need to address the issue of integration of immigrants in a more comprehensive, integrated and strategic manner. In the revised common objectives for the second round of the Social Inclusion Process (Copenhagen European Council, December 2002), the emphasis to be given to the situation of ethnic minorities and immigrants was, therefore, reinforced, with member states agreeing to 'highlight more clearly the high risk of poverty and social exclusion faced by some men and women as a result of immigration'. Finally, in the 2004 Joint Report on Social Inclusion, the Commission prescribed six priorities on which the member states were expected to focus in their social policies over the next two years. The report established '[m]aking a drive to reduce poverty and social exclusion of immigrants and ethnic minorities' as priority number six.[64] The issue of exclusion among immigrants and ethnic minorities was recognized as an 'increasingly significant issue'.[65]

With respect to the member states' performance, the Joint Report 2004 states that, in many national action plans, only a brief reference is made to migrant and ethnic groups being at risk, 'with little attempt to analyse their situation or factors which lead to exclusion and poverty. Only a few countries attempt to identify trends, negative or positive, in the living and working conditions of these groups.'[66] Moreover, the Report finds that only very few member states make a direct link between discrimination and social cohesion issues. Few countries link fighting discrimination and legislative measures.[67] In conclusion, the Report states that too little attention is paid 'to promoting the access of immigrants and ethnic minorities to resources, rights, goods and services, in particular to social protection schemes, to decent and sanitary housing, to appropriate healthcare and to education'. The Report finds it particularly astonishing that there is so little emphasis on a rights-based approach in the member states.[68] Moreover, it repeats that the lack of detailed data and indicators, let alone common indicators, hinders any thorough analysis of the situation facing these vulnerable groups. The report concludes that the specific situation of immigrants and ethnic minorities faced with poverty and exclusion will require greater effort and analysis 'if we are to increase their labour market participation to the same levels as the majority population, and to promote their participation in social, cultural and political life'.[69] In fact, the report of 2005 puts, in its 'key policy priority' number seven, explicit emphasis on the aspect of 'overcoming anti-discrimination' of these groups and underlines that the fight against high levels of exclusion involves 'a mixture of increasing access to mainline services and opportunities, enforcing legislation to overcoming discrimination and developing targeted approaches'. Special reference is made to Roma.[70] However, it should be noted that the question of minority protection is conspicuously absent from the most recent Report on Social Protection and Social Inclusion from 2007.[71]

As with the Employment Strategy, the Social Inclusion Process seems primarily concerned with migrants and, as such, with new minorities as opposed to the so-called 'old' minorities. The 'impact of increased migration and growing ethnic diversity' is identified as one of six core structural changes that are impacting on poverty and social exclusion.[72] In the context of the new member states, a certain emphasis is also placed on the Russophone minorities and Roma, whereas – due to the considerably lower levels of immigration – migrants play a lesser role.[73] In general, however, the integration of third-country nationals seems to be gaining more and more attention as a concern of the EU. The general belief of the Commission is that the failure to develop an 'inclusive and tolerant society which enables different ethnic minorities to live in harmony with the local population of which they form a part' will lead to 'discrimination, social exclusion and the rise of racism and xenophobia'.[74]

Minorities and migration/integration policy

This position of the Commission is also reflected in the fact that the question of integration is becoming an essential pillar within the EU's migration policy. It is worth recalling that the European Council of Tampere (October 1999) postulated a 'more vigorous integration policy' aiming at granting migrants 'rights and obligations comparable to those of EU citizens'.[75] This would seem to indicate that the EU was heading for an integration policy through provisions of hard EU law. In fact, the Commission was thinking of a proper 'concept of civic citizenship'.[76]

However, to date, there has been only a scattered extension of selected rights to third-country nationals.[77] Even the far-reaching Directive on long-term residents falls far short of providing proper civic citizenship.[78] Contrary to the calls of the Parliament, the Directive does not offer any sort of political participation. Moreover access of third-country nationals to the public services of member states remains more restricted when compared to the legal situation of EU citizens.[79] The issue of integration does not seem to be an issue for (hard) EU law.[80] The Directive explicitly gives great leeway to the states in their implementation of integration measures.[81] This reluctant stance is also present in the Reform Treaty, which calls for the development of a common European immigration policy but states that, in the area of integration of third-country nationals, the EU's role is limited to providing incentives and support for the action of member states, excluding any harmonization of the laws and regulations of the latter.[82] Against, this background it is interesting to note that there seems to be a rapidly increasing engagement of the EU in integrating new minorities by means of soft law and by use of the OMC.

In mid-2003, the Commission handed down its report on immigration, integration and employment.[83] There, the Commission admitted that the characteristics of the host societies and their organizational structures differ 'and there are, therefore, no single or simple answers'. Nevertheless, it stressed that 'much can be learned from the experiences of others'. The Commission identified a need for 'greater convergence' and proposed therefore to develop cooperation and exchange of information within the newly established group of national contact points on integration. The Commission proposed, as the central focus of this necessary coordination exercise between the states, the exchange of experience and ideas regarding introduction programmes for newly arrived immigrants, language training and the participation of immigrants in civic, cultural and political life.[84] The use of the OMC conforms with the fact that migration is, on the one hand, international in nature but raises, on the other hand, 'many sensitive and far-reaching issues which directly affect civil society which need to be discussed openly, at both national and European levels, in order to reach a consensus on policy positions'.[85] Moreover, the application of the OMC is supposed to guarantee that immigration policy is complementary and consistent with other policies, such as the employment strategy and social policies which include, for example, social inclusion and the Community's anti-discrimination strategy.[86]

Equally, it is becoming more and more evident that the member states also recognize the role of the EU in the development of integration policies *vis-à-vis* migrants. The European Council stated at the end of 2004 in its 'Hague Programme' that, for the successful integration of legally resident third-country nationals, a 'comprehensive approach involving stakeholders at the local, regional, national and EU level' is essential in order to prevent isolation of certain groups and in order to create equal opportunities that ensure their full participation in society. The European Council 'underlines the need for greater coordination of national integration policies and EU initiatives in this field'. Most importantly, it calls for the establishment of 'common basic principles underlying a coherent European framework on integration'. The European Council made it clear that a European reading of integration 'includes, but goes beyond, anti-discrimination policy'.[87] Two weeks later, the Justice and Home Affairs Council (JHA) elaborated on the findings of the European Council and presented 11 'common basic principles for immigrant integration policy in the European Union' (CBPs).[88]

The first of these principles is the definition of 'integration' as a 'dynamic, two-way process of mutual accommodation by all immigrants and residents of Member States'. Immigration is described in Principle 4 as 'enrichment' and it is affirmed that 'full respect for the immigrants' language and culture...should be also an important element of integration policy'.[89] Nevertheless, the main emphasis is clearly on the integration of migrants into the respective societies and *not* on the preservation or protection of the migrants' identity. However, with regard to political participation, the Council recommends in Principle 9 that, 'wherever possible', immigrants 'could even be involved in elections'. Furthermore, it does not limit itself to nice ideas but hints also at necessary and costly measures. In the context of Principle 7 – which calls for frequent interaction between immigrants and EU citizens, shared forums and a functioning inter-cultural dialogue – the Council makes clear that this is only possible if the 'image of the people' is changed, which requires improving their living environment 'in terms of decent housing, good health care, neighbourhood safety and the availability of opportunities for education, voluntary work and job training'.

In autumn 2005, the Commission reacted to these 11 principles and presented a 'Common Agenda for Integration', which aims to put the 11 CBPs into practice by providing indicative lists of concrete measures to be taken at national and at European levels for every CBP.[90] In this respect, it is worth stressing that it will be important to put sufficient emphasis on the regional dimension of integration policies in Europe.[91] In 2006, the Commission presented its second handbook on integration. As regards funding opportunities, the Commission designated 2007 as the European Year of Opportunities for All, and 2008 as European Year of Intercultural Dialogue.[92] Moreover, for the period 2007–2013, the Commission has proposed the establishment of a European Fund for the integration of third-country nationals.[93]

Conclusion

It seems that the process of 'internalization' of the minority topic after enlargement went hand in hand with shifting the policy focus from 'old' to 'new' minorities. This is not to say that old minorities were to be excluded from the various dialogues taking place between the European and national levels in the areas of employment, social or migration policy and even less from crucial hard law instruments such as the Race Directive. Rather, the Commission states in its Framework Strategy for Non-Discrimination that the EU 'needs to develop responses to the different needs of new migrants, established minorities of immigrant origin and other minority groups'.[94] However, it does seem that most of the EU's more recent policies and funding instruments are directed primarily at new minorities rather than old minorities. Areas where new forms of governance apply, in particular, employment policy, social policy and migration policy, are characterized by the desire to include potentially segregated, disadvantaged, poor and discriminated groups into society. These features typically characterize migrants and new minorities. New minorities want to *prevent* their 'being different' from becoming a basis for exclusion and discrimination. By contrast, old minorities typically want actively to *preserve* their 'being different' in order to avoid tendencies of assimilation.

In other words, one could say that the EU is more and more concerned with issues of integration, while issues of preservation are left at the discretion of the member states.[95] In fact, the Commission identified social and labour market integration as one of the 'key challenges' that the EU would have to face. The major task for the EU is to 'promote concerted effort by all of the relevant stakeholders in order to maximize the impact and effectiveness' of the various instruments. The means of modern governance described might encourage those involved to look at anti-discrimination legislation, employments strategies, social policies and financial stimuli in an inclusive and interconnecting way. The new High-Level Advisory Group on Social and Labour Market Integration of Disadvantaged Ethnic Minorities might prove helpful in this respect and represents, in any case, a *novum* of considerable symbolic importance, since it will be, next to the traditional Intergroup of the Parliament,[96] the only semi-official EU forum dealing specifically with minority issues.[97]

The EU, OSCE and CoE: creating an 'inter-organizational trialogue'

Introduction

After World War II, nation-states underwent a process of internationalization, meaning that they started to cooperate among each other, shifting tasks (and partly also sovereignty) to various international (if not supranational) organizations. With the beginning of the new century, it seems timely to ask whether international organizations themselves have not reached a level of consolidation that allows and calls for a comparable process. In fact, it has been a source of criticism that the EU, OSCE, CoE and NATO are not only geographically expanding but also steadily extending their tasks and responsibilities and thereby mutually interpenetrating their traditional areas of competence. This 'imperialism of tasks' calls for efficient modes of cooperation and a convincing division of labour between the organizations in order to avoid duplications that would result in loss of synergy, opacity and public misspending.[98] In fact, in Europe, a tendency towards 'inter-organizational' cooperation is becoming more and more visible. The considerable territorial overlap between the three big players (EU, OSCE and CoE) makes this cooperation easier. The EU – holding a dominant share of the 47 member states of the CoE and the 55 participating states of the OSCE – seems adapted to play a significant role in this growing inter-organizational trialogue. The following section provides a brief overall view of the developing EU/OSCE and EU/CoE cooperation.[99]

The dialogue between the EU and the OSCE

Javier Solana recently called the OSCE the 'natural born partner' of the EU.[100] This seems an exaggeration. The mere fact that both organizations were born out of the Cold War and aimed at defusing post-war tensions is hardly enough to speak of natural-born partnership. Rather, what might be considered 'natural' is a certain degree of distance between the two players, which is now fading away. Politically speaking, this distance derives from the fact that the OSCE was born as a forum open to the former communist 'East' whereas the EC/EU was an entirely Western organization. Legally speaking, the two institutions differ crucially in structure and essence. Whereas the CSCE was (and the OSCE still is) a loose forum offering a diplomatic platform for leaders of various states, the Community was (and still is) an increasingly supranational organization, equipped with a Parliament and independent organs such as the Court and the Commission, which deal with and intervene in inter-state realities.

With this background, it is hardly surprising that the EC Treaty traditionally calls on the Community to 'establish all appropriate forms of cooperation with the Council of Europe' but remains silent with respect to the OSCE.[101] Nevertheless, it should be underlined that the political commitments assumed by the states in the framework of the CSCE are not limited explicitly to the CSCE framework itself but bind (if not in a legal sense) the respective states in all the other international forums, the EU included.[102] Therefore, the various CSCE minority commitments reflect shared values that should guide the policies of the EU states both 'individually and collectively'. Moreover, it is underlined that the EC participated from the beginning – next to its member states – in the Helsinki process, which developed into the framework of the CSCE.[103] However, only the *annus mirabilis* brought the two organizations in evident and direct contact. With the fall of the Iron Curtain, both players realized that their aims were converging more and more.

This process of rapprochement also resulted in an institutionally visible cooperation. Since 1989, the President of the Commission and the EU Presidency participate in the OSCE Summits. Since 2003, there has been a formal exchange between the OSCE Secretariat in Vienna and the EU Commission and the General Secretariat of the Council of the EU. In 2002, a specific working party within the Council of the EU was given responsibility for relations with the CoE and the OSCE.[104] Within the European Commission, a specific unit within the External Relations Directorate General is responsible for relations with the OSCE and the CoE. In November 2003, the Council of the EU made further proposals. Building on the 2003 practice, the Council announced that, during each *presidency*, a meeting should take place between the EU troika, the OSCE troika and the OSCE Secretary General. Briefings by the Secretary General/High Representative for the Common Foreign and Security Policy (CFSP) and the European Commissioner for external relations to the Permanent OSCE Council in Vienna should be arranged when deemed necessary. As appropriate, representatives of the OSCE Secretary General and Chairman-in-Office, Heads of Mission and Heads of OSCE institutions should be invited to informal meetings with relevant EU working groups.

In fact, these aims are becoming standard practice.[105] Moreover, the Council proposed the posting of a Council Secretariat liaison officer to Vienna, so as to facilitate communication between the Council Secretariat and the OSCE, and to enhance further cooperation and synergy between the EU and the OSCE.[106] In the OSCE's view, the EU is already 'a permanent participant in day-to-day OSCE business in Vienna and elsewhere', especially through the EU Presidency and the Commission's representation.[107] Regular meetings at staff level[108] and countless examples of cooperation at project level, especially, at the OSCE's Office for Democratic Institutions and Human Rights (ODIHR) and missions in Southeastern Europe, Southern Caucasus and Eastern Europe, as well as Central Asia, complete this picture.[109]

With regard to the protection of minorities – an area where the OSCE holds considerable experience and competence – some observers within the OSCE (but also within the CoE) view the growing engagement of the EU with scepticism.[110] It is therefore important to keep the position of the Council of the EU in mind, which underlines that cooperation between the EU and the OSCE has to 'be based on the principle of avoiding duplication and identifying comparative advantages and added value, leading to effective complementarity'.[111] So far, cooperation in the area of minority protection concentrates on the funding of projects and field missions.[112] Apart from this functional cooperation, the EU is also making regular reference to the standards developed by the OSCE – a fact that was especially evident in the framework of the process of Eastern enlargement, where the High Commissioner on National Minorities was frequently approached by the Commission in order to give an opinion on legal developments in the candidate states. Moreover, the Council also declared in general terms that it would 'take account of OSCE *acquis* with respect to standards, notably on democracy and human rights'.[113] In institutional terms, cooperation has been especially close between the Commission and the High Commissioner on National Minorities, who 'maintains close contacts with various parts of the European Commission, including its Legal Service and the Directorate General for Enlargement'.[114] A formalization of these contacts could help to prevent the dilution of these links in the aftermath of enlargement.

The dialogue between the EU and the CoE

If the OSCE is described as the natural-born partner of the EU, one might talk of the CoE as the EU's natural-born twin. A closely related history and the increasingly shared legal interest in the protection of human rights (symbolized by the judicial dialogue between the two Courts in Strasbourg and Luxembourg) has meant that cooperation between the EU and the CoE has more facets and is closer than that between the EU and the OSCE.

Already, in 1959, the two organizations had decided to exchange annual reports. In 1987, President Delors and Secretary General Oreja signed an

'Arrangement' between the CoE and the European Community that provided for contacts at various levels. Since 1989, the so-called '2+2' meetings have been held. In the latter, the EU Presidency, the EU Commission, the Chair-in-Office and the Secretary General of the CoE come together twice a year in quadripartite meetings. These meetings are complemented by regular meetings between members of the EU Commission with the Secretary General or the Human Rights Commissioner of the CoE. Moreover, at the technical level, the Legal Service and the Directorate General for Justice and Home Affairs of the Commission are cooperating with their counterparts in the CoE.[115]

As regards the substance of this cooperation, the 2001 Joint Declaration on Cooperation and Partnership makes clear that respect for human rights, including the protection of national minorities, forms a prominent part.[116] On 16–17 May 2005, the Heads of State and Government of the member states of the CoE gathered in Warsaw, where they bore 'witness to unprecedented pan-European unity'. They attached to their 'Warsaw Declaration' an action plan that deals in Part IV with the cooperation between the CoE and the two other organizations. With respect to the EU, it is underscored that the two organizations should take the CoE's and the EU's achievements and future standard-setting work into account in each other's activities.[117] Appendix 2 of this action plan lists 10 'Guidelines on the Relations between the Council of Europe and the European Union'. Therein, one reads that the promotion and protection of pluralist democracy, respect for human rights and social cohesion are all matters of common interest that form the basis of the relationship between the two organizations.[118] Enhanced partnership and complementarity should govern the future relationship between them. It is underlined that the 'common objective of a Europe without new dividing lines can best be served by making appropriate use of the norms and standards, as well as the experience and expertise developed in the Council of Europe over half a century'.[119] Not only should the EU accede to the ECHR, but accession to other CoE conventions should also be taken into consideration.[120] This might bring up the question of whether the Community can and should accede to the FCNM.[121] Another remarkable provision deals with 'legal cooperation' between the two organizations. It is submitted that greater complementarity between the EU and CoE legal texts can be achieved by striving to transpose those aspects of CoE conventions into EU law where the EU holds respective competences.[122] This fits well with the functional approach of the Parliament with respect to minority issues described above.

Finally, special emphasis is given in the guidelines to a reinforced cooperation between the specialized CoE bodies and the EU.[123] However, with respect to institutional cooperation, the only concrete proposal of the guidelines is to establish as soon as possible a permanent EU office to the CoE.[124] As regards the area of minority protection, one could perhaps also envisage the usefulness of an institutionalized participation of members of the Parliament and the Commission in the respective debates in the Committee of Ministers and the Advisory Board of the FCNM. One guideline refers to the future Human Rights Agency of the EU as an opportunity 'to further increase cooperation with the Council of Europe, and contribute to greater coherence and enhanced complementarity'.[125] In fact, the current proposal for the establishment of that EU agency states in its considerations that close cooperation between the two organizations will avoid any overlaps.

However, when it comes to concrete mechanisms guaranteeing this strict cooperation, the proposal does not offer anything that would go beyond the current mechanisms existing in the legal structure of the European Monitoring Centre on Racism and Xenophobia (that is, a cooperation agreement between the Agency and the CoE and the participation of the CoE on the boards of the Agency).[126] In this context, it might prove useful to think of the establishment of revamped, permanent and institutionalized channels of communication and participation between the various monitoring bodies such as the Human Rights Agency, the CFR-CDF, the Advisory Board of the FCNM, the Committee of Independent Experts of the Language Charter and the European Commission Against Racism and Intolerance.[127]

So far, interaction between the CoE and the EU in the area of minority protection has concentrated on an ongoing transfer of standards (especially in the context of the Commission's monitoring exercise in the course of the enlargement process)[128] and Joint Programming (several of the joint CoE and EU projects deal with minority issues).[129] It might be timely to complement these two fields of interaction with an institutionalized inter-organizational dialogue on minority issues.

Conclusion: the EU within an integrated system of minority governance

In the late 1980s and the early 1990s, there were certain tendencies in the European Parliament to establish a supranational EC Charter of group rights. These proposals, tabled first by Count Stauffenberg and then by Siegbert Alber (both members of the European Parliament), had no realistic chance of gaining consensus, and were consequently not even voted upon in the respective Committees. However, the arguments used at that time are still heard. People who favour a supranational regime of minority protection in Europe point to the fact that the EU could offer a stringent legal system equipped with direct effect and supremacy and a convincing court system. The EU is seen in this context as a post-national entity that could manage the minorities' cause in a neutral and efficient way.

However, it was Count Stauffenberg himself who noted that the resistance of states against engagement in a system of international minority protection became increasingly persistent the more stringent the law applied.[130] In fact, it is the big advantage of international law that participating states can escape to watered-down solutions, pick and choose approaches and forms of geographic flexibility, and still establish a net of legal obligations. Consequently, it will remain the task of the CoE to respond to possible future *avant-gardes* in the area of minority protection and offer tailored solutions for these states. It can hardly be the task of the EU to provide one-size-fits-all solutions in the area of group rights. This is due not only to legal arguments but to obvious reasons of political legitimacy.[131] Systems providing for group rights intervene in sensitive issues of redistribution and equality perceptions. Such public interventions have to be legitimized by a strong and locally rooted consensus and can hardly be imposed by a supranational top-down approach, which would not conform with the spirit of the principle of subsidiarity.

With respect to group rights, the challenge for the EU in an integrated system of minority governance is to accommodate far-reaching systems of minority protection at the member state level in a way that avoids internal EU frictions. As is well known, the Common Market aims at unlimited mobility and unrestricted access to goods and services, whereas highly developed systems of minority protection tend to restrict access to rare goods such as work places, social housing and the like to certain groups.[132] Consequently, there is a certain tension between the mechanisms of the European Common Market and strong regimes of minority protection at the national level. It is, in this respect, of no relevance whether these regimes are anchored in constitutional law or not. The case law on the supremacy of EC law led to the observation that 'even the most minor piece of technical Community legislation ranks above the most cherished constitutional norm'.[133] There is consequently no reason to believe that in the event of a conflict between Common Market principles and a constitutionally anchored system of minority protection, the latter 'will stand' due only to its constitutional rank.[134] Rather, such provisions have to be based on a specific exemption in primary EU law,[135] as is the case for the Aaland Islands or the specific rights of the Saami.[136] Likewise, the special provisions enshrined in the draft Annan plan that were designed to guarantee the ethnic balance on Cyprus would have to have been anchored in EU primary law in order to be compatible with the Common Market principles.[137] If such an exemption is not available, it is up to the perception and specific application of the EU notions of equality and proportionality to establish a convincing balance between economic mobility and cultural diversity.[138]

Apart from this delicate challenge, within the future integrated system of minority governance in Europe the EU will hardly be confronted with questions of preservation, but primarily with questions of integration. As has been shown above, the EU is becoming more and more involved in questions of inclusion. With the methods of modern governance such as the Open Method of Coordination, the EU has, as the first international organization ever, the means at its disposal to put its member states in a situation of competition for best ideas and practices in areas such as social policy, employment policies and migration policies without exerting legal pressure. The area of human rights may become one such area.

Apart from this politically strong, but legally soft, integration of the EU into the national policies of its member states, the EU has at its disposal extremely far-reaching hard law instruments in the field of anti-discrimination. This is an area where the EU is co-designing the legal reality of the member states. From 2000 to the present day, both hard engagement in the area of anti-discrimination and soft engagement in the area of integration have developed very rapidly, and current dynamics indicate that the EU will continue to gain momentum in these areas.

All of this demonstrates clearly that the EU has internalized its minority engagement. The enlargement experience did not lead only to an even more outspoken engagement of the EU in its external relations, but also provoked a new EU engagement with minorities within the EU territory. Moreover, the enlargement experience has induced a revamped and still developing cooperation between the three international players: the OSCE, CoE and EU. As regards the new internal engagement of the latter, it was argued above that the primary focus has shifted from 'old' to 'new' minorities. However, this corresponds to the fact that, for questions of preservation, the member states remain the primary responsible entities.[139]

In conclusion, therefore, one can say that, after E-day, the EU is not only tidying up its tasks which remain outstanding under former minority engagement, but is assuming a new role in the area of minority protection.

Notes

1. See, for example, G. Sasse, 'Minority Rights and EU Enlargement: Normative Overstretch or Effective Conditionality?', in G.N. Toggenburg (ed.), *Minority Protection and the Enlarged European Union: The Way Forward* (Budapest: LGI Books, 2004), 59–84.
2. See B. de Witte, 'Politics versus Law in the EU's Approach to Ethnic Minorities', in J. Zielonka (ed.), *Europe Unbound: Enlarging and Reshaping the Boundaries of the European Union* (London: Routledge, 2002), 137–60.
3. See, for example, Sasse, 'Minority Rights', *supra* note 1.
4. See, for example, R. Ekeus, 'From the Copenhagen Criteria to the Copenhagen Summit: The Protection of National Minorities in an Enlarging Europe', speech given to the Conference 'National Minorities in the Enlarged European Union'. 5 November 2002.
5. See G.N. Toggenburg, 'A Rough Orientation through a Delicate Relationship: The European Union's Endeavours for (its) Minorities', *European Integration Online Papers* 16 (2000).
6. For an assessment of the possibilities for and limitations on protection within the EU framework, see G.N. Toggenburg, 'Minority Protection in a Supranational Context: Limits and Opportunities', in Toggenburg (ed.), *Minority Protection, supra* note 1: 1–36.

7. See Council of the European Union, 'Council Conclusions on the Application of Conditionality with a view to developing a Coherent EU-Strategy for the Relations with the Countries in the Region', *Bulletin EU* 4 (1997), at 137. In official documents this second generation conditionality is occasionally referred to as 'SAP conditionality' or '1997 conditionality'.

8. Note, however, that – just as in the case of the Europe agreements – the SAAs so far (the SAA with Macedonia entered into force on 1 April 2004 and the SAA with Croatia on 1 February 2005) do not explicitly establish minority protection as an 'essential element' of the agreements (see Article 2 of the respective agreements). However, the agreements mention in their Article 3 that they 'come within the framework of the regional approach of the Community as defined in the Council conclusions of 29 April 1997, based on the merits of the individual countries of the region'.

9. See Article 2, Paragraph 2, lit. b) of Council Regulation (EC) No. 2666/2000 of 5 December 2000 on assistance for Albania, Bosnia and Herzegovina, Croatia, the Federal Republic of Yugoslavia and the Former Yugoslav Republic of Macedonia, repealing Regulation (EC) No. 1628/96 and amending Regulations (EEC) No. 3906/89 and (EEC) No. 1360/90 and Decisions 97/256/EC and 1999/311/EC, OJ L 306, 7 December 2000, 1–6. Note that Article 5 of the Regulation establishes 'minority rights' as an 'essential element for the application of this Regulation and a precondition of eligibility for Community assistance. If these principles are not respected, the Council, acting by qualified majority on a proposal from the Commission, may take appropriate measures'.

10. This is not true for the basic Council Regulation (EC) No. 533/2004 of 22 March 2004 on the establishment of European partnerships in the framework of the stabilization and association process, OJ L 086 as of 24 March 2004, 1–2. However, the Council Decisions of 14 June 2004 on the principles, priorities and conditions contained in the European Partnerships with the relevant countries that are based on that regulation not only contain country-specific recommendations in the area of minority protection but refer also to second-generation conditionality (see point 5 of the pertinent annexes).

11. See, for example, the Commission's reply to written question E-2538/01, in OJ 147 E, 20 June 2002, 27–28: 'In the Commission's opinion, the rights of minorities are part of the principles common to the Member States, listed in the first paragraph of Article 6 of the Treaty on European Union'.

12. See Council document No. 10229/03 (Press 163), Thessaloniki, 21 June 2003, Paragraph 1. Note that in the context of the SAp one often finds references to respect for minority 'rights' as opposed to merely 'minorities'.

13. Council of the European Union, Council Joint Action 2000/717/CFSP of 16 November 2000 on the holding of a meeting of Heads of State or Government in Zagreb (Zagreb Summit), OJ L 290. 17 November 2000, at 54.

14. See B. de Witte, 'The Constitutional Resources for an EU Minority Policy', in G.N. Toggenburg (ed.), *Minority Protection, supra* note 1: 109–24.

15. Compare in this context the so-called 'Package for Europe', a bundle of proposals developed by a team of experts convened by the European Academy Bolzano in 1997. See EURAC, *Package for Europe* (Bolzano/Bozen: European Academy, 1998), at 13–90.

16. The Parliament has a long-standing tradition of being the most minority-minded EU institution. Not only has it issued countless resolutions dealing with minority issues, it also disposes over an Intergroup dealing specifically with these

issues (currently 45 parliamentarians take part in the 'Intergroup for Traditional National Minorities, Constitutional Regions and Regional Languages'). See, for more detail, Toggenburg, 'A Rough Orientation', *supra* note 5.

17. European Parliament Resolution on the Protection of Minorities and Anti-discrimination Policies in an Enlarged Europe, adopted on 8 June 2005 and based on the report A6-0140/2005 as of 10 May 2005 (the so-called 'Moraes report', named after the responsible Rapporteur Claude Moraes).

18. See Moraes Resolution, Paragraph 49, lit. a)–lit. h).

19. Network of Independent Experts in Fundamental Rights (CFR-CDF) (2003). 'Report on the Situation of Fundamental Rights in the European Union and its Member States in 2003'.

20. Compare Article 2 EC, which obliges the Community to establish 'equality between men and women' as an aim of the Community. Compare also Article 141, Paragraph 4, EC.

21. Council Directive 2000/43/EC of 29 June 2000 implementing the principle of equal treatment between persons irrespective of racial or ethnic origin, OJ L 180, 19 July 2000, 22–26; Council Directive 2000/78/EC of 27 November 2000 establishing a general framework for equal treatment in employment and occupation. OJ L 303, 2 December 2000, 16–22; Council Directive 2004/113/EC of 13 December 2004 implementing the principle of equal treatment between men and women in the access to and supply of goods and services, OJ L 373. 21 December 2004, 37–43.

22. Council Decision 2001/51/EC of 20 December 2000 establishing a programme relating to the Community framework strategy on gender equality (2001–2005), OJ L 017, 19 January 2001, 22–29; Council Decision 2000/750/EC of 27 November 2000 establishing a Community action programme to combat discrimination (2001 to 2006), OJ L 303, 2 December 2000, 23–28.

23. See, for example, Council Decision 2002/179/EC of 17 December 2001 concerning the conclusion of a Framework Agreement between the European Community and the Republic of Turkey on the general principles for the participation of the Republic of Turkey in Community programmes, OJ L 061, 2 March 2002, 27–28.

24. See Council Decision 2001/903/EC of 3 December 2001 on the European Year of People with Disabilities 2003, OJ L 335, 19 December 2001, 15–20. The year 2007 is designated to become the European Year of Equal Opportunities for All; see Communication from the Commission containing a proposal for a respective decision of the Parliament and the Council, COM(2005) 225 final, 1 June 2005; 2008 is designated to become the European Year of Intercultural Dialogue, see the Commission's proposal for a respective decision of the Parliament and the Council, COM(2005) 467 final, 5 October 2005.

25. For a description see, for example, G.N. Toggenburg, 'The Race Directive: A New Dimension in the Fight against Ethnic Discrimination in Europe', *European Yearbook of Minority Issues* 1 (2002): 231–44.

26. See CFR-CDF. 'Report on the Situation of Fundamental Rights', *supra* note 19.

27. O. de Schutter and A. Verstichel, 'The Role of the Union in Integrating the Roma: Present and Possible Future', *European Diversity and Autonomy Papers* 2 (2005): 1–43.

28. See de Witte, 'The Constitutional Resources', *supra* note 14.

29. This was a wording proposed by the OSCE; see K. Drzewicki, 'A Constitution for Europe: Enshrining Minority Rights. Words Can Make Worlds of Difference', *OSCE Magazine*, March 2005, 19–21.

30. Note that the English version of the first proposal read as follows: 'human rights, including the rights of persons belonging to minority groups'. The text can be found in CIG 52/03 ADD 1 PRESID 10 (Annex 1) or in Annex I of CIG 60/03 ADD1 PRESID 14 as of 9 December 2003.
31. Treaty of Lisbon amending the Treaty on European Union and the Treaty Establishing the European Community, Article 3 (amending Article 1a).
32. de Witte, 'The Constitutional Resources', *supra* note 14, at 111.
33. See Annex 2 of CONV 528/03 as of 6 February 2003, at 11.
34. In Article I-8 of the Reform Treaty (amending Article I-6 EC), the Charter of Fundamental Rights is recognized as having 'the same legal value as the Treaties'.
35. Emphasis added.
36. However, this article does not provide a 'clear mandate' for the Union 'to act' against discrimination. See K. Topidi, 'European Union Standards and Mechanisms for the Protection of Minorities and the Prevention of Discrimination', in Council of Europe (ed.), *Mechanisms for the Implementation of Minority Rights* (Strasbourg: Council of Europe Publishing, 2004), 183–202, at 197.
37. See Article 13 EC.
38. Note that the Parliament (Moraes Resolution, Paragraph 7) as well as the Network of Independent Experts on Fundamental Rights (Report 2002) sustain the definition used in Council of Europe Recommendation 1201 (1993).
39. For the various submissions and comments in that process, see S. Hölscheidt, 'Artikel 22', in Meyer J. (ed.), *Kommentar zur Charta der Grundrechte der Europäischen Union* (Baden-Baden: Nomos, 2003), 290–8. Note, in particular, the drafting history of Article II-82 CE (the wording of which was identical to Article 22 CFR), which was incorporated as an interim measure during the drafting of the Charter.
40. See on this subject G.N. Toggenburg, '"Unity in Diversity": Searching for the Regional Dimension in the Context of a Somewhat Foggy Constitutional Credo', in R. Toniatti *et al.* (eds), *An Ever More Complex Union: The Regional Variable as Missing Link in the European Constitution* (Baden-Baden: Nomos, 2004), 27–56. See also B. de Witte, 'The Value of Cultural Diversity', *European Diversity and Autonomy Papers* 3 (2005).
41. Similar horizontal clauses can be found also in the current Treaty. See, for example, Article 151, Paragraph 4 EC (obligation of the Community to take cultural aspects into account in its action under other provisions of the Treaty, in particular in order to respect and to promote the diversity of its cultures), Article 6 EC (environmental protection requirements must be integrated into the definition and implementation of the Community policies and activities), Article 153, Paragraph 2 EC (consumer protection requirements shall be taken into account in defining and implementing other Community policies and activities). However, these clauses are weaker in their legal wording.
42. If that had been the aim of this provision, Article III-118 CE would refer to the 17 different forms of discrimination listed in the prohibitive provision in Article II-81 CE (including language and membership of a national minority) and not just to the 9 forms of discrimination listed in the enabling provision in Article III-124 CE.
43. Of course, the aim of combating discrimination in the framework of the respective instrument can only be of secondary nature. If it represents the primary aim of that measure, the latter has to be based on Article III-124 CE and not on the respective policy provision.
44. However, it has to be stressed that the Constitution introduces several elements that are of indirect relevance for minorities. Besides the mentioned

mainstreaming provision, the newly designed procedures to protect the principle of subsidiarity or the new title on 'the democratic life of the Union' serve as examples in this respect.

45. This is also the opinion of the Commission; see the European Commission, Commission Report on the 'Implementation of the Action Plan against Racism: Mainstreaming the Fight against Racism', January 2000.

46. See European Commission, Communication from the Commission 'An Action Plan against Racism'. COM(1998) 183 final, 25 March 1998.

47. See the European Commission, Communication from the Commission on Impact Assessment, COM(2002) 276 final, 5 June 2002.

48. See J. Shaw, 'Mainstreaming Equality in European Law and Policymaking', European Network Against Racism (ENAR), Working Paper, April 2004.

49. See the European Commission, 'Compliance with the Charter of Fundamental Rights in Commission Legislative Proposals: Methodology for Systematic and Rigorous Monitoring', COM(2005) 172 final, 27 April 2005. Note that this new approach is supposed to be supervised by the newly founded Group of Commissioners on Fundamental Rights, Anti-discrimination and Equal Opportunities. One of the declared aims of this enhanced human rights monitoring of the legislative procedure is the promotion of an EU 'fundamental rights culture'. See COM(2005) 172 final, at 3.

50. This goes especially for proposals that include a *limitation* of a fundamental right or that lead to direct or indirect *difference* in treatment or are specifically aimed at *implementing* or *promoting* a particular fundamental right. Such proposals have to include in their explanatory memorandum a standard Charter recital and a statement summarizing the reasons pointing to the conclusion that fundamental rights have been respected. See COM(2005) 172 final, *supra* note 49.

51. In fact, the Charter-based rights cut across all three sectors. The Commission underlines that the creation of a subheading in the chapter on social impacts would 'not adequately reflect the variety of, and balance between, the social, economic and political rights in the Charter'. See COM(2005) 172 final, *supra* note 49, at 5.

52. See European Commission, 'Impact Assessment Guidelines'. SEC(2005) 791, 15 June 2005, Table 3 (Social Impacts).

53. See, for example, the Presidency Conclusions of the Lisbon European Council, 23–24 March 2000, Paragraph 37.

54. The Commission stated quite clearly that the OMC 'should not be used when legislative action under the Community method is possible'. See the European Commission, White Paper, *European Governance'*, COM(2001) 428 final, 25 July 2001, at 22.

55. See, for example, the paper of the Convention Secretariat on 'Coordination of National Policies: The Open Method of Coordination', WG VI WD 015, 26 September 2002.

56. See Council of the European Union, Council Decision 2005/600/EC of 12 July 2005 on Guidelines for the Employment Policies of the Member State, OJ Nr. L 205, 6 August 2005, 21–27.

57. For 1999 and 2000, a reference can be found in Guideline number 9, from 2001 onwards a reference was included in Guideline number 7.

58. Joint Employment Report 1999, Part I: the European Union, as adopted by the Joint Council (Labour and Social Affairs/ECOFIN) at its session on 29 November 1999, at 29 and 46.

59. Joint Employment Report 1999, at 47: 'Member States have interpreted the reference to ethnic minorities in different ways, with some (UK, Netherlands) using a broad definition to encompass "visible minorities" (i.e. people who appear to be of foreign origin, irrespective of their nationality), while others restrict the scope either to non-nationals or non-EU nationals (Germany, Sweden) or to national minorities (Ireland, Finland, Austria).'

60. See Joint Employment Report 2003/2004, as adopted by the Council and the Commission on 4 March 2004.

61. See Background Document for the Joint Employment Report 2004/2005 based on the staff working paper COM(2005) 13 final.

62. Joint Employment Report 2004/2005, as adopted by the Council and the Commission on 3 March 2005, at 16.

63. See European Commission, 'Communication: Strengthening the Implementation of the European Employment Strategy', 7 March 2004, COM(2004) 239 final, at 27.

64. Joint Report on Social Inclusion 2004, at 8.

65. *Ibid.*, at 9.

66. *Ibid.*, at 95.

67. The Commission is referring to the United Kingdom, Sweden, Finland, Belgium, Ireland and France. See Joint Report on Social Inclusion 2004.

68. Note that this remark is to be found only in the German version of the Report; see Gemeinsamer Bericht über die soziale Eingliederung 2004, at 120. However, the Report on the 10 new member states contains a similar remark: 'Little attention is paid to a right-based approach, which can provide a useful framework for the further development of integration policies. Further emphasis must be given to enforcing legislation, notably the laws transposing the Article 13 Directives. The role of the civil society as well as impact of the recent decentralization towards regions has been largely underestimated in this process.' See Report on Social Inclusion 2005, An Analysis of the National Action Plans on Social Inclusion (2004–2006), submitted by the 10 New Member States, at 86.

69. Joint Report on Social Inclusion 2004, at 102.

70. *Ibid.*, at 8.

71. Joint Report on Social Protection and Social Inclusion 2007.

72. Joint Report on Social Inclusion 2004, at 32.

73. However, this is a situation that is expected to change after enlargement. See the Report on the New Member States.

74. See European Commission, 'Communication: Open Method of Coordination for Community Immigration Policy', COM(2001) 387 final, at 11.

75. European Council in Tampere, Council Conclusions, 16 October 1999, Paragraph 18.

76. See, for example, the Communication of the Commission on a Community Immigration Policy, COM(2000) 757 final, 22 November 2000, at 19.

77. See Directive 2003/109/EC and Council Regulation 859/2003/EC extending the provisions of Regulation (EEC) No. 1408/71 and Regulation (EEC) 574/72 to nationals of third countries who are not already covered by those provisions solely on the ground of their nationality, OJ L 124, 20 May 2003, 1–3.

78. Council Directive 2003/109/EC of 25 November 2003 concerning the status of third-country nationals who are long-term residents of 25 November 2003, OJ L 16, 23 January 2004, 44–53. The directive has to be transposed by 23 January 2006.

79. Compare Article 11, Paragraph 1, lit. A) of Directive 2003/109 with the relevant case law of the ECJ.
80. However, it has to be stressed that there is also no EU law on the integration of EU citizens and old minorities. Rather, EU law offers effects of integration through the prohibition of discrimination. See on this subject, G.N. Toggenburg, 'Who is Managing Ethnic and Cultural Diversity in the European Condominium? The Moments of Entry, Integration and Preservation', *Journal of Common Market Studies* 43(4) (2005): 717–37.
81. See Article 5, Paragraph 2 and Article 15, Paragraph 3 of Directive 2003/109/EC. This has been considered as a permission to 'insist on assimilation' and as a possible violation of international minority rights standards. See also S. Peers, '"New" Minorities: What Status for Third-Country Nationals in the EU System?', in Toggenburg (ed.), *Minority Protection, supra* note 1, 149–62.
82. See Article II-65, Paragraph 4 Reform Treaty, providing for a new Article 63(a) EC.
83. European Commission, 'Communication: Immigration, Integration and Employment', COM(2003) 336 final, 3 June 2003.
84. *Ibid.*
85. COM(2001) 387 final, at 5. It is possible that the future parts of this regular dialogue will be regulated in a more formal way. See in this respect the Communication of the Commission for a Council Decision on the Establishment of a Mutual Information Procedure Concerning Member States', Measures in the Areas of Asylum and Immigration, COM(2005) 480 final, 10 October 2005.
86. COM(2001) 387 final.
87. European Commission, Justice and Home Affairs, *The Hague Programme: Ten Priorities for the Next Five Years*, 2005, point 1.5.
   The Hague Programme, point 1.5.
88. Annex attached to the press release regarding the 2618th Council meeting of 19 November 2004.
89. It seems as if the Spanish government has pushed for including a reference to the promotion of the migrants' cultures and languages but did not reach consensus. See *Migration und Bevölkerung* 9 (2004).
90. See European Commission, 'Communication: A Common Agenda for Integration Framework for the Integration of Third-Country Nationals in the European Union', COM(2005) 389 final, 1 September 2005.
91. Note that the Committee of the Regions has drafted an opinion in this regard. See Draft Opinion of the Commission for Constitutional Affairs and European Governance as of 15 February 2006, CdR 53/2006 EN.
92. Compare the European Commission, 'Communication: Non-Discrimination and Equal Opportunities For All: A Framework Strategy', 1 June, COM(2005) 224 final, 2005.
93. See European Commission, 'Communication: Establishing a Framework Programme on Solidarity and the Management of Migration Flows for the period 2007–2013', COM(2005) 123 final, 6 April (2005e). This also contained a proposal for a Council decision establishing the European Fund for the Integration of Third-country nationals for the period 2007–2013 as part of the General programme 'Solidarity and Management of Migration Flows'.
94. See COM(2005) 224 final, *supra* note 93, at 10.
95. See for more detail Toggenburg, 'Who is Managing', *supra* note 80.
96. The Intergroup (to which over 40 MEPs belong) has existed since the 1980s. As is the case with every Intergroup, it has to be refounded at the beginning of

every legislative period. The current 'Intergroup for traditional national minorities, constitutional regions and regional languages' lists the following three as its 'targeted groups': national minorities; nations without a state; and regional languages. It considers as its major tasks issues such as the examination of concrete cases, the elaboration of recommendations or the work on creating a legal basis for minority protection in the EU (see minutes of the meeting on 16 December 2004).

97. See COM (2005) 224 final. The Group consists of 10 experts from different fields. It is supposed to deliver a report with recommendations on how the EU can develop a coherent and effective approach to the problems of social and labour market exclusion for disadvantaged minorities by the end of 2007.

98. Tudyka speaks of 'Zuständigkeits-Imperialismus' and is of the opinion that the Secretariats of the international players are characterized more by jealousy, competition and dominance than by cooperation. See, K.P. Tudyka, 'Die Vernetzung der europäischen Institutionen', *OCSE Handbook* (Opladen: Leske and Budrich, 2002), 87–97, at 89.

99. It is, however, important to stress that there is also a growing cooperation between the OSCE and the Council of Europe that is of crucial interest for minorities. See, in this context, for example, the so-called Common Catalogue ('Relations between the Organization for Security and Co-operation in Europe and the Council of Europe, Common Catalogue of Co-operation Modalities', 12 April 2000). See for more detail H.-P. Furrer, 'OSCE-Council of Europe Relations: Past, Present and Future', in V.-Y. Ghébali, D. Warner and B. Gimelli (eds), *The Future of the OSCE in the Perspectives of the Enlargements of NATO and the EU* (Geneva: PSIO, 2004), 91–121.

100. J. Solana, 'The EU and the OSCE: The Shape of Future Cooperation', Address to the Permanent Council of the OSCE. 25 September 2002.

101. See Article 301 EC. The draft Constitution changes this picture and also makes explicit reference to the OSCE in its Article III-327.

102. This can be seen from CSCE, 'Towards a Genuine Partnership in a New Era', Budapest Summit 1994, Paragraph 2.

103. This can be seen already from the Moro-Declaration attached as Annex 1 to the Helsinki Final Act. Therein Aldo Moro declared: *'En ce qui concerne ces matières, l'expression 'Etats participants', qui figure dans l'acte final, se comprendra donc comme s'appliquant aussi aux Communautés européennes.'''* European Commission, Justice and Home Affairs, The Hague Programme: Ten Priorities for the Next Five Years, 2005, point 1.5.
Note that documents like the Charter of Paris or the Charter for European Security have also been signed by the President of the European Commission.

104. COREPER decision of 19 May 2002, see Progress Report on Joint Cooperation between the European Commission and the Council of Europe, June 2001–May 2003, 19 May 2003.

105. See, for example, the Annual Report on OSCE Activities 2003.

106. See Council of the European Union, 'EU-OSCE Cooperation in Conflict Prevention, Crisis Management and Post-Conflict Rehabilitation', 17 November 2003.

107. OSCE Report 2003, at 171.

108. On 28 May 2003 the first formal staff level meeting between the OSCE Secretariat, the European Commission and the General Secretariat of the Council of the European Union took place. The second meeting took place in November 2004.

109. For an overall view on this cooperation at project level see the OSCE Report 2004.

110. For a similar position in the literature see H. Borchert and D. Maurer, 'Kooperation, Rivalität oder Bedeutungslosigkeit? Fünf Szenarien zur Zukunft der Beziehungen zwischen OSZE und EU', *OSCE Yearbook 2003* (Baden-Baden: Nomos, 2003), 441–55, at 453.
111. Council Conclusions of 17 November 2003, Paragraph 4.
112. See, for a list, the OSCE Annual Report 2003, 171–3.
113. Council Conclusions of 17 November 2003, Paragraph 8.
114. Annual Report on OSCE Activities 2003, at 172.
115. See Progress Report on Joint Cooperation.
116. See Joint Declaration on Cooperation and Partnership between the Council of Europe and the European Commission, signed on 3 April 2001.
117. See the Ministers' Deputies Document, 'Action Plan', CM (2005) final 17 May 2005.
118. See Guideline 1.
119. Guideline 3.
120. Guideline 4. Note that Article I-9, Paragraph 2 CE provides a mandate (if not an obligation) for the EU to accede to the ECHR. Compare in this context also Article 17 of the new ECHR Protocol No. 14.
121. See critically in this respect Toggenburg, 'Minority Protection', *supra* note 6.
122. Guideline 5.
123. Guidelines 6 and 7.
124. Guideline 10.
125. Guideline 8.
126. See Consideration Number 16, Article 6, Paragraph 2, lit. c); Article 9; Article 11, Paragraph 1, lit. c); and Article 11, Paragraph 6 of the proposed regulation establishing a European Union Agency for Fundamental Rights, COM(2005) 280 final as of 30 June 2005.
127. Note that on 1 September 2005, the EUMC, the ECRI, the ODIHR, the CERD and the Anti-Discrimination Unit at the OHCHR convened in Paris for an inter-agency meeting.
128. See, on this, R. Hofmann and E. Friberg, 'The Enlarged EU and the Council of Europe: Transfer of Standards and the Quest for Future Cooperation in Minority Protection', in Toggenburg (ed.), *Minority Protection, supra* note 1: 125–47.
129. See DSP (2004) 21, European Commission/Council of Europe Joint Programmes, Scoreboard Report as of 1 October 2004.
130. See, F.L. Graf von Stauffenberg, 'Der Entwurf einer Volksgruppen-Charta der EG', in F. Ermacora, *et al.* (eds), *Volksgruppen im Spannungsfeld von Recht und Souveränität in Mittel- und Osteuropa* (Vienna: Braumüller, 1993), 245–54.
131. See, for more detail on this problem, Toggenburg. 'Minority Protection', *supra* note 6.
132. See, for more detail on this problem, Toggenburg. 'Minority Protection', *supra* note 6.
133. S. Weatherill, *Law and Integration in the European Union* (Oxford: Oxford University Press, (1995), at 106.
134. This is, however, the opinion of T.H. Malloy, *National Minority Rights in Europe* (Oxford: Oxford University Press, 2005), at 125.
135. An exemption in secondary law would fall under the Damocles sword of possibly infringing its own Common Market principles. Compare, however, Article 15 of Directive 2000/78/EG, which states for Northern Ireland, for example, that '[i]n order to tackle the under-representation of one of the major religious

communities in the police service of Northern Ireland, differences in treatment regarding recruitment into that service, including its support staff, shall not constitute discrimination'.

136. See the so-called 'Aaland protocol' and 'Saami protocol' in OJ C 241, 29 August 1994.

137. In fact, this was the function of the so-called 'Draft act of adaptation to the terms of accession of the united Cyprus republic to the European Union'.

138. For an examination of the system of South Tyrol, see G.N. Toggenburg, 'Europas Integration und Südtirols Autonomie: Konfrontation – Kohabitation – Kooperation?', in J. Marko *et al.* (eds), *Die Verfassung der Südtiroler Autonomie* (Baden-Baden: Nomos, 2005), 451–94.

139. For the wider picture of 'diversity management' in this respect see Toggenburg, 'Who is Managing?', *supra* note 80.

5
The EU and the Management of Ethnic Conflict

Stefan Wolff and Annemarie Peen Rodt

Introduction

The European Union as a collective of its member states has been concerned with ethnopolitical conflicts since its very beginning. This concern can be looked at and analysed from different perspectives. On the one hand, the EU (and its predecessor organizations) has always prided itself on being, among other things, a community of values in which democracy, human rights and the rule of law take on concrete meaning for the benefit of all its citizens, regardless of ethnic, linguistic or religious background. This normative perspective has informed the EU's non-discrimination directives and policies, and has thus been one instrument in the management of minority–majority relations within EU member states.

Yet its success in effectively addressing ethnopolitical conflicts has been limited, both within the Union and, notably, beyond its boundaries. Conflicts in Northern Ireland, the Basque Country and Corsica have persisted at different levels of violence and intensity, causing loss of human life and material damage. The states directly affected by these conflicts, and other countries outside the present boundaries of the EU, share a second area of concern in relation to ethnopolitical conflicts – security. This relates to the physical security of both individual citizens and the state, but also involves a wide range of other security dimensions; for example, ethnopolitical conflict has immediate and longer-term consequences for socio-economic security, to name but one.

The conflicts within the EU as it existed before the 2004 enlargement were relatively well contained and did not pose major threats to the security and stability of the EU as a whole. EU-internal threats had remained relatively contained for decades and member states facing such conflicts generally resented and actively blocked EU involvement in their management.[1] As such, these conflicts were perceived as internal matters that were not to be dealt with at the EU level.

However, the perception of far graver threats in post-communist Europe, large parts of which had aspired to EU membership since the early 1990s, prompted the EU to adopt a much more proactive policy in the management of external ethnopolitical conflicts. Conflicts outside the Union were perceived as far more dangerous, not only in the short term, but in the possible longer term of their becoming EU-internal conflicts by way of enlargement; in other words, they were regarded as potential threats to the EU's 'new' neighbourhood.

A more proactive EU engagement was made possible as a result of the collapse of communism, the end of the Cold War division of Europe, and the greater political and economic leverage that the EU had gained over these countries. All of these developments resulted in the EU beginning to create a framework of policies and institutions for the management of ethnopolitical conflict, which was aimed primarily at non-member states and became most closely associated with the Union's Common Foreign and Security Policy (CFSP). However, it was also, and increasingly, associated with the EU's Enlargement Policy through the Stabilization and Association Process in the Western Balkans, which effectively allowed the EU to impose conditions on candidate states that it did not implement in its own territories.

This chapter will focus exclusively on the European Union's evolving capabilities in the fields of conflict prevention and crisis management and offer an assessment of the current state of affairs. It begins with a brief overview of the Union's early attempts to develop its own mechanisms and policies in this area and then examine in more detail the acceleration of this process in the aftermath of the Kosovo conflict in 1999. Since its Common European Security and Defence Policy (CESDP) became operational in 2001, the European Union has carried out six operations in Europe in 2003, 2004 and 2006, three of which are still ongoing. Two of these fall under military crisis management operations, three under the category of civilian crisis management, and the most recent EU operation remains at the planning stage in preparation of the actual crisis management.[2] Following a brief assessment of the EU's performance in managing ethnopolitical crises in Europe to date, this chapter will conclude by drawing some more general conclusions about the Union's ability to meet the challenges emanating from ethnopolitical conflicts in Europe.

The European Union and the management of ethnic conflict from the collapse of communism to the Kosovo conflict

Conflict prevention and crisis management in the emerging post-Cold War European security architecture

With the end of the Cold War, one fundamental premise of the European security architecture changed: collective security was no longer something to be achieved, in large part at least, through deterrence and the threat of mutual annihilation in the event of a military confrontation between NATO and the Warsaw Bloc. Instead, with the disappearance of the ideological divide in Europe, and the subsequent political and economic liberalization in the former communist bloc, the risk of war between states was diminished greatly – while that of conflict within them increased dramatically. Unsurprisingly, a security architecture predicated upon the need to prevent war between the two blocs was ill equipped to respond rapidly and adequately to the newly emerging threats of ethnic conflict within the (successor) states of the communist bloc.

NATO, the Organization for Security and Cooperation in Europe (OSCE), the Western European Union (WEU), the UN and the Council of Europe – the main building blocs of Europe's Cold War security architecture – survived easily into the 1990s, but they needed to reinvent themselves and to develop new and more effective instruments and policies with which to address the challenges of a changed security situation. The EU could play only a limited role in this emerging security architecture, as it could have an impact on 'low security', but not on 'high security issues'. The EU had, after all, been conceived and developed as a primarily economic union, with little political clout. As time progressed, however, the EU became a very significant political actor in Europe and beyond, as a result both of its economic muscle and of the attraction it held for many countries in Central and Eastern Europe who were eager to join.

Thus, the transition task for the EU was easy and hard at the same time: it had to define its own role in conflict prevention and crisis management, and carve out its own space in an already crowded field at a time when all the established players were about to adjust themselves to a fundamentally altered situation. The EU's initial response to this challenge was the CFSP pillar, established in Article 17 of the Treaty of the European Union, signed in Maastricht in 1992, which was to deal with all issues concerning the security of the Union (CFSP is examined in greater detail later in this chapter). At the height of this period of institutional uncertainty in the early 1990s, the EU and other international organizations concerned with security in Europe were faced with the dual challenges of an initially peacefully dissolving Soviet Union and a violently disintegrating Yugoslavia.

The failure to prevent the latter, and the cascade of wars and human suffering that followed in its aftermath, is, in retrospect, the most obvious illustration that the then prevalent traditional paradigms of conflict prevention and crisis management were wholly inadequate to deal with the post-Cold War situation, despite initial pronouncements by European leaders to the contrary. As crisis erupted in the Western Balkans in the early 1990s, the President of the Council of Ministers, Jacques Poos, announced: 'If one problem can be solved by the Europeans it is the Yugoslav problem. This is the hour of Europe, not the hour of the Americans.' The

President of the European Commission, Jacques Delors, added: 'We do not interfere in American affairs. 'We hope that they will have enough respect not to interfere in ours.' Such statements illustrated the confidence among European leaders that the EC could – and would – solve the Yugoslav crisis in 1991. Over the next decade more than a quarter of a million dead and three million refugees and internally displaced people demonstrated the extent of the failure of European crisis management in the former Yugoslavia.[3]

The EU marginalized

Based on its principle of respect for state sovereignty and its own experiences of ethnic conflict management, the EC's initial response to the Yugoslav crisis was to try and keep the Yugoslav state intact, thereby containing the problem. European leaders faced with ethnic conflicts in their own countries expressed fears that, if they supported the dissolution of Yugoslavia, this might encourage ethnic minorities elsewhere in the region (and beyond) to push for independence, ultimately resulting in increasing levels of ethnic violence. From the beginning of the crisis in Yugoslavia, the EC attempted to take a neutral stance and was reluctant to recognize any one side as the aggressor. Instead, it insisted that the UN impose a general arms embargo on all the Yugoslav republics. This approach was unsuccessful on two counts: not only did the EC fail to send in peacekeeping troops to stop the violence but, by failing to recognize that the Yugoslav National Army was now effectively the armed forces of Serb nationalists, the arms embargo removed the Croat and (to a larger extent) Muslim ability to defend themselves legally against the aggressors.[4]

The EC instead supported President Milošević's plan to reconstruct the Yugoslav federation within its existing borders, and attempted to use its power as an economic heavyweight to broker a peace agreement, by offering aid to those who cooperated and threatening to withhold it from those who did not. As violence broke out in 1991, first in Slovenia and later in Croatia, the EC continued its strategy of attempting to prevent the conflict from spreading throughout the region, but by the end of the year ethnic violence had spread to Bosnia. The EC responded to the increasing violence in Bosnia by freezing all financial aid to the region and sending in its troika of Foreign Ministers (later replaced by a single EC negotiator: Lord Carrington) on a number of peace-negotiating missions.

Following the repeated rejection of these efforts and the growing humanitarian crisis in Bosnia, the EC, against the advice of its own chief negotiator Lord Carrigan (and the UN Secretary-General and the United States), declared itself ready to recognize Slovenian and Croatian independence in December 1991. Recognition was contingent on the meeting of certain conditions in relation to minority protection, peaceful settlement of border disputes and guaranteed government control of their territories, as laid out by the arbitration commission for independence. Germany, however, disregarded the joint EC position and proceeded to recognize the two republics independently, despite the fact that Croatia did not meet EC conditions. EC recognition of both countries followed shortly after, ignoring not only Croatia's non-compliance but also (and perhaps more importantly in this respect) its own diplomatic negotiator, the independence standards it itself had promoted, and thus, effectively, its own foreign policy. This undermined the EC's competence and credibility as an international actor, not only to its own members and allies, but also to the warring parties on the ground. The Serbian side especially questioned the EC's credibility as a neutral mediator and when trade embargoes against Croatia, Slovenia and Macedonia were lifted, while the embargo against the Serbs was kept intact, the Serbian delegation withdrew from the negotiations and the EC peace efforts collapsed.[5]

By 1992 full-scale military conflict had broken out in Bosnia. The EU had recognized the country's independence but refused to send in peacekeeping troops as requested by Bosnian President Izetbegović. Instead, the EU and the UN co-hosted another round of peace negotiations that were again rejected by the Serb delegation. Further sanctions were imposed on Yugoslavia (now consisting of Serbia and Montenegro) and both trade and weapons embargoes remained in force. Under EU pressure, the UN sent protection forces to Croatia, Bosnia and Macedonia, on the assumption that the presence of international troops would calm down nationalist aggression and that the humanitarian purpose of the mission would foster respect for the UN operations. The mandate, however, entitled the troops to use force only in 'self-defence', leaving the soldiers on the ground without a mandate to provide the protection indicated by the mission's name, or to 'create the conditions for peace and security required for the negotiation of an overall settlement of the Yugoslav crisis', which was the stated purpose of the mission according to Security Council Resolution 743 of February 1992. The inability to prevent large-scale disasters such as the 1995 atrocities in the 'UN protectorate' of Srebrenica, demonstrated yet again the complete failure of European-led conflict management efforts.[6] Eventually, the US sidelined the EC by sending in the Contact Group of Five to reach an agreement, but it was not until NATO's military intervention that Presidents Milošević, Tudjman and Izetbegović agreed to the US-brokered Dayton Peace Agreement, ending the war in Bosnia.[7]

At the beginning of the 1990s the EU was unable to reconcile the conflicting views of its member states, which disagreed not only on what to do and how to do it, but also on the very nature of the problem. To mention but a few: France, a historic ally of Serbia and a centralized state itself, favoured keeping the Yugoslav state intact; Italy supported this approach, largely due to its strong links with the Yugoslav government; while Germany, itself unified only a few months earlier and influenced by a strong public opinion supporting the moves for independence in Slovenia and Croatia and with traditionally strong ties to Croatia through the many ethnic Croats living in Germany, stressed what it called 'its moral duty to help other nations coming out of an era of Communism'. The Netherlands, Belgium, Italy and France favoured an early UN intervention in Yugoslavia assuming that the conflicting parties would then agree to a ceasefire. France pushed for the Western European Union (WEU) to take action, but without support from any other members. The UK was reluctant to send in troops, in light of its recent experience in Cyprus and Northern Ireland, which had illustrated the difficulty of withdrawing troops once they were sent in, and Germany was still forbidden from sending troops into any area outside NATO.

These are just a few examples of how EU member states perceived both the nature of the problem and its solution in very different ways. The disagreements between its member states gave rise to the perception of the EU as an indecisive, inconsistent and effectively weak international actor, dismissed by US President Clinton as 'incompetent' in handling the Yugoslav crisis. This was due at least partially to the EU's structural deficiencies. It is, however, important to stress that what the EU was lacking more than anything in the early 1990s was the political will of its member states to act – and to act in unison. The EU's early failures in Yugoslavia were arguably the result, not only of its inability to take the joint decisions required to stop the fighting, but also of its unwillingness to do so.[8]

The Dayton Agreement did not put an end to ethnic violence in the former Yugoslavia, which culminated in fierce clashes between ethnic Albanians and ethnic Serbs in the Kosovo province between 1998 and 1999. The EU, still unable to put weight behind its warnings to President Milošević, was once again sidelined by the US-led NATO intervention. The Kosovo crisis underscored yet again the main structural shortcoming of EC (and later EU) conflict management in the Western Balkans in the 1990s; the EU struggled with its own inexperience in providing 'soft' as well as 'hard' security, it lacked the military strategy and strength to back up its threats and the infant CFSP was simply not ready to deal with a problem as complex as Yugoslavia.

The European Union did, however, go through a learning process in the Balkans. After the Dayton Agreement the EU gradually began a more coherent and effective response to political stabilization and economic recovery in the region. The EU assumed a modest role in the first three years of the international protectorate in Bosnia and Herzegovina and contributed significantly in terms of humanitarian aid and assistance in post-conflict reconstruction in the wider region, but it was not until after the Kosovo campaign, that the EU re-emerged with a comprehensive vision for the Western Balkans and a renewed claim to the leadership it had so boldly – however prematurely – proclaimed in 1991. Today the EU, heavily engaged in conflict prevention and crisis management, is widely recognized as one, if not the most important, of the international actors in the region.[9]

Rebuilding the European security architecture and the credibility of the EU

Gradually, the lessons of European failure were learnt and a new European security architecture is beginning to emerge, in which different international organizations play their part and contribute to a cooperative, rather than merely collective, security order. Characterized by the principles of task- and burden-sharing, this new cooperative security structure, emerging at the beginning of the twenty-first century, includes the same core security institutions, that is, the UN, OSCE, NATO and EU, but with a new set of mandates, instruments and policies that will (in principle) enable them to face existing and emerging security challenges. Within this new European security architecture the EU occupies a central role: enlarged to 27 member states in 2007, strengthened in its political weight through the enlargements, accession and association processes, and diplomatically and militarily more capable as a result of the development of its security and defence identity and policy.

Towards a European security and defence identity: from the Petersberg Tasks to the 1999 Cologne Summit

European Political Cooperation (EPC) was set up by the EC foreign ministers in 1970 as a framework for loose and voluntary collaboration between its member states on foreign policy issues. The EPC, which was created without a treaty basis, operated on an *ad hoc* basis outside the formal institutional structures and legislative processes of the EC. It aimed to foster intergovernmental communication, consultation and mutually agreed shared actions on the basis of consensus among governments. The EPC was formally recognized in the Single European Act (Title III), signed in Luxembourg in 1986, which stated that member states should seek to formulate and implement a shared European foreign policy. In practice, however, it resulted in little more than rather vague declarations.

The 1992 Maastricht Treaty on European Union (TEU)[10] introduced the current three-pillar structure of the European Union and brought the notion of CFSP from EPC into the formal institutional structures of the European Union. The first pillar, or Community dimension, incorporated all arrangements set out in the earlier European Community Treaty, European Coal and Steel Community Treaty and the Euratom Treaty, such as matters of Union citizenship, Community policies, Economic and Monetary Union, free movement of persons and humanitarian aid provided through the European Office for Emergency Humanitarian Aid (ECHO). Decision-making in this pillar is characterized by a supranational element which accords the Council and the European Parliament the status of legislative bodies through joint decision-making. The second pillar, dealing exclusively with Common Foreign and Security Policy (CSFP), was established under Title V TEU, and is strictly inter-governmental in its decision-making procedure, in other words, decisions can be taken by only the Council. This is partly a reflection of the shortcomings (if not failure) of the Presidency system, which included foreign policy, then referred to as European Political Cooperation until the revisions introduced by the TEU. The third pillar, dealing with cooperation in the areas of justice and home affairs (principally police and judicial cooperation in criminal matters), which was also established by the TEU (Title VI) also falls under the decision-making competence of the Council.[11]

Crisis management is a policy area within the Common Foreign and Security Policy (CFSP) Pillar and the Common European Security and Defence Policy (CESDP),[12] as it was established by the TEU and revised by the Treaty of Amsterdam (1997), but owing to the complexity of the tasks, it also requires input from policy areas in Pillars 1 and 3 (see Figure 5.1). Specifically, the Treaty of Amsterdam expanded a range of tasks of the Union to 'humanitarian and rescue tasks, peacekeeping tasks and tasks of combat forces in crisis management, including peacemaking' (Article 17). These so-called Petersberg Tasks have their origin in the June 1992 Ministerial Council of the Western European Union (WEU) at which the WEU member states agreed to make available military units for tasks conducted under WEU authority.[13]

For the military component of crisis management, the European Council in Helsinki (1999) followed up on the decisions made at the Cologne Council meeting earlier the same year.[14] Comparing existing capabilities with the ambitious Petersberg Tasks, the Heads of State and Government agreed on the Helsinki Headline Catalogue, which determined 144 areas in which capabilities and assets needed to be developed in order to enable the Union to fulfil the Petersberg Tasks:

- Commitment by the member states to make available 50,000–60,000 military personnel deployable within 60 days and sustainable for up to 12 months;
- Establishment of coordinating political and military structures within the Union's single institutional framework;
- Development of a framework for cooperation with NATO and third states.

Subsequent meetings of the European Council contributed to the further development of EU crisis management policy, particularly in relation to the improvement of its civilian component. The 2000 Feira European Council determined four priority areas for the improvement of the Union's civilian crisis management capabilities:

- Police (commitment to the deployment of up to 5,000 officers and training of local forces);
- Strengthening of the rule of law (identification of 200 experts readily available for deployment, development of common training modules for human rights monitors);

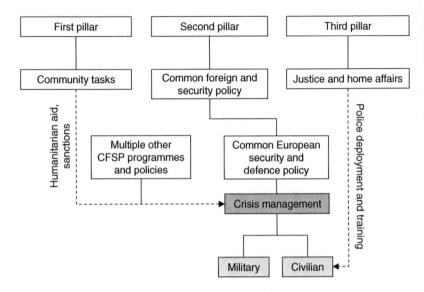

Figure 5.1   The place of crisis management in EU policy

- Civilian administration;
- Civil protection.

If ratified, the Treaty of Lisbon or 'Reform Treaty', signed in December 2007, will introduce two significant institutional changes to the TEU: the creation of the office of a High Representative of the Union for Foreign Affairs and Security Policy and of a European External Action Service. As far as the decision-making process is concerned, the principle of unanimity has been largely confirmed for CFSP, thus preserving member states' ability to cast a veto on specific policy proposals. The Reform Treaty limits the available CFSP instruments to European decisions (on actions and positions taken by the Union and their implementation) and international agreements. The concept of common strategies found in the TEU has been preserved in the Reform Treaty as strategic interests and objectives.[15]

Developing European crisis management: civilian and military capabilities

Shortly after taking office in October 1999, Lord Robertson, the Secretary-General of NATO (until the end of 2003), emphasized that the three most important elements for securing the future of the Alliance were 'capabilities, capabilities, capabilities'. What is true for NATO, the most powerful military

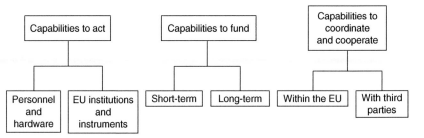

Figure 5.2   The EU's 'capabilities, capabilities, capabilities' problem

alliance (albeit largely dependent on the US in this context) is equally valid for the EU's crisis management capabilities, be they military or civilian in nature. In the EU context, the 'capabilities, capabilities, capabilities' dogma can be broken down into three main areas: capability to act, capability to fund and capability to cooperate and coordinate (see Figure 5.2).[16]

In terms of capability to act, issues of personnel and hardware were addressed by several European Council meetings following the inauguration of crisis management as a distinct policy under CESDP in Cologne in 1999. Specifically, the Helsinki European Council in 1999 agreed on the Helsinki Headline Goal, which was to set up the rapid response capabilities needed to fulfil the Petersberg Tasks (see above). By the time the Heads of State and Government of EU members met again in Laeken in 2001, the Headline Goal had, in their view, been partially met, and they found that 'through the continuing development of the ESDP, the strengthening of its capabilities, both civil and military, and the creation of appropriate structures within it and following the military and police Capability Improvement Conferences held in Brussels on 19 November 2001, the Union is now capable of conducting some crisis management operations'.[17] However, the Council also recognized that there were a large number of deficiencies in areas crucial for the EU's ability to take on more demanding operations and emphasized that the Union had to improve coordination between the resources and instruments of military and civilian crisis management, strengthen its military capabilities, finalize agreements with NATO to gain access to resources (planning, military assets, command options), and implement pre-existing arrangements with other non-NATO partners.[18]

It should be borne in mind that strengthening EU military capabilities was on the agenda well before the more recent development of EU crisis management policies. Since the inauguration of the EU's CFSP, there had been agreement on both sides of the Atlantic that it was necessary to develop a European Security and Defence Identity (ESDI), and to do so within the context of NATO. Thus, since the early 1990s, there has been support in NATO for strengthening EU military capabilities, and developments such as the Berlin Plus Agreement, should be seen in this context of a longer-term agenda, pursued jointly by both organizations, rather than as *ad hoc* reactions to an abruptly discovered capability gap on part of the EU.

Subsequently, NATO–EU cooperation has made significant progress.[19] On the 16 December 2002, the Berlin Plus Agreement comprised, together with a joint EU–NATO declaration on European Security and Defence Policy (ESDP) the various arrangements put in place between NATO and the EU since the 1999 NATO Washington Summit. This declaration was meant to institutionalize a mutually reinforcing strategic partnership in the realm of military capabilities and crisis management activities, built on transparent consultation and cooperation structures, equality in decision-making, appreciation for all member states of both organizations and respect for the principles of the UN Charter. In the agreement, both organizations recognized the need for such an arrangement to ensure the coherent, transparent and mutually reinforcing development of the capability requirements that they shared. The European Union ensured the fullest possible involvement of non-EU European NATO members within the ESDP, and NATO guaranteed its support to the ESDP, in accordance with the previous Washington Summit decisions, and assured EU access to NATO planning capabilities, as set out in the North Atlantic Council decisions on 13 December 2002.

The EU–NATO partnership was put into force by a Framework Agreement consisting of an exchange of letters between the EU's High Representative for CFSP, Javier Solana, and NATO's Secretary-General, Lord Robertson, on 17 March 2003. Since then, the EU, as required by the Laeken European Council, has had access to NATO assets and capabilities, including planning capabilities. There are also clear EU–NATO consultation arrangements in place for EU crisis management operations for which NATO makes available its assets and capabilities.[20] In addition to the Berlin Plus Agreement, NATO and the EU have also signed an Agreement on Security of Information in March 2003, which enables the two organizations to implement common security standards for the handling of sensitive data and to share classified information.

While dependency on NATO resources may pose a potential problem for the EU's ability to decide upon and implement its (military) crisis management operations autonomously, cooperation between the two organizations makes a lot of sense for a number of reasons: the vast majority of the EU's member states are also members of NATO (21 out of 27 EU member states are also members of NATO); the declared security concerns of both organizations and their member states are very similar (for example, regional conflicts, terrorism, proliferation of weapons of mass destruction, state failure and organized crime); and, under the current cooperation arrangements, the strengthening of EU capabilities benefits both EU and NATO, simultaneously increasing their abilities to engage independently of one another in crisis management operations.

At the same time, however, the role of NATO as a defence ally may continue to decrease, leaving EU capabilities even more vulnerable. Following the attacks of 11 September 2001, NATO has been effectively sidelined by the United States in its war on terrorism when the Bush administration decided not to avail itself of the opportunities of an Alliance operation under Article V. NATO enlargement, too, might contribute to turning the Alliance into an increasingly political rather than military organization. In this context, the process of building up EU crisis management capabilities has also not been helped by a refocusing of national defence spending on 'homeland security' issues across most EU member states.[21] Thus, despite existing agreements between the EU and NATO and their common security interests, the Union may sooner or later come to depend more on its own resources. However, as far as military assets are concerned, to date these hardly exist independently of NATO. Nevertheless, the creation of the European Defence Agency, and plans for the development of the Union's own airlift capacity – the A400M project – indicate that this dependency has been recognized and is being addressed.

The development of appropriate institutions and policy instruments progressed much faster and more successfully. The creation of the post of Secretary-General of the European Council and High Representative for CSFP (and the appointment of former NATO Secretary-General Javier Solana to that post) was a significant step forward and indicated that the Union was prepared to follow up on its intentions with substantive commitments.[22] Of the plethora of other institutions involved in CFSP under the authority of the European Council, several are directly relevant to EU crisis management operations (see Figure 5.3), especially the EU Political and Security Committee, the EU Military Committee and the EU Military Staff, all of which were made permanent under the provisions of the Nice Treaty. This institutional structure has, to date, proved reasonably efficient and effective. Initial antagonism between different EU institutions concerned with foreign policy in the wider sense (such as the Presidency, the President of the Commission, the Commissioners for External Affairs, Enlargement, Trade and Development) were handled reasonably well, and the new institutional arrangement has boosted the status of the EU as an international actor.[23] As for EU policy instruments, and emphasizing the multi-faceted nature of CFSP, Hill has aptly summarized the situation: '[t]he arrival of Joint Actions, Common Positions and now Common Strategies in the CSFP has spawned new initiatives such as the Stability Process in South-East Europe'.[24] In addition to these three policy instruments, 'statements' also form part of the range of options available to the Council for the conduct of its CFSP.[25]

Capabilities to fund various crisis management operations in the short and the long term do exist within the EU. As discussed below, the provision of long-term funds for CFSP activities is not usually problematic; certainly, it has not been a shortage of financial means that has impeded EU policy towards the Western Balkans. However, the complicated system within the Union to make the use of its funds transparent and accountable often hindered their rapid disbursement. An important contribution to the improvement of the EU's short-term funding capabilities, therefore, has been the creation of the Rapid Reaction Mechanism (RRM) in February 2001. Its main aim is to 'allow the Community to respond in a rapid, efficient and flexible manner, to situations of urgency or crisis or to emergence of crisis'.[26] The RRM covers six dimensions of EU crisis management: 'assessment of possible Community responses to a crisis; conflict prevention in countries and regions showing significant signs of instability; acute crisis management; post-conflict reconciliation; post-crisis reconstruction; and the fight against terrorism'.[27] Actions financed with funds from the RRM may be carried out by 'authorities of Member States or of beneficiary countries and their agencies, regional and international organisations and their agencies, NGOs and public and private operators with appropriate specialised expertise and experience' (Art. 6) and must be implemented within six months. The RRM has a fixed amount of funds at its disposal each year, determined annually by the budgetary authority (Art. 8). In 2001, this was €20 million and in 2002 €25 million. Of the 2001 funds, 64 per cent were spent on the Former Yugoslav Republic of Macedonia[28] alone, while in 2002 all new activities financed by the RRM took place outside the Western Balkans, where the last programmes approved in 2001 were completed in September 2002. This being primarily a reflection of the assessment of the situation on the ground as not requiring immediate intervention beyond the programmes already running, the RRM proved a very useful financing tool for crisis management operations in Macedonia in 2001, that is, both before and after the conclusion of the Ohrid Agreement (Macedonia, 2001).

Coordination and cooperation capabilities within the EU have two dimensions: a horizontal one (coordination among the three pillars) and a vertical one (between the EU as a supranational organization with its own institutional structures and the EU member states). As demonstrated below, both dimensions of coordination and cooperation have worked reasonably well in the Western Balkans of late. This is partly the result of lessons learned from earlier shortcomings, especially in the vertical dimension (recognition of Slovenia and Croatia), and partly also that of virtually identical interests between the EU and its member states (stabilization and closer integration), and of the fact that crisis management operations in the Western Balkans are integrated into a broader comprehensive strategy towards the region in which institutions in all three pillars play a legitimate role.

At a more general level, internal cooperation and coordination capabilities have been enhanced by the more secure institutional infrastructure that crisis management has been given since 1999, and especially since the 2000 Treaty of Nice (see Figure 5.3). This is the case, in particular, with regard to the Political and Security Committee, which has effectively replaced the Political Committee and taken over many functions held by it previously.

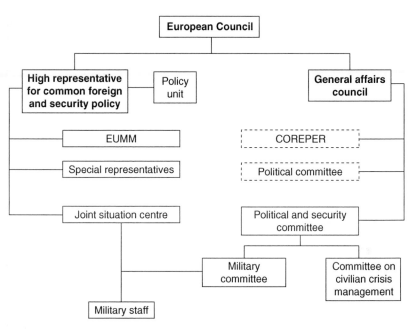

Figure 5.3   The institutional infrastructure of crisis management for the Balkans

At the external level, coordination and cooperation is essential, particularly with NATO (see above) and, while potentially increasing EU dependency on NATO resources, has worked well so far. Especially in the Western Balkans there has been a longer tradition of cooperation anyway (Bosnia and Herzegovina, Macedonia, Kosovo), and the Union took over SFOR (Stabilization Force in Bosnia and Herzegovina) in 2004 after having already assumed responsibility in Macedonia from an earlier NATO force. Cooperation with third countries (that is, non-EU and non-NATO members) and international organizations (UN, OSCE, UNHCR (United Nations High Commissioner for Refugees), non-governmental organizations [NGOs]) is accorded high priority by the Union. This is so for two reasons: the EU is strongly committed to a multilateral approach and recognizes the mutual benefits of cooperation, given that different organizations 'specialize' in different crisis management (and conflict prevention) tasks. In the case of cooperation with NATO, permanent consultation structures have been created in the wake of the Berlin Plus Agreement; in the case of cooperation with third parties, the EU has clear procedures for coordination, including the establishment of so-called committees of contributing countries meant to give third parties an adequate role in the day-to-day running of a particular crisis management operation, while leaving responsibility for overall strategic direction with the relevant institutions inside the Union. In addition, as recent experience in the Western Balkans indicates, the EU also uses its ability to conclude bilateral agreements with third parties as a mechanism for putting crisis management cooperation on a solid legal foundation.

Testing the new capabilities

The EU Police Mission in Bosnia and Herzegovina

The European Union Police Mission (EUPM) in Bosnia and Herzegovina, established on 1 January 2003, is the first mission ever launched as part of the ESDP and, as such, falls under the Union's civilian crisis management operations. It is also part of a comprehensive programme of measures aimed at establishing and stabilizing the rule of law in Bosnia and Herzegovina; it is envisaged that it will have accomplished its tasks by the end of 2007. It is the successor of the United Nation's International Police Force and, although it is led by the EU and more than 50 per cent of its annual €38 million budget is provided directly by Brussels, Mission personnel consists of 207 staff from 34 countries, including the EU27. Roughly 85 per cent (175) of the personnel is supplied from EU25 countries with France, Germany and the UK as the biggest contributors, while the remaining 15 per cent comprises police officers from third countries, with Turkey as the biggest contributor. From an international legal perspective, EUPM derives its legitimacy in part from Security Council Resolution 1396 of 5 March 2002 and an earlier decision by the Steering Board of the Peace Implementation Council on 28 February 2002 to accept the EU's offer to provide the police mission following the end of the mandate of the UN Mission in Bosnia and Herzegovina (UNMIBH).

In a European Council Joint Action, adopted on 11 March 2002, Heads of State and Government agreed the terms of the EUPM. The Mission Statement appended to this Joint Action makes it explicit that the EUPM 'will not include executive powers or the deployment of an armed component' and names among its political and strategic goals:

- The preservation of existing levels of institutional and personal proficiency;
- The enhancement, through monitoring, mentoring and inspection of police managerial and operational capacities;
- The strengthening of professionalism at high levels within the ministries, as well as at senior police officer levels;
- Monitoring of the exercise of appropriate political control over the police.

The Mission Statement also details how this general and long list of operational goals is to be achieved, including methods such as the co-location of mission personnel alongside local police commanders at various levels and in relevant institutions within Bosnia and Herzegovina, the ability to recommend to the High Representative for Bosnia and Herzegovina the removal from office of police officers obstructing the achievement of the EUPM's goals, coordination with the Office of the High Representative and other organizations working towards establishing and consolidating the rule of law in Bosnia and Herzegovina and ensuring support from EUFOR on public security issues.

The Joint Action further specifies that the EUPM is a crisis management operation and, as such, has a unified command structure within the single institutional framework of the Union, comprising the European Council and its Secretary Genetral/High Representative, the Political and Security Committee and the EU Special Representative for Bosnia and Herzegovina (EUSR). The Head of Mission/Police Commissioner leads the EUPM and is in charge of its day-to-day operations, reporting to the SG/HR through the EUSR and receiving guidance from the SG/HR through the EUSR.

Given the current challenges to the rule of law in Bosnia and Herzegovina, the EUPM has two priorities – fighting organized crime and ensuring the security of returnees. Apart from technical and professional assistance and training, EUPM is therefore also involved in the creation and consolidation of institutional structures that will enable local police forces to achieve better results in the fight against organized crime and in protecting returning refugees. Such structures were already specified in the Council Joint Action of March 2003 at entity, inter-entity and state levels, for example, the Steering Board for Returnee and Refugee Return, the Ministry of Security, and the State Information and Protection Agency and the State Border Service.

Operation Concordia in Macedonia

Operation Concordia, established on 31 March 2003, was, like the EUPM, an EU-led follow-on mission from a previous international effort with a similar task, in this case NATO's operation Allied Harmony. The background of both missions was to ensure sufficient levels of security and stability in Macedonia in order to enable the implementation of the 2001 Ohrid Agreement, which was brokered by the EU between the Macedonian government and representatives of the Albanian minority in the country following a brief spell of violence in the summer of 2001 after a long period of inter-ethnic tension (in other words, to provide military protection to observers monitoring implementation of the Ohrid Agreement on the ground). It derived its legitimacy from a request by Macedonian President Boris Trajkowski and had further legal basis in UN Security Council Resolution 1371.

Operation Concordia fell within the remit of military crisis management operations of the Union, and was the first ever deployment of EU military forces under the terms of its security and defence policy. It comprised 400 soldiers from 26 countries, thus again including non-EU contributor states. Operation Concordia was also the first case for EU–NATO cooperation in the framework of the Berlin Plus Agreement, in other words, the EU made use of NATO capabilities in conducting Operation Concordia.

Initially only expected to last for six months, Operation Concordia was subsequently extended at the request of the Macedonian government until 15 December 2003. Command of the operation now rested with EUFOR headquarters.[29] This also meant that the Operations Field Commander of Operation Concordia was a member of the military staff of EUROFOR, but was nevertheless part of the command structure of this particular EU crisis management operation. He reported to the EU Operation Commander, in this case NATO's Deputy Supreme Allied Commander for Europe. The EU Military Committee and its Chairman monitored the conduct of the military operation and received reports from the Operation Commander, in addition to providing the first point of contact for him in relation to the Council. This meant that, even though the Operation Commander held a position simulta-neously within the NATO command structure, he reported only to EU bodies and the entire chain of command remained under the EU's political control and strategic direction, as determined in a European Council Joint Action of 27 January 2003, in particular the Political and Security Committee and the European Council. In contrast to the EUPM, the Special Representative of the EU to Macedonia, at the time Alexis Brouhns, was not part of the command chain, but acted, together with the SG/HR, as the primary point of contact for Macedonian authorities and as key liaison for EU commanders in the field.

Contributions to Operation Concordia were made by 23 of today's EU27 member states[30] and 4 non-EU members.[31] A budget of €6.2 million was contributed by the EU directly with non-common costs borne by the participating states directly.

As part of the day-to-day management structures, a Committee of Con-tributors was established following a decision of the Political and Security Committee of 18 February 2003. This committee had a consultative role in the decision-making procedure regarding Operation Concordia. It took its decisions on day-to-day management, as well as on any recommendations to the Political and Security Committee, on the basis of unanimity.

Operation Proxima in Macedonia

Launched in December 2003, Operation Proxima became the second EU police mission in the Western Balkans after EUPM in Bosnia and Herzegov-ina. The establishment of the mission followed an invitation on 16 September 2003 by Macedonia's Prime Minister. Its implementation was closely linked to the execution of the Ohrid Agreement of 2001, in which the Macedonian government and political representatives of the ethnic Albanian community in the country agreed on a settlement on minority rights and political partici-pation in the country. The mission was extended beyond its initial 12-month period by a Council Joint Action of 22 November 2004, again following a request by then Macedonian Prime Minister, Hari Kostov, of 1 October 2004, and was completed on 14 December 2005.

The mission personnel comprised 184 international staff from 24 EU member states and 3 non-member states (Switzerland, Turkey and Ukraine). Together with 138 local staff, they were deployed to five locations across Macedonia, including the country's capital Skopje. According to its mandate, the international staff of Operation Proxima were 'monitoring, mentoring and advising' Macedonia's police force and 'promoting European policing standards' through programmes that supported:

- The consolidation of law and order, including the fight against organized crime, focusing on the sensitive areas;
- The practical implementation of the comprehensive reform of the Ministry of Interior, including the police;
- The operational transition towards, and the creation of a border police, as part of the wider EU effort to promote integrated border management;
- The local police in building confidence within the population; and
- Enhanced cooperation with neighbouring states in the field of policing.[32]

The Operation Proxima budget was €7.3 million for start-up costs and €7 million for 2004 running costs to be financed from the Community budget. For the 12-month extension after 2004, a budget of €15.95 million was agreed.

Operation Althea in Bosnia and Herzegovina

On 12 July 2004, the European Council decided to take over responsibility from NATO for securing the conditions for the implementation of the Dayton Peace Agreement in Bosnia and Herzegovina.[33] Following a Council Decision in November of the same year,[34] Operation Althea was launched, marking the transition from NATO-led SFOR to EU Force (EUFOR). Apart from the short-term goal of ensuring a smooth handover period between the two forces, Operation Althea had two further political objectives. In the medium term, the operation was meant to support Bosnia and Herzegovina's progress towards EU integration, initially with the aim of concluding a Stabilization and Association Agreement. This, in turn, was to contribute to the long-term objective of peace and stability in the country and its eventual accession to the European Union.

The initial budget for the operation's common costs was determined at €71.7 million. These were administered by the so-called ATHENA mechanism, which relied on financial contributions by EU member states determined on a GDP basis.

In addition to the 24 EU member states participating in this operation, 11 non-member states have also contributed to the approximately 7,000 troops comprising the mission's personnel: Albania, Argentina, Canada, Chile, Morocco, New Zealand, Norway, Switzerland and Turkey.[35]

Perhaps more than any other ESDP operation by the EU to date, Operation Althea exemplifies the importance of cooperation among the international organizations making up Europe's security architecture. The European Council's decision in July 2004 to take over from NATO in Bosnia and Herzegovina was only possible following the work of NATO's SFOR in the country and the resulting improvements in the general security environment that led NATO heads of states and government to decide, at the Istanbul Summit in June 2004, to end their operation and prepare for a transfer of responsibility to an EU-led mission in the context of the Berlin Plus arrangements.[36] This decision by NATO was itself based on positive experiences gained in the context of Operation Concordia in Macedonia in 2003, after which the EU and NATO agreed to make permanent the so-called European Union Staff Group at Supreme Headquarters Allied Powers Europe (SHAPE). This was meant to provide guidance to NATO's Deputy Supreme Allied Commander for Europe on European issues, as the holder of this office was potentially also the EU Operation Commander, as well as to provide the core staff of an EU Operations Headquarters at SHAPE. When the European Council confirmed in December 2003 that the EU was prepared to conduct a military ESDP-mission in Bosnia and Herzegovina under the Berlin Plus arrangements, consultations with NATO began in 2004, which led to the establishment of Operation Althea.[37]

Thus, the EU has been able to rely on NATO common assets and capabilities. NATO's Deputy Supreme Allied Commander Europe was appointed as the Operation Commander for the military component of Operation Althea, and SHAPE – simultaneously became the EU Operation Headquarters. The command structure of Operation Althea also underlines the close cooperation between NATO and EU: under the political control and strategic direction of the EU's Political Security Committee, the EU Operation Headquarters at SHAPE in Mons (Belgium), the EU Command Element at the Allied Joint Forces Command in Naples (Italy) and the Headquarters of EUFOR at Camp Butmir in Sarajevo (Bosnia and Herzegovina). The EU Command Element at the Allied Joint Forces Command in Naples is a particularly crucial element in the coordination process with NATO, as it ensures the EU's operations in the Balkans conform to the EU's regional approach, on the one hand, and cooperate closely with NATO operations in the Balkans, on the other.

The regional element in the EU's approach also means coordination with other international organizations active in the Western Balkans. This relates primarily to the UN and the OSCE, both of which continue to play a role in Bosnia and Herzegovina. EUFOR operates on a Chapter VII mandate, and in a resolution of November 2004 the UN welcomed the EU's intention to launch an EU military operation and authorized those UN member states 'acting through or in cooperation with the EU to establish for an initial planned period of 12 months a multinational stabilization force (EUFOR) as a legal successor to SFOR' and 'to take all necessary measures to effect the implementation of and to ensure compliance with Annexes 1-A and 2 of the Peace Agreement', recognizing their right 'to take all necessary measures to defend themselves from attack or threat of attack'.[38]

In addition, the EU coordinates closely actions taken under its military mission – Operation Althea – with those taken under its police mission – EUPM. As both of these operations are meant to contribute to the full implementation of the Dayton Peace Agreement, cooperation with the Peace Implementation Council and the Office of the High Representative is also essential. This is, among other things assured by the fact that the EU's Special Representative for Bosnia and Herzegovina also serves as High Representative.

EU planning team in Kosovo

Since April 2006 the EU has been maintaining an operation under the name of the European Union Planning Team in Kosovo. This operation, which is currently limited to a planning team, is meant to prepare the ground for a European crisis management mission to take over tasks from the United Nations Interim Administration Mission in Kosovo (UNMIK). The planning team, the mandate of which was extended into 2008, is involved mainly in providing technical assistance to UNMIK.[39]

Meeting the challenges of present and future ethnopolitical conflict in Europe

In 1993, Christopher Hill predicted six future functions of the then European Community (EC) as an international actor, including that of 'regional pacifier' and 'mediator of conflicts'.[40] In each case, he made explicit reference to former Yugoslavia and pointed out that it fell to the EU 'to act as mediator/coercive arbiter when the peace of the whole region seems under threat' and that there had been 'considerable diplomatic effort and creativity in the early stages of the Yugoslav imbroglio'. However, judging by the EU's performance in the 1990s, it was only after the NATO intervention in Kosovo in 1999 that the EU came to play an increasingly important role as regional pacifier and mediator of conflicts in the Western Balkans, and with varying success over time. No matter which perspective one takes on the Union's crisis management policy, which has with few exceptions to date[41] remained confined to the Western Balkans, it remains the largest donor and the organization with the biggest presence throughout this region, having contributed significantly (partly in cooperation with third parties) to the stabilization of the countries in the region and their reconstruction to date. This general view testifies, at least in part, to the existence of EU crisis management capabilities in the Western Balkans.

However, a closer look at the operations conducted there allows us to make more informed statements about the status of capability development in general. Current EU capabilities appear to be sufficient to take on tasks of the kind required in the Western Balkans. The EU was able to mobilize adequate personnel, hardware and the funds to sustain them, it had the institutional framework and instruments available to make the necessary decisions and it proved itself capable of a certain level of cooperation and coordination within its own structures, as well as with third parties.

This relatively positive assessment of EU crisis management capabilities in the Western Balkans after 1999, however, must not necessarily be taken as a general indication of the readiness of the Union to manage crises elsewhere and with a similar degree of success. While it is undoubtedly true that the 'CFSP, through the position of the HR for CFSP, has experienced in a very short time a substantial improvement in its coherence and visibility',[42] improved coherence and visibility do not necessarily translate into effectiveness. With respect to the Western Balkans one could question whether the Union has indeed been successful. In Macedonia, for example, it could be argued that early-stage crisis management, despite the mobilization of significant resources, failed, and that it was only once violent conflict erupted that the EU (through crisis management measures) succeeded in brokering a deal between the fighting factions.[43]

Taking into account the complexity of the situation the EU had, and has, to deal with in the Western Balkans and the intensity of the crises it has had to manage (in post-Dayton Bosnia and Herzegovina and in Macedonia), the Union has demonstrated that its development of an institutional framework and a set of policies have enabled it to make decisions quickly, to provide adequate funds and personnel, and to cooperate and coordinate activities with third parties in ways that enhance its own capabilities and maximize the chances of successful crisis management. It is equally important in this context to bear in mind that, since the failure of crisis management in the early and mid-1990s, the Union's capabilities have been improved significantly, enabling it now to undertake both civilian and military operations; in other words, it is able now to back up its diplomatic efforts with credible threats of force where necessary.

However, it is suggested that the EU's relative success of late in the Western Balkans has its source not only in improved crisis management capabilities. It is argued that the Union's experience in the Western Balkans cannot be generalized easily. The distinct advantage that the EU has in this region is that its policy of conditionality is much more effective *vis-à-vis* countries where the promise of closer association with, and potentially accession to, the EU is credible, and where both political elites and the general public are ready to make significant compromises in order to attain what many believe to be a panacea for all their problems, even though there is now growing euroscepticism in Croatia, Serbia and Bosnia and Herzegovina, because the imagined solutions are not forthcoming as quickly as envisaged.

In other words, the success of EU crisis management in the Western Balkans must be seen in a larger context, in which crisis management is only one element in a comprehensive EU approach to a region. As Javier Solana pointed out as early as 2000, '[t]he European Union is uniquely placed for comprehensive action in the Western Balkans' and is 'the only institution capable of comprehensive action, ranging from trade, economic reform and infrastructure, humanitarian assistance, human rights and democratization, justice and police to crisis management and military security'.[44] Without the clear long-term commitment of the EU to the Western Balkans' prospect of EU membership, the incentives for political elites and the various ethnic groups they represent would be less powerful, thereby diminishing the Union's ability to elicit short- and long-term compliance, which has been to date a major factor in the success of its crisis management operations.

A second note of caution regarding the EU's readiness to engage successfully in crisis management operations elsewhere concerns the availability of personnel and especially military assets. The commitments made by EU member states have not yet been tested to the full – the two police missions in Bosnia and Herzegovina and Macedonia have required only about 10 per cent of the total number of police officers committed by EU member states, and the two military operations Concordia and Althea similarly have required only around 12 per cent of total committed troops. At the same time, the EU is now, for better or worse, locked into a framework of cooperation with NATO which will perpetuate its dependency on NATO resources.[45] This may significantly decrease the Union's capability of autonomous action in situations where NATO resources are stretched or where disagreement within NATO prevents the use of certain resources by the EU.

A final factor which limits our ability to draw generalized conclusions from the relative success of recent EU crisis management operations in the Western Balkans is, simultaneously, one of the very reasons for this success – the increasing familiarity with, and sensitivity towards, the situation in the region and the countries concerned; a long-standing network of information sources (EU Monitoring Mission); and previous experience in dealing with the political elites and populations in the area. One of the main shortcomings of EU capabilities, identified by the Director General of the European Union Military Staff, General Rainer Schuwirth, as 'shortfalls in all areas of intelligence gathering' and a lack of a 'common system for intelligence fusion', could be at least partially neutralized therefore.[46]

Nevertheless, even the limited crisis management operations that the EU is currently conducting in the Western Balkans are very valuable for its future role as a serious international actor. While it might be too early to proclaim the overall success of EU conflict management in the region, there are some indicators that success might not have eluded the Union on this occasion.[47] First of all, there has been the proven success of institutional reforms within the Union and of the development of credible policies and instruments for crisis management. Second, the overall approach of the EU to the conduct of international affairs has been fruitful: there has been increased commitment to multilateralism (within the EU and with its partners elsewhere),[48] constructive and long-term engagement with crisis regions, the combination of short-term crisis management with long-term structural conflict prevention and a fair balance between civilian and military strategies to maximize the short- and long-term impact of its policies. Third, by highlighting any remaining deficiencies in EU crisis management capabilities, the Union now has an opportunity to draw lessons for the future before engaging in more ambitious and demanding operations elsewhere in the world.

Notes

1. This is not to deny that the EU has had two successive programmes in support of the Northern Ireland peace process since the mid-1990s (PEACE I from 1995 to 1999, and PEACE II from 2000 to 2006) and that European integration has provided institutional structures and incentives for cross-border cooperation both in Northern Ireland and in South Tyrol that have had a generally positive, albeit hardly quantifiable impact on conflict resolution in both of these cases.

2. There have been further ESDP civilian, police and military operations in the South Caucasus, South-east Asia, the Middle East and Africa, and in April 2006 the Council signed a joint action establishing an EU planning team (EUPT) for a possible future EU crisis management operation in the field of rule of law (and possible other areas) in Kosovo.

3. See E. Faucompret, *The Dismemberment of Yugoslavia and the European Union* (Antwerp: University of Antwerp, 2001); and V. Meier, *Yugoslavia* (London: Routledge, 1999).

4. Preoccupied with the end of the Cold War security structures, the reunification of Germany, the break-up of the Soviet Union and US intervention in Kuwait and with only one year to go before the presidential elections, the Bush administration happily left Yugoslavia for the Europeans to resolve. As James Baker (then US Secretary of State) often expressed it: 'We don't have a dog in this fight' (quoted in R. Holbrooke, *To End a War* (New York: Random House, 1999), 27).

5. See N. Morris, *Humanitarian Intervention in the Balkans*, in J. Welsh (ed.), *Humanitarian Intervention and International Relations* (Oxford: Oxford University Press, 2004); and A.G. Kintis, 'The EU's Foreign Policy and the War in Former Yugoslavia', in M. Holland (ed.), *Common Foreign and Security Policy* (London: Pinter, 1997).

6. Kintis, 'The EU's Foreign Policy', *supra* note 5; L. Silber and A. Little, *The Death of Yugoslavia* (London: Penguin Books, 1996).

7. It is estimated that between 7000 and 8000 Muslim men and boys were killed by Serb nationalists in Srebrenica in 1995 (Silber and Little. *The Death of Yugoslavia*, *supra* note 6).

8. Kintis, 'The EU's Foreign Policy', *supra* note 5; Morris, *Humanitarian Intervention*, *supra* note 5; P.C. Pentland, 'The EU and Southeastern Europe after Dayton', Europe-Russia Working Chapters, Europe-Russia Conference Series (Ottowa: Carleton University, 2003).

9. Faucompret, *The Dismemberment of Yugoslavia*, *supra* note 3.

10. F. Cameron, 'The European Union's Role in the Balkans', in B. Blitz (ed.), *War and Change in the Balkans* (Cambridge: Cambridge University Press, 2006); Faucompret, *The Dismemberment of Yugoslavia*, *supra* note 3; Silber and Little, *The Death of Yugoslavia*, *supra* note 6.

11. The Treaty was negotiated during 1991, officially signed in February 1992 and entered into force on 1 November 1993 (European Union 1992).

12. R. Jones, *The Politics and Economics of the European Union* (Cheltenham: Edward Elgar Publishing, 2001).

13. Initially simply referred to as ESDP in the Presidency Conclusions of the Cologne European Council in June 1999, the Helsinki Council of December 1999 introduced the acronym of CESDP 'to signify the determination, on the part of the EU member states, to develop a distinct European politico-military project, with its own institutional infrastructure and a significant military capacity'. J. Howorth, 'Britain, NATO and CESDP: Fixed Strategy, Changing Tactics', *European Foreign Affairs Review* 5(3) (2000): 377–96, at 377.

14. The Petersberg Declaration was the WEU's response to calls for greater burden-sharing within NATO through the elaboration of a coherent European Security and Defence Identity (ESDI) built around the WEU. In the context of the European Convention, important amendments and revisions to the Petersberg Declaration were proposed by the so-called Barnier Report (European Convention 2002).

15. The Cologne Summit, importantly, happened just at the end of NATO's intervention in the Kosovo crisis which in turn visibly influenced the decision-making by Heads of State and Government in Cologne.

16. Cf. Draft Treaty of Lisbon amending the Treaty on European Union and the Treaty establishing the European Community, Article I-19; Article I-22; Article I-27, amending Article V-11 TEC; Article I-29, amending Article V-13 TEC; Article I-30; Articles I-49 to I-53.

17. For a somewhat different take on the capabilities problem, see U. Schneckener, *Developing and Applying EU Crisis Management: Test Case Macedonia*, ECMI Working Paper No. 14 (Flensburg: European Centre for Minority Issues, 2002), 37–9.

18. Presidency Conclusions, European Council Meeting in Laeken, 14 and 15 December 2001, SN 300/1/101 REV 1, Paragraph 6.

19. *Ibid.*, Annex II.

20. More recently, the 2005 proposal by some EU members (notably France and Germany) to create an EU planning capability might threaten this progress in the future, as it potentially not only duplicates existing NATO planning capabilities, but also clearly contravenes earlier agreements between EU and NATO to develop EU capabilities within, rather than as a potential rival outside NATO. This has also created additional tensions in the transatlantic relationship, in the relationship between advocates and opponents of this plan within the EU, and also puts a strain on the negotiations of the new constitutional treaty in the CSFP area.

21. NATO assets essentially means US assets as the only real collective assets NATO has are not always sufficient for crisis management operations requirements (e.g., AWACS planes, bunker systems, etc.). This poses a potential problem for the EU as the US also has gaps in its military portfolio and will prioritize its own needs over EU requirements. Thus, agreement on EU access to NATO assets does not necessarily guarantee their actual availability at a given moment in the future. (We are grateful to Jenny Medcalf for pointing this out.)

22. T. Garden, 'EU Crisis Management: A British View', Paper presented to a Colloquy held at the Ecole Militaire, Paris, 31 May 2002.

23. This has also been emphasized by Piana in relation to the crisis in Macedonia: 'The creation of the post of High Representative definitely brought the visibility/continuity element that was lacking in the CFSP', C. Piana, 'The EU's Decision-Making Process in the Common Foreign and Security Policy: The Case of the Former Yugoslav Republic of Macedonia', *European Foreign Affairs Review* 7(2) (2002): 209–26, at 211.

24. The potential downside of this 'personal' cooperation is, of course, its lack of institutionalization (cf. D. Hannay, 'Europe's Common Foreign and Security Policy: Year 1', *European Foreign Affairs Review* 5(3) (2000): 275–80, at 279). For relevant policy papers on the role of, and by, the SG/HR and the Commissioner for External Relations, see A. Missiroli, 'European Security Policy: The Challenge of Coherence', *European Foreign Affairs Review* 6(2) (2001): 177–96, at 187–9.

25. C. Hill, 'The EU's Capacity for Conflict Prevention', *European Foreign Affairs Review* 6(3) (2001): 315–33, at 328.

26. Note the proposed limitation on policy instruments in the Constitutional Treaty.

27. European Council, Council regulation on creating a rapid reaction mechanism, (EC) No. 381/2001, 26 February 2001.

28. European Commission, 'Information Note: The Rapid Reaction Mechanism Supporting the European Union's Policy Objectives in Conflict Prevention and Crisis Management' (2002) <http://www.europa.eu.int/comm/external_relations/cfsp/doc/rrm.pdf>

29. Hereinafter, Macedonia.

30. EUROFOR was established in 1995 in Lisbon as a military force under the Petersberg Tasks. Contributing nations are France, Italy, Portugal and Spain. Operational since 1998 and listed in the force catalogues of EU, NATO, OSCE and UN, it has been part of NATO Operation Allied Guardian in Albania in 2000.

31. The EU15 members (except Ireland and Denmark) plus Bulgaria, Czech Republic, Estonia, Hungary, Latvia, Lithuania, Poland, Slovakia, Slovenia and Romania.

32. Canada, Iceland, Norway and Turkey.

33. European Council, Council Joint Action on the European Union Police Mission in the former Yugoslav Republic of Macedonia, 2003/681/CFSP, 29 September 2003.

34. European Council, Council Joint Action of 12 July 2004 on the European Union military operation in Bosnia and Herzegovina, 2004/570/CFSP, 2004.

35. European Council Decision of 25 November 2004 on the launching of the European Union military operation in Bosnia and Herzegovina, 2004/803/CFSP, 2004.

36. This means that two European non-EU member states of NATO – Norway and Turkey – contribute to the operation, as well as one non-European NATO member – Canada.

37. This was in many ways similar to what had happened one year earlier in relation to the EU's Operation Concordia taking over from NATO's Operation Allied Harmony in Macedonia.

38. SHAPE, 'SHAPE–EU Cooperation: Background Information', http://www.nato.int/shape/issues/shape_eu/background.htm (last accessed 16/05/2008), 2004.

39. United Nations Security Council, Resolution 1575, S/RES/1575, 2004 <http://consilium.europa.eu/cms3_fo/showPage.asp?id=1100&lang=en>

40. Hill, 'The EU's Capacity for Conflict Prevention', *supra* note 25, 312f.

41. These exceptions so far were, compared to the Union's engagement in the Western Balkans, relatively short-term and less costly. They include AMM (Aceh, Indonesia), EUBAM and EUPOL COPPS (Palestinian territories), AMIS II assistance (Darfur,

Sudan), EUSR border teams (Moldova/Ukraine), EUPOL KINSHASA, EUFOR and EUSEC (DR Congo) and EUJUST THEMIS (Georgia).

42. G. Müller-Brandeck-Bocquet, 'The New CFSP and ESDP Decision-Making System of the European Union', *European Foreign Affairs Review* 7(3) (2002): 257–82, at 278.

43. This is the problem of CFSP as a 'moving target'. See F. Cameron, 'The European Union's Growing International Role: Closing the Capability – Expectations Gap', Paper presented at the Conference on the European Union in International Affairs, National Europe Centre, Australian National University, July 2002.

44. J. Solana, Report on the Western Balkans Presented to the Lisbon European Council by the Secretary-General/High Representative together with the Commission, Brussels, SN 2032/2/00/REV2, 21 March 2000.

45. For example, the decision to extend Operation Concordia in Macedonia was contingent upon a decision of the North Atlantic Council to extend the availability of NATO assets to the EU.

46. R. Schuwirth, 'Hitting the Helsinki Headline Goal', *NATO Review*, Autumn 2002.

47. The two big (known) unknowns in this respect are the closure of the Office of the High Representative in Bosnia and Herzegovina and the outcome, and impact, of the Kosovo final status negotiations.

48. The preference of a multilateral approach to crisis management can also be deduced from the fact that in both current crisis management operations in the Western Balkans and in the brief military operation in the Danish Refugee Council, the European Council either did not move before the UN (DRC) or explicitly inferred the legitimacy of its operation, at least in part, from a *preceding* UN resolution, cf. M.E. Smith, 'Diplomacy by Degree: The Legalisation of EU Foreign Policy', *Journal of Common Market Studies* 39(1) (2001): 79–104, at 99.

6
The Enlargement of the European Union and the OSCE High Commissioner on National Minorities

Krzysztof Drzewicki

The mandate of the High Commissioner on National Minorities

Before embarking upon an examination of the consequences of the enlargement of the EU on the activities of the OSCE High Commissioner on National Minorities (HCNM), the mandate of the latter institution warrants some introductory comments.

The post of HCNM was established within the Organization for Security and Cooperation in Europe (OSCE) in 1992 as a highly autonomous and independent political body.[1] It was set up at a time when interethnic conflicts were erupting throughout Central and Eastern Europe at the end of the Cold War during the course of the painful process of restoring democratic governance to post-communist Europe. Tensions of an interethnic nature need to be addressed using a multidimensional approach. The mandate of the HCNM was conceived to reflect just such a response through the application of a preventive perspective and means.[2] To this end, when determining the HCNM's mandate, it was envisaged that the 'High Commissioner [would] thus be an instrument of conflict prevention at the earliest possible stage'.[3] To achieve this end, the HCNM was to provide 'early warning' and, as appropriate, 'early action' upon the discernment of tensions involving national minority issues, particularly those that, 'in the judgment of the High Commissioner, [had] the potential to develop into a conflict within the OSCE area, affecting peace, stability or relations between participating states'.[4] Consequently, the HCNM's function was both to identify and to seek early resolution of ethnic tensions that might threaten peace and stability.

Based on OSCE principles and commitments, the HCNM works in confidence and acts independently of all parties directly involved in the tensions.[5] In his or her assessment of different situations, the High Commissioner 'will take fully into account the availability of democratic means and international instruments to respond to it, and their utilization by the parties involved'.[6]

Bearing in mind the above provisions stipulated in the mandate, one might conclude that the HCNM was created as an international instrument for security, more specifically as a conflict prevention instrument, and not as a mechanism within the human dimension. Thus, according to the mandate, the involvement of the HCNM does not extend to all minority-related issues and situations, but is limited to those having security aspects or implications.

The HCNM's mission is basically two-fold: 'first, to address and de-escalate tensions before they ignite and, second, to act as a "tripwire", meaning that he is responsible for alerting the OSCE whenever such tensions threaten to develop to such a level that he cannot alleviate them with the means at his disposal'.[7]

As indicated above, characterizations of the mandate tend to result in the rather categorical conclusion that it was created as a conflict prevention instrument, and not as a human dimension mechanism. However, the mandate's focus on conflict prevention has neither deprived the HCNM of, nor prevented him or her from becoming involved in a concomitant monitoring of human dimension commitments, including those on minority rights. This stems, first, from the interpretation of Paragraph 6 of the mandate,[8] whereby the HCNM may take into account fully the availability of democratic means and international instruments and their utilization by the parties involved. However, this implies nothing but an assessment of a range of potentially applicable monitoring-like opportunities (for example, by recommending governments to resort to them). Secondly, the HCNM cannot ignore the concept of 'comprehensive security' which defines security and cooperation within a broader formula of three baskets: political and security questions, economic and environmental cooperation, and the 'human dimension' (democratic governance, the rule of law, human rights and fundamental freedoms, and humanitarian issues).[9] Thirdly, a practical analysis of the first decade of the HCNM's activities demonstrates that the human dimension approach has become an integral part of the 'tool-box' of preventive diplomacy, which, in turn, often entails an indirect protective effect.[10]

One may safely conclude, therefore, that the mandate of the HCNM has been designed for the needs of conflict prevention, which provide a set of human dimension commitments and can be applied, with the mutual consent of the parties involved, through systems of dialogue, confidentiality and quiet diplomacy.

Evolution of the powers of the EC/EU and the OSCE

The European Community (EC) and, later, the European Union (EU), has also been involved modestly in the field in which the HCNM has been granted his or her mandate. For decades, both organizations have demonstrated a typically functional asymmetry.

On the one hand, the EC was, from its inception (1950–1957), a small club of six Western European states which, although technically focused on economic cooperation and integration, was also, broadly speaking, intent on achieving those goals in such a way as to prevent the occurrence of yet another war in Europe. European cooperation and integration after 1945 were rooted deeply in the pre-1939 failures of liberal democracy and market economy, and in the tragic lessons of the Second World War.[11] Over time, the club was gradually expanded, both in membership and in its substantive field of competence. On the other hand, the OSCE was, from its inception, a regularly held pan-European conference, which developed into an organization focused on Euro-Atlantic security and human dimensions, but with the primary aim of preventing wars. Nevertheless, in spite of differences in membership, fields and methods of action, both the EC/EU and the OSCE have shared one common perspective – the prevention of wars, autocratic governance and instability.[12] It needs to be noted, however, that infrastructure for democratic human-rights governance has, in the meantime, gradually been created by the Council of Europe (CoE), established in 1949 as a result of the same pan-European movement.[13]

As far as minority rights and human rights issues were concerned, the two organizations adopted different approaches, at different stages, and with varying results. For decades, human rights, including minority rights, were not a priority at all within the organizational and functional frameworks of the EC/EU. This is not particularly surprising in the context of the fundamentally different mandate of the EC/EU. Neither was the protection afforded to human and minority rights of a comprehensive nature, due to the predominant focus on economic integration.

However, the extension of the powers of the EC and the establishment of the EU contributed greatly to the increased visibility of human rights on the EU agenda. Part of this process and its achievements emanated from the rulings of the European Court of Justice, which, after years of reticence, acknowledged that respect for fundamental rights formed an integral part of the general principles of Community law. The protection of these rights, consonant with the constitutional traditions common to member states, had to be assured within the context and aims of the Community.[14]

Initial deficiencies, like the absence of a list of fundamental rights and the lack of an explicit provision making the observance of human rights a requirement for admission of new members, were remedied at a later stage.[15] Most notably, accession criteria were spelt out explicitly and, subsequently, a catalogue of human rights appeared with the adoption of the EU Charter of Fundamental Rights on 7 December 2000 in Nice. The future role of the Charter of Fundamental Rights of the European Union, in spite of its non-binding character, may prove to be more far-reaching than initially envisaged due to the inclusion of the Charter into the Treaty establishing a Constitution for Europe, adopted by consensus by the European Convention (in Part II) on 13 June and 10 July 2003 in Brussels. In spite of the failure of the Constitution, its successor, the Reform Treaty not only recognizes the rights, principles and freedoms contained in the Charter but accords it 'the same legal value as the Treaties'.[16] As such, it is clear that, overall, one can conclude that human rights issues have evolved within the EC/EU from a modest, concomitant aspect to one that features among the most dynamic items on its present and future agendas.

Unlike the EC/EU, the OSCE has been preoccupied with human and minority rights issues from the very beginning, as part of the human dimension (formerly known as the 'third basket') as a result of close interaction between the three 'baskets'. Although the role of the second basket (economic and environmental cooperation) was, in spite of Eastern European expectations, very modest (as a 'carrot' usually is), a link between security and human dimension issues was probably the strongest factor and, eventually, the most successful contribution of the OSCE, in bringing the Cold War to its end.

It was a few decades before the two organizations – the EC/EU and the OSCE having gradually developed their preventive approaches and human rights systems – realized that the natural thing to do was to approach one another. The end of the twentieth century has been marked, therefore, by a quest for the best possible ways of achieving peaceful coexistence, cooperation and coordination.

Enlargement of the European Union and the quality status of newcomers

On 1 May 2004, the EU experienced an enlargement of its membership with the inclusion of 10 states: two Mediterranean Republics (Malta and Cyprus) and eight countries from Central and Eastern Europe (Czech Republic, Estonia, Hungary, Latvia, Lithuania, Poland, Slovakia and Slovenia). This extended the membership of the EU from 15 to 25 states, followed by the addition of Bulgaria and Romania early in 2007, with Turkey and Croatia remaining on the waiting list and others hoping to follow.[17] Against the background of changes in membership, the question arises as to whether and how this might affect the activities of the HCNM.

In attempting to give a tentative answer to this question, one should recall a number of pertinent points. First, all the members of the EU are among the 55 participating states of the OSCE and are committed to the goals of the OSCE and the HCNM. Significantly enough, all the EU member states are also members of the CoE.[18] Second, there is nothing in the new post-enlargement situation that would absolve the office of HCNM from its responsibilities to continue to operate as an instrument of conflict prevention in regard to all 55 participating states. Third, although the HCNM has had virtually no involvement in the territories of countries 'west of Vienna', it should not be inferred from this that there is a policy of '55 minus 15'. The absence of the HCNM 'west of Vienna' was never determined by the fact of EU membership, but by a lack of sufficient prerequisites for involvement there. Thus, it would be misleading to conclude that the accession of 12 new members to the EU rendered them outside the realm of the HCNM's mandate. Just as there was no '55 minus 15' policy, likewise, there cannot be one of '55 minus 27'.

Within this context, the question of what changes the latest accessions might entail for the HCNM becomes even more valid. One way to address this question is to examine the quality status of newcomers, since this will highlight the types of problems, if any, that might be encountered by states newly admitted to the EU.

An assessment of the 12 new members of the EU prompts a distinction to be made between '10 and 2'. The latter – Malta and Cyprus – have exhibited a great deal of similarity in their evolution towards democratic governance after gaining their independence from British colonial rule. Recognized as representative democracies, respecting the rule of law and human rights, they were both admitted to the CoE shortly after attaining independence (Cyprus in 1961 and Malta in 1965).

From the perspective of the mandate of the HCNM, Malta has not posed any specific problems with regard to minorities, an assessment reaffirmed during the thorough monitoring procedure under the FCNM, and the final (positive) Opinion issued by the Advisory Committee.[19]

Similarly, Cyprus is a strong democracy with governance based upon the rule of law and human rights. However, Cyprus entered the EU with an unresolved problem in its Northern territory, which has remained under Turkish administration since 1974. Importantly, this is not only an international and constitutional problem, but it also has a bearing on the issue of national minorities. Ethnic, religious and linguistic divisions between Greek Cypriot and Turkish Cypriot communities were at the root of original tensions and the eventual armed intervention by Turkish troops. Until a viable solution is found for the coexistence of both communities, one cannot ignore the fact that, under the present circumstances, a minority of Greek Cypriots is unprotected and, in some respects, subject to rights violations. This issue was examined by the European Court of Human Rights in the judgment of *Cyprus v. Turkey* of 10 May 2001.[20] The execution of this complex judgment is under regular supervision by the Committee of Ministers.[21]

As far as the Eastern and Central European countries are concerned, the group constitutes a specific aggregate of states with a great many similarities originating from their communist legacy and their divergent experiences in historical traditions. The process of democratization of these countries is best illustrated perhaps by reference to the process of their admission to the CoE after 1989. Two major models of transition from communist rule to democracy can be identified tentatively:[22]

(1) The Iberian model: so termed due to apparent similarities with the peaceful transformation of the Iberian Peninsular states (Spain and Portugal) from autocratic governance under, respectively, Franco and Salazar.

Within this model, negotiations have prevailed over resort to the use of force, and reforms of political and economic systems of governance have been pursued with a high degree of social legitimization and power-sharing between ex-communists and groups of democratic opposition; and

(2) Other models characterized by: elements of large-scale resort to violence against democratic opposition (the 'Tiananmen Square' syndrome), the persistence of regular tensions and conflicts on ethnic and religious grounds (Balkan 'malaise' or 'Lebanese syndrome') and the continuation of governance by communist 'nomenclature' strongholds as a revamped scenario of autocratic rule under the guise of superficial democratic reforms.

It is submitted here that all newly admitted Central and Eastern European members belong to the first group/model. Significantly, they avoided openly violent conflicts and ensured, in a dialogue with ruling communist elites, a peaceful, albeit painful, transition to democracy. Not unimportant was the presence of a decent level of political culture supported by a degree of democratic tradition and past experience. All these determinants were factors conducive to initiating the reconstruction of democracy but, indispensably, were to be followed subsequently by profound and comprehensive reforms towards a market economy, notably, through privatization of the state-run sector and viable democratic governance.[23]

This characterization of the two different group models relating to Central and Eastern European states has been confirmed, with the final results evident in the admission process to the CoE.[24] This elaborate procedure, consisting of substantive and political stages of assessment, did not result in major frustrations or failure on the part of the CoE. The first wave of candidates was admitted after a relatively short duration (Hungary in 1990, Czechoslovakia and Poland in 1991), while other countries were accepted within the following few years (Lithuania, Estonia and Slovenia in 1993, and Latvia in 1995).[25] There was an understanding that these countries were expected to make a great many reforms, so that, among other things, they could ratify the European Convention on Human Rights and other treaties monitoring compliance with European standards. The latter requirements oblige states to submit themselves to a regular – and sometimes rigorous – supervision process (for example, binding judgments of the European Court with a possible adjudication of compensation). The above conclusion concerning the states belonging to the first model admitted to the CoE has been reaffirmed further in the examination of subsequent applications for membership, particularly those of states whose admission was effected largely on political rather than substantive grounds.[26]

Two conclusions can be drawn from the assessment of the quality status of new members of the EU. First, we have been dealing with states that have successfully met a single set of CoE membership criteria and have accepted post-admission monitoring procedures. In this way they have achieved democratic legitimacy, which, in turn, bolstered their bid for accession to the EU. It is in this context that one can argue correctly that the way to Brussels is through Strasbourg.[27] Hence, a state that receives a *laissez passer* to the CoE and, subsequently, to the EU, continues to be subject to the CoE monitoring mechanisms.

Second, there is a need to continue and to strengthen the application of the membership criteria to any subsequent candidates for EU membership. This speaks in favour of the further development of post-admission monitoring mechanisms and their scrupulous application with regard to both 'old' and 'new' members. For its part, the EU should consistently apply its own accession criteria, bearing in mind the results of the monitoring mechanisms of the CoE and the OSCE.

Accession of new members and their legacies in regard to minority issues

These conclusions concerning the quality status of new EU member states are insufficient if we fail to examine the end result of enlargement from another perspective: namely, that of the legacies of newcomers. One cannot reasonably claim that accession will solve all problems relating to minorities. Clearly, national minority issues will remain the subject of disputes, tensions and even conflicts. What, then, are the new and potentially sensitive dimensions to these issues that the 10 new members to the EU might bring with them? Three types of situations, notably from the perspective of the HCNM, can be identified tentatively.

The first is where a set of minority problems, which were already in existence to a limited extent in the 'old' EU, is increased and intensified due to the expansion in volume. This particular dimension is illustrated by the example of Roma communities whose size, when viewed collectively in Slovakia and Hungary, assumes a far greater potential for conflict than before. The EU will have to decide whether such a dimension will require its engagement and, if so, what form this should take, bearing in mind the principle of subsidiarity. The Office of the HCNM, in its conflict prevention capacity, will be bound to follow these developments.

The second dimension consists of situations of interstate tensions concerning minorities, which, following enlargement, have become internal matters of the EU. These may be interstate tensions between new members (for example, Slovakia and Hungary) or between new and old EU members (for example, Slovenia and Austria). The question of how to approach and manage such tensions is yet another issue for discussion and commendably coordinated action of the HCNM and the EU.

The third dimension concerns minorities that have been brought into the EU by the accession of its new members, and the relations of those minorities with their neighbours or with other third states (for instance, Latvian and Estonian relations with Russia, or Cyprus with Turkey). It may be assumed that, due to constitutional arrangements within the EU, such situations fall under external policy and, as such, become problems for Brussels.

The above overview of possible 'added dimensions' to problems and situations brought about by the accession of new member states to the EU demonstrates the need for a thorough debate before any specific action is taken. One should, however, be aware that, with regard to all three of the above-mentioned dimensions, the EU's *acquis* is currently weak and insufficient. A more solid legal base and policy guidelines for EU action in the field of national minorities are essential, particularly in light of the EU's increasing involvement in human rights and fundamental freedoms. The fate of accession criteria is a good reflection of emerging challenges.

Accession to the European Union criteria and a 'minority clause'

In June 1993, the Copenhagen European Council, while recognizing the right of the countries of Central and Eastern Europe to join the EU, stipulated in regard to non-economic criteria that 'membership requires that the candidate country has achieved stability of institutions guaranteeing democracy, the rule of law, *human rights and respect for and protection of minorities*'.[28] With this stipulation, the European Council reached a decision on its extension towards the East. For the first time, the accession process was to deal with former communist countries. Significantly, the Central and Eastern European candidates were both similar (autocratic states) and dissimilar (as 'communist' economies they had virtually no experience of operating within a market economy) to Spain and Portugal. Therefore, the Community clarified that accession by any new members ought to be based on economic criteria, as well as on guaranteeing a stable democracy, the rule of law, human rights and respect for minorities. During the accession procedure, the EU could rely to a large extent on the regular monitoring mechanisms of the CoE and the OSCE. This was a realistic approach given that political admission/accession criteria to the CoE and the EU are actually identical, though formulated in different ways and with different emphases.[29]

As far as the issue of minorities is concerned, their protection by the CoE has traditionally been regarded as part of human rights.[30] However, the Copenhagen criteria upgraded the position of the minorities issue by separating it and putting it on an equal footing with human rights ('human rights *and* respect for and protection of minorities')[31]. Furthermore, requiring both 'protection of' and 'respect for' minorities – with the latter meaning broadly both promotion of respect and prevention of discrimination – strengthens this formulation. Thus, the EU spelt out explicitly the absolute necessity of 'respect for and protection of minorities' in terms of admission criteria. None of the four politico-legal requirements have ever been contested and, more significantly, together they constitute a concrete normative basis for the lengthy admission process of Central and Eastern European countries into the EU. These requirements should continue to serve as admission criteria, notably because of the strong message contained therein concerning the importance of the minorities issue for the stability of democracy and its powerful impact on the domestic law and policies of candidate states.

However, in the course of recent standard setting in the EC/EU, the issue of minorities was not regarded as having the same importance. There is no mention of any specific minority rights provisions in the EU Charter of Fundamental Rights adopted during the Nice meeting of the European Council (7–8 December 2000).[32] Further disappointment was discernible in other major reforms of the EU, which envisaged the drafting of a European Constitution. On 10 July 2003, the Convention on the Future of Europe, set up under the Laeken Declaration (2001) and termed 'the European Convention', completed its task and submitted a draft of the European Constitution, which included in Chapter II the entire and unmodified text of the EU Charter of Fundamental Rights.[33] Regrettably, the draft submitted by the European Convention was silent on the rights of minorities, in spite of some earlier positive developments.

However, prior to the signing of the Treaty establishing a Constitution for Europe in Rome on 29 October 2004, EU heads of state and government gave their agreement to the text of a number of modified provisions of the Draft Constitution for Europe, at their meeting on 18 June 2004. Among the amended provisions was the reformulation of Article I-2, which stated that:

> The Union is founded on the values of respect for human dignity, liberty, democracy, equality, the rule of law and respect for human rights, **including the rights of persons belonging to minorities**. These values are common to the Member States in a society in which pluralism, non-discrimination, tolerance, justice, solidarity and equality between women and men prevail.[34]

In spite of the failure of the Constitution, this provision was carried over into its successor, the Reform Treaty, signed in Lisbon in December 2007.[35]

It is safe to say that the ratification of such a clause would strengthen, not only the legal basis and standing of minority issues within the EU legal order, but equally would bring the mandate of the OSCE High Commissioner closer to the EU field of action. Given its mandate, the Office of the High Commissioner cannot remain indifferent to these developments in EU standard-setting and operational programmes on and for national minorities. Generally, the more the EU becomes involved in the minority issues of its members and citizens, and areas within its neighbourhood, the more it can learn and benefit from the experience of the High Commissioner in conflict prevention and the protection of minority rights.

In fact, during the whole post-Maastricht stage of the evolution of the EU, human rights issues were strengthened significantly. The Amsterdam Treaty proclaimed solemnly that the EU is founded on 'the principles of liberty, democracy, *respect for human rights and fundamental freedoms,* and the rule of law',[36] these principles being common to all member states.[37] The enumeration of these principles is essential in itself but is more than just 'window dressing': they have been linked to the EU membership criteria.

It was precisely this philosophy that was behind the observation concerning the 'missing link', at issue in the Reform Treaty. The Treaty sets forth that: 'Any European State which respects the values referred to in Article 1a and is committed to promoting them may apply to become a member of the Union.'[38] This provision sets out conditions of eligibility and procedures for accession to the EU by direct reference to the EU's values. The legal significance of such an approach is emphasized further by the provisions of Article I-9 Reform Treaty, whereby a European decision might be adopted in the event of the Council's determination of a 'clear risk of a serious breach by a Member State of the values mentioned in Article 1a'. Likewise, a similar European decision might be adopted if the Council determines the 'existence of a serious and persistent breach by a Member State of the values mentioned in Article 1a'.[39]

In order to avoid a double-standard approach and to ensure the enhancement of the protection of minorities, the EU would have been well advised to adopt its standards for the protection of minorities and to apply those standards equally to all of its members. Consequently, the application of equal standards regarding minorities should extend to candidate states as well as to actual member states of the EU. Moreover, the experience of the CoE has confirmed the need for and the usefulness of an ongoing assessment of membership criteria after the admission of new states. Indeed, this was the reason behind the Council's establishment of two post-admission monitoring procedures – one by the Committee of Ministers and the other by the Parliamentary Assembly.[40]

Restoring explicit standards on minority rights to the EU's list of values would have permitted fair application of the arrangements for membership suspension in cases of alleged breach of the values mentioned in Article Ia.[41] However, another aspect should be noted: in Article I-8 of the Reform Treaty, the EU accedes to the European Convention on Human Rights 1950 (ECHR) and states that the fundamental freedoms guaranteed therein 'shall become general principles of EU law'.[42] Of particular relevance to minority rights is Article 14 ECHR, which cites 'association with a national minority' as one of the prohibited grounds of discrimination; national minorities appear again, autonomously, in Article 1 of Protocol No. 12 to the ECHR, which applies the current expansive and indefinite grounds of prohibited discrimination in Article 14 to the exercise of any legal right and to the actions (including the obligations) of public authorities.[43] Again, this presents at least an opportunity for closing the gap or remedying inconsistencies between European law made in Brussels and its Strasbourg counterpart.

Another important question concerned the external relations of the EU. According to Article I-24 of the Reform Treaty, the issue of values in the EU's external action was referred to in Paragraph 1 to the effect that:

> The Union's action on the international scene shall be guided by the principles which have inspired its own creation, development and enlargement, and which it seeks to advance in the wider world: democracy, the rule of law, **the universality and indivisibility of human rights and fundamental freedoms**, respect for human dignity, the principles of equality and solidarity, and respect for the principles of the United Nations Charter and international law.[44]

Although this provision avoids explicit mention of a minority clause, it contains many prerequisites that indicate that minority issues are part of the principle of 'indivisibility of all human rights', notably in the context of the so-called holistic approach to human rights.[45] Yet another encouraging aspect was included in Article I-24 Reform Treaty whereby:

> The Union shall ensure consistency between the different areas of its external action and between these and its other policies. The Council of Ministers and the Commission, assisted by the High Representative of the Union for Foreign Affairs and Security Policy, shall ensure that consistency and shall cooperate to that effect.[46]

Although this creates a convenient basis for preventing inconsistencies and double standards, it would have been preferable to include a clause on minority rights in order to generate far-reaching effects beyond the EU itself, rendering those standards applicable throughout the rest of Europe and elsewhere. From the perspective of the HCNM, it is important to take into account that a number of OSCE participating states will not – either in the near future or perhaps ever – become members of the EU. Therefore, an explicit minority clause promotes the application of EU values and standards in those countries through trade, other agreements and policies. The same is true with regard to the whole range of conventions along the lines of the so-called Lomé Convention of 1976 which linked trade issues with those of human rights in EU relations with developing countries. Precisely for these reasons, a legal stipulation is required to provide for a single and consistent system of values and standards.

Due to these and other developments, the HCNM was encouraged to undertake an official intervention by addressing a letter to the Irish Minister for

Foreign Affairs during the latter's presidency of the EU.[47] In it, the HCNM advocated the continued validity of the so-called Copenhagen political criteria for EU membership and proposed two alternative amendments to the Draft Constitution aimed at restoring an express clause on the rights of minorities. It was proposed that Article I-2 on 'The Union's Values' be supplemented, following the words 'respect for human rights', by either 'including minority rights' or 'including the rights of persons belonging to minorities'. The latter option was proposed in order to eliminate any possible arguments implying a collective dimension of 'minority rights'.[48]

It should be noted that both the proposed versions for an amendment to the Draft Constitution reflected yet another commendable change to the original formulation of the Copenhagen criteria for membership. While the latter enumerated separately 'democracy, the rule of law, human rights and respect for and protection of minorities', the former recommended inserting 'the rights of persons belonging to minorities' as an integral part of human rights (this is why the term 'human rights' is followed by the word 'including' to restore an adequate balance to the formulation of Article I-2 by pointing out that the rights of persons belonging to minorities constitute merely a *lex specialis* regulation within the international law of human rights.

The Reform Treaty has retained the language proposed in Article I-2 of its predecessor. The Reform Treaty now features Section 3, providing for a new Article 1a of the TEU, which lists the Union's Values as follows:

> The Union is founded on the values of respect for human dignity, freedom, democracy, equality, the rule of law and respect for human rights, **including the rights of persons belonging to minorities.**[49]

Concluding remarks

The enlargement of the EU has brought with it the potential for a great many changes and the opportunity for significant improvements. However, the accession of 12 new members does not absolve the Office of the HCNM from its responsibilities in the whole OSCE area, in respect of all EU and non-EU members, and it will continue to exercise its conflict prevention mandate in relation to tensions involving national minorities. Some of the minority problems addressed by the HCNM will also become part of the EU's involvement, though from a different perspective. Therefore, in its continued involvement in newly admitted states, the Office of the HCNM naturally would expect to enjoy enhanced support from the EU. Thus, greater synergy between the High Commissioner and the EU may legitimately be anticipated as a result of their combined powers, achievements and established authority. It is anticipated that the issue of national minorities will not disappear from the EU's agenda. In view of the inadequacy of approaching minority issues solely from the point of view of the general human rights structure and its fundamental principles of equality and non-discrimination, there is a need both for reaffirmation and further development of standards concerning minorities. Specific policies must be adopted and pursued, notably in sectors such as media, education, languages, public participation and socio-economic life.

In such a common area of activity under differently conceived mandates, the Office of the High Commissioner has been particularly aware in its own activities of the prominent position given to the minority issue in the Copenhagen criteria with regard to accession by candidate states. These criteria have become a powerful tool in generating appropriate changes in domestic law and policies on national minorities. This is why the High Commissioner was so concerned about the absence of the minority clause of the Copenhagen criteria in the Treaty establishing a Constitution of Europe drawn up by the European Convention in 2003. His criticism stemmed from the fear that the accession criteria might lose their persuasive impact. Furthermore, there was a perceptible risk that double standards might be applied: those pertaining to candidate and other third states, and those pertaining solely to actual members. These anxieties prompted him to submit his official intervention to the EU Irish presidency, successfully advocating the restoration of a stipulation on the minority issue in the Constitution prior to its finalization and signature.

All in all, it seems legitimate to expect that effective promotion and protection of minority rights will bring about the full integration of minorities within the systems of governance based on democracy, the rule of law and human rights, including the rights of persons belonging to national minorities. It is the great challenge of our generation to build a new Europe, one that is not just a European *house*, that is, not simply as a structural design but, rather, a European *home*; in other words, a place where its inhabitants can enjoy life with dignity, freedom and solidarity.

Notes

1. Established in 1973 as a Conference on Security and Cooperation in Europe (CSCE) and developed into the Organization for Security and Cooperation in Europe (OSCE) in 1995 with, initially, 35 participating states, and presently numbering 55; this increase was generated by the collapse of the USSR, Czechoslovakia and Yugoslavia. For more detailed information see W. Kemp *et al.* (eds), *OSCE Handbook*, 3rd edn (Vienna: Secretariat of the Organization for Security and Cooperation in Europe, 1999).
2. See Concluding Document of Helsinki – The Fourth Follow-up Meeting, 10 July 1992 (hereinafter, Helsinki Document 1992), Chapter II. For more on the background of the post see R. Zaagman and H. Zaal, 'The CSCE High Commissioner on National Minorities: Prehistory and Negotiations', in A. Bloed (ed.), *The Challenges of Change: The Helsinki Summit of the CSCE and its Aftermath* (Dordrecht: Martinus Nijfhoff, 1994), 95–111.

3. Helsinki Document 1992, *supra* note 2, Chapter II, Paragraph 2.
4. *Ibid.*, Paragraph 3.
5. *Ibid.*, Paragraph 4.
6. For more on the content of the mandate see R. Zaagman, 'The CSCE High Commissioner on National Minorities: An Analysis of the Mandate and the Institutional Context', in Bloed (ed.), *The Challenges of Change, supra* note 2, 113–75; J. Packer, 'The OSCE High Commissioner on National Minorities', in G. Alfredsson *et al.* (eds), *International Human Rights Monitoring Mechanisms: Essays in Honour of Jacob Th. Möller* (The Hague: Martinus Nijhoff Publishers, 2001), 641–56; and Y.I. Diacofotakis, *Expanding Conceptual Boundaries: The High Commissioner on National Minorities and the Protection of Minority Rights in the OSCE* (Athens/Brussels: Sakkoulas, Bruylant, 2002), 15–29.
7. See OSCE, *Annual Report on OSCE Activities 2003: Security and Cooperation for Europe* (Vienna: OSCE, 2003). at 138. More information on the HCNM's mandate may be found at <www.osce.org/hcnm/>
8. Helsinki Document 1992, *supra* note 2.
9. For more details see T. Buergenthal, 'CSCE Human Dimension: The Birth of a System', in A. Clapham and F. Emmert (eds), *Collected Courses of the Academy of European Law*, Volume I-2 (Dordrecht: Martinus Nijhoff, (1992), 160–209; and M. Estébanez, 'The OSCE and Human Rights', in R. Hanski and M. Suksi (eds), *An Introduction to the International Protection of Human Rights: A Textbook*, 2nd revised edn (Turku/Åbo: Institute of Human Rights, Åbo Akademi University, 1999), 329–50.
10. In this respect, some scholars conclude in even stronger terms by pointing out that 'it goes without saying that the HCNM is deeply involved in the monitoring of minority rights in those states where he has become active', A. Bloed, 'Monitoring the Human Dimension of the OSCE', in Alfredsson *et al.* (eds), *International Human Rights Monitoring Mechanisms, supra* note 6, 633–41, at 636.
11. Western Europe took the idea of preventing war and maintaining peace extremely seriously, as reflected in the words of the UN Charter: '[T]o save succeeding generations from the scourge of war, which twice in our lifetime has brought untold sorrow to mankind' (Paragraph 1 of the Preamble to the UN Charter).
12. Prevailing submissions among social scientists are that 'no wars have been fought between independent nations with elective governments'; 'democracies do not fight each other'; and 'wars (or even military conflicts short of war) are non-existent (or very rare) among democracies'. For more information on this debate see N. Gleditsch, 'Democracy and Peace: Good News for Human Rights Advocates', in D. Gomien (ed.), *Broadening the Frontiers of Human Rights: Essays in Honour of Asbjørn Eide* (Oslo: Scandinavian University Press, 1993), 290–1.
13. On post-war endeavours to create an economic and political union see A.H. Robertson, *European Institutions: Cooperation, Integration, Unification*, 3rd edn (London: Stevens and Sons, 1973).
14. See *Internationale Handelsgesellschaft*, Case C-11/70.17.12.1970; and *Nold*, Case C-4/73. 14.05.1973. For comments see A. Rosas, 'The Legal Sources of EU Fundamental Rights: A Systemic Overview', in N. Colneric, D. Edward, J.-P. Puissochet and D. Ruiz-Jarabo Colomer (eds), *Une communauté de droit: Festschrift für Carlos Rodríguez Iglesias* (Berlin: Berliner Wissenschafts-Verlag, 2003), 87–90.
15. A.H. Robertson and J. G. Merrills, *Human Rights in Europe: A Study of the European Convention on Human Rights*, 3rd revised edn (Manchester: Manchester University Press, 1993). The authors noted, however, a large number of matters within the powers of the Communities that were directly concerned with human rights,

particularly in the social and economic spheres. More broadly on human rights policy in the European Union, see P. Alston and J.H.H. Weiler, 'An 'Ever Closer Union' in Need of a Human Rights Policy: The European Union and Human Rights', in P. Alston *et al.* (eds), *The EU and Human Rights* (Oxford: Oxford University Press, 1996), 3–66.

16. Treaty of Lisbon amending the Treaty on European Union and the Treaty establishing the European Community (hereinafter, Reform Treaty), Article I-8, amending Article I-6 TEU.

17. For more information on the accession process see H. Hörburger, (ed.), *EU-Enlargement – Our Neighbour's Views* (Marburg: Schüren Verlag, 2003).

18. Since the admission of Monaco in October 2004, the Council of Europe has been made up of 46 member states (see <www.coe.int>). This brings the CoE to the limits of its European membership, with Belarus as the only state remaining outside the CoE but which is a participating state of the OSCE. Further differences with the OSCE concern two North American states (USA and Canada), the Holy See (untypical, non-territorial, subject of international law) and five Central Asian Republics (Kazakhstan, Kyrgyzstan, Tajikistan, Turkmenistan and Uzbekistan). For more information see <www.osce.org>

19. One major problem stems from the Maltese reservation whereby there are no minorities on the island in the sense of the Framework Convention. In its Resolution 2001 (7), however, the CM recommended to continue the dialogue with the Advisory Committee on the existing, albeit limited, potential for application of certain provisions of the FCNM.

20. Appl. No. 25781/94.

21. See F.G.E. Sundberg, 'Control of Execution of Decisions under the ECHR – Some Remarks on the Committee of Ministers' Control of the Proper Implementation of Decisions Finding Violations of the Convention', in Alfredsson *et al.* (eds), *International Human Rights Monitoring Mechanisms*, *supra* note 6, 561–85.

22. For more on the models of transformation see K. Drzewiecki, 'Protection of Human Rights and the Formation of Civil Society', in R. Dehousse (ed.), *An Ever Larger Union? The Eastern Enlargement in Perspective* (Baden-Baden: Nomos Verlagsgesselschaft, 1998), 47–53; and K. Drzewicki, 'Institutional Arrangements for Pan-European Human Rights Protection', in Z. Kędzia, A. Korula and M. Nowak (eds), *Perspectives of an All-European System of Human Rights Protection. The Role of the Council of Europe, the CSCE and the European Communities. Proceedings and Recommendations of an International Conference. Poznań, Poland, 8–11 October 1990* (Kehl: N.P. Engel, 1991), 75–8.

23. While political and economic reforms enjoyed the support of large sectors of the populations in the region, this cannot be said about changes made to the system of accepted values. Social values remained largely intact. See K. Drzewicki, 'Implementation of Social and Economic Rights in Central and Eastern Europe Transforming from Planned Economy to Market Economy', *Nordic Journal of International Law* 64 (1995): 373–9.

24. For more information on the admission requirements see K. Drzewicki, 'Future Relations between Eastern Europe and the Council of Europe', in A. Bloed and W. de Jonge (eds), *Legal Aspects of a New European Infrastructure* (Utrecht: Europa Instituut and Nederlands Helsinki Comité, 1992), 41–60.

25. In the case of Latvia, a certain amount of prolongation of the admission procedure was due largely to the need for the adoption of a number of amendments to legislation concerning acquisition of citizenship.

26. Admittedly, admission of some countries reflected a priority given to political urgency over substantive assessment of the three admissibility criteria, a priority politically exercised by the EU itself.
27. See Drzewicki, 'Protection of Human Rights', *supra* note 22.
28. Emphasis added. Further conditions for accession were: a functioning market economy, incorporation of the Community *acquis* and adherence to the various political, economic and monetary aims of the EU. The Madrid European Council in 1995 also added the importance of adapting the applicant countries' administrative structures to create the conditions for a gradual harmonious integration. Regrettably, although it has an extensive catalogue and far-reaching human dimension commitments (see Copenhagen Document of 1990), the OSCE has no criteria similar to those of the CoE; it thus applies UN-like membership criteria: respect for obligations and to be 'peace-loving countries'.
29. According to the Statute of the Council of Europe, a member state must ensure: pluralist and representative democracy, the rule of law, protection of human rights and fundamental freedoms and show its peaceful and European vocation. See Drzewicki, 'Future Relations', *supra* note 24.
30. It was only in 1995 that the CoE adopted a distinct and binding instrument with its own supervisory mechanism: the Framework Convention for the Protection of National Minorities (in force since 1998). See an extensive study on this issue by P. Thornberry and M. Estébanez, *Minority Rights in Europe: A Review of the Work and Standards of the Council of Europe* (Strasbourg: Council of Europe Publishing, 2004), 39–135.
31. Emphasis added.
32. See G. Pentassuglia, *Minorities in International Law: An Introductory Study* (Strasbourg: Council of Europe Publishing, 2002), 150–1. The exceptions are the provisions on equality before the law and a general clause prohibiting discrimination, which traditionally pervade the whole human rights system.
33. See the full text on the EU website (www.zeuropa.eu.int/) and in *Human Rights Law Journal* 24(1–4) (2003): 1–79.
34. Emphasis in bold in this instance occurs in the original document of the Conference of the Representatives of the Governments of the Member States, Brussels, 16 June 2004, CIG 81/04, at 7 (Annex 2) and it indicates the modified parts of the provision.
35. Treaty of Lisbon amending the Treaty on European Union and the Treaty establishing the European Community, Article I-3.
36. Emphasis added.
37. Article 6, Paragraph 1, ex Article F, Paragraph 1.
38. Article I-57 DRT, amending Article 49 TEU.
39. Article I-9 Reform Treaty, amending Article I-7 of the TEU, Paragraphs 1 and 2.
40. For more on the development of monitoring procedures see A. Drzemczewski, 'Monitoring by the Council of Europe', in Alfredsson *et al.* (eds), *International Human Rights Monitoring Mechanisms, supra* note 6, 525–32.
41. See Article I-9 Reform Treaty, amending Article I-7 of the TEU.
42. Article I-8 Reform Treaty, amending Article 6 TEU.
43. Note that Protocol 12 ECHR entered into force in April 2005 but, in December 2007, had still not been signed by the following states: Andorra, Bulgaria, Denmark, France, Lithuania, Malta, Poland, Sweden, Switzerland and the UK. All except Andorra and Switzerland are EU member states.
44. Article I-24 Reform Treaty, inserting Article 10A into the revised Title V TEU on General Provisions on the Union's External Action. Emphasis added.

45. In a similar context, such provisions were termed 'open-ended references to human rights', which would anyway be perfectly able to absorb new developments such as the EU Charter. For more on this submission, see J. Wouters, 'The EU Charter of Fundamental Rights: Some Reflections on its External Dimension', *Maastricht Journal of European and Comparative Law* 1 (2001): 3–10; Institute for International Law, Working Paper No. 3, May 2001: 6–8.
46. Article I-24 Reform Treaty, inserting Article 10A into the revised Title V TEU on General Provisions on the Union's External Action.
47. See the letter of 14 January 2004 from Ambassador Rolf Ékeus, the OSCE High Commissioner on National Minorities to H. E. Mr Brian Cowen, Minister for Foreign Affairs of Ireland.
48. It seems that similar proposals for inclusion of a minority clause in Article I-2 of the Draft Constitution for Europe were submitted by the governments of Hungary and Romania. For the wording of Article 1 of the Framework Convention whereby the collective rights were excluded, see Explanatory Report thereto, Paragraphs 30–31.
49. Reform Treaty. Article I-3. Emphasis added.

7
The Future of Minority Issues in the Council of Europe and the Organization for Security and Cooperation in Europe

Rainer Hofmann

Introduction

The visibility of minority issues within the wider Europe has increased significantly over the past 10 to 15 years. Initially, attention was drawn to these issues in the context of the violent dissolution of the former Yugoslavia. Interethnic conflict in other parts of Europe, including the Caucasus, only reinforced the view that minority issues required urgent engagement. A number of strategies were adopted to manage this process. These included the creation of a network of bilateral treaties, the confirmation of existing borders and the addressing of minority issues and the establishment of the OSCE High Commissioner on National Minorities (HCNM). In addition, the Council of Europe (CoE) accelerated its involvement in minority rights protection.

With the inclusion of several of the states of Central and Eastern Europe in the EU – states that were initially the subject of action under these mechanisms – and the likely addition of further new members, the question arises as to whether the focal point on minority issues will lie with the OSCE, the CoE, or will gradually migrate to the EU. This chapter will consider the development of minority rights standards thus far, the practice of implementing these standards and the future of their protection within the wider Europe. It predicts that the CoE will continue to play a leading role in this area, especially if the European Court of Human Rights (ECtHR) gradually becomes less reluctant over time to address minority issues as minority issues.

New standards for minority issues in the Council of Europe and the OSCE

The major purpose of this chapter is to identify those substantive standards of minority issues that have evolved – or are evolving – in Europe over the last 17 years as a result of, on the one hand, the Copenhagen Document on the Human Dimension of the Conference on Security and Cooperation in Europe (CSCE) of 29 June 1990 and the decision taken in July 1992 to establish the position of an HCNM and, on the other hand, the pertinent activities pursued within the CoE; the (cautious) jurisprudence of the ECtHR, based on the European Convention on Human Rights and Fundamental Freedoms (ECHR); and the monitoring activities of the Committee of Ministers and the Advisory Committee under the Framework Convention for the Protection of National Minorities (FCNM). However, before embarking upon this task of the identification of the substantive standards presently applicable to minority issues in Europe, it seems worthwhile briefly to indicate the main features of the procedural aspects of standard setting, both within the CoE and the OSCE, since the various procedures have an impact on the legal – and political – quality of the substantive standards.

Standard setting

Procedural aspects of standard setting

Before describing and assessing the procedural aspects of standard setting with regard to minority issues in the CoE and the OSCE, it is appropriate to make a few general introductory remarks on the various ways and means of standard setting in international law, and the legal implications of these differing approaches.

At the outset, it should be recalled that standard setting in the field of minority rights as part of the international protection of human rights is effected by various actors and by different means: first, there are states – the traditional subjects of international law – which, by enacting domestic legislation, create the factual and legal basis for identifying international standards, which, by a comparative analysis, might eventually come to constitute customary international law. Since World War II, states have continued to bind themselves, at least from a legal perspective, by ratifying bilateral and multilateral treaties, the contents of which contribute significantly to the identification of international legal standards.

Second, there are international organizations, founded by states in order to pursue and implement common goals such as, for example, the international protection of human rights in general and minority rights in particular, as provided for in the respective treaties or other legal documents establishing such international organizations as independent subjects of international law. These international organizations are often given the task of constituting a forum to draft international treaties aimed specifically at the international protection of human rights, including minority rights. Again, analysis of the contents of such treaties – both the founding treaties of an international organization or, in particular, the treaties or other legal documents drafted within and under the auspices of such international organizations – might help to identify applicable international standards in the field of human and minority rights.

The task of identifying these international standards is facilitated further if the relevant treaties provide for some kind of international monitoring mechanism for controlling and ensuring respect for the legal obligation incurred by states parties to implement and apply, within their domestic jurisdiction, the provisions of the treaties. The 'strongest' kind of international supervision – from a legal point of view – consists of a judicial system, for example, the one provided for under the ECHR, whereby a court, acting upon individual complaints or applications by states parties, is entitled to hand down binding judgments based upon a binding interpretation of the applicable treaty provision. To put it more clearly: such systems result in hard jurisprudence based upon hard law. It should be mentioned, however, that these systems give rise to a setback with regard to the task of identifying standards: since judgments are concerned, by their very nature, with individual cases, it might be difficult to establish standards which are of a general character, unless there exists a kind of settled jurisprudence based upon a number of judgments.

The 'weakest' – again, from a strictly legal point of view – kind of international supervision consists of a non-judicial system, for example the one provided for under the OSCE with its 1990 Copenhagen Document, or that spawned by the CoE with its European Committee against Racial Intolerance (ECRI). Under this type of set-up, a body of experts either produces (legally non-binding) guidelines on specific issues, as formulated by experts upon invitation by the HCNM, or it authors country-specific reports (that are not based upon a legal document and have no legally binding force), as is the case with ECRI. Such guidelines and general country reports might indeed contribute to identifying international standards, particularly if they refer to binding legal instruments. Their major relevance, however, lies in their potential to influence domestic policies and legislation – in other words, in their persuasive authority.

A third – intermediate – kind of international supervision consists of a quasi-judicial system, akin to the one provided for under the FCNM, by which a body of experts authors a (legally non-binding) opinion, based upon an examination and assessment of the legal and factual compliance of a state party with its obligations flowing from participation in an international treaty, that then serves as the basis for a legally binding decision of the competent monitoring body (in the case of the FCNM, the resolutions of the Committee of Ministers). As long as such resolutions reflect the major thrust of the underlying opinion, these documents together might be considered as soft jurisprudence based upon hard law and will, as a rule, contribute significantly to identifying general standards.

Council of Europe

As regards CoE instruments and mechanisms of potential relevance for identifying general standards for minority issues, this chapter focuses on two instruments: the European Convention on Human Rights (ECHR) and the Framework Convention for the Protection of National Minorities (FCNM).

(a) Standard Setting under the European Convention on Human Rights

For many decades, the ECHR – as interpreted and applied by the ECtHR and, until the entry into force of the 11th Additional Protocol in 1999, the European Commission of Human Rights (EComHR) – had only very limited relevance for the protection of the rights of persons belonging to national minorities. Until the mid-1990s, the only pertinent statement was formulated by the ECtHR in the *Alta River* case,[1] when it said that Article 8 ECHR might have some impact for the protection of the traditional lifestyle of persons, in that case the Saami of Northern Norway. Since the judgment of the ECtHR in the *Buckley* case in 1996,[2] the situation has changed slightly: a growing body of jurisprudence has been concerned with the protection of the traditional lifestyle of national minorities, in particular British Roma and 'Travellers', under Article 8 ECHR,[3] or the protection of the freedom of opinion and association of persons belonging to national minorities under Articles 10 and 11 ECHR.[4]

The substance of these decisions[5] will be taken into account in the following section on the (evolving) substantive standards concerning the protection of national minorities. At this point, it is, however, important to stress that the failure of political initiatives, in the early 1990s, to draft an Additional Protocol to the ECHR on the rights of persons belonging to national minorities[6] resulted in quite a fundamental change with regard to the procedure and character of standard setting on minority issues in the CoE. The entry into force of an Additional Protocol on Minority Rights in the ECHR had invested the ECtHR with the competence and responsibility to hand down binding judgments on a wide range of minority issues – in other words, hard jurisprudence based upon hard law. The decision taken at the 1993 Vienna Summit of CoE Heads of State and Governments to draft a Framework Convention for the Protection of National Minorities, resulted eventually in a fundamentally different procedure and character of standard setting: as was mentioned above, and is to be developed in the following subsection, standard setting under the FCNM, while being based on (relatively) hard law, results in soft jurisprudence, for example, the country-specific resolutions of the Committee of Ministers based upon the pertinent opinions of the Advisory Committee.

This is not the place to discuss the political wisdom of this decision; however, it should be emphasized here that the ECHR does provide the ECtHR, in many of its articles, with sufficient legal basis to contribute considerably to the protection of the rights of persons belonging to national minorities and, by extension, to produce hard jurisprudence based upon hard law. Admittedly, this is the case with regard to only a limited number of issues, but these are issues of considerable relevance for national minorities. As will be demonstrated later, however, the ECtHR has been rather reluctant to make use of this potential, at least to date, and has not acted as an important player in this regard, as is reflected in the judgments concerning aspects of the traditional lifestyle of British Roma and 'Travellers' and, in particular, the *Gorzelik* case. In the end, there might be good reasons of judicial policy for such a cautious approach; it is, however, important to stress here that the ECtHR could play a much more proactive role and thereby contribute to standard setting on minority issues by producing more hard jurisprudence based on hard law.

(b) Standard Setting under the Framework Convention for the Protection of National Minorities (FCNM)

Since the monitoring system under the FCNM has been described in detail elsewhere,[7] a short overview is considered sufficient here.

According to Articles 24 and 26 FCNM, the ultimate evaluation of the implementation of the FCNM by the states parties is entrusted to the Committee of Ministers, which is assisted in this task by an Advisory Committee. Under Article 25 FCNM, the states parties are required to submit a report, giving full information on legislative and other measures taken to give effect to the principles of the FCNM, within one year of its entry into force for the relevant state party. Further reports are due every five years and whenever the Committee of Ministers so requests.

Immediately upon receipt of a state report by the Secretariat of the CoE, it is transmitted to all members of the Advisory Committee. The members of the country-specific working group set up within the Advisory Committee will set out an opinion based on information contained in the state report and received from other sources[8] before and during a visit to the relevant country.[9] At the end of these country visits, the working group identifies the essential aspects of its draft opinion, which is then transmitted to the plenary of the Advisory Committee for a first reading and, with amendments agreed, put to a vote. It should be stressed that the opinions to date have always been adopted with overwhelming majorities, quite often unanimously.[10] The opinions are then transmitted to the governments concerned and the Committee of Ministers.

The actual discussion of the opinions of the Advisory Committee, as well as of the comments that both the government of the relevant state party and other governments wished to submit, take place in the Rapporteur Group on Human Rights (GR-H), a sub-body of the Committee of Ministers. The opinions are introduced by representatives of the Advisory Committee, who are also invited to be available for an ensuing exchange of views with the members of the GR-H.

In its conclusions and recommendations, the resolutions adopted show clearly that the Committee of Ministers is guided to a large extent by the opinions of the Advisory Committee. Thus, it is important to stress that all of the country-specific resolutions so far adopted by the Committee of Ministers reflect clearly the pertinent findings of the Advisory Committee.[11] In fact, it must be emphasized that all the issues identified by the Advisory Committee, in the concluding remarks of its opinions, as being of particular relevance were also addressed in the conclusions of the Committee of Ministers. Furthermore, the Committee of Ministers consistently recommended to states that they take appropriate account of the various findings of the Advisory Committee, to continue their dialogue with it and to keep it regularly informed of new developments, in particular about the measures taken in order to implement the conclusions and recommendations set out in the resolutions. Together, not only do these practices illustrate the high relevance that the Committee of Ministers accords the Advisory Committee in the context of the monitoring of the implementation of the state obligations flowing from the FCNM, but they also justify the conclusion that the findings of the Advisory Committee should be regarded as particularly relevant with regard to the interpretation of the substantive provisions of the FCNM and might, consequently, be considered as soft jurisprudence based upon hard law.

The OSCE

The first OSCE HCNM, Max van der Stoel, called upon internationally recognized independent experts to draft recommendations and guidelines on issues and themes that had become the subject of his attention during his work in a number of states. The main purpose of these recommendations and guidelines was to achieve an appropriate and coherent application of relevant minority rights in the OSCE area that could serve as a reference for policy- and law-makers in OSCE member states. They sought to clarify the content of existing rights and aimed to provide states with some practical guidance on developing policies and laws that fully respected the letter and spirit of internationally agreed standards. At the same time, although they were by no means legally binding documents, they intended to reflect existing international legal standards and might be considered a kind of soft law. They are, in any case, a useful, if only additional, means to identify precisely the legally binding international standards.

As of now, the following documents have been elaborated: the 1996 Hague Recommendations regarding the Education Rights of National Minorities, the 1998 Oslo Recommendations regarding the Linguistic Rights of National Minorities, the 1999 Lund Recommendations on the Effective Participation of National Minorities in Public Life (as further developed by the 2001 Warsaw Guidelines to Assist National Minority Participation in the Electoral Process), the 2003 Guidelines on the Use of Minority Languages in the Broadcast Media and the 2006 Recommendation on Policing in Multi-Ethnic Societies.[12]

Conclusion

Based upon the preceding considerations, it seems justified to determine the following documents as sources for the subsequent task of identifying (evolving) substantive standards for minority protection. First, we might examine the judgments of the ECtHR, which constitute hard jurisprudence based upon hard law. However, these are still rather infrequent and, in view of the limited relevance of the ECHR for minority issues, relate to only a small number of rights relevant for minority protection. Therefore, the major source for the findings of the following section will be the opinions of the Advisory Committee, which, at least insofar as they are explicitly or implicitly supported by the Committee of Ministers, constitute soft jurisprudence based upon hard law, and concern all the rights that are relevant for minority protection. An additional source is the recommendations and guidelines on issues of particular relevance for minority protection that are elaborated by independent experts upon request by the HCNM, notwithstanding that they constitute only soft law (if they can be said to constitute 'law' at all).

The evolving substantive standards for minority protection

Based upon an analysis of the above-mentioned sources, this section will group the (evolving) substantive standards for minority protection into the following categories: aspects of the right of national minorities to a distinct identity, non-discrimination and effective equality, intercultural dialogue and tolerance, political rights, media rights, linguistic rights, educational rights, participatory rights and free transboundary contacts. In the context of the discussion of these different aspects, this section will also approach the question of whether recent developments within the CoE and the OSCE have contributed to the clarification of two very basic and quasi-eternal issues of international minority protection: who is entitled to minority rights (in other words, the issue of the definition of the term 'national minority'), and are those rights individual or group rights?

The right to a distinct identity: self-identification, protection and promotion of the distinct identity, and prohibition against forced assimilation

The right to – and respect for – the distinct identity of a national minority is the most fundamental right in the field of minority protection; it is its *Grundnorm*, its *conditio sine qua non*. There can be no minority protection without recognition of this right and it seems that there is no controversy as to the existence of this rule as such. The real and equally fundamental problem is, however, the following: under what conditions does a group of persons constitute a national minority in the sense of international law?

The definition of the term 'national minority' This leads to the above-mentioned issue of the definition of the term 'national minority' in international law. It is well known that, notwithstanding serious efforts, there does not exist, as yet, any such definition that is accepted by all concerned, in particular by the states and minorities themselves. However, there seem to be some basic elements that are common to all such definitions and that may be traced back to the proposal made by Francesco Capotorti in the late 1970s:[13] they usually include some objective and one subjective elements. The basic element is, of course, constituted by the distinctive features of the relevant minority group as contrasted with the majority population of a given state, for example, history, language, religion, ethnicity, lifestyle, and so on. Additional objective elements are the numerical inferiority of minorities and their non-dominant position. The necessary subjective element can be labelled the common will of a group's members to preserve their distinctive characteristics, which is generally implicit in cooperative efforts to preserve and to defend their ethnic, religious or linguistic identity, and their refusal to be assimilated by the majority.

While these elements seem to be recognized in principle by all parties concerned, the current discussion relates primarily to the following two issues: does a group need to have resided for a minimum period of time on the territory in which they live (in other words, do they need to have a certain historic link to that territory) and do persons who have the citizenship of the state in which they – and the minority – live count as belonging to a national minority? This question is also known as the issue of 'old versus new minorities' and it should be stressed that the recent practice of European states within the CoE and the OSCE does not allow for any clear answer but only for the identification of a certain trend.

Ultimately, however, this issue seems to boil down to the question of whether the existence of the subjective element (to recall, the common will of the persons concerned to preserve what they consider to constitute their distinct identity) is sufficient, or whether state authorities have the power to deny such persons recognition as a national minority based on the argument that (some of) the objective criteria are not fulfilled. In other words, we are faced with the issue of 'self-identification versus state recognition'.

Analysis of the recent practice of the ECtHR under the ECHR and the Advisory Committee and Committee of Ministers under the FCNM does not provide any clear guidance on these issues. As concerns the jurisprudence of the ECtHR, it must be pointed out that it did not need to address this problem until its judgment in the *Gorzelik* case and, even here, the Court dealt with the issue only in the context of its control of the 'margin of appreciation' held by national authorities when applying the provisions of the ECHR. In the series of cases involving aspects of the traditional lifestyle of Travellers in the United Kingdom,[14] the question was not whether the latter had recognized this group as a national minority, but only whether the measures applied (resulting in a lack of adequate camping sites for 'Travellers' or the prohibition of the Horsmonden Horse Fair) constituted unlawful interferences with the right to private life protected under Article 8 ECHR or the freedom of assembly guaranteed under Article 11 ECHR, or whether they could be considered to remain within the 'margin of appreciation' and, as such, did not amount to any violation of these provisions. As is well known, the ECtHR decided in favour of the latter alternative.

Similar questions had to be dealt with by the ECtHR in cases involving the prohibition of a political party, the refusal to register an association, and the prohibition of a manifestation by an organization, all of which was aimed at hindering the interests of national minorities. Again, at least in the *United Communist Party of Turkey*, *Sidiropoulos* and *Ilinden* cases, the issue to be decided was not the recognition of a Kurdish minority in Turkey or a Macedonian minority in Greece or Bulgaria, but was limited – at least in the understanding of the ECtHR – to the question of whether the relevant measures were proportionate and, as such, compatible with Article 11 ECHR, or whether the national authorities had transgressed their 'margin of appreciation'; here, the ECtHR decided in favour of the former alternative and declared that the measures involved constituted violations of Article 11 ECHR.

The real test, however, was expected to be the *Gorzelik* case. Here, the Polish authorities had refused to register an association that, according to its memorandum of association, identified itself as an association of the 'Silesian national minority'. The major argument of the Polish authorities, which had been accepted by the Polish Supreme Court in its judgment of 18 March 1998, was that the Silesians did constitute a distinct 'ethnic group' but not a 'national minority' in the sense of Polish domestic law. The Polish authorities and courts also relied on the argument that such registration would result in a non-existent national minority taking advantage of the privileges conferred on genuine national minorities, in particular under the 1993 Elections Act.[15] The ECtHR, sitting as a Grand Chamber, proclaimed that, in view of the very different factual situations of national minorities in Europe, there was no uniform pan-European definition of the term 'national minority'; therefore, the ECtHR concluded that it was both inevitable and consistent with the adjudicative role vested in them for the national courts to be left with the task of interpreting the notion of 'national minority' as distinguished from an 'ethnic minority', within the meaning of the Constitution, and assessing whether the applicants' association qualified as an 'organisation of a national minority'.[16]

It was therefore decisive whether the refusal to register the association represented by Mr Gorzelik was justified as 'necessary in a democratic society'.[17]

In this regard, the Grand Chamber first declared that the Polish authorities had acted within their margin of appreciation:

> The Court accepts that the national authorities, and in particular the national courts, did not overstep their margin of appreciation in considering that there was a pressing social need, at the moment of registration, to regulate the free choice of associations to call themselves an 'organisation of a national minority', in order to protect the existing democratic institutions and election procedures in Poland and thereby, in Convention terms, to prevent disorder and to protect the rights of others.[18]

The second and final point, then, was to assess whether the refusal to register the association was proportionate; in this regard, the Grand Chamber stressed that this measure was aimed not at preventing the association from pursuing its goal to promote the distinctive features of the Silesians but only at preventing the abuse of privileges contained in Polish electoral law:

> [I]t was not the applicants' freedom of association *per se* which was restricted by the State. The authorities did not prevent them from forming an association to express and promote distinctive features of a minority but from creating a legal entity which, through registration under the Law on Associations and the description it gave itself in paragraph 30 of its memorandum of association, would inevitably become entitled to a special status under the 1993 Elections Act. Given that the national authorities were entitled to consider that the contested interference met a 'pressing social need' and given that the interference was not disproportionate to the legitimate aim pursued, the refusal to register the applicants' association can be regarded as having been 'necessary in a democratic society' within the meaning of Article 11 §2.[19]

When analysing this judgment, it becomes clear that the ECtHR was not prepared to contribute substantially to the discussion on the conditions under which a distinct group of persons constitutes a national minority in the legal sense. Instead, it sought for ways and means to circumvent that decision – an attitude for which, while there might indeed exist valid arguments of 'judicial policy', there remains a deep feeling of an opportunity missed.

However, when comparing the judgments in *United Communist Party*, *Sidiropoulos* and *Ilinden*, on the one hand, and *Gorzelik*, on the other hand, the following conclusions might be drawn: the intention to take measures in favour of a national minority does not *per se* threaten national security and, therefore, does not *as such* justify restrictive state measures. In contrast, *Gorzelik* dealt with a situation where the registration of an association would have implied the enjoyment of certain privileges, of certain positive measures, not mandated by international law. It seems that the ECtHR is of the opinion that, at least in the latter circumstances, it is not only the primary responsibility of the national authorities to decide whether a certain group fulfils the necessary criteria to benefit from such positive measures but that, in such situations, the ECtHR will give the national authorities a wider margin of appreciation. Although this is, of course, pure speculation at this moment in time, it is possible to imagine that the ECtHR would only declare a state's margin of appreciation to have been overstepped if the refusal of the national authorities to register an association as an organization of a national minority was, in light of the factual situation, clearly unjustified or arbitrary and therefore, in comparison with other (recognized) national minorities, amounted to discrimination. To give an example taken from German electoral law: to accord a political party representing the Danish minority the privilege provided for in Section 6(6) of the German Federal Elections Act 1956 (exemption from a 5 per cent electoral threshold), but not to accord it to a political party representing the Frisian or Sorbian minority, would be clearly unjustified.

To conclude the analysis of the *Gorzelik* judgment, it is important to note that the Grand Chamber held explicitly that, since international law does not provide for a generally accepted definition of the term 'national minority', states are under no international legal obligation to apply, in their domestic legal order, any such specific definition derived from international law, but can instead rely on any definition provided for in their domestic legislation. This might indeed be interpreted as if the ECtHR had joined the ranks of those who argue that 'self-identification' alone is not sufficient to oblige states to recognize a certain group as a national minority (at least as long as such a status results in certain benefits or privileges or positive measures). Indeed, there might be good reason to accept that, while the decision of whether a group constitutes a national minority usually depends upon the self-identification of the persons within that group, in a situation where a particular state has enacted legislation that accords positive measures to national minorities, it is to be expected that the question of whether a group constitutes a national minority for the purpose of that legislation is taken by the authorities of that state (state recognition). In the latter case, it would also be anticipated that the decision would be subject to only limited international scrutiny, whether it was arbitrary or not.

It is interesting to note that the approach of the ECtHR here is reminiscent of the one taken by the Advisory Committee in situations in which states refuse to recognize certain groups as national minorities for the purposes of the FCNM. The Advisory Committee considers that, in the absence of a definition of the term 'national minority' in the FCNM, the states parties must examine the personal scope of application to be given to the FCNM in each country. The position of any government, as reflected in declarations made upon ratification or statements in a state report on the personal applicability of the FCNM, is deemed to be the outcome of this examination. In this respect, states parties have a certain margin of appreciation to take into account the specific circumstances prevailing in their countries; on the other hand, this margin of appreciation must be exercised in accordance with general principles of international law and the fundamental principles set out in Article 3 FCNM. In particular, the implementation of the FCNM must not be a source of arbitrary or unjustified distinctions. Therefore, the Advisory Committee considers it part of its duty to verify that no such arbitrary or unjustified distinctions have been made. If, in the view of the Advisory Committee, this was clearly the case, that assessment would be spelled out in the relevant country-specific opinion.[20] In less obvious situations, the Advisory Committee calls upon the states parties involved to discuss the issue with representatives of the group concerned – as it did in its opinion on Poland with respect to the Silesians.[21]

Finally, as regards the issue of 'new' minorities (that is, those persons who are not citizens of their country of residence or who belong to a group that has only recently moved to the area in which it resides), no clear answer can be given. The situation under domestic law seems to be quite varied, as is also reflected in the pertinent statements made by states parties to the FCNM, either upon its ratification or in the relevant state report. Whereas the ECtHR has not, as yet, been faced with this problem, the Advisory Committee has consistently held that some of the provisions of the FCNM – such as Article 11(3), with its explicit reference to areas traditionally inhabited by persons belonging to a national minority – would obviously be applicable only to 'old' minorities. By contrast, it is clear that Article 6 FCNM applies to 'all persons living on the territory' of a given state party and, thus, also to persons belonging to 'new' minorities.[22] Furthermore, it is possible to argue that other provisions, such as Articles 3, 5, 7 and 8 FCNM could, at least in certain circumstances, be applicable to persons belonging to 'new' minorities. Based upon this analysis, the Advisory Committee has opted for a flexible approach that makes it possible to consider the inclusion of persons belonging to such groups in the application of the FCNM on an article-by-article basis. As a result, the Advisory Committee expressed its opinion that the competent state authorities should consider the issue in consultation with those concerned.[23] It made it clear, however, that it favours strongly an inclusive approach, and would either welcome such an approach by a government[24] or support developments towards the *de facto* implementation of such an approach.[25]

Likewise, the Office of the HCNM has consistently favoured an inclusive approach; on the other hand, it should be noted that it has been concerned mainly with situations in which 'new' minorities had only recently come into existence, usually as a result of the restoration of the independence of the Baltic states, or the dissolution of the Soviet Union, or the break-up of former Yugoslavia. Indeed, there might be good reason to differentiate between, on the one hand, persons who came to a specific area as citizens of the state of which that area was then a part and – even more so – who were born there and, on the other hand, persons who moved to another country as migrant workers and perhaps never expected to develop close links with the state in which they resided. However, it seems justified to state that there is an increasing tendency to favour an inclusive approach that would make it possible, be it on a right-by-right or article-by-article basis, to extend the personal applicability of minority rights to persons belonging to such 'new' minorities.

Two further issues should be mentioned briefly. In the international discussion on the term 'national minority' there is no unanimous view as to whether persons who differ from the majority population in only their religion are to be considered as forming a national minority and, as such, fall under the personal scope of application of international instruments aimed at the protection and promotion of the distinct identity of national minorities. At least as regards the FCNM, this issue has been solved by the practice of the Advisory Committee: in its opinion on Cyprus, it dealt extensively with the situation of the Maronites and, to a lesser extent, with other religious groups such as the Latin and Armenian communities,[26] and made it clear that it considered religious minorities to be national minorities for the purposes of the FCNM. This position was later shared by the Committee of Ministers.

Another highly controversial issue is the question of whether persons belonging to an 'indigenous people' can be considered a 'national minority' in the legal sense. In this regard, the Advisory Committee was of the opinion that the recognition of a group of persons as an 'indigenous people' did not exclude persons belonging to that group from benefiting from the protection afforded by the FCNM, since the fact that a group of persons might be entitled to one form of protection does not, of itself, justify their exclusion from other forms of protection.[27]

Right to self-identification and prohibition of forced assimilation   The right to freely identify oneself as a person belonging to a national minority – or not belonging to a national minority – and the corresponding prohibition on any measures of forced assimilation constitute further fundamental principles of international law with respect to national minorities, as reflected in Paragraph 32 of the 1990 OSCE Copenhagen Final Document and Articles 3(1) and 5(2) FCNM.[28]

As yet, there does not seem to have evolved a large number of standards in this respect. The one exception concerns the issue of collecting personal data for statistical purposes, particularly in the context of censuses. It is clear, at least in the case of Article 3(1) FCNM, that while persons should be encouraged to identify themselves as belonging to a national minority, it would be incompatible with this provision to include in census questionnaires mandatory questions concerning a person's ethnic or national affiliation. On a more general plane, it was held that any collection of such data on the ethnic or national affiliation of a person by state officials without the explicit and informed consent of the persons concerned would be incompatible with Article 3(1) FCNM.

The obligation to protect and to promote the distinct identity of national minorities, including by positive measures.   Another cornerstone of international minority rights law is the (legal) obligation of states to protect and to promote the distinct identity of national minorities, including by positive measures, as reflected in Paragraphs 32 and 33 of the 1990 OSCE Copenhagen Final Document and Articles 4(2) and 5(1) FCNM.[29]

Throughout its practice, the Advisory Committee has welcomed state measures in support of the cultural activities of national minorities and stressed that they should be identified and implemented in close contact with the persons concerned.[30] Moreover, it has called strongly for a solution to the Saami land rights issue,[31] and noted with concern the absence of adequate stopping sites for 'Travellers' and the effect this has on the latter's ability to maintain and develop their culture and to preserve the essential elements of their identity, of which travelling is an important aspect.[32] The Advisory Committee has also expressed its deep concern about the forced dissolution of Horno, a municipality with Sorbian character, aimed at allowing lignite quarrying to continue, as such measures are likely to make the preservation of the Sorbian minority identity more difficult due to the population displacement involved.[33]

Minority rights: individual or group rights?   For some time, scholars and politicians have discussed whether minority rights should be construed as group rights – as was the case during the inter-war period under the system of minority rights protection established by the League of Nations – or as individual rights, which nonetheless might be exercised in community with others. For the time being, this discussion seems to be closed at the European level: both the 1990 OSCE Copenhagen Final Document, in its Paragraph 32, and Article 3(2) FCNM state clearly that persons belonging to national minorities may exercise their rights individually or in community with others. Thus, they recognize the possibility of a joint exercise of those rights and freedoms, but this is distinct from the notion of 'group' or 'collective' rights. The fact that this discussion seems to be more or less closed is also reflected in the fact that the issue has never been raised in the opinions of the Advisory Committee.

In addition, it should be stressed that this situation corresponds to the vast majority of domestic legal systems in Europe: with very few exceptions, such as Hungary and Slovenia, OSCE and CoE member states construe their domestically guaranteed minority rights as individual rights, although these might be exercised in community with others.[34] It must be stressed, however, that there are no international legal impediments to a state according collective or group rights to the national minorities residing on its territory.

Non-discrimination and effective equality

The prohibition of discrimination and the right to effective equality are not only a fundamental element of international human rights law in general, but are also of obvious and particular relevance for persons belonging to national minorities. In the European context, this was already reflected clearly in Paragraphs 31 and 33 of the 1990 OSCE Copenhagen Final Document and Article 4 FCNM[35] and was strengthened further upon entry into force of the 12th Additional Protocol to the ECHR. This added to the accessory right already provided for in Article 14 ECHR an independent right to non-discrimination, similar to that found in Article 26 of the International Covenant on Civil and Political Rights.

The Advisory Committee has stressed consistently that Article 4 FCNM requires not only the enactment of legislation protecting all persons against discrimination, both by public authorities and private entities, but also effective remedies against such acts of discrimination.[36] In addition, it noted the existence of wide discrepancies, in some countries, between government statistics concerning the number of persons belonging to those national minorities and the estimates of the national minorities themselves. Since the absence of accurate data could seriously hamper the ability of the state to target, implement and monitor measures ensuring the full and effective equality of persons belonging to national minorities, the Advisory Committee has called upon governments to identify ways and means of gathering reliable statistical data,[37] even in states where, in view of the historical context and the particularly sensitive political and security climate, exhaustive statistical data pertaining to national minorities cannot be collected.[38] More specifically, the Advisory Committee has stressed that, in some countries, Roma are disproportionately affected by a broad range of socio-economic problems. Therefore, it has welcomed pertinent government action in that area and stressed that, when implementing such programmes, particular attention should be paid to the situation of Roma women.[39]

Finally, while refraining from addressing general issues of citizenship legislation, the Advisory Committee has welcomed legislative developments that, in some states, have contributed to the elimination of difficulties faced in an inequitable manner by persons belonging to national minorities as regards attempts to invoke relevant norms in order to clarify citizenship issues.[40]

Intercultural dialogue and tolerance

The obligation of states to promote intercultural dialogue and interethnic tolerance, which includes, at times, having to respond to acts of incitement to racial hatred, anti-Semitism, xenophobia and persecution based on the victims' affiliation with particular groups, belongs to the universally accepted norms of general international law. In Europe, this is reflected in particular in Paragraphs 30 and 40 of the 1990 OSCE Copenhagen Final Document, Article 6 FCNM[41] and in the work carried out by ECRI.

Notwithstanding these principles of international law, the existence of pertinent domestic legislation, and the almost unanimous view of politicians of the necessity to combat such incidents, the Advisory Committee has identified, as an apparently rather widespread and disconcerting phenomenon, ongoing discrimination against Roma in many societal settings, for example, in admission to places of entertainment and in the field of employment and housing.[42] It has also noted with concern instances of physical violence or threats against Roma and the existence of anti-Roma sentiment among members of police forces amounting to acts of police brutality against Roma.[43]

This serious situation has been aggravated further by the fact that some media continue to present information in such a way as to strengthen existing negative stereotypes of minorities, and in particular the Roma. Consequently, the Advisory Committee has called upon governments consistently to support measures aimed at promoting accurate and balanced reporting on minority questions, while recognizing the relevance of freedom of expression as the most fundamental basis for any democratic society.[44]

Finally, in line with the above-mentioned wide scope of personal applicability of Article 6 FCNM, the Advisory Committee has identified a number of serious problems faced by non-citizens, including asylum-seekers and migrant workers. These pertain, in particular, to incidents of xenophobia, discrimination as concerns access to work and remuneration, over-representation in special schools for under-achievers and, correspondingly, under-representation at institutions of secondary and tertiary education.[45]

Freedom of religion and political rights (freedom of assembly, association, expression, thought and conscience)

It is a truism that freedom of religion and political rights such as freedoms of assembly, association, expression, thought and conscience are the very basics of any truly democratic society. Moreover, in view of the special situation of national minorities, they have particular relevance for persons belonging to such minorities. Therefore, it is important that they are guaranteed not only in the pertinent articles of the ECHR, but also in those referred to in Paragraph 32 of the 1990 OSCE Copenhagen Final Document and protected under Articles 7 and 8 FCNM.[46]

As regards freedom of religion, there seems to be little specific practice concerning the special situation of national minorities. The main point might be that, under both the OSCE principles and the FCNM, it has been recognized that 'religious' minorities constitute 'national' minorities in the legal sense.[47] Moreover, as the ECtHR held in the *Metropolitan Church of Bessarabia* case, the refusal of state authorities to register the church of a religious minority might amount to a violation of Article 9 ECHR.[48] Whereas the pertinent practice of the Advisory Committee relates primarily to very specific issues often connected with disputes concerning the property rights of churches and other religious monuments, it is useful to stress that the Advisory Committee, while recognizing that Article 8 FCNM does not exclude all differences in the treatment of religious entities, is of the opinion that such differences must not result in undue limitations of the rights of persons belonging to national minorities.[49] More specifically, it has held that the absence of comprehensive legislation to protect individuals from religious discrimination or religious hatred has an adverse effect on persons belonging to national minorities, notably, if blasphemy laws are restricted solely to one religion.[50] Furthermore, the Advisory Committee, while considering that a state church system is not, in itself, in contravention of Article 8 FCNM and that the latter does not entail an obligation *per se* to fund religious activities, nevertheless was of the opinion that, where such funding exists, it must be in conformity with the principle of equality before the law and equal protection of the law as guaranteed under Article 4 FCNM.[51]

With respect to political rights, freedom of association and assembly have been of particular relevance for the jurisprudence of the ECtHR relating to national minorities. From the pertinent jurisprudence in the *United Communist Party*, *Sidiropoulos* and *Ilinden* cases[52] it might be deduced, as an important conclusion, that the activities of political organizations aimed at the promotion of the distinct identity of national minorities do not *per se* constitute a threat to national security and, therefore, must not be prohibited unless there are additional reasons, such as indications that such aims shall be achieved by non-democratic means. The same approach has been followed by the Advisory Committee.[53] Of particular relevance is the view that domestic legislation prohibiting, as such, the establishment of political parties of national minorities raises considerable problems as to its compatibility with Article 7 FCNM.[54]

Media rights

Media rights, including, in particular, the right to have adequate access to – and visibility in – public audio-visual media and to establish private print and audio-visual media (radio and television broadcasting) clearly are of fundamental relevance for the protection and promotion of the distinct identity of national minorities. In an era in which societal developments are largely influenced by the media, information on – and by – national minorities is essential for the understanding of these distinct identities, both by the majority population and by the persons belonging to minorities themselves. Moreover, since most national minorities in Europe have – as one, and potentially the most important, criterion to distinguish them from the majority population – their own distinct language, print and audio-visual media in those languages are also essential for the learning of such languages, as well as for keeping them alive. The fundamental importance of media rights so described is, in addition to the general provisions of Article 10 ECHR, well reflected in Paragraph 32 of the 1990 OSCE Copenhagen Final Document and Article 9 FCNM.[55]

The media rights of national minorities have, as yet, not been of any major relevance for the jurisprudence of the ECtHR under Article 10 ECHR. As regards the practice of the Advisory Committee, it is important to note that the bulk of its concerns relate to situations of insufficient access of national minorities to public radio and television broadcasting programmes and the uneven allocation of financial and other resources to different national minorities concerning private radio and television programmes.[56] However, the Advisory Committee has not yet found itself in a position to develop clear criteria that could be used to determine issues such as insufficient access to or insufficient coverage by public media, or insufficient financial funding of private radio and television programmes run by national minorities. Further work in this respect is needed, and it is to be hoped that the Advisory Committee will find the time to continue its work on thematic issues, which could eventually result in the express identification of good practices or the establishment of standards that might then assist state parties in developing their domestic legislation and practice.[57] On the other hand, it is equally important to keep in mind that the large factual and legal differences characterizing the situation of national minorities in FCNM member states might make it difficult to draft precise standards that could be universally applied. This might make it inevitable that the Advisory Committee focuses on situations that it deems to be incompatible with Article 9 FCNM.[58]

If, however, the Advisory Committee should embark upon the task of standard setting in the field of audio-visual media, valuable guidance might be found in the above-mentioned Guidelines on the use of Minority Languages in the Broadcast Media, which were elaborated under the auspices of the HCNM by independent experts, and were adopted in October 2003.[59] These guidelines – which might be considered as a kind of soft law and consist of an enumeration of general principles, such as freedom of expression, cultural and linguistic diversity, protection of identity, equality and non-discrimination – are concerned with pertinent state policies which should, *inter alia*, include the establishment of independent regulatory bodies and be geared towards the inclusion of persons belonging to national minorities; deal with the issue of regulation by emphasizing, among other things, that states may not prohibit the use of any language in the broadcast media and, while promoting the use of some languages, must not discriminate against minority languages; and assert that any regulation should take into account the factual situation and contain proposals for promoting the use of minority languages in the broadcast media.

While it seems justified to state that, as regards the situation in the audio-visual media, there remains considerable potential for substantial improvement, a more positive assessment applies in the field of print media. There are only a limited number of critical statements, concerning mainly the lack of financial support for print media owned by and catering for the needs of persons belonging to national minorities.[60]

Linguistic rights

Since most national minorities in Europe are characterized by their language, linguistic rights are of essential relevance to the protection and promotion of the distinct identity of such minorities. As a consequence, both the 1990 OSCE Copenhagen Final Document, in its Paragraph 32, and the FCNM, in its Articles 10 and 11, provide for guarantees of such linguistic rights.[61]

These linguistic rights include the right to use one's own language in the private and public sphere and, to some extent, in contact with administrative and judicial bodies; the right to use one's own name in the minority language and the right to official recognition thereof; and the right to display, in a minority language, signs of a private nature and, under specific conditions, to display topographical signs in a minority language.

At the outset, it must be stressed that the Advisory Committee has, on several occasions, expressed its view that the FCNM does not preclude the existence of a state language. It has also recognized the legitimacy of measures to promote and to protect such a state language, provided that such initiatives are implemented in such a way that the rights of persons belonging to national minorities are safeguarded.[62] With respect to several states, the Advisory Committee has concluded that there existed considerable problems as to the practical implementation of domestic legislation providing for the use of minority languages in official dealings with administrative authorities.[63] More specifically, it has welcomed explicitly legislation in Austria, Romania and Slovakia that allows for the use of minority languages in areas in which the minority population represents 10 per cent (Austria) or 20 per cent (Romania, Slovakia) of the overall population,[64] while, by contrast, it has declared a similar quota of 50 per cent as too high.[65] These statements might indeed be indicative of the future approach of the Advisory Committee as regards the formulation of generally applicable standards. Finally, it should be mentioned that the Advisory Council has emphasized that the fact that persons belonging to national minorities also have a command of the (dominant) language is not decisive, as the effective use of minority languages remains essential in consolidating the presence of minority languages in the public sphere.[66]

As to the right to use one's own name in the form of the minority language, the Advisory Committee has strongly welcomed pertinent legislative reforms[67] and criticized cases in which persons were forced to use versions of their names in the state language.[68] With respect to the right to display in a minority language 'signs and other information of a private nature to the public', it concluded that certain Estonian legislation was incompatible with Article 11(2) FCNM in that it was overly restrictive.[69] As concerns topographical signs, the Advisory Committee has welcomed relevant possibilities available in certain states,[70] but criticized in some instances a lack of clarity of the pertinent legislation.[71] More specifically, it welcomed strongly a judgment of the Austrian *Verfassungsgerichtshof*, in which it ruled that, if a national minority formed more than 10 per cent of the total population in an area over a long time, this was sufficient to entitle the inhabitants to display bilingual topographical indications.[72] The same positive assessment was given to Czech legislation by virtue of which bilingual topographical signs could be displayed providing 10 per cent of the population residing in a municipality considered themselves to be persons belonging to the national minority concerned and, of these, at least 40 per cent so requested.[73] In contrast, it considered a quota of 50 per cent an obstacle to the effective exercise of such right[74] and held – not surprisingly – the absence of any possibility to display bilingual topographical signs as being incompatible with Article 11(2) FCNM.[75] These numbers might indeed be indicative of the future formulation of generally applicable standards in this field.

In the process of formulating such standards, valuable guidance might also be drawn from the above-mentioned Oslo Recommendations regarding the Linguistic Rights of National Minorities,[76] elaborated by a group of independent experts under the auspices of the HCNM and made public in February 1998. Particular attention should be given to the explanatory report annexed to the recommendations.

Educational rights

It is a truism that education is the key to the successful protection and promotion of any cultural identity and, in particular, of that of national minorities. Since, as stated above, national minorities in Europe are usually defined by their distinct language and culture, the right to learn one's mother tongue is an absolute *conditio sine qua non* for the survival of any national minority. Therefore, educational rights are clearly of central relevance for the international protection of national minorities. However, for a state policy aimed at the preservation and promotion of the distinct identity of a national minority, the learning – and teaching – of a minority language to pupils who belong to that minority is not enough: it is equally important that these pupils are familiarized with their history and culture, as well as with the language, history and culture of the majority population. Finally, it is also necessary to acquaint pupils – and the general public – belonging to the majority population with the history and culture of the national minorities residing in the country concerned and to enable them, if they so wish, to learn minority languages.

Thus, it is clear that the issue of educational rights of persons belonging to national minorities ranks highly among the issues dealt with in the field of minority rights protection. This assessment is reflected in the pertinent provisions of Paragraphs 32 and 34 of the 1990 OSCE Copenhagen Final Document, which resulted in the guarantee of educational rights in Articles 12, 13 and 14 FCNM.[77] Furthermore, educational rights were already the subject, in 1996, of the above-mentioned Hague Recommendations regarding the Educational Rights of National Minorities, drafted by independent experts under the auspices of the HCNM.[78]

Whereas such rights have, as yet, not been of particular significance for the jurisprudence of the ECtHR,[79] this is, of course, not the case as regards the practice of the Advisory Committee. With respect to the rights guaranteed under Article 12 FCNM, the Advisory Committee has had to accord particular attention to the situation of Roma children. Not only has the Advisory Committee expressed its deep concern about the abnormally high level of absenteeism among Roma pupils,[80] but also about an apparently widespread practice of placing Roma children in special educational groups or even schools designed for mentally disabled children, due to either real or perceived language and cultural differences between the Roma and the majority. The Advisory Committee stressed that such placement should only occur when absolutely necessary on the basis of consistent, objective and comprehensive tests.[81] More generally, it noted that, notwithstanding commendable efforts to improve the situation, a shortage of both textbooks available in minority languages and of qualified teachers persists in some countries.[82]

With respect to the right to instruction of – or instruction in – the mother tongue, as provided for by Article 14 FCNM, the Advisory Committee stressed that, when decisions are taken concerning the continuation or closure of schools, particular attention must be paid to the fact that schools with instruction in, or of, a minority language contribute, by their very existence, to the preservation of the distinct identity of the national minority concerned.[83] It also emphasized that state parties should, when embarking upon a far-reaching reform of their educational system, resulting in a decrease of instruction in minority languages, introduce detailed guarantees as to how persons belonging to national minorities will be provided with adequate opportunities to be taught the minority language and to receive instruction in that language; it also recommended that such reforms should always be planned and implemented in close consultations with those primarily concerned.[84]

Finally, from a more general perspective, it should be mentioned that the Advisory Committee indicated, in some instances, that it considered a truly bilingual education to be the most appropriate way of implementing the obligations flowing from Article 14 FCNM.[85] This leads to one issue that the Advisory Committee dealt with in the course of the second cycle of monitoring: an in-depth discussion in order to formulate a general approach to educational rights. In view of the crucial importance of such rights for the protection and promotion of the distinct identity of national minorities described above, this was certainly called for. One issue was the question of whether the fundamental approach that was followed implicitly – and sometimes more explicitly – during the first cycle of monitoring, and that was based upon the assumption that pupils belonging to a national minority should be integrated as far and as fast as possible into the general educational system while providing for sufficient possibilities to learn – or to be instructed in – the mother tongue, should be continued or modified. Indeed, there might be situations where separate schools or classes constitute a viable option, provided such a system is established in accordance with the wishes of those concerned and is organized in such a way as to guarantee sufficient knowledge of the languages of both the majority and minority and does not result in segregation. The second aspect discussed relates to the question of whether the article-by-article approach followed to date by the Advisory Committee should be replaced by the so-called '4-A' scheme, as developed by Katarina Tomaszewski in her capacity as Special Rapporteur on the Right to Education of the United Nations Commission on Human Rights and subsequently adopted by the United Nations Committee on Economic, Social and Cultural Rights in General Comment No. 13. Under this scheme, the right to education comprises four elements: availability, accessibility, acceptability and adaptability.[86] In any case, there can be no doubt that standard setting in the field of educational rights is of utmost importance for the future of national minorities and the existing monitoring systems alike.

Participatory rights

The right to effective participation in cultural, economic and social life, and in public affairs is another principle essential for the proper functioning of any democratic society. In view of the potentially vulnerable situation of national minorities, it is of particular relevance for the survival of their distinct cultures and identities. This principle seems to be generally accepted, as reflected in Paragraph 35 of the 1990 OSCE Copenhagen Final Document, and by its guarantee in Article 15 FCNM.[87] It has also been the subject of the above-mentioned 1999 Lund Recommendations on the Effective Participation of National Minorities in Public Life, as specified by the quite detailed 2001 Warsaw Guidelines to Assist National Minority Participation in the Electoral Process.[88] The particular relevance of the issue of effective participation results from the correct understanding that only members of those national minorities who feel that the state in which they reside is also 'their' state – that it 'belongs to them' – will be prepared to integrate themselves fully into that state and its structures; this, in turn, will contribute to stability and peaceful minority–majority relations. To achieve this end, effective participation is clearly another *conditio sine qua non.*

In its pertinent practice, the Advisory Committee noted that, in some countries, the representation of national minorities on local, regional and central level legislative bodies was low and recommended that governments examine ways and means to improve this situation.[89] In particular, they should ensure that, if advisory or consultative bodies are established, they represent national minorities in an adequate manner.[90] More generally, the Advisory Committee underlined the relevance of territorial autonomy for the preservation and promotion of the distinct identity of national minorities,[91] which means that changes to the administrative structures of a country that might have detrimental effects on the situation of national minorities must be avoided.[92]

Furthermore, the Advisory Committee found that, in a number of countries, persons belonging to national minorities were clearly under-represented in a wide range of public sector services,[93] and that unemployment rates were often higher amongst persons belonging to national minorities.[94] In addition, it stressed that language proficiency requirements should be limited carefully to situations where they were necessary to protect a specific public interest; the same considerations applied to candidates running for elections.[95]

Finally, the Advisory Committee expressed its concern about the shortcomings that remain, notwithstanding a number of commendable efforts made by the governments concerned, with regard to the effective participation of Roma in social and economic life and the negative impact that these shortcomings have on the social and economic living conditions of this minority in general and of Roma women in particular.[96]

Attempts to identify precisely the criteria for effective participation (procedural aspects only and/or a result-oriented assessment) should figure prominently among the issues to be dealt with by the Advisory Committee in its future work on standard setting. Specific attention should also be devoted to mechanisms related to the electoral process;[97] in this context, the above-mentioned 2001 Warsaw Guidelines will provide most valuable guidance.

Free transboundary contacts

In view of the geographic distribution of most national minorities, free transboundary contacts with persons belonging to the same group are of considerable relevance for the preservation and promotion of the distinct culture of national minorities. This assessment explains the introduction of this right into Paragraph 32 of the 1990 OSCE Copenhagen Final Document and into Article 17 FCNM.[98] Notwithstanding the problems connected with some aspects of activities carried out by some kin-states,[99] the assistance of kin-states, if provided for in a non-discriminatory manner, might indeed contribute to an improvement of the situation of persons belonging to national minorities in areas such as, for example, the field of education.

Another issue highlighted in the practice of the Advisory Committee is the recent introduction, as a result of some states' accession to the European Union, of rather strict visa regimes. In this context, the Advisory Committee called upon governments to implement visa requirements for citizens of neighbouring countries in a manner that does not cause undue restrictions to the right of persons belonging to national minorities to establish and maintain contacts across frontiers.[100]

Concluding remarks

The above contribution shows the existence of mechanisms to establish generally applicable standards in the field of minority protection. However, some of them, in particular the monitoring system under the FCNM, need more time to be able to finalize such work; in view of the complex nature of this task, it is recommended that the Advisory Committee implements its intention by working on standards in the field of media, educational and participatory rights. For the foreseeable future, the resulting soft jurisprudence will constitute the backbone of this procedure of standard setting. Furthermore, it is to be hoped that the ECtHR will discontinue its rather reluctant approach to deal with the minority-related aspects of its caseload and take on a more proactive role by adding some hard jurisprudence to the soft jurisprudence produced by the Advisory Committee and the Committee of Ministers. All three organs should take due account of the previous and future standard setting within the OSCE; although certainly not binding in any legal sense, the guidelines and recommendations it has produced constitute a valuable resource for the formulation of generally applicable standards.

Notes

1. EcommHR, *G. and E. v. Norway*, Appl. Nos 9278/81, 9415/81, 03.10.1983.
2. EctHR, *Buckley v. United Kingdom*, Appl. No. 20348/92, 25.09.1996.
3. See, in particular: EctHR, *Chapman v. United Kingdom*, Appl. No. 27238/95, 18.01.2001; and EctHR, *The Gypsy Council and Others v. United Kingdom*, Appl. No. 66336/01, 14.05.2002.
4. See, in particular, ECtHR, *United Communist Party and Others v. Turkey*, Appl. No. 19392/92, 30.01.1998; EctHR, *Sidiropoulos and Others v. Greece*, Appl. No. 26695/95, 10.07.1998; EctHR, *Stankov and the United Macedonian Organization Ilinden v. Bulgaria*, Appl. Nos. 29221/95, 29225/95, 02.10.2001; and EctHR, *Gorzelik v. Poland*, Appl. No. 44158/98, 20.12.2001.
5. For reviews of the jurisprudence of the ECtHR in matters concerning national minorities see, for example, G. Pentassuglia, 'Minority Issues as a Challenge in the European Court of Human Rights: A Comparison with the Case Law of the United Nations Human Rights Committee', *German Yearbook of International Law* 46 (2003): 401–51; and R. Hofmann, 'Nationale Minderheiten und der Europäische Gerichtshof für Menschenrechte', in J. Bröhmer *et al.* (eds), *Festschrift für Georg Ress* (Köln: Heymann, 2004), 1011–26. See also R. Medda-Windischer, 'The Jurisprudence of the European Court of Human Rights', in European Centre for Minority Issues, *European Yearbook of Minority Issues* 1 (Flensburg: ECMI, 2001/2002), 487–534; R. Medda-Windischer, 'The Jurisprudence of the European Court of Human Rights', in European Centre for Minority Issues, *European Yearbook of Minority Issues* 2 (Flensburg: ECMI, 2002/2003), 445–69.

6. See, in particular, Recommendation 1201 (1993) of the Parliamentary Assembly of the Council of Europe on a Draft Protocol on Minority Rights in the ECHR.

7. See, R. Hofmann, 'The Framework Convention for the Protection of National Minorities: An Introduction', in M. Weller (ed.), *The Framework Convention for the Protection of National Minorities: A Commentary* (Oxford: Oxford University Press, 2005), 1–24, at 7–11.

8. Such sources include, in particular, reports of other monitoring bodies, such as the UN Human Rights Committee, the Committee under CERD or ECRI and of international organizations such as the OSCE; documents provided by international NGOs such as Minority Rights Group (MRG) or the International Helsinki Federation, as well as national NGOs, which, due to their specific insight, are of special relevance.

9. During the first cycle of monitoring, such visits have been conducted to the following states parties (in chronological order): in 1999, to Finland and Hungary; in 2000, to Slovakia, Denmark, Romania, Czech Republic, Croatia, Cyprus and Italy; in 2001, to Estonia, the United Kingdom, Germany, Moldova, Ukraine, Armenia and Austria; in 2002, to Slovenia, the Russian Federation, Norway, Albania, Switzerland, Lithuania and Sweden; in 2003, to Ireland, Azerbaijan, Poland, Serbia and Montenegro, the Former Yugoslav Republic of Macedonia and Bulgaria; the visit to Bosnia-Herzegovina took place in 2004. Regrettably, only the government of Spain did not invite the relevant working group to conduct a visit. In view of the specific situation in Liechtenstein, Malta and San Marino and the information available, the relevant working groups felt that their work on the state reports could be completed without country visits. Moreover, in September 2005, the Advisory Committee visited Kosovo as provided for by the specific Agreement concluded between UNMIK and the Council of Europe; on this issue, see R. Hofmann, 'Protecting Minority Rights in Kosovo', in K. Dicke *et al.* (eds), *Weltinnenrecht: Liber amicorum Jost Delbrück* (Berlin: Duncker and Humblot, 2005), 347–79. As concerns the second cycle of monitoring, which started for some countries in spring 2004, country visits to the following states parties had been conducted, as of 1 July 2006: Croatia, Hungary, Moldova, Czech Republic and Estonia in 2004; Italy, Slovenia, Finland and Romania in 2005; and Germany, Norway, Armenia, the Russian Federation and Ireland in 2006.

10. As of 1 July 2006, the Advisory Committee had adopted the following 34 opinions during the first cycle of monitoring: on 22 September 2000 on Denmark, Finland, Hungary and Slovakia; on 30 November 2000 on Liechtenstein, Malta and San Marino; on 6 April 2001 on Croatia, Cyprus, Czech Republic and Romania; on 14 September 2001 on Estonia and Italy; on 30 November 2001 on the United Kingdom; on 1 March 2002 on Germany, Moldova and Ukraine; on 16 May 2002 on Armenia and Austria; on 12 September 2002 on Albania, Norway, the Russian Federation and Slovenia; on 21 February 2003 on Poland, Serbia and Montenegro, and Spain; on 28 May 2004 on Bosnia and Herzegovina, Bulgaria and the Former Yugoslav Republic of Macedonia. Thus, the Advisory Committee has, as concerns the first cycle of monitoring, concluded its work on 34 out of 38 states parties – the state report by Portugal, which was due on 1 September 2003, was received on 23 December 2004, whereas the first state reports of the Netherlands, Latvia and Georgia are due on 1 June 2006, 1 October 2006 and 1 April 2007, respectively. It should also be mentioned that, on 24 November 2006, the Advisory Committee adopted its first opinion on Kosovo. On 1 October 2004, the Advisory Committee adopted its first opinions under the second cycle of monitoring, namely on

Croatia and Liechtenstein; they were followed by opinions on Denmark, Hungary and Moldova (on 9 December 2004); on Czech Republic, Estonia and Italy (on 24 February 2005); on Slovakia and Slovenia (on 25 May 2005); on Malta and Romania (on 24 November 2005); on Finland, Germany and San Marino (on 2 March 2006); and on Armenia and the Russian Federation (on 12 May 2006). All these opinions are available at <http:///www.coe.int/T/E/human_rights/minorities>

11. As of 1 July 2006, the Committee of Ministers had adopted resolutions, as concerns the first cycle of monitoring, with respect to the following states parties: Denmark and Finland (on 31 October 2001); Hungary and Slovakia (on 21 November 2001); Liechtenstein, Malta and San Marino (on 27 November 2001); Croatia and Czech Republic (on 6 February 2002); Cyprus (on 21 February 2002); Romania (on 13 March 2002); Estonia and the United Kingdom (on 13 June 2002); Italy (on 3 July 2002); Armenia, Germany and Moldova (on 15 January 2003); Ukraine (on 5 February 2003); Norway (on 9 April 2003); the Russian Federation (on 10 July 2003); Lithuania, Sweden and Switzerland (on 10 December 2003); Austria (on 4 February 2004); Ireland (on 5 May 2004); Azerbaijan (on 13 July 2004), Poland and Spain (on 30 September 2004); Serbia and Montenegro (on 17 November 2004); Albania and Bosnia and Herzegovina (on 11 May 2005); on the Former Yugoslav Republic of Macedonia (on 15 June 2005); Slovenia (on 28 September 2005); and Bulgaria (on 5 April 2006). Moreover, on 21 June 2006, it adopted its resolution on Kosovo. As concerns the second cycle of monitoring, the Committee of Ministers adopted resolutions on Croatia (28 September 2005); on Liechtenstein and Moldova (on 7 December 2005); on Denmark and Hungary (on 14 December 2005); on Estonia (on 15 February 2006); on the Czech Republic (on 15 March 2006); on Italy and Slovenia (on 14 June 2006); and on Slovakia (on 21 June 2006). All these resolutions are available at <http://www.coe.int/T/E/human_rights/minorities>

12. All accessible at <www.osce.org/hcnm/documents.html>

13. F. Capotorti, 'Study on the Rights of Persons belonging to Ethnic, Religious and Linguistic Minorities', UN Doc. E/CN.4/Sub.2/384/Rev. 1, 1979.

14. See the judgments in the *Buckley*, *Chapman* and *Gypsy Council* cases, *supra* notes 2, 3 and 3, respectively.

15. See Paragraph 36 of the ECtHR judgment in the *Gorzelik* case, *supra* note 4.

16. *Ibid.*, Paragraph 70.

17. Within the meaning of Article 11(2) ECHR.

18. See Paragraph 103 of the ECtHR judgment in the *Gorzelik* case, *supra* note 4.

19. See *ibid.*, paragraph 106.

20. See, for example, Paragraphs 17–22 of the Opinion on Albania, where the Advisory Committee held that the *a priori* exclusion of the Egyptians as a group that had resided for centuries in Albania from the personal scope of application of the FCNM was incompatible with Article 3, FCNM ACFC/INF/OP/I(2003)00, 18.02.2002; and Paragraphs 13–25 of the (first) Opinion on Denmark, where the same conclusion was reached with respect to, *inter alia*, the Roma (ACFC/INF/OP/I(2001)005, 31.10.2001) – a conclusion that was explicitly confirmed in the pertinent Resolution of the Committee of Ministers. In view of the continued unwillingness of the Danish authorities to grant protection to the Roma under the FCNM, the Advisory Committee repeated and thus confirmed its above conclusion in Paragraphs 50–53 in its (second) Opinion on Denmark (ACFC/INF/OP/II(2004)005, 11/05/2005), which was again backed by the Committee of Ministers in its (second) Resolution on Denmark.

21. See Paragraph 28 of the Opinion on Poland, ACFC/INF/OP/I(2004)005, 30.09.2004; see also, for example, Paragraphs 12–20 of the Opinion on Austria concerning inhabitants of Vienna of Polish origin, ACFC/INF/OP/I(2002)009, 07.11.2002; Paragraphs 14–18 of the (first) Opinion on Romania concerning the Csangos, ACFC/INF/OP/I(2002)001, 10.01.2002; Paragraphs 24–25 of the (first) Opinion on Slovenia concerning the German-speaking minority, ACFC/INF/OP/I(2005)002, 14.03.2005 – a concern echoed in Paragraph 36 of the (second) Opinion on Slovenia, ACFC/INF/OP/II(2005)005, 01.12.2005; Paragraphs 23–24 of the Opinion on Spain concerning the population of Ceuta and Melilla, ACFC/INF/OP/I(2004)004, 30.09.2004; Paragraphs 13–19 of the Opinion on Sweden concerning the inhabitants of Scania and Gotland, ACFC/INF/OP/I(2003)006, 25.08.2003; Paragraphs 24–25 of the Opinion on the Former Yugoslav Republic of Macedonia concerning Bosniacs and Egyptians, ACFC/INF/OP/I(2005)001, 02.02.2005; Paragraphs 13–16 of the Opinion on Ukraine concerning the Rusyins, ACFC/INF/OP/I(2002)010, 27.11.2002; and Paragraphs 11–16 of the Opinion on the United Kingdom concerning the Cornish people, ACFC/INF/OP/I(2002)006, 22.05.2002. All these opinions can be accessed electronically via the CoE website at <http://www.coe. int/t/e/human_rights/minorities/Country_specific_eng. asp#P829_44467>

22. See, for example, Paragraph 35 of the Opinion on Austria, *supra* note 21; Paragraph 76 of the (second) Opinion on Denmark, *supra* note 20; Paragraphs 137–140 of the (first) Opinion on Germany, ACFC/INF/OP/I(2002)008, 12.09.2002; Paragraph 40 of the (first) Opinion and Paragraph 78 of the (second) Opinion on Italy, ACFC/INF/OP/I(2002)007, 03.07.2002 and ACFC/INF/OP/II(2005)003. 25.10.2005, respectively; Paragraph 36 of the Opinion on Norway, ACFC/INF/OP/I(2003)003, 13.02.2003; and Paragraph 37 of the Opinion on Sweden, *supra* note 21.

23. See, for example, Paragraph 20 of the Opinion on Austria, *supra* note 21; Paragraph 25 of the Opinion on Bosnia and Herzegovina, ACFC/INF/OP/I(2005)003, 11.05.2005; Paragraph 18 of the (first) Opinion on Germany, *supra* note 22; Paragraph 14 of the (first) Opinion on Hungary, ACFC/INF/OP/I(2001)004, 14.09.2001; Paragraph 17 of the (first) Opinion on Italy, *supra* note 22; Paragraph 29 of the Opinion on Poland, *supra* note 21; Paragraph 24 of the Opinion on Serbia and Montenegro, ACFC/INF/OP/I(2004)002, 02.03.2004; Paragraph 24 of the Opinion on Switzerland ACFC/INF/OP/I(2003)007, 21.08.2003; and Paragraph 25 of the (first) and Paragraphs 40–41 of the (second) Opinion on Slovenia, *supra* note 21.

24. See, for example, Paragraph 14 of the Opinion on the United Kingdom, *supra* note 21.

25. See, for example, Paragraph 20 of the Opinion on Azerbaijan, ACFC/INF/OP/I (2004)001, 26.01.2004; Paragraph 17 of the (first) and Paragraphs 27–30 of the (second) Opinion on Croatia, ACFC/INF/OP/I(2002)003, 06.02.2002 and ACFC/INF/OP/II(2004)002, 13.04.2005, respectively; Paragraphs 25–29 of the (second) Opinion on the Czech Republic, ACFC/INF/OP/II(2005)002, 26.10.2005; Paragraph 17 of the (first) and Paragraphs 25–27 of the (second) Opinion on Estonia, ACFC/INF/OP/II(2005)001, 22.07.2005; and Paragraph 16 of the Opinion on Sweden, *supra* note 21.

26. See Paragraphs 18–21 of the Opinion on Cyprus, ACFC/INF/OP/I(2002)004, 21.02.2002; see also Paragraph 19 of the (first) Opinion on Armenia with respect to the Yesidi, ACFC/INF/OP/I(2003)001, 15.01.2003.

27. See Paragraphs 21–29 of the (first) Opinion on Finland (Saami). ACFC/INF/OP/I (2001)002. 06.07.2001; Paragraphs 9 and 19 of the Opinion on Norway (Saami). *supra* note 22; Paragraph 26 of the (first) Opinion on Russia (numerically small nations of the north), ACFC/INF/OP/I(2003)005, 10.07.2003; and Paragraph 18 of the Opinion on Sweden (Saami), *supra* note 21.

28. On Article 3(1) FCNM see the commentary by H.J. Heintze, 'The Principle of Non-Intervention: A Link to Human Rights', in Weller (ed.), *The Framework Convention*, *supra* note 7: 107–37; and on Article 5(2) FCNM the commentary by G. Gilbert, 'Non-assimilation: The Development of Identity', in Weller (ed.), *The Framework Convention*, 172–5.

29. On Article 4(2) FCNM see the commentary by G. Alfredsson, 'The Principle of Equality', in Weller (ed.), *The Framework Convention*, 141–52; and on Article 5 (1) FCNM see Gilbert, 'Non-assimilation', *supra* note 28.

30. See, for example, Paragraphs 24–27 of the Opinion on Austria, *supra* note 21; Paragraphs 60–67 of the (second) Opinion on the Czech Republic, *supra* note 25; Paragraphs 27–28 of the (first) and Paragraphs 60–62 of the (second) Opinion on Estonia, *supra* note 25; Paragraphs 25–28 of the (first) Opinion on Germany, *supra* note 22; Paragraphs 37–39 of the (first) and Paragraphs 66–70 of the (second) Opinion on Italy, *supra* note 22; Paragraphs 38–40 of the (first) and Paragraphs 52–54 of the (second) Opinion on Moldova, ACFC/INF/OP/II(2004)004, 24/05/2005; Paragraphs 42–43 of the Opinion on Poland, *supra* note 21; Paragraphs 30–31 of the (first) Opinion on Romania, *supra* note 21; Paragraphs 46–48 of the (first) Opinion on the Russian Federation, *supra* note 27; Paragraphs 22–24 of the (first) Opinion on Slovakia, ACFC/INF/OP/I(2001)001, 06.07.2001; and Paragraphs 43–45 of the Opinion on the Former Yugoslav Republic of Macedonia, *supra* note 21.

31. See Paragraphs 21–23 of the (first) Opinion on Finland, *supra* note 27; Paragraph 38 of the Opinion on Norway, *supra* note 22; and Paragraphs 30–32 of the Opinion on Sweden, *supra* note 21.

32. See Paragraphs 48–55 of the Opinion on Ireland, ACFC/INF/OP/I(2004)003, 05.05.2004; Paragraph 58 of the (second) Opinion on Italy, *supra* note 22, Paragraph 47 of the Opinion on Spain, *supra* note 21; Paragraphs 34–38 of the Opinion on Switzerland, *supra* note 23; and Paragraphs 40–42 of the Opinion on the United Kingdom, *supra* note 21. See also the ECtHR decision in the *Buckley* case.

33. See Paragraphs 29–32 of the (first) Opinion on Germany, *supra* note 22.

34. On this issue, see, for example, R. Hofmann, 'Minority Rights: Individual or Group Rights? A Comparative View on European Legal Systems', *German Yearbook of International Law* 40 (1998), 356–382.

35. On Article 4(1) FCNM see Alfredsson, 'The Principle of Equality', *supra* note 29.

36. See, for example, Paragraph 21 of the Opinion on Austria, *supra* note 21; Paragraph 24 of the Opinion on Azerbaijan, *supra* note 25; Paragraphs 33–36 of the Opinion on Bosnia and Herzegovina, *supra* note 23; Paragraphs 21–25 of the (first) and Paragraph 42 of the (second) Opinion on Croatia, *supra* note 25; Paragraphs 23–24 of the Opinion on Cyprus, *supra* note 26; Paragraphs 24–26 of the (first) and Paragraph 39 of the (second) Opinion (welcoming important improvements) on the Czech Republic, *supra* note 25; Paragraph 25 of the (first) Opinion on Denmark, *supra* note 20; Paragraph 22 of the (first) Opinion on Germany, *supra* note 22; Paragraph 31 of the Opinion on Serbia and Montenegro, *supra*

note 23; Paragraph 17 of the (first) Opinion on Slovakia, *supra* note 30; Paragraphs 26–28 of the (first) Opinion on Slovenia, *supra* note 21; Paragraphs 25–28 of the Opinion on Spain, *supra* note 21; Paragraphs 28–29 of the Opinion on the Former Yugoslav Republic of Macedonia, *supra* note 21; and Paragraphs 26–28 of the Opinion on Ukraine, *supra* note 21.

37. See, for example, Paragraph 22 of the Opinion on Austria, *supra* note 21; Paragraph 27 of the Opinion on Azerbaijan, *supra* note 25; Paragraph 29 of the (first) Opinion on Croatia, *supra* note 25; Paragraph 28 of the (first) Opinion on the Czech Republic, ACFC/INF/OP/I(2002)002, 25.01.2002; Paragraph 69 of the (first) Opinion on Hungary, *supra* note 23; Paragraph 35 of the Opinion on Poland, *supra* note 21; Paragraph 26 of the (first) Opinion on Romania, *supra* note 21; Paragraph 44 of the Opinion on Serbia and Montenegro, *supra* note 23; Paragraph 21 of the (first) Opinion on Slovakia, *supra* note 30; and Paragraphs 41–42 of the Opinion on the Former Yugoslav Republic of Macedonia, *supra* note 21.

38. See, for example, Paragraph 21 of the (first) Opinion on Germany, *supra* note 22; Paragraph 27 of the Opinion on Norway, *supra* note 22; and Paragraph 41 of the Opinion on Spain, *supra* note 21.

39. See, for example, Paragraphs 44–51 of the Opinion on Bosnia and Herzegovina, *supra* note 23; Paragraphs 69–74 of the (second) Opinion on Croatia, *supra* note 25; Paragraphs 28–30 of the (first) and Paragraphs 49–59 of the (second) Opinion on the Czech Republic, *supra* note 25; Paragraphs 18–19 of the (first) Opinion on Hungary, *supra* note 23; Paragraphs 55–60 of the (second) Opinion on Italy, *supra* note 22; Paragraphs 33–36 of the (first) and Paragraphs 43–48 of the (second) Opinion on Moldova, *supra* note 30; Paragraphs 36–39 of the Opinion on Poland, *supra* note 21, Paragraphs 27–29 of the (first) Opinion on Romania, *supra* note 21; Paragraphs 39–43 of the Opinion on Serbia and Montenegro, *supra* note 23; Paragraphs 20–21 of the (first) Opinion on Slovakia, *supra* note 30; Paragraphs 62–74 of the (second) Opinion on Slovenia, *supra* note 21; and Paragraphs 31–38 of the Opinion on Spain, *supra* note 21.

40. See, for example, Paragraph 31 of the (first) Opinion on the Czech Republic, *supra* note 25; Paragraph 27 of the (first) and Paragraphs 28–30 of the (second) Opinion on Croatia, *supra* note 25; Paragraph 26 of the (first) and Paragraphs 46–50 of the (second) Opinion on Estonia, *supra* note 25; Paragraphs 30–31 of the Opinion on Lithuania, ACFC/INF/OP/I(2003)008, 25.09.2003; Paragraphs 37–38 of the (first) Opinion on the Russian Federation, *supra* note 27; Paragraph 32 of the Opinion on Serbia and Montenegro, *supra* note 23; Paragraphs 30–32 of the (first) and Paragraphs 56–59 of the (second) Opinion on Slovenia, *supra* note 21; Paragraphs 36–37 of the Opinion on the Former Yugoslav Republic of Macedonia, *supra* note 21; and Paragraph 29 of the Opinion on Ukraine, *supra* note 21.

41. On Article 6 FCNM see Gilbert, 'Non-assimilation', *supra* note 28.

42. See, for example, Paragraphs 67–69 of the Opinion on Bosnia and Herzegovina, *supra* note 23; Paragraphs 35–38 of the (first) and Paragraphs 96–98 of the (second) Opinion on the Czech Republic, *supra* note 25; Paragraph 33 of the (first) Opinion on Germany, *supra* note 22; Paragraph 25 of the (first) Opinion on Finland, *supra* note 27; Paragraphs 35–43 of the Opinion on Ireland, *supra* note 32; Paragraph 25 of the (first) Opinion on Italy, *supra* note 22; Paragraph 27 of the (first) Opinion on Romania, *supra* note 21; Paragraph 39 of the Opinion on Serbia and Montenegro, *supra* note 23; Paragraph 18 and 39 of the (first) Opinion on Slovakia, *supra* note 30; Paragraph 32 of the Opinion on Spain, *supra* note 21;

Paragraph 24 of the Opinion on Sweden, *supra* note 21; and Paragraph 52 of the Opinion on the Former Yugoslav Republic of Macedonia, *supra* note 21.

43. See, for example, Paragraph 40 of the Opinion on Albania, *supra* note 20; Paragraph 70 of the Opinion on Bosnia and Herzegovina, *supra* note 23; Paragraphs 39–43 of the (first) and Paragraph 97 of the (second) Opinion on the Czech Republic, *supra* note 25; Paragraph 85 of the (second) Opinion on Italy, *supra* note 22; Paragraphs 40–41 of the (first) Opinion on Romania, *supra* note 21; Paragraph 58 of the Opinion on Serbia and Montenegro, *supra* note 23; Paragraph 28 of the (first) Opinion on Slovakia, *supra* note 30; Paragraph 56 of the Opinion on Spain, *supra* note 21; Paragraph 38 of the Opinion on Sweden, *supra* note 21; and Paragraph 53 of the Opinion on the Former Yugoslav Republic of Macedonia, *supra* note 21.

44. See, for example, Paragraph 32 of the Opinion on Austria, *supra* note 21; Paragraph 66 of the Opinion on Bosnia and Herzegovina, *supra* note 23; Paragraph 33 of the (first) and Paragraph 84 of the (second) Opinion (welcoming important improvements) on Croatia, *supra* note 25; Paragraph 37 of the (first) and Paragraph 90 of the (second) Opinion on the Czech Republic, *supra* note 25; Paragraph 35 of the (first) and Paragraphs 80–82 of the (second) Opinion on Italy, *supra* note 22; Paragraphs 34–35 of the (first) Opinion on Romania, *supra* note 21; Paragraph 62 of the (first) Opinion on the Russian Federation, *supra* note 27; Paragraph 61 of the Opinion on Serbia and Montenegro, *supra* note 23; Paragraph 26 of the (first) Opinion on Slovakia, *supra* note 30; Paragraphs 40–41 of the (first) and Paragraph 100 of the (second) Opinion on Slovenia, *supra* note 21; Paragraph 41 of the Opinion on Switzerland, *supra* note 23; and Paragraph 55 of the Opinion on the Former Yugoslav Republic of Macedonia, *supra* note 21.

45. See, for example, Paragraphs 33–35 of the Opinion on Austria, *supra* note 21; Paragraphs 76–84 of the (second) Opinion on Denmark, *supra* note 20; Paragraph 35 of the (first) Opinion on Germany, *supra* note 22; Paragraph 40 of the (first) and Paragraph 77 of the (second) Opinion on Italy, *supra* note 22; Paragraph 44 of the Opinion on Lithuania, *supra* note 40; Paragraph 49 of the Opinion on Spain, *supra* note 21; Paragraph 44 of the Opinion on Switzerland, *supra* note 23; and Paragraphs 47–51 of the Opinion on the United Kingdom, *supra* note 21.

46. On Articles 7 and 8 FCNM see Z. Machnyikova, 'Freedom of Assembly Association, Expression, Thought and Religion', in Weller (ed.), *The Framework Convention*, *supra* note 7, 193–224; and Machnyikova, 'Religion', in *ibid.*, 225–61.

47. See Paragraphs 18–21 of the Opinion on Cyprus, *supra* note 26; see also Paragraph 19 of the (first) Opinion on Armenia with respect to the Yesidi, *supra* note 26.

48. EctHR, *Metropolitan Church of Bessarabia and Others v. Moldova*, Appl. No. 45701/99, 13.12.2001.

49. See, for example, Paragraph 38 of the (first) and Paragraph 101 of the (second) Opinion (welcoming important improvements) on Croatia, *supra* note 25; Paragraphs 79–81 of the (second) Opinion on Moldova (concerning difficulties to register religious organizations), *supra* note 30; and Paragraph 67 of the Opinion on Serbia and Montenegro, *supra* note 23.

50. See Paragraphs 57–61 of the Opinion on the United Kingdom, *supra* note 21.

51. See Paragraph 29 of the (first) and Paragraph 110 of the (second) Opinion on Denmark, *supra* note 20; and Paragraph 29 of the opinion on Finland, *supra* note 27.

52. See *supra* text accompanying note 15.

53. See, for example, Paragraphs 43–45 of the Opinion on Azerbaijan, *supra* note 25; and Paragraph 49 of the (first) Opinion on Moldova, ACFC/INF/OP/I(2003)002, 15.01.2003.

54. See Paragraphs 68–70 of the (first) Opinion on the Russian Federation, *supra* note 27.

55. On Article 9, see the commentary by J. Packer and S. Holt, 'Expression and the Media', in Weller (ed.), *The Framework Convention*, *supra* note 7, 264–300; see also K. Jakubowicz, 'Persons Belonging to National Minorities and the Media', *International Journal of Minority and Group Rights* 10 (2003): 291–314.

56. See, for example, Paragraphs 47–49 of the Opinion on Albania, *supra* note 20; Paragraphs 47–50 of the (first) Opinion on Armenia, *supra* note 26; Paragraphs 38–40 of the Opinion on Austria, *supra* note 21; Paragraphs 50–52 of the Opinion on Azerbaijan, *supra* note 25; Paragraphs 40–42 of the (first) and Paragraphs 107–109 of the (second) Opinion on Croatia, *supra* note 25; Paragraphs 53–54 of the (first) and Paragraphs 107–109 of the (second) Opinion on the Czech Republic, *supra* note 25; Paragraphs 116–120 of the (second) Opinion on Denmark, *supra* note 20; Paragraphs 55–57 of the (first) and Paragraph 85 of the (second) Opinion on Estonia, *supra* note 25; Paragraphs 44–47 of the (first) Opinion on Germany, *supra* note 22; Paragraphs 88–92 of the (second) Opinion on Italy, *supra* note 22; Paragraphs 56–57 of the (first) and Paragraphs 89–91 of the (second) Opinion on Moldova, *supra* note 30; Paragraphs 62–65 of the Opinion on Poland, *supra* note 21; Paragraphs 76–78 of the (first) Opinion on the Russian Federation, *supra* note 27; Paragraph 62 of the Opinion on Spain, *supra* note 21; Paragraphs 42–43 of the Opinion on Sweden, *supra* note 21; Paragraph 62 of the Opinion on the Former Yugoslav Republic of Macedonia, *supra* note 21; and Paragraphs 43–47 of the Opinion on Ukraine, *supra* note 21.

57. See Jakubowicz, 'Persons Belonging', *supra* note 55: at 304.

58. See, for example, Paragraph 144 of the (first) Opinion on the Russian Federation where it finds that the 'overall *a priori* exclusion of the use of the languages of national minorities in federal radio and TV broadcasting, implied in the Law on Languages of the Peoples of the Russian Federation, is overly restrictive and not compatible with Article 9', *supra* note 27. See also for a similar prohibition – and assessment – Paragraph 50 of the Opinion on Azerbaijan, *supra* note 25.

59. See *supra* note 12.

60. See, for example, Paragraph 51 of the (first) Opinion on Armenia, *supra* note 26; Paragraph 52 of the Opinion on Lithuania, *supra* note 40; Paragraph 44 of the Opinion on Norway, *supra* note 22; Paragraph 64 of the Opinion on Spain, *supra* note 21; and Paragraph 46 of the Opinion on Sweden, *supra* note 21.

61. On Articles 10 and 11 FCNM see the commentaries by F. de Varennes, 'Use of Language', in Weller (ed.), *The Framework Convention*, *supra* note 7, 301–27; and de Varennes, 'Use of Names and Signs', in *ibid.*, 329–63, respectively. For a general survey of the contents of linguistic rights see F. de Varennes, 'Enhancing Linguistic and Cultural Diversity', in J. Kühl and M. Weller (eds), *Minority Policy in Action: The Bonn–Copenhagen Declarations in a European Context 1955–2005* (Aabenraa: Institute of Border Region Studies, 2005), 217–35.

62. See, for example, Paragraphs 53–55 of the Opinion on Azerbaijan, *supra* note 25; Paragraph 39 of the (first) and Paragraph 92 of the (second) Opinion on Estonia, *supra* note 25; Paragraph 70 of the Opinion on Lithuania, *supra* note 40; Paragraph 81 of the (first) and paragraph 95 of the (second) Opinion (welcoming

considerable improvements) on Moldova, *supra* note 30; and Paragraph 63 of the Opinion on Ukraine, *supra* note 21.

63. See, for example, Paragraphs 57–59 of the (first) Opinion on Armenia, *supra* note 26; Paragraphs 56–57 of the Opinion on Azerbaijan, *supra* note 25; Paragraphs 54–56 of the Opinion on Lithuania, *supra* note 40; Paragraphs 66–67 of the Opinion on Poland, *supra* note 21; Paragraphs 80–85 of the (first) Opinion on the Russian Federation, *supra* note 27; Paragraphs 48–50 of the Opinion on Sweden, *supra* note 21; and Paragraph 56 of the Opinion on Switzerland, *supra* note 23.

64. See Paragraphs 44–46 of the Opinion on Austria, *supra* note 21; Paragraph 10 of the (second) Opinion on the Czech Republic (explicitly welcoming new legislation), *supra* note 25; Paragraph 49 of the (first) Opinion on Romania, *supra* note 21; Paragraph 36 of the (first) Opinion on Slovakia, *supra* note 30; and Paragraph 68 of the Opinion on the Former Yugoslav Republic of Macedonia, *supra* note 21.

65. See Paragraphs 79–81 of the Opinion on Bosnia and Herzegovina, *supra* note 23; Paragraphs 43–45 of the (first) Opinion on Croatia but see Paragraphs 111–113 of the (second) Opinion on Croatia where the Advisory Committee explicitly welcomed the lowering of the applicable threshold to one third of the population of the administrative unit concerned, *supra* note 25; Paragraphs 39–41 of the (first) Opinion on Estonia but see Paragraphs 95–98 of the (second) Opinion on Estonia where the Advisory Committee explicitly welcomed pertinent improvements, *supra* note 25; Paragraph 62 of the (first) Opinion on Moldova, *supra* note 53; and Paragraphs 49–53 of the Opinion on Ukraine, *supra* note 21.

66. See, for example, Paragraph 49 of the (first) Opinion on Germany, *supra* note 22.

67. See, for example, Paragraph 58 of the (first) and Paragraph 122 of the (second) Opinion on the Czech Republic, *supra* note 25; and Paragraphs 58–59 of the Opinion on Norway, *supra* note 22.

68. See, for example, Paragraph 55 of the Opinion on Albania, *supra* note 20; Paragraph 37 of the (first) Opinion on Slovakia, *supra* note 30; and Paragraphs 54–56 of the Opinion on Ukraine, *supra* note 21.

69. See Paragraph 43 of the (first) and Paragraph 104 of the (second) Opinion on Estonia, *supra* note 25; see also Paragraph 99 of the Opinion on Azerbaijan, *supra* note 25; and Paragraph 70 of the Opinion on Poland, *supra* note 21

70. See, for example, Paragraph 100 of the (second) opinion on Estonia, *supra* note 25; Paragraph 35 of the (first) Opinion on Finland, *supra* note 27; Paragraph 52 of the (first) Opinion on Italy, *supra* note 22; Paragraph 59 of the (first) Opinion on Slovenia, *supra* note 21; and Paragraph 51 of the Opinion on Sweden, *supra* note 21.

71. See, for example, Paragraph 56 of the Opinion on Albania, *supra* note 20; Paragraph 58 of the Opinion on Lithuania, *supra* note 40; and Paragraph 87 of the (first) Opinion on the Russian Federation, *supra* note 27.

72. See Paragraph 50 of the Opinion on Austria, *supra* note 21.

73. See Paragraph 126 of the (second) Opinion of the Czech Republic, *supra* note 25; these figures constitute a further improvement as compared to the previous situation. See also Paragraph 59 of the (first) Opinion on the Czech Republic, *supra* note 37; and Paragraph 73 of the Opinion on the Former Yugoslav Republic of Macedonia where the Advisory Committee welcomes legislation allowing for bilingual topographical signs in areas with a minority population exceeding 20 per cent of the total population, *supra* note 21.

74. See Paragraph 57 of the Opinion on Ukraine, *supra* note 21; see also Paragraph 82 of the Opinion on Bosnia and Herzegovina, *supra* note 23.

75. See Paragraphs 71–72 of the Opinion on Poland, *supra* note 21.
76. *Supra* note 12.
77. On Articles 12 and 13 FCNM see the commentaries by P. Thornberry, 'Education', in Weller (ed.), *The Framework*, *supra* note 7: 365–93; and Thornberry, 'Identity', in *ibid.*, 395–406, respectively; and on Article 14 FCNM see the commentary by Thornberry and F. de Varennes, 'Language Education', in *ibid.*, 407–28; see also D. Wilson, 'Educational Rights of Persons Belonging to National Minorities', *International Journal on Minority and Group Rights* 10 (2003): 315–79.
78. *Supra* note 12.
79. With the noteworthy exception of the judgment in *Case Relating to Certain Aspects of the Laws on the Use of Languages in Education in Belgium* (Appl. Nos. 1474/62, 1677/62, 1691/62, 1769/63, 1994/63, 2126/64, 23.07.1968) where the Court held that the state has a right to determine the official languages of instruction in public schools and denied that there was a right to instruction in the language of one's choice. For a discussion of more recent developments concerning the ECHR and minority rights in education see Wilson, 'Educational Rights', *supra* note 77, at 323.
80. See, for example, Paragraphs 88–89 of the Opinion on Bosnia and Herzegovina, *supra* note 23; Paragraph 55 of the (first) and Paragraph 114 of the (second) Opinion on Italy, *supra* note 22; Paragraph 118 of the (second) Opinion on Moldova, *supra* note 30; Paragraph 81 of the Opinion on Serbia and Montenegro, *supra* note 23; Paragraph 70 of the Opinion on Spain, *supra* note 21; Paragraph 78 of the Opinion on the Former Yugoslav Republic of Macedonia, *supra* note 21; and Paragraphs 81–83 of the Opinion on the United Kingdom, *supra* note 21.
81. See, for example, Paragraph 49 of the (first) Opinion on Croatia but see Paragraph 129 of the (second) Opinion on Croatia where the Advisory Committee strongly welcomed the discontinuation of such practices, *supra* note 25; Paragraphs 61–63 of the (first) Opinion on the Czech Republic but see Paragraphs 145–149 of the (second) Opinion on the Czech Republic, *supra* notes 37 and 25, respectively; Paragraph 41 of the (first) Opinion on Hungary, *supra* note 23; Paragraph 77 of the Opinion on Poland, *supra* note 21; Paragraphs 57–59 of the (first) Opinion on Romania, *supra* note 21; Paragraphs 89–90 of the Opinion on Serbia and Montenegro, *supra* note 23; Paragraphs 39–40 of the (first) Opinion on Slovakia, *supra* note 30; and Paragraphs 63–65 of the (first) Opinion on Slovenia, *supra* note 21. On this issue see also the recent judgment of 7 February 2006 of the Second Chamber of the ECtHR, *D.H. and Others v. The Czech Republic* (Appl. No. 57325/00, 07.02.06) where it was noted that several organizations, including Council of Europe bodies, had expressed concern about the placement of Roma children in special schools; however, the ECtHR held that, while the relevant statistics disclosed worrying figures, the pertinent measures did not amount to discrimination and, thus, found no violation of Article 14 ECHR, taken together with Article 2 of Protocol No. 1.
82. See, for example, Paragraphs 63–65 of the (first) Opinion on Armenia, *supra* note 26; Paragraph 48 of the (first) and Paragraph 126 of the (second) Opinion on Croatia, *supra* note 25; Paragraph 117 of the (second) Opinion on Estonia, *supra* note 25; Paragraph 110 of the (second) Opinion on Italy, *supra* note 22, Paragraph 74 of the (first) and Paragraph 117 of the (second) Opinion on Moldova, *supra* note 30; Paragraph 74 of the Opinion on Poland, *supra* note 21; Paragraphs 87–88 of the Opinion on Serbia and Montenegro, *supra* note 23; Paragraph 62 of the (first) and Paragraph 141 of the (second) Opinion on Slovenia, *supra* note 21;

Paragraphs 76–77 of the Opinion on the Former Yugoslav Republic of Macedonia, *supra* note 21; and Paragraph 59 of the Opinion on Ukraine, *supra* note 21.

83. See, for example, Paragraph 63 of the Opinion on Austria, *supra* note 21; Paragraphs 59–61 of the (first) Opinion on Germany, *supra* note 22; and Paragraph 73 of the Opinion on Lithuania, *supra* note 40.

84. See, for example, Paragraphs 50–52 of the (first) Opinion and Paragraphs 138–140 of the (second) Opinion on Estonia welcoming certain positive amendments of the applicable legislation, *supra* note 25; Paragraphs 70–72 of the Opinion on Lithuania, *supra* note 40; Paragraphs 81–83 of the (first) and Paragraphs 132–134 of the(second) Opinion on Moldova, *supra* note 30; and Paragraphs 63–65 of the Opinion on Ukraine, *supra* note 21.

85. See, for example, Paragraphs 61–65 of the Opinion on Austria, *supra* note 21; Paragraph 51 of the (first) Opinion on Estonia; and Paragraph 72 of the Opinion on Switzerland, *supra* note 23.

86. On this scheme and for a discussion on its potential for the future work of the Advisory Committee see Wilson, 'Educational Rights', *supra* note 77, at 317.

87. On Article 15 FCNM see the commentary by M. Weller, 'Effective Participation', in Weller (ed.), *The Framework Convention, supra* note 7, 429–61; see also J.A. Frowein and R. Bank, 'The Participation of Persons Belonging to National Minorities in Decision-Making Processes, *Zeitschrift für ausländisches öffentliches Recht und Völkerrecht* 61 (2001): 1–28; and M. Weller, 'Creating the Conditions Necessary for the Effective Participation of Persons Belonging to National Minorities', *International Journal on Minority and Group Rights* 10 (2003): 265–90.

88. *Supra* note 12.

89. See, for example, Paragraphs 69–70 of the Opinion on Albania, *supra* note 20; Paragraphs 76–77 of the Opinion on Azerbaijan, *supra* note 25; Paragraphs 58–62 of the (first) and Paragraphs 161–163 of the (second) Opinion on Croatia welcoming significant improvements in this sphere, *supra* note 25; and Paragraphs 69–70 of the Opinion on Ukraine, *supra* note 21.

90. See, for example, Paragraphs 71–74 of the Opinion on Albania, *supra* note 20 Paragraphs 77–80 of the (first) Opinion on Armenia, *supra* note 26; Paragraphs 57–58 of the (first) and Paragraph 154 of the (second) Opinion on Estonia, *supra* note 25; Paragraphs 77–79 of the Opinion on Lithuania, *supra* note 40; Paragraphs 85–89 of the (first) and Paragraphs 136–139 of the (second) Opinion on Moldova, *supra* note 30; Paragraphs 101–108 of the (first) Opinion on the Russian Federation, *supra* note 27; and Paragraphs 105–109 of the Opinion on Serbia and Montenegro, *supra* note 23.

91. See, for example, Paragraph 36 of the (first) Opinion on Denmark, *supra* note 20; Paragraph 47 of the (first) Opinion on Finland, *supra* note 27; Paragraphs 61–62 of the (first) Opinion on Italy, *supra* note 22; Paragraph 91 of the (first) Opinion on Moldova, *supra* note 53; Paragraphs 111–112 of the Opinion on Serbia and Montenegro, *supra* note 23; Paragraph 75 of the Opinion on Spain, *supra* note 21; and Paragraph 74 of the Opinion on Switzerland, *supra* note 23.

92. See Paragraphs 158–168 of the (second) opinion on Denmark, *supra* note 20.

93. See, for example, Paragraph 75 of the Opinion on Albania, *supra* note 20. Paragraph 117 of the Opinion on Bosnia and Herzegovina, *supra* note 23; Paragraphs 55–57 of the (first) and Paragraphs 156–159 of the (second) Opinion on Croatia, *supra* note 25; Paragraph 66 of the (first) Opinion on Italy, *supra* note 22; Paragraph 103 of the Opinion on Serbia and Montenegro, *supra* note 23; Paragraph

99 of the Opinion on the Former Yugoslav Republic of Macedonia, *supra* note 21; and Paragraph 96 of the Opinion on the United Kingdom, *supra* note 21.

94. See, for example, Paragraph 79 of the Opinion on Azerbaijan, *supra* note 25; Paragraph 59 of the (first) Opinion on Estonia, *supra* note 25; Paragraph 109 of the (first) Opinion on the Russian Federation, *supra* note 27; Paragraph 118 of the Opinion on Serbia and Montenegro, *supra* note 23; and Paragraphs 74–75 of the Opinion on Ukraine, *supra* note 21.

95. See, for example, Paragraphs 55–60 of the (first) and Paragraphs 163–166 of the (second) Opinion on Estonia strongly welcoming legislation removing such language proficiency requirements with respect to elections and, at the same time, calling for a review of the still existing requirement in the private employment sector; and Paragraph 106 of the (first) Opinion on the Russian Federation, *supra* note 27.

96. See, for example, Paragraph 75 of the Opinion on Albania, *supra* note 20; Paragraph 71 of the Opinion on Austria, *supra* note 21; Paragraph 108–110 of the Opinion on Bosnia and Herzegovina, *supra* note 23; Paragraph 65 of the (first) and Paragraphs 146–147 of the (second) Opinion on Croatia; Paragraph 71 of the (first) and Paragraph 182 of the (second) Opinion on the Czech Republic, *supra* notes 37 and 25, respectively; Paragraph 66 of the (first) Opinion on Germany, *supra* note 22; Paragraph 54 of the (first) Opinion on Hungary, *supra* note 23; Paragraph 65 of the (first) Opinion on Italy, *supra* note 22; Paragraph 63 of the (first) Opinion on Norway, *supra* note 22; Paragraph 69 of the (first) Opinion on Romania, *supra* note 21; Paragraph 47 of the (first) Opinion on Slovenia, *supra* note 21; Paragraph 47 of the (first) Opinion on Slovakia, *supra* note 30; Paragraph 79 of the Opinion on Spain, *supra* note. 21; Paragraph 77 of the Opinion on Switzerland, *supra* note 23; and Paragraph 102 of the Opinion on the Former Yugoslav Republic of Macedonia, *supra* note 21.

97. See, in particular, Weller, 'Creating the Conditions', *supra* note 87, at 268.

98. On Article 17 FCNM see the commentary by J. Jackson-Preece, 'Cross-frontier Contacts', in Weller (ed.), *The Framework, supra* note 7, 487–506.

99. On this issue see, for example, R. Hofmann, 'Preferential Treatment of Kin-Minorities and Monitoring of the Implementation of the Framework Convention for National Minorities', European Commission for Democracy through Law, *The Protection of National Minorities by Their Kin-State* (Strasbourg: Council of Europe, 2002), 235–60.

100. See, for example, Paragraph 63 of the (first) and Paragraphs 171–172 of the (second) Opinion on Estonia welcoming the conclusion of an agreement between Estonia and the Russian Federation allowing for the introduction of a simplified visa regime, *supra* note 25; Paragraph 56 of the (first) Opinion on Hungary, *supra* note 23; Paragraph 83 of the Opinion on Lithuania, *supra* note 40; Paragraph 92 of the Opinion on Poland, *supra* note 21; and Paragraph 50 of the (first) Opinion on Slovakia, *supra* note 30.

Part III

Minority–Majority Relations in Practice in an Enlarged EU

8
Minority Protection in Central Europe and Accession to the EU
*Wojciech Sadurski**

It is a euphemism to say that the post-communist states of Central and Eastern Europe (CEE) have been less than enthusiastic about promoting a strong, robust policy for the promotion of minority rights. While this has not placed them in stark contrast with many of their West European counterparts – consider the official policy of France or Greece – it has nevertheless been a source of concern for many observers and experts fearing that, if these new democracies fail to establish fair and stable bases for minority–majority relations, they might become vulnerable to disintegrating internal tensions and 'export' those problems to the West.

At the same time, there has been a growing perception of the limited and imperfect resources that the European institutions – in particular the EU, but also the Council of Europe (CoE) and Organization for Security and Cooperation in Europe (OSCE) and their networks – have at their disposal *vis-à-vis* CEE states when it comes to their minority-related policies and legislation. EU 'conditionality' has proved to be of very limited effectiveness in this regard, the OSCE (in particular, the High Commissioner on National Minorities (HCNM)) has intervened mainly when ethnic tensions have posed a threat to international stability and the CoE instruments (in particular, the Framework Convention on the Protection of National Minorities, or FCNM) have provided a very minimal threshold for the protection of minority rights. Such minimal thresholds have quickly turned into ceiling limits, thereby defying hopes for them to constitute the starting points for more ambitious and

*I am very grateful to Professor John Packer for his extremely important and comprehensive remarks, which I have not been able to take fully on board in the present contribution but which will serve as valuable inspiration in my future thinking on the subject.

progressive arrangements for minority–majority relations in those countries. As Will Kymlicka observed:

> These minimal international standards [as attributable to the FCNM and OSCE recommendations] are not being treated as the preconditions needed to democratically negotiate the forms of power-sharing and self-government appropriate to each country, but rather are viewed as eliminating the need to adopt, or even to debate, forms of power-sharing and self government. When minority organizations raise questions about substantive minority rights, post-communist states respond 'we meet all international standards', as if that foreclosed the question of how states should treat their minorities.[1]

If Kymlicka is right – and he emphatically is – the problem to address is: what accounts for this reticence on the part of CEE states to use the minimal standards of European norms on minority protection as a starting point for a more generous and robust approach to minority rights, in particular in the areas of language rights, territorial autonomy (where appropriate, that is, where the territorially identifiable minorities live) and self-government through, for example, proportional representation of minorities at all levels of government? Two broad answers are available and this chapter will examine them in turn. First, the Europeanization of political and legal norms – and, in particular, conditionality – related to the process of accession to the EU has been singularly unimpressive in the field of minority rights. The candidate EU states (as they were then), in addition to those who saw themselves as future candidates, had very little reason, incentive or capacity to venture expansively and bravely into the sphere of minority relations; they had very little to emulate, so why bother? Second, their domestic institutional resources, designed and set up to counter the majoritarian, populist and illiberal tendencies of these newly democratized states, proved largely unwilling and incapable of acting forcefully in this sphere. As a result of these two phenomena, there has been no synergy between external and domestic factors – which have proved reasonably effective in many other areas related to the democratization and liberalization of post-communist countries, such as the autonomy of central banks, the independence of the judiciary or freedom of the media.

The impact of EU conditionality on minority protection

In the burgeoning literature on the impact of EU conditionality (and, more generally, on the impact of 'Europeanization', broadly understood) upon the standards and norms adopted in the post-communist states, it became a commonplace view that the effectiveness of conditionality is a function, among other things, of the degree of resonance between 'European norms' and the preferences, policies and interests that prevail in the domestic political life of CEE states, *and also* of the coherence, clarity and compelling nature of the European norms themselves. Thus, the first section of this chapter will discuss the effectiveness of the implantation of European norms within the CEE states, while the second section will examine why the CEE states have been relatively reluctant to emulate these norms in their legal and political orders.

If one considers different areas to which EU political conditionality has applied, one realizes that the degree of specificity and solidity has varied from one domain to another, and has been much more effective in those cases where there was a determined set of rules that candidate states were expected to observe than in those cases in which the criteria laid down could be characterized, at best, as a vague template. For example, Antoaneta Dimitrova found a generally high effect of conditionality on civil service reform[2] while, by contrast, Martin Brusis, who explored the regionalization reforms in CEE states, established that conditionality mattered little in that area: if it *were* relevant, one would have trouble explaining the significant differences in the regionalization politics between countries as similar as the Czech Republic and Slovakia.[3] In addition, the legitimacy of conditionality demands has varied depending on whether they corresponded to the seriousness and determination with which the EU held its own member states to those standards; when the EU set certain political conditions that were not already part of the EU legal system and, as such, were not actually shared by the member states themselves, the credibility – and, hence, effectiveness – of this area of conditionality must have been suspect. Apart from the legitimacy and 'double standards' problem, the candidate states, even when acting in good faith, could not know exactly what was expected of them because neither the current practice of member states nor the *acquis* provided any clear guidance.

Minority rights provide a significant example of low-efficiency conditionality areas. Although 'respect for and protection of minorities' figure prominently among the Copenhagen political criteria,[4] these precepts lack any basis in EU law and, as such, are not directly translatable into the *acquis communautaire*. It might be hypothesized that the inclusion of these criteria reflected 'widespread Western perceptions and security concerns *vis-à-vis* CEE where the post-communist potential for ethno-regional conflict amidst multi-faceted transition processes appeared to be high'.[5] This absence of clear standards, both in EU law and in the practice and law of EU member states, yielded not only a strong charge of hypocrisy and double standards,[6] but also led to difficulties in gauging the real meaning of these criteria. While the Treaty of Maastricht did recognize respect for fundamental rights as one of the underlying values of the EU, and the Treaty of Amsterdam did incorporate *almost* all of the values set out by the EU in the Copenhagen political criteria, reference to minority protection is conspicuously absent from both treaties. Clearly, there is no consensus among the older EU member states as to the requisite standards of minority protection: some member states officially recognize the existence of minorities in their population while others (France and Greece) do not; some (the UK) reserve the term 'minority' to describe the immigrant population, while others apply the term to historically rooted ethnic groups (the Slovenes in Austria; the Slovenes, French and Germans in Italy); some have ratified the 1995 FCNM while others have not,[7] and so on.

Analysis of the European Commission's annual reports on applicant states' progress towards fulfilling the 'minority protection' criterion suggests ambiguities and inconsistencies in the process of scrutinizing the practice of candidate states. As Gwendolyn Sasse has observed, the regular reports consistently emphasized the plight of only two of the minority groups in the region (the Roma population and the Russian-speaking population in the Baltic states), notwithstanding the pervasive nature of minority–majority problems in CEE countries. This selectivity suggests that the main issues addressed by the drafters of the reports were those of an extrinsic nature (that is, a fear of uncontrollable migration to Western countries, in the case of the Roma, and a concern for Russian political sensibilities, in the case of the Baltic states), and not of an intrinsic concern for the plights of disadvantaged minorities.

For an example of a real and dramatic situation of minorities that has remained invisible in the reports and, largely, to public opinion in the West,[8] consider the plight of the Slovenian residents originating from other former Yugoslav republics (mainly Serbs, Croats and Bosnian Muslims, summarily called the 'Yuzhniks', meaning 'people from the South') who constitute around 10 per cent of the Slovenian population. Under the 1991 nationality law, passed soon after the declaration of Slovenian independence, all those born outside Slovenia, regardless of how long they had lived in Slovenian territory, were required to apply for citizenship. Due to the very short timeframe within which applications could be lodged and some very demanding bureaucratic requirements, around 30,000 residents missed out on this opportunity and were crossed off the register of permanent residents in 1992. Since then, some 18,000 of those stateless people who stayed in Slovenia (around 11,000 left the country) have been denied basic welfare and other entitlements. Successive laws enacted to solve the situation have not resulted in any significant improvements. In 1999, the ruling centre-right coalition passed a law aimed at a conclusive solution to this problem, but its many provisions (including a three-month deadline for the lodging of applications and the punitive requirement of having to prove a continuous residence in Slovenia over the past eight years) clearly were aimed at limiting the benefits of the law to as few people as possible.[9] This is one dramatic example of how the device of citizenship has been used to exclude people from their rights, essentially for discriminatory reasons.[10] Significantly, the situation of Slovenian minorities was never registered in the EU Annual Reports, which kept simply repeating the mantra: 'The overall situation regarding the protection of minorities in Slovenia can be considered to be good.'[11]

Generally, the emphasis in the reports was on formal measures (such as the adoption of certain laws, the setting up of institutions and the launching of governmental policies) rather than on their implementation; the assessment of countries' records had a rather formulaic, schematic character.[12] Often, the real problems were watered down with bureaucratic language, which tended to gloss over difficulties and leave unclear the reality of what actually happened. Consider this statement: 'The issue of the legal obligation to use the Lithuanian alphabet in spelling the names of persons belonging to national minorities is *being addressed constructively* in particular in the framework of the cooperation between the Lithuanian and Polish authorities.'[13] What does 'being addressed constructively' actually mean? Are non-Lithuanian citizens still compelled to spell their names in the Lithuanian alphabet or not, or only sometimes? The reader cannot guess. Most importantly, when it came to identifying the yardstick of assessment, the reports referred vaguely to 'international' or 'European' standards, often without specifying what these were.

The question is, of course: *are* there any European standards of minority protection? The only instrument that can be described as roughly identifying these standards is the FCNM but, even there, doubts of two kinds arise as to how easily it can be said to define identifiable benchmarks of common European minimum standards. First, it has not been signed, much less ratified, by all European states so it is hard to call the standards included therein 'common'. Second, its language is vague, aspirational and rather minimalist,[14] and its implementation is not judicial but of a combined political–expert style.[15] By far the most comprehensive – and broadly adopted – human rights instrument in Europe, the European Convention on the Protection of Human Rights and Fundamental Freedoms (ECHR), does not contain any reference to protection of minority rights and the closest it comes to referring to minorities is in its prohibition of discrimination (Article 14) which lists 'association with a national minority' as one of the prohibited grounds of discrimination.[16] There is also the Charter for Regional and Minority Languages, which evidently concerns an important but limited aspect of minority rights,[17] although the list of countries that have ratified it is less than comprehensive[18]; the CSCE so-called Copenhagen Document of 1990, which served as an early 'code' of the CSCE/OSCE in this area; the set of EC anti-discrimination directives, in particular, the Race Discrimination Directive of 2000;[19] and – last *and* least – a pious expression of concern for cultural, religious and linguistic diversity in the EU Charter of Fundamental Rights (Article 22).

The overall picture, therefore, is of a patchwork of norms of a largely programmatic and non-specific character, few of which enjoy a comprehensive and consensual support in Western Europe. Even with the best will in the world, the CEE states would be hard pushed to determine what specific blueprint they were supposed to comply with. However, that 'best will' was unlikely to emerge when the Western attitude smacked of hypocrisy and double standards, factors which in turn undermined the seriousness with which the minority prong of Copenhagen criteria were made. Given that none of the EU candidate states housed the sort of ethnic tensions that would constitute a direct and severe threat to regional stability, they realized that anything they did in this domain, however perfunctory and ritualistic, would be considered a 'plus' and would not be subjected to overly severe scrutiny. The two persistent themes in the annual reports of the Commission – the Roma situation and the Russian-speaking minority in the Baltic states – never led to any serious questioning of the candidate states' credentials as bona fide democratic and rights-respecting states eligible for membership in the EU. With regard to the situation of the Roma population, the EU member states have a less-than-perfect record themselves, so their credibility in depicting the faults of candidate states was questionable from the outset.[20] As far as the Russian-speaking population in the Baltic states is concerned, the worst aspects of discrimination have been properly remedied in time – thanks to the persistence of the HCNM. The other problem areas in the field of minority protection have occasionally prompted gentle castigation on the part of the EU, but nothing more serious than this.[21] The general feeling is that none of the parties – neither Western scrutinizers nor the candidate states – took this part of political conditionality particularly seriously; a mutual, if unspoken, understanding developed that the scrutinizers would not be too harsh and the scrutinized would not openly question their scrutinizers' credentials.

Domestic constitutional resources for minority protection in CEE

However, the weakness of external factors is not sufficient explanation for the (non-)adoption of a 'European norm' by a state wanting to be accepted into the European club. The opacity and thinness of European norms would not be fatal if there were strong institutional resources in CEE states displaying a firm commitment to countering societal preferences and political pressures. In some cases, 'Europe' was successful in having its norms emulated in CEE states, not merely because the meaning of the European norms was clear and forceful, but also because there were local, political and legal resources that favoured their adoption. Economic liberalization and accompanying rule-of-law reforms (including judicial independence), as well as the autonomy of central banks, were successful to the degree to which they were perceived as beneficial to the emerging business community. These reforms were supported by an institutional design that strengthened the implementation of the relevant norms and rendered the reforms almost irreversible. Has there been a similar normative resonance and favourable institutional design in the case of minority rights?

This section of the chapter will attempt to demonstrate that, notwithstanding a by-and-large minority-friendly constitutional design ('Constitutional design of minority rights'), the central institutions set up to articulate and interpret the meaning of constitutional provisions – namely constitutional courts – have been reluctant to use those provisions in an expansive way ('Institutional articulation of minority rights'). This indicates that the anxieties that accompanied the process of state formation and state consolidation in the wake of the fall of communism had a centralizing effect upon the behaviour of all institutions, including constitutional courts ('Ideological predispositions and commitments').

Constitutional design of minority rights

The only constitution in the region that fails to mention minority rights is the Constitution of Bulgaria.[22] All the others list various catalogues, with special prominence given to language and educational rights and the right to preserve one's cultural and religious identity, among others. Clearly, the protection of minority language is of central focus within minority rights regimes (to be discussed in more detail below). For example, the Constitution of Latvia provides that: 'Persons belonging to ethnic minorities have the right to preserve and develop their language and their ethnic and cultural identity.'[23] The catalogues of minority rights are often more elaborate, as in this provision of the Romanian constitution: 'The state recognizes and guarantees the right of persons belonging to national minorities, to the preservation, development and expression of their ethnic, cultural, linguistic and religious identity.'[24]

In some cases, certain minority rights – in particular, the right to education in one's own language – are framed as positive rights and, as such, impose an active obligation on the state to ensure that they are guaranteed. For example, in Hungary, the Constitution states that: 'The Republic of Hungary shall provide for the protection of national and ethnic minorities ... [and] education in their native languages.'[25] Positive state duties are sometimes restricted to particular obligations, especially in the sphere of official communications and the interaction of citizens with governmental bodies. For example, in Estonia, there is a very specific regulation concerning the official use of language, which provides: 'In localities where at least half of the permanent residents belong to an ethnic minority, everyone shall have the right to receive answers from state and local government authorities in the language of the ethnic minority.'[26] Finally, some constitutions provide for the rights of minorities *qua* minorities to participate in public affairs. The Hungarian constitution proclaims that 'national and ethnic minorities will be assured collective participation in public affairs' and that '[t]he laws of the Republic of Hungary shall ensure representation for the national and ethnic minorities living within [the] country'.[27]

The constitutions do not, on the whole, attempt a definition of the term 'minority', nor refer to a definition enshrined in any other international document (which is not surprising, given the lack of any such precise definitions in the major international agreements on this subject).[28] The Constitution of Slovenia distinguishes between different types of minority groups in its provisions on the protection of minorities. For example, it states, in Article 61, that '[e]ach person shall be entitled to freely identify with his national grouping or autochthonous ethnic community, to foster and give expression to his culture and to use his own language and script'. However, in addition to this, there are specific rights subsumed under the heading 'Special Rights of the Italian and Hungarian Ethnic Communities in Slovenia'.[29] Here, these groups are given additional rights, such as '[entitlements] to establish organizations, to foster economic, social, scientific and research activities ... to plan and develop their own curricula [for education] ... In those areas where the Italian and Hungarian ethnic communities live, their members shall be entitled to establish autonomous organizations in order to give effect to their rights.'[30] As mentioned earlier, while Italians and Hungarians may be seen as 'indigenous' groups in Slovenia, given their centuries-long inhabitancy in the area, they are not the most numerous ethnic minorities: Croats, Serbs and Muslims constitute proportionally larger minorities in Slovenia than do the Italians and Hungarians.[31] The only explanation for this apparent abnormality is that the issue of the relationship between ethnic Slovenians and ethnic Italians and Hungarians in Slovenia is less politically explosive than the relationship between the members of ethnic groups that made up the former Yugoslavia. Hence, it was safer to accord a special, elaborate and advantageous minority status to Italians and Hungarians than to Serbs and Croats. Different treatment is also accorded to the Roma people. Article 65 of the Slovenian Constitution states that '[t]he status and rights of Gypsy communities living in Slovenia shall be such as are determined by statute'. This suggests that they do not fall within the general provisions on minorities and are not considered to be a minority group.

Most of the constitutions of the region phrase minority rights in the language of *individual rights,* as held by 'persons belonging to national minorities'.[32] In some cases, however, the language of group rights is used. For example, the Hungarian Constitution states: 'National and ethnic minorities shall have the right to form local and national bodies for self-government.'[33] Slovenia also takes this approach, albeit in relation to the rights of *Hungarian and Italian minorities only* (the others are treated as individual rights).[34] Thus, these states create constitutionally guaranteed group rights. Several constitutions use the languages of both group and individual rights in terms of minorities, depending on the nature of the right proclaimed. For example, the Polish Constitution uses group rights language with regard to the establishment of educational and cultural institutions for national minorities,[35] and individual rights language when dealing with the freedom to maintain one's customs, tradition and culture.[36] What difference does this make? A brief *excursus* on group versus individual rights for minorities is perhaps in order.

The main constitutional dilemma with regard to the protection of minorities is whether the best way of protecting members of (national, ethnic, religious, etc.) minorities is simply through strong protection of individual rights backed up by a robust non-discrimination principle, or whether there should be a constitutional principle (or set of principles) that confers special rights upon minority members. The former approach dominates thinking on the protection of minorities in the United States: the idea is that if every citizen, regardless of their (*inter alia*) national or ethnic group membership, benefits from the same strong civil and political rights then any special group-based protection is redundant.[37] This may be called a 'liberal-neutralist' (or individualistic) approach. In the continental European setting, however, this approach has been seen as largely ineffective and insufficient; there has been much less faith in the beneficial effects of the extension of individualistic liberal principles to a situation in which anti-minority prejudices and hostility are deeply ingrained, and are displayed in equal measure by those who are entrusted with the enforcement of general rules.

In principle, the liberal-individual approach is considered well-suited to the particular situation of immigrant societies, where the dominant concern of new minorities is to enjoy the same rights as the older population and to integrate themselves into a larger society governed by neutral rules. In contrast, when the claims for protection come from groups that have been present in a given territory for a long time or that find themselves sharing the same nation-state due to changing borders or forced movements of population (hence, forced rather than voluntary migration), the purely individualistic method appears much less capable of providing real and effective protection to minorities.[38]

Probably the main reason why the liberal-individualist approach to minority protection is more entrenched in Anglo-American constitutional systems (in particular, in the United States and, to a lesser degree, in countries such as Canada, Australia and New Zealand) than in Europe is that, in the former, one encounters a problem that has traditionally given liberal theorists a headache: how to reconcile a universal commitment to individual human rights (including the right to autonomy) with a proper respect for the traditions of minorities that do not practise autonomy in their internal life and that are (by liberal standards) oppressive towards their members. This is arguably the fundamental liberal dilemma when it comes to minority rights. On the one hand, a liberal is committed to extending certain fundamental dignity-based rights to everyone. On the other hand, those minorities – often indigenous ones – that do not respect fundamental equality between men and women, that practise corporal punishment and that do not respect the individual's right to control his or her life to the degree deemed necessary by liberals, pose a threat to these fundamental values. Hence, the liberal theorist is concerned with the position of the most vulnerable members of those minorities – often women and children – who are threatened with deprivation of all those individual rights that non-minority citizens take for granted.

Collective rights aimed at the protection of the identity of the group as a whole accord that group a degree of immunity from interference by the wider community in its 'internal affairs'. As noted by Brian Barry:

> [I]t seems overwhelmingly plausible that some groups will operate in ways that are severely inimical to the interests of at any rate some of their members. To the extent that they do, cultural diversity cannot be an unqualified good. In fact, once we follow the path opened up by that thought, we shall soon arrive at the conclusion that diversity is desirable to the degree, and only to the degree, that each of the diverse groups functions in a way that is well adapted to advance the welfare and secure the rights of its members.[39]

The *prima facie* hostility of Anglo-American legal systems to minority rights stems in large part from this quandary. However, in the continental European setting and, in particular, in CEE states, this dilemma is much less acute: the problem just identified simply does not ring true in the context of CEE societies to the same degree that it does in the United States, Canada or Australia. The pattern of relations between an ethnic majority and minority (or minorities) does not fit as easily into the category of 'liberal majority versus oppressive minority';[40] as Nenad Dimitrijević noted: 'All post-communist states of the region claim adherence to liberal constitutionalism, and *no national minority ... would question main liberal tenets*'.[41] Therefore, the fundamental philosophical reason for distrusting the very idea of minority rights does not apply (or applies to a much lesser degree) to the CEE, and more broadly, European situation. Obviously, this does not negate the fact that a 'multicultural' solution, with an explicit recognition of separate minority rights, is often seen as a threat to the culture of the majority and to state sovereignty.

The problem, then, is not whether a liberal-neutralist model or a diversity-accommodating model (that is, a pluralist model) should be adopted; this dilemma seems to have been answered overwhelmingly in favour of the latter. As one Serbian legal scholar concludes:

> [E]xperience in [CEE] countries has shown that ethnocultural neutrality and group-neutral regulation cannot accommodate cultural pluralism, and cannot guarantee stability and peace between ethnic majorities and minorities. Traditional liberal attitudes lack empathy towards maintaining diversity, and cannot provide solutions in traditionally multicultural

environments where equality presumes an equal right to maintain one's distinct identity.[42]

It is significant that virtually the same argument has been endorsed officially in Hungarian law, namely in the 1993 Act on the Rights of Ethnic and National Minorities, which proclaims in its introduction that 'minority rights cannot be fully guaranteed within the bounds of individual civil rights; thus, they are also to be formulated as rights of particular groups in society'.[43]

Institutional articulation of minority rights

As noted above, the specific design of minority rights in CEE states varies from one country to the next but, overall, the constitutional texts provide a promising starting point for progressive policies and laws towards minorities. However, the actual implementation of those broad constitutional provisions has tended towards their confinement rather than their expansion, and the institutions that are hailed elsewhere as courageous and imaginative devices for the protection of constitutional rights – constitutional courts – frequently have handed down restrictive interpretations of constitutional provisions aimed at the protection of minority rights.

The question of language rights is perhaps the most instructive here because, as is known, they are directly related to a number of other rights, including the right of participation in the democratic process. The well-known case of Russian-speaking minorities in the Baltic states provides an example of the constitutional courts' very weak role (if any) in protecting language and other rights of minorities. Estonia's saga with its own Language Law is worth looking at because it illustrates the point well. The Constitutional Review Chamber (CRC) in Estonia was asked to decide on the constitutionality of imposing Estonian language requirements on electoral candidates running in national and local elections.[44] The 1997 amendments to the Language Act provided for language requirements of electoral candidates (as well as the tightening of Estonian language proficiency requirements for non-Estonian employees in the public and private sectors). As one commentator notes, the law had been 'motivated by nationalist desires to make sure that no non-Estonian-speaking person could be elected to parliament or a local council'.[45] The challenge to the law by the president was not based on minority rights grounds but rather on technicalities (the vagueness of language requirements and the delegation of the task to control the language proficiency to the executive branch, which breached the separation of powers). The court followed this narrow line of reasoning, adding the argument that one of the duties of the state was to preserve the Estonian nation and culture, as evidenced in the constitutional preamble and state language provisions. On the basis of these provisions and, additionally, of the provision that everyone has the right to address the authorities in Estonian and to receive answers in Estonian,[46] the court inferred that the challenged requirement of proficiency in the Estonian language for the candidates to parliament and councils was not unreasonable.

As a matter of fact, the court did put forward an 'activist' or 'expansive' interpretation, but one that actually undermined any possible claims for minority language rights. On the basis of the constitution's preamble (incidentally, a non-typical basis for a constitutional court's reasoning), which declares that the state will guarantee 'the preservation of the Estonian nation and culture through the ages' (note there is no mention of the language) and on the further basis of the principle that Estonia is a democratic republic,[47] the Chamber concluded that language requirements for electoral candidates could be justified. It was, therefore, on narrow technical grounds that the Chamber eventually struck down the controversial provisions. It agreed with the challenger that the law was impermissibly vague insofar as the requirements for employment were concerned and also that, by delegating the power to regulate the language requirements for election candidates to the government, it was contrary to the separation of powers: decisions connected with electoral rights should be made by the legislature and not the executive.

Unsurprisingly, the Parliament properly viewed the Constitutional Review Chamber's decision (and an analogous decision handed down a few months later)[48] as a 'green light ... to legislate language requirements for electoral candidates',[49] which it did, in November 1998, by passing amendments to the electoral law, which the president soon promulgated despite protests from Russian community leaders. These language requirements were eventually repealed in November 2001, but only under direct pressure from the OSCE and not as a result of a constitutional challenge.

In other post-communist countries, very few ethnicity-related decisions have been made by constitutional courts and, where they have, they would hardly support the thesis that those courts play a central role in shaping a regime of tolerance. For instance, in Romania in 1995, UDMR (the Hungarian minority party), along with some other opposition parties, attempted to introduce a provision promulgating the right of the Hungarian minority to have a state Hungarian-language university into the draft law on education. They did not succeed in the legislative process and challenged the bill before the constitutional court in an *ex ante* review procedure. However, the challenge failed.[50] Another example, taken from beyond the pool of candidate states, is a decision of the Ukrainian Constitutional Court in December 1999, in which the court strengthened the constitutional position of the Ukrainian language in Ukraine, and established an affirmative duty on all public bodies to use only Ukrainian throughout the country (even though in eastern and southern regions the Russian language is widely used in both private and public contexts).

It might be said at this point, in defence of constitutional courts, that they have very narrow scope for manoeuvre as they are bound by constitutional provisions which set up the 'official language'. This is true to some extent – indeed, in almost all candidate states (with the exception of Czech Republic and Hungary) there are constitutional provisions stipulating the official language of the state. On the other hand, the contours of the rights and duties entailed by the 'official language' rule are not self-evident and need to be articulated more clearly by those applying it. In addition, all these constitutions contain provisions stating that minorities are allowed to use their own language. It is, therefore, the task of constitutional courts, when faced with the relevant demand, to negotiate the borderline between the official language rule and the linguistic rights of the minorities. In those few cases in which the language rule was litigated before the courts, the results proved not particularly helpful to minorities.

Consider the example of the Polish Constitutional Tribunal and its only encounter, to date, with the official language rule. Poland provides an unwholesome example of a rigid, homogenizing constitutional attitude towards the official state language. The constitutional provision that declares that 'Polish is the official language'[51] leaves no room for the introduction of any minority languages into official fora, even in a restricted manner. While there is an additional sentence in this article, to the effect that the official language rule 'shall not infringe upon national minority rights resulting from ratified international agreements', at least one prominent critic of this constitutional provision has argued that it adds nothing to the first sentence and does not open up the possibility of introducing official minority languages.[52] It is therefore not an exception to the rigid rule: '[N]ational minorities have not acquired in this Constitution a right to depart from a general rule that Polish is the official language.'[53] The above-quoted critic has reviewed all of the international treaties between Poland and its neighbouring states and has concluded that none contains a rule permitting a minority to have its language officially recognized in Poland. If the drafters of the Constitution had wanted to allow for such a possibility, they would have said so explicitly in the official language provision.[54]

The only occasion when the Tribunal came to consider the meaning of the 'official language' provisions was in its 'interpretive decision' of 14 May 1997.[55] The Tribunal was asked by the President of the Supreme Audit Chamber to provide an interpretation of the official language provisions by setting out to whom exactly they applied, and also to which types of official actions they pertained. The direct trigger for the decision was unrelated to minority languages, however. Nonetheless, at the end of its lengthy decision (which confirmed that the requirement to use the official language applies to all state institutions and to all of their official actions), the Tribunal hinted that, as far as citizens were concerned, the official language rules were applicable only 'indirectly' (in their communications with state bodies) and that constitutional rights and freedoms defined the limits of the duty of state bodies to communicate in the official language. As the Tribunal stated in the very last sentence of its decision: 'A citizen, whenever he wants to exercise his fundamental freedoms and rights, cannot be forced to comply with the provisions establishing the official language'.[56] Unfortunately, this pronouncement was left in a vacuum: no specific criteria were identified regarding how to reconcile the official language provisions with the rights of members of minority groups.[57] However, the limits on these rights seem very strong and rigid. As noted by the authoritative commentator cited above: under the present constitution, the right to use a minority language in public 'does not imply that state organs have a duty to issue official certificates (e.g. birth certificates) or conduct court proceedings in the language of [an] ethnic minority'.[58] In other words, no duties upon state bodies were inferred from the 'fundamental freedoms and rights' to which the Constitutional Tribunal alluded and which established, allegedly, the limits of the official language provisions.

Another important aspect of the promotion of minorities within the political system of a country is the making of special arrangements for facilitating or assuring their representation in the political branches of the government and, in particular, in self-government and representative institutions.[59] Mild types of such facilitation take the form of a more lenient election 'threshold', as in Poland[60] or Lithuania.[61] Romania goes one step further: its constitution reserves a seat in the parliament for each ethnic minority organization that fails to obtain a sufficient number of votes to get elected in the normal manner, though the electoral law clarifies that this is subject to obtaining at least 5 per cent of votes.[62] In Slovenia, the Hungarian and Italian minorities can elect at least one candidate each to the National Assembly.[63]

In Hungary, apart from the constitutional right to be represented in national and local bodies, national and ethnic minorities have a constitutional right to form their own minority self-governments. By the mid-1990s, it had been reported that over 800 such minority self-government units existed in Hungary,[64] although it must be added that serious doubts have been expressed as to the resources available to, and the powers and effects of, these bodies.[65] However, when it comes to the formal parliamentary representation of ethnic minorities, despite an impressive number of assorted legislative proposals aimed at designing an acceptable system,[66] there has emerged as yet no political consensus that permits the adoption of a statute to regulate this issue – even though the Hungarian Constitutional Court declared unconstitutional the absence of mechanisms to implement the constitutional requirement for parliamentary representation of minorities.[67]

The Slovak Constitutional Court provides an example of constitutional court intervention that actually prevents a system of ethnic representation.[68] In that country, where the Constitution is silent on the question of the political representation of minorities, there was an attempt to introduce by legislation a rule of proportional representation of ethnic groups (an admittedly controversial idea, which is not meant to be endorsed here). A local self-government electoral law of 1998 stipulated that, in towns and villages where national minorities or ethnic groups lived, the total number of deputies in local elections must be divided proportionally, resulting in a faithful reflection of the ratio between Slovaks and individual minorities. The law was challenged before the Constitutional Court, which found that a quota system was contrary to the constitutional rule of equal access to public offices, to the principle of equal dignity and to the constitutional provision that stated that the regulation of political rights must facilitate political competition in a democratic society. In effect, the Court rejected any idea of 'preferential quotas' in order to improve the status of a national minority or ethnic group, opting instead for the individual-civic principle: all citizens are equal in the exercise of their political rights, regardless of group membership.

Overall, one must conclude that the record of constitutional courts in the sphere of the promotion and protection of minority rights has been a mixed bag in CEE states. There have been, no doubt, some important and positive (though rather limited) contributions made by constitutional courts in this regard, such as those decisions by the Slovenian court on the restrictive nationality law, mentioned above, or by the Hungarian court on the constitutional failure to enact the statute implementing the constitutional rule of representation of minorities at a national level. In addition, there was the extremely important and courageous decision by the Bulgarian Constitutional Court, which saved the Turkish party (MRF) from being banned.[69]

On the other hand, as elaborated above, there have been decisions that displayed a failure to grasp the opportunity to provide an expansive, pro-minority interpretation of constitutional rules. This suggests that the contribution of these new constitutional courts to the area of minority rights protection has been much less impressive than initial high hopes would have anticipated. The barriers against an expansive approach to minority rights have remained powerful, despite the fact that the constitutional design provided for counter-majoritarian mechanisms that have proved reasonably effective in many other areas of constitutional interpretation.

Ideological predispositions and commitments

The explanation for this reluctance of major institutional actors in CEE countries to adopt an expansive approach to minority rights is to be found in the role played by nationalism and an appeal to the dominant ethnic idea within state-building and state-consolidation efforts in CEE states. After the fall of communism, national identity (often perceived in an ethnic rather than civic fashion) has probably been the most powerful social factor, other than those identified with the social foundations of the *ancien régime*, capable of injecting a necessary degree of coherence into society and of countervailing the *anomie* of a disintegrated, decentralized and demoralized society. An expectation, expressed in particular in the 1970s and 1980s by democratic opposition, that 'civil society', constructed on the basis of spontaneous social solidarity, responsibility and strong informal networks between the state and the family, would play the role of a unifying force, turned out to be little more than wishful thinking.

In some of these societies (notably, in Poland), the dominant religion played this role to a limited degree and for a limited period of time, but faced its own problems given the need to reconstitute its social role in a situation in which it was no longer the only free political space in an otherwise oppressed society. Hence, virtually the sole common force capable of supporting the social coherence required for state-building after the fall of communism was a national ideal related in these countries to the idea of sovereignty of the nation state.[70] As Claus Offe has noted: 'The sheer absence of imagined as well as institutionalized collectivities such as classes, status groups, professional or sectoral associations, constituted religious groups, etc. moves the ethnic code into a prominent position.'[71]

One might deplore this fact, but nationalism has turned out to be an indispensable factor in providing the basis for societal mobilization without which the processes of state-building and state transformation would not have occurred, or would have been even less successful than they were in CEE countries. This confirms the analysis that John Breuilly developed in his study of the relationship between nationalism and the modern state.[72] Breuilly identifies three main functions of nationalist ideologies *vis-à-vis* the state that render nationalism a particularly effective component of political action: those of coordination, mobilization and legitimacy.[73] The mobilization function is of particular relevance in our context: while Breuilly carefully emphasizes that the general process of mobilization in the modern state does not give rise necessarily to nationalistic politics, especially when different social groups find effective ways of expressing their interests to government, nevertheless, in circumstances where civil society actors articulate their interests poorly and where the representation of social interests by parties based on class or special interest is either blocked or underdeveloped, nationalism becomes a convenient device for political mobilization. This – we might observe – is precisely the case in post-communist societies and the words written by Breuilly in relation to colonial situations apply equally to post-communist CEE states: 'In such cases the appeal to cultural identity is often a substitute for the failure to connect politics with significant social interests'.[74] Furthermore, it needs to be remembered that a significant number of the accession states are, literally speaking, 'new' states (all three Baltic states, the Czech Republic, Slovakia and Slovenia). It is natural and understandable (if deplorable) that 'new states' make a strong appeal to national identity, both as a way of asserting their legitimacy in the international order, and to match a new territorial polity to an ideology that provides the necessary degree of coherence and mobilization to make a new political elite sufficiently legitimate. It is also in the new states that nationalist movements – often in opposition to a dominant elite – find particularly fertile ground for development (as there is always a degree of territorial-ethnic mismatch inherited from the older state), and push the dominant elite towards a more nationalist policy.

This, it is argued, is the main explanation for the chronic resistance of institutions in the post-communist states to a more expansive interpretation of minority rights. In particular, when combined with anxieties of perceived 'loss of sovereignty' relating to accession to the EU, the patterns of incentives among political actors in CEE states have not favoured pro-minority policies. This often combined with more specific, contingent factors (such as resentment of Russian-speaking minorities in Baltic states related to the forced Russification of these countries in the immediate past) and, as a result, created a situation in which the opportunities for pro-minorities approaches were meagre. Whenever such opportunities arose, they were grasped – as in Hungary, which had its own reasons to lead by example in providing its minorities with a thick structure of local representation – but, even in these circumstances, the policy was often tainted by less benign, more nationalist motives, as reflected in the Hungarian Status Law, at least as originally conceived.

Conclusions

As argued at the outset, the impact of Europeanization and, more specifically, of conditionality, upon the positive changes in the law and politics of CEE states has been most impressive in cases where there has been a synergy between external factors (clear, coherent and credible norms supported by the established practices of the Western states in a given domain) and internal ones (institutional support and proper incentives to act in favour of the adoption and implementation of those norms). In the case of minority protection, such a synergy has occurred only to a very limited degree. As demonstrated in the first section of this chapter, the minority protection norms that the Western states expected CEE states to follow were opaque and rarely implemented in a coherent way throughout Western Europe. As illustrated in the second section, the institutions charged with the development and articulation of constitutional norms in CEE had no incentives or ideological predisposition to push the articulation of minority rights in an expansive direction.

Where does this leave EU conditionality with regard to the protection of minority rights? There are two schools of thought.[75] The first suggests that standards of minority protection will decrease following the formal end to conditionality which resulted from accession of the 'candidate states' to the EU.[76] As minority protection is not part of the EU competence, the new member states (just as all other member states) will be free of any special scrutiny in this regard; they will be able to revert to their old ways – unless properly checked by other European institutions (of course, this has been the case regardless of EU conditionality). The second suggests a phenomenon of 'reverse conditionality' or a 'boomerang effect': the standards articulated in the conditionality instruments (and, in particular, despite all their weaknesses, in the Commission's regular reports on the progress of candidate states towards accession) will inform thinking about minority rights and minority protection across the board in the newly enlarged EU. As the then OSCE's HCNM Rolf Ekeus proclaimed in 2002 (as a normative ideal rather than a prediction): 'the standards on which the Copenhagen criteria are based should be universally applicable within and throughout the EU, in which case they should be equally – and consistently – applied to all Member States'.[77]

It is very hard today to speculate as to which of these two scenarios will prevail, but it is not unlikely that future developments will strike a middle path between the extremes. On the one hand, it is unlikely that the EU will take 'minority protection' on board: with the enlargement of the EU (and, therefore, with a larger overlap between the EU and CoE membership base), the voices urging a clear delineation of tasks between the two organizations will intensify and the case for the EU to sideline those goals that the CoE or OSCE are (reasonably) good at achieving will become even stronger. It is, therefore, likely that the moderate voices of scholars like Bruno de Witte, who argue that the EU should not adopt the 'holistic' approach of detailed standard-setting as regards minority protection, will prevail; the EU will confine itself to a piecemeal approach, by incorporating concern for minorities into EU cultural and educational policies (including the promotion of minority languages), through cultural diversity policies, and so forth.[78]

On the other hand, however, it is unreasonable to expect – and it would certainly be regrettable – that the standards and experience written into the EU's institutional memory relating to political conditionality were to be erased altogether with the passing of accession. While no clear and substantial norms can be attributed to the standards used in conditionality, there are a number of problem areas, information, suggestions and complaints deposited in this institutional memory and, more specifically, in the Commission's annual reports on candidate states' progress towards accession. These may continue to haunt those misbehaving – and this would be a good thing. Under the general rules for monitoring rights developments within the member states and, in particular, under Article 7 of the Treaty on European Union on sanctions against a member state found to be in a serious and persistent breach of democracy, human rights and the rule of law, one can anticipate a higher degree of sensitivity towards the new entrants than towards the older member states. This is because some of these solutions have been registered in European public opinion – and in the EU conditionality context more specifically – as being vulnerable to serious objections regarding their treatment of minorities. This being said, the above is only a very minimal threshold for international scrutiny.

Notes

1. W. Kymlicka, 'The Evolving Basis of European Norms of Minority Rights: Rights to Culture, Participation and Autonomy', Paper presented at the Conference 'Nations, Minorities and European Integration', European University Institute, Florence, 7–8 May 2004, at 21–2. See also Chapter 2 of this volume.
2. A.L. Dimitrova, 'Conditionality Meets Post-communism: Europeanization and Administrative Reform in Central and Eastern Europe', Paper presented at the workshop on 'The Europeanization of Eastern Europe: Evaluating the Conditionality Model', The Robert Schuman Centre for Advanced Studies at the European University Institute, 4–5 July 2003, at 33.
3. See M. Brusis, 'Instrumentalized Conditionality: Regionalization in the Czech Republic and Slovakia', Paper presented at the Workshop 'The Europeanization of Eastern Europe: Evaluating the Conditionality Model', The Robert Schuman Centre for Advanced Studies at the European University Institute, 4–5 July 2003, at 13–14.
4. The European Council, held in Copenhagen in 1993, established that in order to be successful in its pursuit of full membership the applicant state must enjoy, *inter alia*, 'stability of institutions guaranteeing democracy, the rule of law, human rights and respect for and protection of minorities'.
5. G. Sasse, 'EU Conditionality and Minority Rights in Central and Eastern Europe', Paper presented at the European Forum Meeting. The Robert Schuman Centre for Advanced Studies at the European University Institute, Florence, 15 April 2004, at 1.
6. See M. Johns, ' "Do As I Say, Not As I Do": The European Union, Eastern Europe and Minority Rights', *East European Politics and Societies* 17 (2003): 682–99.
7. Belgium, Greece and Luxembourg have not ratified the Convention; France has not yet signed it.
8. The matter only recently came to public attention when, in the beginning of April 2004, the overwhelming majority of those taking part in the referendum in Slovenia rejected the idea of restoring the citizenship rights to those formerly 'erased' from the registers.
9. A. Balcer, 'Słowenia i mniejszości narodowe', *Gazeta Wyborcza* (Warsaw), 28 April 2004, <http://serwisy.gazeta.pl/wyborcza/2029020,34475,2047285.html>. Please note that the law was eventually struck down as unconstitutional by the Slovenian Constitutional Court in 2003.
10. I am grateful to John Packer for this observation.
11. See, for example, European Commission, 'Regular Report on Slovenia's Progress towards Accession 2002', Commission Report. COM(2002) 700 final – SEC(2002) 1411, <http://ec.europa.eu/enlargement/archives/pdf/key_documents/2002/sl_en.pdf> at 27.
12. See Sasse, 'EU Conditionality', *supra* note 5.
13. European Commission, 'Regular Report on Lithuania's Progress Towards Accession 2002', Commission Report. COM(2002) 700 final – SEC(2002) 1406: at 29. Emphasis added.
14. Thornberry lists the objections by the critics of the Convention as addressed to 'its loose 'framework' structure of 'programme type' provisions, its avoidance of the language of collective rights, its textual silence on autonomy, the 'softness' of the language, and the ensemble of qualifiers attached to key provisions'. P. Thornberry, 'A Critique of European Standards on Minority Rights', Paper presented at the

European Forum Meeting of the Robert Schuman Centre for Advanced Studies, European University Institute, Florence, 22 April 2004, at 9.

15. The monitoring of its implementation is carried out by the Committee of Ministers assisted by an Advisory Committee consisting of 'recognized experts in the field of protection of national minorities'.

16. The results of litigation under this article have been meagre and, consequently, the ECHR has been a limited instrument as far as minority protection is concerned. See Thornberry, 'A Critique', *supra* note 14, at 7. See also, generally, G. Gilbert, 'The Burgeoning Minority Rights Jurisprudence of the European Court of Human Rights', *Human Rights Quarterly* 24 (2002): 736–80.

17. An important limitation of the Charter is that it explicitly refuses to apply to 'the languages of migrants' and it does not indicate when a language ceases to be regarded as a language of migrants. See Thornberry, 'A Critique', *supra* note 14, at 7.

18. Belgium, Greece, Ireland and Portugal have not signed it; Italy and France have not ratified it.

19. Council Directive 2000/43 [2000]OJ L180/22.

20. On discrimination against Roma in Spain and Germany, see OSI/EUMAP, *Monitoring the EU Accession Process: Minority Protection*, Vol. 1 (Budapest: OSI EU Accession Monitoring Programme, 2002), 37–49.

21. These include: failure by local authorities in Slovakia to set up a faculty for Hungarian teachers (see the 2002 Report on Slovakia, citation below); the refusal of the Latvian Parliament to ratify the Framework Convention for the Protection of National Minorities (see the 2002 Report on Latvia, citation below); and some mild misgivings about the Hungarian Status Law (see, for example, the 2002 Report on Hungary, citation below); European Commission, 'Regular Report on Slovakia's Progress towards Accession 2002', Commission Report, COM(2002) 700 final – SEC(2002) 1410: at 30; *ibid.*, 'Regular Report on Latvia's Progress towards Accession 2002', Commission Report COM(2002) 700 final – SEC(2002) 1405: at 30; *ibid.*, 'Regular Report on Hungary's Progress towards Accession 2002', Commission Report COM(2002) 700 final – SEC(2002) 1404: at 30.

22. Constitution of the Republic of Bulgaria 1991.

23. Constitution of the Republic of Latvia 1922, Article 114.

24. *Ibid.*, Article 6.

25. Constitution of the Republic of Hungary 1949, Article 68(2). See also the constitutions of Albania (Article 20), Belarus (Article 50), Czech Charter (Article 25), Hungary (Article 68), Macedonia (Article 48(4)), Slovakia (Article 34), Romania (Article 32(3)), Ukraine (Article 53), Serbia and Montenegro Charter (Article 52), Montenegro (Article 68) and Serbia (Article 32). Full texts of all of the above can be found online at <http://www.legislationline.org//search.php>

26. Constitution of the Republic of Estonia 1992, Article 51(2).

27. Constitution of the Republic of Hungary, *supra* note 25, Article 68(2) and (3).

28. See Gilbert, 'The Burgeoning Minority Rights', *supra* note 7, at 738.

29. Constitution of the Federal Republic of Slovenia 1991, Article 64.

30. *Ibid.*, Article 64.

31. See A.L. Pap, 'Representation or Ethnic Balance: Ethnic Minorities in Parliaments', *Journal of East European Law* 7 (2000): 261–339, at 289.

32. This particular quote is taken from Article 6 of the Constitutional of Romania 1991. The following constitutions have similar provisions: Albania (Article 20); Croatia (Article 15); Czech Charter (Article 25); Georgia (Article 38); Latvia

(Article 114); Lithuania (Article 37); Macedonia (Article 48); Poland (Article 35(1), although Section 2 of the same article uses the language of group rights); Romania (Article 6); Slovakia (Article 34); Slovenia (Article 61, although note the exception relating to Hungarian and Italian minorities); Ukraine (Article 53); and Serbia (Article 32). Full texts of all of the above can be found online at <http://www.legislationline.org//search.php>

33. Constitution of the Republic of Hungary, *supra* note 25. Article 68(4). Note, however, that the statute on the rights of national and ethnic minorities adopted on 7 July 1993 uses both the language of collective and individual rights. See P. Paczolay, 'Human Rights and Minorities in Hungary', *Journal of Constitutional Law in Eastern and Central Europe* 3 (1996): 111–26, at 123.

34. Thus, Article 64 states that: 'The autochthonous Italian and Hungarian ethnic communities and their members shall be granted the right to ... ', Constitution of the Federal Republic of Slovenia, *supra* note 29.

35. Constitution of the Republic of Poland 1997, Article 35(2).

36. *Ibid.*, Article 35(1). For other examples of the mixed use of both group and individual rights language, see the Constitution of the Republic of Estonia, *supra* note 26, Articles 49–51.

37. As an account of the actual, authoritative legal situation of the United States this is certainly an oversimplification: the rejection of group rights is not absolute in US law. For example, when the US Supreme Court allowed Amish families to keep their children out of school up to a certain age (see *Wisconsin v. Yoder*, 406 US 205 (1994)) or when it upheld Native American tribal law that imposed patrilineal kinship rules which limited women's marital choices (see *Santa Clara Pueblo v. Martinez*, 436 US 49 (1978)), it clearly recognized the legal weight of group-based claims for treatment different to that accorded by universally binding legal rules. Similar group-based thinking is visible in the enhanced legal protection of those who are victims of crimes motivated by hatred of a group (in the form of enhanced punishment for hate crimes, see *Wisconsin v. Mitchell*, 508 US 476 (1993)). On the qualified nature of the group/individual rights distinction in US law, see J. Greenberg, 'Affirmative Action in Higher Education: Confronting the Condition and Theory', *Boston College Law Review* 43 (2002): 521–621, at 580–1.

38. See D. Petrova, 'Racial Discrimination and the Rights of Minority Cultures', in S. Fredman (ed.), *Discrimination and Human Rights: The Case of Racism* (Oxford: Oxford University Press, 2001), at 65; and M.J. Aukerman, 'Definitions and Justifications: Minority and Indigenous Rights in a Central/East European Context', *Human Rights* 22 (2002): 1011–50, at 1029–30.

39. B. Barry, *Culture and Equality* (Cambridge: Polity, 2001), at 134.

40. There are some exceptions, of course, such as that of the Roma population in Europe.

41. N. Dimitrijević, 'Ethno-Nationalized States of Eastern Europe: Is there a Constitutional Alternative?', *Studies in East European Thought* 54 (2002): 246–69, at 247. Emphasis added.

42. T. Várady, 'On the Chances of Ethnocultural Justice in East Central Europe', in W. Kymlicka and M. Opalski (eds), *Can Liberal Pluralism be Exported? Western Political Theory and Ethnic Relations in Eastern Europe* (Oxford: Oxford University Press, 2001), 135–49, at 147–8.

43. Quoted in S. Deets, 'Reconsidering East European Minority Policy: Liberal Theory and European Norms', *East European Politics and Societies* 16 (2002): 30–53, at 49.

44. Constitutional Chamber of the Supreme Court of Estonia, Decision concerning the constitutionality of the 'Amendment Act to the Language Act and the State Fees Act', 4 November 1998, <http://www.legislationline.org/legislation.php?tid=57&lid=2225&less=false>
45. V. Pettai, 'Democratic Norm Building and Constitutional Discourse Formation', Paper presented at the Workshop 'Rethinking the Rule of Law in Post-Communist Europe', European University Institute, Florence, 22–23 February 2002, at 26.
46. Constitution of the Republic of Estonia, *supra* note 26, Article 51(1).
47. *Ibid.*, Article 1.
48. In November 1998 the Constitutional Review Chamber considered a challenge, which reached it via a lower court, to the original Language Act (not the 1997 amendments) requirements for local deputies. See Pettai, 'Democratic Norm Building', *supra* note 45, at 28–9.
49. *Ibid.*, at 29.
50. Of course, one may suggest that it was due to the general weakness of the Romanian Constitutional Court and that a stronger constitutional court would have taken on the legislature more aggressively but it is an unverifiable speculation.
51. Constitution of the Republic of Poland, *supra* note 35, Article 27.
52. J. Trzciński, 'Remarks about Article 27', in L. Garlicki (ed.), *Konstytucja Rzeczypospolitej Polskiej: Komentarz* (Warsaw: Wydawnictwo Sejmowe, 1999). (Loose leaf.)
53. *Ibid.*, at 4 (quoting J. Boć with approval).
54. *Ibid.*, at 4.
55. The decision was handed down before the new constitution entered into force, which declared in its Article 27 that 'Polish is the official language'. The subject-matter of the Tribunal's interpretation was a 1945 decree on the official language (previous Polish Constitutions had not dealt with the issue at all); however, according to authoritative commentators, this decision also applies to the new constitution and can thus be seen as a statement of the current official position of the Constitutional Tribunal on the issue of the 'official language'.
56. Trzciński, 'Remarks about Article 27', *supra* note 52, at 796.
57. To be fair, the Tribunal was not asked to do so in this particular interpretative decision.
58. Trzciński, 'Remarks about Article 27', *supra* note 52, at 4–5.
59. For a very good survey and discussion see Pap, 'Representation or Ethnic Balance', *supra* note 31.
60. Electoral committees representing ethnic minorities do not have to pass the 5 per cent threshold to achieve parliamentary representation.
61. The organizations representing ethnic minority parties were exempt (until the 1996 amendment to the 1992 election law) from the 4 per cent threshold needed to elect candidates under the proportional rules (which apply to half of the MPs, the remaining half being elected through a majoritarian system).
62. See Pap, 'Representation or Ethnic Balance', *supra* note 31, at 286–8.
63. Constitution of the Federal Republic of Slovenia 1991, *supra* note 29, Article 80 (3).
64. Paczolay, 'Human Rights and Minorities', *supra* note 33, at 125.
65. Deets, 'Reconsidering East European Minority Policy', *supra* note 43, at 49–51.
66. See Pap, 'Representation or Ethnic Balance', *supra* note 31, at 320–4.
67. See European Commission, 'Regular Report on Hungary', *supra* note 21, at 20.

68. Decision 19/98 of 15 October 1998, summarized in *Bull Constitution Case Law* 3 (1998): 460–2, SVK-1998-3-010.
69. The decision of the Bulgarian Constitutional Court of 22 April 1992 on the status of the Movement of Rights and Freedom. For a discussion of the decision, see E. Konstantinov, 'Turkish Party in Bulgaria Allowed to Continue', *East European Constitutional Review* 1(2) (1992): 11–12.
70. Of course, the link between nationalism and celebration of sovereignty is contingent; the national idea (even in its strong forms) can thrive without, or even against, the context of a sovereign state. In countries such as Poland or the Baltic States, where the memories of the loss of sovereignty are strong, the two happen to come in a package. I will return to this point below.
71. C. Offe, 'Ethnic Politics in European Transitions', Working Paper of Zentrum für Europäische Rechtspolitik an der Universität Bremen, Bremen, February 1993, at 26, footnote omitted.
72. J. Breuilly, *Nationalism and the State* (New York: St. Martin's Press, 1982), at 349.
73. *Ibid.*, at 365–73.
74. *Ibid.*, at 371.
75. See, for example, B. de Witte, 'The Impact of Enlargement on the Constitution of the European Union', in M. Cremona (ed.), *The Enlargement of the European Union* (Oxford: Oxford University Press, 2003), 209–52, at 240; and Sasse, 'EU Conditionality', *supra* note 5, at 32.
76. Of course, conditionality will continue *vis-à-vis* Bulgaria, Romania, Turkey and other future potential member states.
77. Speech in Copenhagen on 5 November 2002, quoted in Johns, ' "Do As I Say" ', *supra* note 6, at 699.
78. B. de Witte, 'The Constitutional Resources for an EU Minority Protection Policy', in G.N. Toggenburg (ed.), *Minority Protection and the Enlarged European Union: The Way Forward* (Budapest: OSI/LFI, 2004), 107–25.

9
Enlargement and Interethnic Power-Sharing Arrangements in Central and Eastern Europe*

Martin Brusis

Introduction

The surge of ethnic wars on the European continent during the 1990s led the European Union (EU) to put particular emphasis on protecting national minorities in Central and Eastern Europe. The enlargement process endowed the EU with far-reaching powers in those countries that applied for EU membership. This chapter is less interested in how those powers facilitated the implementation of minority protection standards in accession countries, and focuses instead on the impact exerted by the EU on arrangements of domestic interethnic politics, that is, on the institutionalized relations between political actors representing ethnic minorities and majorities. The motivation to adopt this perspective is the assumption that 'politics matters' for the situation of national minorities because international norms of minority protection continue to be only weakly developed and specified. Faced with normative uncertainty, even actors in a weak position politically, such as the accession countries in relation to the EU, have a wide margin of discretion and can tailor normative reasoning to the needs of the political game.

This chapter begins by explaining how the EU's policy on the protection and rights of minorities in accession countries is composed in the absence of an EU minority rights *acquis*. Despite its incoherence, this policy has been very effective, due to the 'loose coupling' of advice and accession conditionality. The following section investigates the impact of the accession constellation on interethnic power relations in three Central and Eastern European (CEE) countries: Bulgaria, Romania and Slovakia. In all three, ethnic minority parties participate in government, albeit in different forms and

---

*This contribution was elaborated in the context of a project on 'issues and consequences of EU enlargement', jointly managed by the Bertelsmann Foundation and the Center for Applied Policy Research. The author wishes to thank Elitsa Markova, Gerhard Seewann and the library of the Südost Institute in Munich for their indispensable support and advice.

degrees, and it is argued that the EU has contributed to the emergence of these models of consociational power-sharing. The final section draws conclusions for interethnic relations in the new member states of an enlarged EU, and reflects upon the 'liberal individualist–pluralism' debate. Consociational power-sharing, it is argued, is to be preferred over a territorialization of interethnic relations and sectoral policies relevant for minorities that may be coordinated among EU member states.

What minority protection policy does the EU have in the accession process?

This section analyses the policy of the EU with respect to the protection of national minorities in accession countries. Whereas the other accession criteria defined by the 1993 European Council of Copenhagen were integrated into the Treaty of Nice 2003 and were reflected in secondary legislation, the meaning of 'respect for and protection of minorities' has not been developed further in EU law.[1] Lacking a detailed and codified *acquis* on minority protection, EU institutions such as the Commission, the Council of Ministers and the European Parliament have used five main 'reference points' to define their policy and to assess whether accession countries fulfil the 'minority criterion' or protect national minorities effectively.[2]

First, insofar as minority protection can be viewed as the outcome of anti-discrimination policies, a legal frame of reference has been created with the extension of anti-discrimination provisions in the Treaty on the European Communities[3] and the adoption of the so-called Race Directive implementing the 'principle of equal treatment between persons irrespective of racial or ethnic origin'.[4] This Race Directive uses a comprehensive notion of ethnic and racial discrimination and is not limited to employees who experience discrimination at the hands of public authorities. The Directive applies also to legal persons, to discrimination in the fields of education, social protection and the provision of public goods, and includes discriminatory rules created in the private sector.[5] Since 2000, the EU has expected the accession countries to incorporate and implement the Directive within their domestic legislation and practice.[6] The Directive provides a comprehensive legal base from which to address negative discrimination, and facilitates positive discrimination in its statement that the principle of equal treatment 'shall not prevent any Member State from maintaining or adopting specific measures to prevent or compensate for disadvantages linked to positive actions at the national level'.[7] However, it does not detail specifically how or in what ways states should go about adopting such measures.

Second, EU institutions have been able to specify standards of minority rights protection where a general policy consensus existed among EU member states. For example, there was broad political agreement on the need to grant full citizenship status to Russian-speaking non-citizens in Estonia and Latvia. While the EU has not rejected the basic position of the Estonian and Latvian governments, according to which international minority protection standards do not apply to their non-citizens, it has continued to pressure the two countries for a quicker naturalization of this group. Similar shared EU policy aims are the social integration of the Roma minority and good relations between states with national minorities and the neighbouring ethnic kin-states of these minorities. The latter aim, for example, provided one of the reference points for the Commission's critique of the way Hungary prepared its Status Law supporting ethnic Hungarians in neighbouring countries.[8] However, it is rare that the scope of the policy consensus in the EU is delineated clearly; furthermore, its legitimacy depends largely on unanimity among the member states and, as such, is liable to be fluid over time.

Third, the EU institutions have referred to legal standards of minority protection established by the Council of Europe (CoE), notably, the Framework Convention on the Protection of National Minorities (FCNM) and the European Charter for Regional and Minority Languages (ECRML). However, this legal framework cannot be said to be universal: in the first place, the FCNM has not even been ratified by a number of the CoE member states, four of them members of the EU,[9] with the ECRML encountering even less support. Furthermore, the FCNM contains few concrete prescriptions to be monitored or enforced and it defines minority protection largely as a task to be fulfilled by states, and not as a set of objective rights that accrue to all national minorities or individuals belonging to national minorities.

In its regular reports monitoring progress made by the candidate countries in meeting the criteria of EU accession (Progress Reports), the Commission seemed to expect the candidates to ratify the FCNM prior to EU accession, although neither did it declare this explicitly to be a general requirement nor has the FCNM become part of the accession negotiations. For example, the 2002 Progress Report stated that 'Latvia is urged to ratify the [FCNM]'.[10] The Report on Turkey also noted that it had not signed the FCNM.[11] The Progress Reports also referred to ways in which the Committee of Ministers of the CoE and the Advisory Committee to the FCNM assessed the implementation of the Framework Convention in accession countries. Contrary to the FCNM, the implementation of the ECRML was not anticipated by the Commission; it neither monitored its ratification systematically for all candidates nor criticized its non-implementation. The European Parliament referred to the FCNM in its resolutions on the enlargement negotiations and the Council mentioned 'international standards' as a general point of reference in its 'Accession Partnerships', that is, in its decisions setting out priorities for the candidate countries' preparation for accession.[12]

Fourth, in their assessments, the EU institutions have reflected norms developed by the Organization for Security and Cooperation in Europe (OSCE) and its High Commissioner on National Minorities (HCNM).[13] The

EU has 'in effect delegated to the HCNM the task of judging whether [Central and Eastern European] countries have "done enough" in terms of minority rights'.[14] In the case of Estonia and Latvia for example, the EU and its member states concluded Europe Agreements that contained 'the commitment to [the] further development of Estonia's [and Latvia's] new economic and political system which respects – in accordance *inter alia* with the undertakings made within the context of ... the Organization for Security and Cooperation in Europe (OSCE) – the rule of law and human rights, including the rights of persons belonging to minorities'.[15] The subsequent Accession Partnerships for the two countries referred to these clauses, which assigned a more enhanced role to the OSCE than the Europe Agreements with other accession countries. Despite this specific legal formulation, however, OSCE documents and the Recommendations of the HCNM did not furnish firm standards for the accession process as they were not legally binding and were concerned primarily with issues of security and not with the aim of setting universal standards of justice.

Finally, the Commission and the Parliament also used domestic constitutional provisions and legislation as points of reference. They interpreted these domestic rules as self-commitments undertaken by an accession country, and addressed implementation deficits or called for compliance with these rules. For example, its 2002 Progress Report on Romania stated that the Law on Local Public Administration, which regulated the official use of minority languages, had been 'successfully applied despite the reticence of some prefectures and local authorities'.[16] Relying on domestic rules and agreements is advantageous as it enables the EU institutions to focus their policy on the local situation in a specific country, but it risks having the parameters of the situation determine the normative assumptions underlying EU policies. To take the above-mentioned Romanian example, for instance, where the use of the minority language as an official language is permitted in municipalities with more than 20 per cent of the residents belonging to the relevant minority, the FCNM and other international standards lack a central point of reference and do not specify a threshold. Furthermore, by linking their evaluation to the domestic context, EU institutions tend to replace a justice-based assessment with a security-based approach aimed at consensual conflict settlement.[17] Thus, whereas domestic political conflicts over the use of the minority language, minority education or culture were noted with concern, the absence or resolution of major disputes was evaluated positively and represented an indicator of compliance with the accession criteria.

From the above discussion it is clear that, although these five points of reference and the political positions derived from them make sense individually, clearly they do not add up to a coherent policy.[18] The EU has been perceived as promoting both anti-discrimination and minority protection objectives, but the extent to which anti-discrimination policies may achieve or replace sufficient minority protection is not clear. The EU did not support group rights as an approach to minority protection expressly, but neither did it demonstrate a clear preference for individual rights.[19] Despite the emphasis placed on the minority protection criteria during the enlargement process, no specific commitments or expectations were enshrined in the Accession Treaty for the first new member states from Central and Eastern Europe, in force from 1 May 2004. Likewise, the protection of minorities was absent from the treaty granting membership to Bulgaria and Romania, adopted roughly a year after the first accession wave and entering into force from 1 January 2007.[20]

A security-based interest in consensual conflict settlement has taken priority over the development of fair and just standards. With the exceptions of Slovakia and Turkey, candidate countries that did not take into account EU critiques of their minority policy were not sanctioned in any way. However, the absence of sanctions might also be regarded as an indicator of behavioural compliance and of effective EU policy-making. In other words, the EU has been able to allow itself diffuse and ambiguous minority rights norms because, effectively, its accession criteria induced the governments of accession countries to align their policies with EU expectations, irrespective of their incoherence.

It is inappropriate to interpret EU statements on minority protection as 'normative judgments', that is, as inferences drawn from a coherent set of norms and linked to certain necessary consequences.[21] Rather, they represent 'moral suasion', advice that has been coupled only loosely with the decision on whether or not an accession country is to be accepted as a member state. Statements from the Progress Reports, Accession Partnerships or Resolutions of the European Parliament indicate the way an accession country should go but do not limit the discretion of the EU and its member states to decide whether the political criteria have been met or whether an accession country can enter. The loose coupling of (bad) evaluations with (negative) enlargement decisions has worked as a strong incentive for accession countries to approximate EU expectations and it has provided the EU with maximum flexibility.

Bulgaria, Romania, Slovakia: EU-induced consociationalism?

This section studies how the EU has influenced interethnic power relations in Central and Eastern European countries. It is confined to Bulgaria, Romania and Slovakia – the two most recent EU member state and a member state from the 2004 wave of accessions with significant ethnic minorities – which were selected mainly for their apt illustration of consociational methods of power-sharing. Consociationalism has been defined by Arend Lijphart as a model of democracy and government for societies with ethnic, religious or cultural cleavages.[22] Characteristics of the consociational model are government by a grand coalition of the political leaders of all significant segments of a plural society, veto rights of all partners involved in the governing coalition, a high degree of autonomy for each segment to run its own internal affairs, and proportionality as the principal standard of political participation, civil service appointments and allocation of public funds.[23] Consequently, the following paragraphs elaborate briefly on these elements of consociationalism in each of the three countries.

Bulgaria

In Bulgaria, the parliamentary elections of 2001 resulted in a coalition between the National Movement Simeon II (NDSV) and the party seeking to represent Bulgaria's 9.4 per cent ethnic Turkish citizens, the Movement for Rights and Freedoms (DPS).[24] DPS was in a veto position, as the NDSV required the support of DPS deputies to achieve a majority in parliament. The DPS participated in the cabinet of Prime Minister Simeon Sakscoburggotski with a Minister of Agriculture, a Minister without Portfolio and deputy ministers in the Ministries of Defence, Agriculture and Forestry, Ecology, and Regional Development and Urban Planning. The DPS had also played a pivotal role in the survival of several previous governments. It supported the first and second governments led by the United Democratic Forces in 1991–92 and 1997, respectively. In addition, the DPS was mandated to form the government of Lyuben Berov in 1992 and supported his government until its resignation in 1994.[25]

The Bulgarian Constitution does not mention the existence of national minorities and forbids the creation of political parties on ethnic grounds. This constitutional provision caused several political initiatives to ban the DPS as a party organized on ethnic grounds. However, the failure of these attempts has led to a certain *modus vivendi*, whereby the major Bulgarian parties accepted the DPS in exchange for its self-restraint with regard to radical ethnopolitical demands.

While the majority of DPS voters are ethnic Turks, the party has neither fully mobilized the entire ethnic Turkish community nor has it established a monopoly of representation. Its electoral share in parliamentary elections increased from 5.7 per cent in 1990 to 7.55 per cent in 1991, but declined to 5.44 per cent in the 1994 elections following internal power struggles and scandals.[26] Electoral support rose again to 7.6 per cent in 1997, when DPS participated in an electoral coalition, and reached 7.45 per cent in the 2001 elections. The DPS does not consider itself an ethnic party and seeks to promote minority concerns by strengthening the civic elements of the Bulgarian state and nation.[27] Its electoral manifesto for the parliamentary and local elections in 2001 and 2003 emphasized liberal values such as individual rights and freedoms and non-discrimination, supporting in particular the decentralization of government and rural economic development.[28] The party was successful in achieving some improvements for national minorities in Bulgaria. For example, the parliament simplified the procedure for re-establishing Turkish names, and the government declared its intention to set up an agency for national minorities supporting the National Council for Ethnic and Demographic Issues.[29] Regional, and some local, councils on ethnic and demographic questions were established to advise the regional state administration.[30]

The ethnic Turkish community enjoys segmental autonomy in Bulgarian society, though its autonomy in terms of ethnic self-consciousness, cultural self-assertion, education and self-government is much weaker than that of ethnic Hungarian communities in Romania and Slovakia. There is a discernible social distance between the ethnic Turkish and ethnic Bulgarian communities, expressed in the low number of people willing to marry a member of the other community.[31] Most ethnic Turks are also Muslims, live in rural areas in the Kurdzhali and Razgrad regions of south-eastern and north-eastern Bulgaria and form a local majority in Kurdzhali. In 2001/2002, 520 schools in ethnic Turkish settlement areas offered the Turkish language as a subject of instruction, and cultural institutions, as well as media, operate in the Turkish language.[32] Under the Sakskoburggotski government, DPS politicians held the posts of parliamentary secretary in the Ministry of Agriculture and Forestry, secretary-general in the Foreign Affairs Ministry, regional governors in 2 of 28 regions and heads of executive agencies. Since the local elections of November 2003, mayors affiliated with DPS have headed 29 municipalities (*obshtini*) with a high share of ethnic Turkish residents, amounting to approximately 11 per cent of all municipalities (262). In general, however, ethnic Turks are underrepresented in public administration.

This did not change significantly in the parliamentary elections of 2005. Even though the coalition of NDSV and DPS had to admit defeat by an alliance of eight political parties, minorities remained underrepresented. In addition, while the OSCE has hailed the latest elections as a sign of the consolidation of democracy in Bulgaria, it also reported organized attempts to systematically influence the vote in Bulgaria's Roma communities, which is evidence that they are still on the margins of an otherwise increasingly stable democracy.[33]

Romania

In Romania, the Democratic Alliance of Magyars in Romania (UDMR) participated in government between 1996 and 2000, and again since December 2004. The UDMR supported the social democrat minority government in parliament between 2000 and 2004.[34]

The UDMR was represented by four ministers in the four-party government that was established in December 2004 and was headed by Călin Popescu Tăriceanu, a senior minister supervising education and European integration activities; a minister for telecommunication and information technology; a minister in charge of public works and territorial planning;

and a minister responsible for trade. Four candidates of the democratic Union of Hungarians in Romania (RMDSZ became prefects, representing the government in Romania's regions.

As a coalition partner to the various cabinets led by prime ministers from the liberal-conservative Democratic Convention of Romania (CDR), the UDMR nominated two ministers, ten state secretaries, two prefects and eight deputy prefects.[35] A UDMR minister headed the Department for the Protection of National Minorities that was established in 1997 and subordinated to the prime minister. The fact that the UDMR ceased to participate in the governing coalition in 2000 did not entail the end of consociational power-sharing.[36] Subsequent agreements between the Social Democratic Party of Romania (PSD) and the UDMR set out a mechanism for obligatory consultation of the UDMR on important political issues and numerous policy concessions in exchange for UDMR abstention from non-confidence motions or votes in parliament. These agreements ensured *de facto* involvement of the UDMR in governance, endowed the UDMR with a veto position and envisaged a 'civic multicultural model' for interethnic relations in Romania, comprising strong elements of consociationalism.[37] The social democrat government assigned the Department for the Protection of National Minorities to the Ministry of Public Information, thereby excluding the head of the department from participation in cabinet meetings. However, the minority departments in the Ministries of Education and Culture were retained and the UDMR also kept the posts of deputy prefects.

The UDMR's involvement in the government was institutionalized in two other executive bodies: an Interministerial Committee for National Minorities (created in 1998) and a consultative Council for National Minorities (2001). Based on the idea of a nation-state, the Romanian Constitution does not assign a special status to the ethnic Hungarian or other minorities. It envisages that the state should guarantee the development of the ethnic identity of persons belonging to national minorities but restricts positive discrimination towards these individuals.

Constant vote shares in subsequent parliamentary, regional and local elections – roughly equivalent to the proportion of ethnic Hungarians in Romania (7 per cent) – indicate that the UDMR has been able to mobilize and integrate the ethnic Hungarian electorate. The UDMR considers itself to be the party representing the interests of the ethnic Hungarian community in Romania. It has sought to integrate all political and social milieus into this community and its political strategy aims at increasing the segmental autonomy of the ethnic Hungarian minority. During the local and parliamentary elections in 2004, the UDMR successfully managed to defend its monopoly of representation against political competitors such as the Hungarian Civic Alliance, a newly established party affiliated with Hungary's right-wing Hungarian Civic Party. Only a few weeks prior to the local and national elections, Romania's Parliament tightened the conditions for registration of new parties so that the new party failed to collect a sufficient number of signatures.

During the CDR-led governments, the UDMR was able to achieve major amendments to the education and self-government laws. In municipalities in which more than 20 per cent of the residents belonged to a national minority, the use of the minority language in public administration was legalized, bilingual signs were introduced and the minority language became a language of instruction.

Agreements between the UDMR and the PDS government were renewed annually and extended to the local and regional organizations of the two parties. On the basis of these agreements, the use of the Hungarian language was legally guaranteed, education and media in the Hungarian language was extended and steps were taken towards fiscal decentralization. In 2001, the Parliament adopted a Law on Local Public Administration that permitted the use of the minority language as an official language in municipalities in which more than 20 per cent of the residents spoke (the same) minority language (hereafter, 'minority areas').[38] The constitutional amendment of October 2003 obliged the state to enable the use of minority languages in contact with public administration bodies in minority areas, and persons belonging to national minorities were entitled by the Constitution to use their mother tongue in court proceedings. The 2002 law on the status of police officers envisaged the recruitment of police officers with minority language skills in minority areas. This provision indicates that ethnic proportionality has gained importance as an organizing principle in Romanian public administration, although the Romanian government did not promote it expressly.[39] A private university was established in Cluj, which taught a number of disciplines in Hungarian. Laws were adopted on the restitution of individual, church and community property nationalized by the communist regime. Tax revenue shares allocated to local and regional government were increased.[40]

Traditionally, the ethnic Hungarian community has been more organized and articulate than the ethnic Turkish community in Bulgaria. Ethnic Hungarians constitute approximately 20 per cent of the population in the Transylvania region of Western Romania and they form local majorities in the counties of Harghita and Covasna (*Székelyföld*). In areas of ethnic Hungarian settlement, local self-government entities are managed by ethnic Hungarian mayors. In addition, 133 schools use Hungarian as a language of instruction, a private Hungarian-language university has been set up, and cultural institutions and media are accorded segmental autonomy.

However, comparative sociological research on social relations between ethnic Hungarians and ethnic Romanians has shown that conflict perceptions are more intense in Transylvania than between ethnic Hungarians and ethnic Slovaks in Southern Slovakia.[41]

Slovakia

In Slovakia, the Slovak Magyar Coalition Party (SMK) has been involved in the governing coalitions led by Prime Minister Mikuláš Dzurinda since 1998. From 1998 until 2002, SMK provided the Deputy Prime Minister responsible, *inter alia*, for minority protection, two ministers and a state secretary in the Ministry of Education. In the four-party coalition government established in October 2002, the SMK again held the posts of Deputy Prime Minister responsible for minority protection and Minister of Environmental Protection. SMK politicians also acted as Deputy Chairman of Parliament, Minister of Agriculture, Minister of Regional Development and as state secretaries in the Ministries of Economics, Finance, Education, Culture, Foreign Affairs and Regional Development.[42] Whereas the first Dzurinda government (1998–2002) did not require the support of SMK deputies to ensure a majority in parliament, the second government (2002–2006) had to rely on SMK votes. To solve intra-coalition conflicts and coordinate policy, the government established a coalition council consisting of one minister for each governing party and the chairpersons of the parliamentary groups and parties.[43] Council decisions required unanimity among the coalition parties.

While the Slovak Constitution does not assign special group rights to national minorities, it does stipulate subjective rights of persons belonging to national minorities with respect to, *inter alia*, establishing associations, using the minority language, education and culture.

The continued governmental involvement of the SMK has improved significantly the institutional environment necessary for segmental autonomy of the ethnic Hungarian community in Slovakia. The governing majority adopted a new law regulating the use of the minority languages and enhanced the status of the consultative Government Council for National Minorities and Ethnic Groups in 1999. In contrast to Bulgaria and Romania, Slovakia ratified the European Charter for Regional and Minority Languages and adopted legislation to decentralize administrative competences and establish regional self-government in 2001. In October 2003, the parliament approved a private university that was located in Komárno and offered courses taught in Hungarian. In addition, the second Dzurinda government's programme declaration envisaged the adoption of a new law regulating, among other things, the funding of minority cultures.[44]

The SMK considers itself as a party that aggregates the interests of the ethnic Hungarian community in Slovakia (9.7 per cent of the population) and tries to represent the entire spectrum of political positions articulated by ethnic Hungarians. Stable electoral results equalling the size of the ethnic Hungarian electorate and opinion poll data confirm that most ethnic Hungarians consider themselves represented by the SMK.[45] As in Romania, a network of Hungarian-language schools, media and cultural institutions reflect the segmental autonomy of the ethnic Hungarian community in Slovak society. In 2003, the heads of regional state administration were appointed in accordance with the proportions of governing parties.[46] Two of the eight regions in Slovakia were headed by civil servants nominated by the SMK. Approximately 15 per cent of the deputies in regional assemblies were affiliated with the SMK. The share of ethnic Hungarian or SMK-affiliated mayors corresponds roughly to the share of the ethnic Hungarian community; no concrete figures are known about the ethnic composition of the civil service. Similar to the Romanian and Bulgarian cases, governments have not aimed to institutionalize the principle of ethnic proportionality but acknowledge the importance of minority representation in the administration of ethnically heterogeneous areas.

Clearly, some further qualifications need to be made with regard to the reality of the consociational model in the three country cases: this chapter uses a wide definition of consociationalism, which does not take into account situations in which more than two ethnic groups exist or those in which none of the ethnic groups are in a dominant position. While many Bulgarian, Romanian or Slovak parties might not consider themselves expressly to be the representatives of the dominant ethnic group and, as such, do not conform to the consociational model,[47] they do represent the ethnic majorities in terms of voter alignments. The same applies to the DPS in Bulgaria, which does not consider itself an ethnic party.

In a formal sense, none of the three countries was governed by a grand coalition including all segments of society, and the Roma community was not represented in any of the governing coalitions. However, the volatility of party systems and the changing social structure in the three countries resulted in shifting non-ethnic alignments of voters. This induced the larger governing parties to emulate grand coalitions by choosing broad representational strategies aimed at various segments of society. Despite these necessary qualifications, numerous elements of their political systems – minority veto, interethnic coalition, proportionality and segmental autonomy – are all components of a consociational model of power-sharing.[48]

The overview has demonstrated that domestic circumstances can account for the emergence of the consociational model. The Bulgarian movement for Simeon II, the Romanian social democrats and the liberal and centre-right parties in Slovakia did not attain an absolute majority in parliament and thus required the support of parties representing mainly the most numerous ethnic minorities. These coalitions were facilitated by proportional electoral systems in all three countries. Yet, this chapter argues that these domestic factors are not sufficient explanation for the creation and stabilization of the consociational model in the three countries, and there are three reasons to assume that the EU and the accession constellation have made an important contribution.

First, the EU provided an electoral platform for parties representing ethnic minorities and majorities.[49] Since the large majority of the citizens in each of the three countries supported European integration and EU membership, citizens expected political parties to reflect European values and to meet the normative expectations of the EU. Parties therefore had an incentive to demonstrate their European value orientation to their constituencies by taking moderate political positions and building compromises around European norms of interethnic reconciliation and coexistence. Notwithstanding the rise of Eurosceptic parties or movements,[50] to date pro-European parties have competed more successfully for electoral support in both minority and majority communities than their anti-European counterparts.

Second, parties advocating either minority or majority issues both claimed to be served by membership of the EU.[51] Representatives of ethnic minorities supposed that minority communities would benefit from more permeable borders, multi-level contacts with neighbouring ethnic kin-states, and through the limitation and scrutiny of state sovereignty in the EU framework. Advocates of ethnic majority concerns – who often claim to represent the general interests of the state or nation – had good reason to believe that EU institutions would be in a much weaker position *vis-à-vis* the member state after accession and, given the lack of a minority rights *acquis*, would interfere far less in states' treatment of their minorities. In the pre-accession phase, these interests of ethnopolitical actors converged and thus facilitated arrangements of joint governance.

Third, the previous section argued that EU policy tends to favour a security-based approach aimed at consensual settlements and the enforcement of universal norms. This policy approach has been particularly conducive to interethnic coalitions, since it has caused political leaders of ethnic groups to abandon principled positions unlikely to be appreciated by the EU. Political representatives of ethnic majorities know that concessions to ethnic minorities were appreciated by EU institutions and minority representatives know that moderate positions would garner more support from Brussels. In contrast, the normative ambiguity and vagueness of EU statements left both sides uncertain as to whether a rights-based policy, even if it appeared convincing and legitimate, would be backed by the EU.

These arguments have sought to illustrate the significant impact of the EU on the development of consociational models of power-sharing. In addition, they are complemented by empirical evidence of EU interest in maintaining interethnic power-sharing arrangements. In Slovakia, the EU intervened directly to sustain the governing coalition during the crisis over the adoption of the territorial–administrative reform laws in August 2001, when the SMK threatened to leave the government after deputies of the governing coalition parties had voted together with opposition deputies to reject a government proposal dividing the country into twelve instead of eight regional self-governing entities. Political representatives of the ethnic Hungarian community favoured smaller regions as a better institutional safeguard of local-level autonomy. A few days prior to the meeting of the SMK Republican Council, in which it was to determine whether to remain within the governing coalition or not, the Commissioner for Enlargement, Günter Verheugen, highlighted the importance that a stable government, which included representatives of the ethnic Hungarian minority, would have for the country's accession to the EU.[52] His warning prompted the SMK to accept the law on regional self-government and induced the coalition partners to accept the conditions set by the SMK for its participation in government.

In Bulgaria and Romania, political intervention of the EU was not targeted directly at the continuation of interethnic cooperation, but nevertheless EU policy has shaped a milieu fostering consociational power-sharing arrangements.

Implications for an enlarged EU and its new member states

This section asks how interethnic relations in CEE states are likely to have developed after accession to the EU. If the accession constellation contributed to the emergence of consociational power-sharing in Bulgaria, Romania and Slovakia, will these arrangements be less stable once the EU relinquishes its power position? If the EU has been able to pursue a diffuse and ambiguous minority rights policy successfully because of functioning accession conditionality, will its policy fail when conditionality ceases to be effective? Does the EU need then to develop and clarify its own normative standards?

Whether or not the basis exists for the development of common norms on interethnic relations in an enlarged EU is addressed in Will Kymlicka's attempt to develop a liberal theory of group rights.[53] A central tenet of this theory is that ethnocultural justice requires states – which are *per se* nation-building in that they embody the majority culture – to accept the nation-building activities of ethnic minorities. States may restrict minority nation-building only by ensuring individual liberties. The norm of justice between minority and majority cultures leads Kymlicka to consider territorial autonomy as a possible and legitimate arrangement for the protection of national minorities. In addition, he supports territorial autonomy for CEE states by giving empirical and functional reasons: 'the trend in the West is in fact towards *greater* territorialization of minority rights regimes for national minorities'.[54] '[Territorial autonomy] has worked well in the West and is worthy of serious consideration in [Eastern and Central Europe]'.[55]

It is doubtful whether territorial autonomy for national minorities can be derived from principles of liberal democracy, since liberal democratic norms of justice and freedom apply to individuals and include their right to determine to which culture they belong. Liberal democracy has to ensure the individual the right of cultural self-determination and an adequate decentralization of power which guarantees a balance of powers and local or regional self-government rights. However, the granting of territorial autonomy to a national minority means transferring functionally unspecified, territorially defined state power to a group simply because of its ethnic distinctiveness. The right to cultural self-determination pertaining to individuals of this group justifies a functionally specified autonomy to protect their cultural self-determination but does not legitimize territorial self-government rights that go beyond the self-government rights exercised by other citizens.

Beyond these normative doubts, functional and empirical arguments militate against territorial autonomy. Fragile statehood traditions and recent wars in CEE states have meant that minority rights are framed in the discourse of loyalty and secession, and not in that of fairness and justice.[56] Territorializing minority rights regimes or conceding the possibility of secession reinforces the predominant 'security risk' perception of majorities and is likely to exacerbate conflicts. Kymlicka does not take this effect seriously enough, nor does he take into account the presence of neighbouring ethnic kin-states in Central and Eastern Europe when he argues for territorial autonomy as a long-term guarantee against the assimilation of minority diasporas outside the autonomous territory.[57] A kin-state like Hungary performs functions for ethnic Hungarian minorities in the neighbouring countries of Hungary that can be compared to the functions of Quebec for francophone Canadians outside Quebec.

This chapter has identified a trend towards consociational power-sharing in three CEE countries: Bulgaria, Romania and Slovakia. For both normative and functional reasons, it argues that consociationalism is better suited to long-term arrangements of interethnic relations in Central and Eastern Europe than the territorialization of minority issues, that is, the granting of territorial rights to a minority group for no reason other than its status as a minority. It is argued that the non-territorial, cultural, personal and functional autonomy regulations facilitated by consociationalism are far more compatible with the principles of liberal democracy. One could even argue that consociational arrangements are a functional equivalent to regimes of personal autonomy (*Personalautonomie*) in the narrower legal sense of minority self-government endowed with certain public functions and prerogatives in minority-relevant areas. A functionally specified autonomy protects the individual right of cultural self-determination, a right that is more acceptable on the basis of liberal democracy than a group right of nation-building. Since consociational arrangements institutionalize the participation of minority representatives in the joint governance of public affairs, they do not frame minority issues as questions of loyalty and secession. In contrast with territorial autonomy, consociational arrangements support a perception of minority issues as problems of justice amongst groups or citizens across policy sectors. They can thus contribute to the consolidation of democracy in CEE societies with ethnic cleavages.

Consociational power-sharing has been criticized as an ineffective strategy of conflict prevention when compared with Donald Horowitz's ideas about institutions facilitating cross-ethnic alignments.[58] However, this juxtaposition does not reflect the reality in the CEE cases studied here. First, as the party systems in Romania, Slovakia and, to a minor extent, Bulgaria have frozen the ethnic cleavages of these societies, any conflict prevention strategy has had to take this into account. Institutional designs that aim to eliminate ethnic cleavages tend to underestimate the resilience of the actors involved. Second, the theories of Horowitz and Lijphart do not represent mutually exclusive conflict prevention strategies: existing consociational elements can be combined with institutions facilitating cross-ethnic alignment and, in fact, are often linked to such institutions in the three countries examined above.

Taken together, analysis of the debates on liberal pluralism and conflict prevention suggests normative and functional considerations that promote consociational power-sharing arrangements. The remainder of this section analyses, in a somewhat speculative fashion, whether an enlarged EU might pay attention to such considerations. After enlargement, the EU institutions are no longer in an authoritative position to monitor the protection of minorities and to expect consensual conflict settlements. As a consequence, domestic political actors will have fewer incentives to develop consociational arrangements and resuscitating conflictual politics may become a more likely option for them. Yet, the future of consensual arrangements will also depend on whether, *inter alia*, majority relations in parliament necessitate broad political coalitions. Parties representing nationalist voters within the ethnic majority will probably be interested in escalating conflicts with ethnic minorities. Nationalist minority politicians, however, will be less successful in rallying support for a more confrontational policy if power-sharing arrangements yield tangible benefits. In any case, one has to take into account the fact that current power-sharing arrangements in the three countries differ from Western examples of consociationalism (such as those of Belgium or Switzerland) in that they lack a strong and positively commemorated tradition of power-sharing on which political actors can build.

With the Treaty of Nice and, in view of its experience with Austria, the EU is now furnished with a legal instrument permitting intervention in the event of a member state violating principles of liberty, democracy, human rights, fundamental freedoms or the rule of law.[59] The EU has not created a minority rights *acquis* beyond the anti-discrimination rules and an enlarged EU seems unlikely to codify its own specific common standards of minority protection, given the persistent diversity of national approaches and the sensitivity of minority issues in old and new member states.[60] EU institutions will certainly not actively promote a coalition government that bridges ethnic cleavages in the member states.

Nonetheless, functionally legitimized and specified arrangements supporting the development of minority culture do appear to be a viable option for a common EU policy, as they are derived from the individual right of cultural self-determination and the EU's commitment 'to respect and to promote the diversity of its cultures'.[61] The EU could use the Open Method of Coordination (OMC) to develop cultural diversity, since this new procedure respects the variety of member states' political practices. OMC aims at encouraging cooperation, the exchange of best practice and agreeing common targets and guidelines for member states. It relies on regular monitoring of progress to meet those targets, allowing member states to compare their efforts and learn from the experience of others. The method was applied first in the 'Lisbon process' on the modernization of social and employment policies, and was extended to migration policies in 2001. An OMC for cultural diversity could set common targets for improving education in the minority language, bilingualism of minorities and majorities, interethnic dialogue mechanisms, the management of multi-ethnic local communities or the advancement of minorities on the labour market. In addition, soft pressure exerted by peer reviews and the good example of other member states might induce governments to increase their efforts to promote cultural diversity. While OMC would preserve the discretion of governments, it could shape a milieu supportive of interethnic power-sharing.

Conclusion

The core argument of this chapter is that the EU has supported the emergence of consociational power-sharing arrangements between political actors that have accommodated ethnic cleavages in accession countries. This was done unintentionally via the mechanism of the accession criteria, since its minority protection policy has been guided largely by a security-based approach that prioritized the consensual settlement of disputes over the enforcement of universal norms. However, the enlargement of the EU has rendered redundant the accession criteria that underpinned this particular policy of minority protection. While, in the case of Slovakia, this has removed an important incentive for domestic political actors to engage in power-sharing, the future of consociational arrangements will also depend on other domestic factors, for example electoral outcomes. Since consociational power-sharing arrangements are more compatible with liberal democratic principles than territorial autonomy arrangements, and seem to function better in a CEE environment, ideas and norms supporting these arrangements could diffuse into EU policies. Although the principal obstacles to collectivizing minority rights have persisted in an enlarged EU, the promotion of cultural diversity might still become a point of departure for an EU policy that aimed to support and develop the framework conditions needed for interethnic power-sharing.

Notes

1. B. de Witte, *Politics versus Law in the EU's Approach to Ethnic Minorities'*, Working Paper (Florence: EUI RSC, 2000).
2. See the extensive discussion of the EU's monitoring of minority protection in E. Heidbreder and L. Carrasco, *Assessing the Assessment: A Review on the Application*

Criterion Minority Protection by the European Commission, Working Paper 03/W/04 (Maastricht: EIPA, 2003), at <www.eipa.nl>

3. Article 13 TEC.
4. Council Directive 2000/43/EC of 29 June 2000 implementing the principle of equal treatment between persons irrespective of racial or ethnic origin (hereafter, 'the Race Directive'), OJ L 180, 19 July 2000.
5. G. Schwellnus, '"Much Ado About Nothing?": Minority Protection and the EU Charter of Fundamental Rights', *Constitutionalism Web-Papers* 5, <http://les1. man.ac.uk/conweb/> 2000; G.N. Toggenburg, 'A Rough Orientation through a Delicate Relationship: The European Union's Endeavours for (its) Minorities', *European Integration Online Papers* 4(16) (2000), <http://econpapers.repec.org/ article/erpeiopxx/p0059.htm>
6. Open Society Institute, *Monitoring the EU Accession Process: Minority Protection* (Budapest: Open Society Institute, 2001).
7. The Race Directive, *supra* note 4, Article 5.
8. European Commission, 'Regular Report on Hungary's Progress Towards Accession 2002', Commission Report COM(2002) 700 final – SEC(2002) 1404.
9. Belgium, France, Greece and Luxemburg, see <http://www.greekhelsinki.gr/bhr/ english/special_issues/fcnm_guide.html>
10. European Commission, 'Regular Report on Latvia's Progress Towards Accession 2002', Commission Report COM(2002) 700 final – SEC(2002) 1405: at 42. All the progress reports can be accessed online at <http://ec.europa.eu/enlargement/ archives/pdf/key_documents/2002/lv_en.pdf>. Except Latvia and Turkey, all other candidate countries have already ratified the FCNM. In spite of the opening of accession negotiations in October 2005 Turkey had still not signed the Convention.
11. European Commission, 'Regular Report on Turkey's Progress Towards Accession 2002', Commission Report, COM(2002) 700 final – SEC(2002) 1412.
12. See the European Parliament Resolution on the state of enlargement negotiations (A5-0190/2002, 13 June 2002) and the Council Decisions on the 13 Accession Partnerships of 28 January 2002 (OJ L 44, 14 February 2002).
13. See the 2002 Regular Report on Latvia, *supra* note 10, or the Parliament's 2001 Resolutions on Latvia (A5-0252/2001, 05.09.2001) and Estonia (A5-0251/2001, 05.09.2001).
14. K. Kymlicka, 'Reply and Conclusion', in W. Kymlicka and M. Opalski (eds), *Can Liberal Pluralism Be Exported? Western Political Theory and Ethnic Relations in Eastern Europe* (Oxford: Oxford University Press, 2001), 347–413, at 375.
15. OJ L68 of 9 March 1998, 3–4 and OJ L26 of 2 February 1998, 3–4.
16. European Commission, 'Regular Report on Romania Progress Towards Accession 2002', Commission Report COM(2002) 700 final – SEC(2002) 1409: at 35.
17. For a thorough discussion of the differences between the contextual, security-based minority rights track and the universal, justice-based minority rights track, see Kymlicka, 'Reply and Conclusion', *supra* note 14.
18. P. Vermeersch, 'EU Enlargement and Minority Rights Policies in Central Europe: Explaining Policy Shifts in the Czech Republic, Hungary and Poland', *Journal of Ethnopolitics and Minority Issues in Europe* 1 (2003).
19. Riedel's assertion that the EU tends to advocate collective rights through its accession requirements cannot be substantiated on the basis of official EU statements. S. Riedel, 'Minorités nationales en Europe et protection des droits de l'homme: un enjeu pour l'élargissement', *Politique étrangère* 3 (2002): 647–64.

20. Treaty between the Member States of the European Union and Bulgaria and Romania 2005.
21. Brunner's critique of the voluntarism (*Beliebigkeit*) manifested in the Commission's Reports tends to take a coherent set of norms as the framework of reference. See G. Brunner, 'EU-Minderheitenpolitik und kollektive Minerheitenrechte: Eine Replik auf Sabine Riedel', *Ostereuropa* 52(2) (2002): 220–8.
22. A. Lijphart, *Democracy in Plural Societies: A Comparative Exploration* (New Haven, CT: Yale University Press, 1977), 25–52.
23. For a discussion of the consociationalist model with respect to the prevention of ethnopolitical conflicts, see U. Schneckener, *Auswege aus dem Bürgerkrieg: Modelle zur Regulierung ethno-nationalistischer Konflikte in Europa* (Frankfurt: Suhrkamp, 2002); T.D. Sisk, *Power Sharing and International Mediation in Ethnic Conflicts* (Washington, DC: United States Institute of Peace Research, 1996); and J. Snyder, 'Managing Ethnopolitics in Eastern Europe: An Assessment of Institutional Approaches', in J.P. Stein (ed.), *The Politics of National Minority Participation in Post-Communist Europe: State-Building, Democracy, and Ethnic Mobilization* (Armonk, NY: Sharpe, 2000), 269–86.
24. The minor coalition partner, DPS, is an alliance of three parties led by the party naming itself DPS.
25. C. Johnson, 'Democratic Transition in the Balkans: Romania's Hungarian and Bulgaria's Turkish Minority (1989–99)', *Nationalism and Ethnic Politics* 8(1) (2002): 1–28; and R.V. Vassilev, 'Post-Communist Bulgaria's Ethnopolitics', *The Global Review of Ethnopolitics* 1(2) (2001): 37–53.
26. Ilchev, I. 'Emigration and the Politics of Identity: the Turkish Minority in Bulgaria', in Stein (ed.), *The Politics of National Minority Participation, supra* note 23: 237–68.
27. See the statements of DPS leaders reported by the US-sponsored NGO, Project on Ethnic Relations, *The Bulgarian Ethnic Experience* (Princeton, NJ: Project on Ethnic Relations, 2002).
28. Bûlgariia – Evropa, Nestandarten pût na razvitie; programna deklaracija 2003, <www.dps.bg>
29. See 'Upravlenska programa na pravitelstvoto na Republika Bûlgariia', at <www.government.bg>; and L. Petkova, 'The ethnic Turks in Bulgaria: Social Integration and Impact on Bulgarian Turkish Relations 1947–2000', *Global Review of Ethnopolitics* 1(4) (2002): 42–59.
30. Report submitted by Bulgaria pursuant to Article 25, Paragraph 1 of the Framework Convention for the Protection of National Minorities, Council of Europe, Strasbourg, 9 April 2003, at 36.
31. Ilchev, 'Emigration', *supra* note 26.
32. Cf. notes 26 and 80.
33. OSCE Office for Democratic Institutions and Human Rights, 'OSCE-ODIHR Election Assessment Mission Report' (Vienna: OSCE, 2005).
34. Z. Csergő, 'Beyond Ethnic Division: Majority–Minority Debate about the Post-communist State in Romania and Slovakia', *East European Politics and Societies* 16(1) (2002): 1–29; Centre for Documentation and Information on Minorities in Europe – Southeast Europe (CEDIME-SE), *Hungarians of Romania* (Kifisia, 2001).
35. W. Kostecki, *Prevention of Ethnic Conflict: Lessons from Romania*, Occasional Paper (Berlin: Berghof Research Center for Constructive Conflict Management, 2002); and N. Medianu, 'Analysing Political Exchanges between Minority and Majority Leaders in Romania', *Global Review of Ethnopolitics* 1(4) (2002): 28–41.
36. Compare, however, Kostecki, *Prevention of Ethnic Conflict, supra* note 35, at 39.

37. Egyezmény a Romániai Magyar Demokrata Szövetség és a Szociális Demokrácia Romániai Pártja között, Megállapodás a Szociáldemokrata Párt és a Romániai Magyar Demokrata Szövetség együttműködésére a 2002/2003, évben.

38. RMDSZ, 'Ez a mi munkánk. Fontosabb változások a magyar közösség helyzetében 2000 és 2004 között' (Kolozsvár/Cluj: RMDSZ, 2004).

39. In addition, Article 81 of the Law No. 188/1999 on the Status of the Public Servant stipulated that some public servants shall know the minority language in areas with a share of more than 20 per cent of the citizens belonging to a national minority.

40. RMDSZ, 'Ez a mi munkánk', *supra* note 38.

41. G. A. Örkény Csepeli and M. Székelyi, 'Konfliktusok Erdélyben és Dél-Szlovákiában', *Szociológiai Szemle* 4 (1999): 100–13.

42. Koaličná dohoda medzi SDKÚ, SMK, KDH a ANO, 8.10.2002, <www.smk.sk>

43. G. Pridham, 'Coalition Behaviour in New Democracies of Central and Eastern Europe: The Case of Slovakia', *Journal of Communist Studies and Transition Politics* 18(2) (2002): 75–103.

44. Programové vyhlásenie vlády Slovenskej republiky, 4.11.2002: 31 <www.vlada.sk>

45. O. Gyárfašová and M. Velšic, 'Verejná mienka', in M. Kollár and G. Mesežnikov (eds), *Slovensko 2001: Súhrnná správa o stave spolocnosti* (Bratislava: IVO, 2002), 241–84.

46. G. Mesežnikov, 'Vnútropolitický vývoj a systém politických strán', in Kollár and Mesežnikov (eds), *Slovensko 2001, supra* note 45, 19–112.

47. Medianu, 'Analysing Political Exchanges', *supra* note 35.

48. In the first parliamentary elections after EU accession the Social Democrat party received most votes but had to cede the government to a coalition of three centre-right parties.

49. See also the general argument made by M. Vachudová, *The Leverage of International Institutions on Democratizing States: Eastern Europe and the European Union* (Florence: European University Institute Working Paper, 2001), at 5.

50. A. Grzymała-Busse and A. Innes, 'Great Expectations: The EU and Domestic Political Competition in East-Central Europe', *East European Politics and Societies* 17(1) (2003): 64–73.

51. Kymlicka, 'Reply and Conclusion', *supra* note 14.

52. Mesežnikov, 'Vnútropolitický vývoj', *supra* note 46, 21–112, at 52.

53. W. Kymlicka, *Multicultural Citizenship* (Oxford: Oxford University Press, 1995); and Kymlicka and Opalski (eds), *Can Liberal Pluralism Be Exported?*, *supra* note 14.

54. Kymlicka, 'Reply and Conclusion', *supra* note 14, at 365. Emphasis in original.

55. *Ibid.*, at 362.

56. Kymlicka and Opalski, *Can Liberal Pluralism?*, *supra* note 14.

57. Kymlicka, 'Reply and Conclusion', *supra* note 14.

58. D. Horowitz, *Ethnic Groups in Conflict* (Berkeley: University of California Press, 1985); Sisk, *Power Sharing, supra* note 23; and Snyder, 'Managing Ethnopolitics', *supra* note 23.

59. Article 7.

60. For a discussion of the role of the Treaty establishing a Constitution for the European Union and the Reform treaty see the chapter by Toggenburg in this volume (Chapter 4).

61. Schwellnus, 'Much Ado about Nothing', *supra* note 5; and Toggenburg, 'A Rough Orientation', *supra* note 5.

10
The Europeanization of Minority–Majority Relations in the Greece–Turkey–Cyprus Triangle

Nathalie Tocci

Introduction

Minority–majority relations in Greece, Turkey and Cyprus have been shaped largely by the wider relationships between these three countries. Indeed, their very establishment and subsequent evolution has been critically defined by conflict, war and rapprochement with one another. In addition, over the last decade, the Eastern Mediterranean triangle has been set increasingly within a wider European and, more precisely, European Union (EU) framework. With Greece and Cyprus in the EU (since 1981 and 2004, respectively) and Turkey commencing accession negotiations (in October 2005), minority–majority relations in the region have been affected by the changing politics of Europeanization. Yet the causal relationships at play in the processes of Europeanization are complex and heavily intertwined, as different EU-inspired mechanisms of change interact with changing domestic and regional dynamics.

This chapter attempts to untangle these causal relationships, pointing both to the main areas of change and to their limits, as well as to their respective causes. In so doing, two main provisos need to be clarified from the outset. The first concerns the very definition of minority–majority relations when it comes to the specific case of Cyprus. Defining and describing relations between the Greek Cypriot and the Turkish Cypriot communities as minority–majority often entails a specific reading of the conflict and its solution. Like other ethnopolitical conflicts in the European neighbourhood (from Abkhazia to Nagorno-Karabakh, Transdniestria or Kosovo), the vast majority of Turkish Cypriots vehemently reject their definition as a minority. Likewise, they abhor any solution based simply on the institutionalization of their minority rights. To the Turkish Cypriots, the relationship is based on intercommunal political equality and a just settlement would codify such a relationship constitutionally. In the post-1974 partition era, many Greek Cypriots, while rejecting any form of secession, have accepted this premise of a future solution, if only orally. Taking this into account, this chapter analyses how the external and domestic parties have sought to accommodate the numerical minority–majority relationship within a federal–confederal constitutional settlement providing for political equality.

The second proviso relates to the question of 'which minorities?' When it comes to Cyprus and Greece the answer is relatively clear-cut. In Cyprus, the Greek Cypriot–Turkish Cypriot relationship is the key issue of interest (despite the small number of Latinos, Armenians and Maronites, who are integrated, for the most part, into the Greek Cypriot community, as well as the rising number of immigrants). In Greece, despite increased immigration and the traditional presence of small religious and ethnic minorities (Catholics, Evangelicals, Old Calendarists, Jews, Armenians and Slavo-Macedonians), the main minority is the Turkish/Muslim minority of Western Thrace. However, when it comes to Turkey, the minority question becomes far more complex. The 1923 Lausanne Treaty accorded minority status to only three non-Muslim communities, namely the Greek Orthodox community, the Armenian Orthodox community and the Jews. However, the Turkish societal mosaic comprises many other non-recognized minorities. These include both religious groups, such as the Christian Syriacs or the Muslim Alevis, as well as ethnic groups, such as the Laz, the Abkhaz, the Circassians, the Albanians and, naturally, the Kurds. In other words, a discussion of Turkey's minorities would require a study of its own, deviating from the principal theme of this chapter. Hence, when it comes to Turkey, the sections below discuss minority and cultural rights policy in general and then draw specific examples from the situation of Turkey's Greek Orthodox community.

This chapter begins by setting out the historical context of minority–majority relations in Greece, Turkey and Cyprus. It does so by mapping out the principal causal relationships at play and by drawing particular attention to the way in which relations between these three countries have affected the domestic standing of their respective minorities. It then documents the current situation in minority–majority relations, including recent improvements, attempted solutions and the remaining problems and shortcomings.

The remaining sections are devoted to an analysis of the underlying causes of the status quo. In particular, how has the Europeanization of the Eastern Mediterranean affected minority–majority relations there? The concept of Europeanization or 'EUization' has been a particularly fuzzy one, as authors have used the concept in different ways and with different definitions, depending on the specific research field to which the concept has been applied.[1] Two key mechanisms of EUization have been identified as 'conditionality' and 'socialization'.[2] Conditionality has been, and remains, a principal instrument of externally inspired domestic change, particularly within the accession process. This has been evident in Central and Eastern Europe and is increasingly true for Turkey.[3] Within the EU itself, direct pressure and conditionality no longer apply (especially in the field of minority rights). Yet, legally binding decisions that affect minorities both directly and indirectly, as well as the more diffuse process of socialization into EU norms and values, can affect politics and policy within member states. This has been true for Greece and may become true for EU member Cyprus in the years to come.[4]

Rarely, however, does the process of Europeanization affect domestic politics through a direct causal relationship. Rather, it does so through domestic and regional developments that either support, legitimize or hinder existing trends.[5] As such, this chapter will endeavour to map out the principal features of the two-way causal interaction between external EU-inspired drivers of change and domestic and regional dynamics.

The emergence and consolidation of minority–majority relations in the Eastern Mediterranean

Following the defeat of the 1922 Greek campaign in Anatolia, the Republic of Turkey was established through the 1923 Treaty of Lausanne. The Treaty and its accompanying conventions foresaw the compulsory exchange of populations between Greece and Turkey. In the early twentieth century, reciprocal ethnic cleansing had been an often-used instrument for 'solving' minority questions in the disintegrating Ottoman Empire (for example, the 1913 population exchange between Bulgaria and Turkey or the 1919 exchange between Greece and Bulgaria). The underlying premise of the exchanges was the view, widespread during that period, that minorities represented a threat or hindrance to the ongoing nation-state building projects in the region. Yet the key difference between previous exchanges and the Greek–Turkish one was the latter's compulsory rather than voluntary nature.[6] Taking place after the Greek irredentist campaign in Asia Minor, a defeated Greece accepted the demands of the new Turkish state. These demands stemmed in turn from the fear that the Greek minority could threaten once again the state's territorial integrity in future. Thereafter, both Greece and Turkey, through different means and approaches, set out to forge united, indivisible and homogenous nation-states, in which unassimilated ethnic or religious minorities remained at the periphery of the nation.

In the Greek–Turkish Convention on the Exchange of Population that saw the mass transfer of 1.4 million Greeks and 0.5 million Turks, the only exceptions were the Turkish Muslims of Western Thrace (Greece) and the Orthodox Greeks of Istanbul and of the Turkish islands of Imbros and Tenedos (Gökçeada and Bözcaada, respectively). The Lausanne Treaty and the ensuing 1930 Greek–Turkish Conventions accorded Turkish citizenship and residency to approximately 103,000 Greeks and Greek citizenship to approximately 110,000 Turkish Muslims. The Lausanne Treaty and Conventions also accorded minority rights to the Greek and Turkish communities. Not unlike the *millet* system under Ottoman rule, under the Lausanne Treaty (Articles 37–45), the Republic of Turkey committed itself to provide its Greek (as well as

Jewish and Armenian) minorities with equality before the law; the free exercise of religion and use of language; the right to establish and run charities, schools, religious and social institutions; and the right to manage religious affairs and family and personal status law. Greece committed itself to similar undertakings *vis-à-vis* its Turkish/Muslim minority.

Since then, the status and condition of the Turkish and Greek minorities in law and practice has been largely a function of Greek–Turkish relations. Indeed, the situation of minorities was at its best between 1930 and 1955, during the years of Greek–Turkish friendship, ushered in by Mustafa Kemal Atatürk and Eleftherios Venizelos.[7] By contrast, in the post-1955 period, the Greek and Turkish minorities suffered greatly as a result of the escalating crisis between Greece and Turkey, predominantly due to developments in Cyprus. As will be discussed below, the situation has improved significantly once again since a Greek–Turkish rapprochement was relaunched in 1999.

Cyprus, too, was once part of the Ottoman Empire. During the three centuries of Ottoman rule, the predominantly Greek Orthodox local population witnessed the immigration of Muslim Turks to the island, leading to a demographic ratio of 180,000 Greek Cypriots to 46,000 Turkish Cypriots in the late nineteenth century. However, initially Cyprus was saved from the waves of nationalism, war and ethnic cleansing that swept across the Eastern Mediterranean and the Balkans, as the Ottoman Empire progressively disintegrated. This was not least because, since 1878, the Ottomans had ceded control of the strategically located island to the British Empire, in return for its protection against Tsarist Russia.

Yet, while British colonial rule might have prevented ethnic cleansing in Cyprus in the nineteenth century, it did little to stop (and indeed it spurred) violent ethnic conflict in the early and mid-twentieth century. The inter-communal struggle in Cyprus emerged between the 1930s and 1950s, when the Greek Cypriot community, supported by Greece, articulated its struggle for self-determination in terms of *enosis*, or union, between Greece and Cyprus. Initially, the British were adamant that they retain control of the Eastern Mediterranean island and, in their attempts to thwart the *enosis* movement, they spurred the Turkish Cypriot community and Turkey to mount a reactive counter-*enosis* campaign. By the mid-1950s, the Turkish positions crystallized in the diametrically opposed position of *taksim*, or partition of the island into Greek and Turkish zones. Violent inter-communal clashes erupted in 1955–59 between the Greek Cypriot EOKA movement (Ethniki Organosis Kypriou Agoniston) and the Turkish Cypriot TMT (Turk Mukavemet Teşkilati).

Inter-communal violence in Cyprus also took its toll in Greece and Turkey. In 1955, in response to the events in Cyprus, large-scale anti-Greek demonstrations and violence erupted in Istanbul in Izmir (later found to have been instigated by the then Menderes government in Turkey), destroying thousands of Greek properties and shops, and precipitating a renewed Greek exodus from Turkey. After 1955, Greek pressure and discrimination against its Muslim Turkish minority, while less violent, was no less deleterious. Land owned by Turks was expropriated, professional licences were denied, citizens were forced or induced to emigrate through the unilateral revocation of citizenship (via application of the infamous Article 19 of the Citizenship Law, that used ethnic origin as a ground for revoking citizenship) and religious freedoms were curtailed. In terms of land ownership, while in the 1920s the Turks had owned most of the land in Western Thrace, by the 1990s the Turkish land share amounted to 20 per cent. Insofar as the Turkish minority worked mainly in agriculture, loss of land amounted to loss of livelihood.

In 1960, a compromise was reached in Cyprus. The British ceded sovereignty of the island (while retaining two large sovereign military bases there) and allowed Cyprus to become an independent bi-communal republic. The 1959–1960 Constitution and Treaties provided for a complex power-sharing formula on the island and accorded Greece, Turkey and the UK guarantor rights *vis-à-vis* the new republic. Yet, the Greek Cypriot leadership remained implicitly devoted to *enosis*. By 1963, the bi-communal republic had collapsed with a constitutional breakdown and a renewed wave of ethnic violence directed mainly at the smaller Turkish Cypriot community.

In 1964, Turkey was on the verge of intervening on the island but was deterred by US President Johnson, who threatened not to come to Turkey's rescue should its actions trigger a Russian defence of the Greek Cypriots. Although it refrained from setting foot on Cypriot territory, Turkey retaliated against its own Greek community. In response to Greek Cypriot violence and discrimination against the Turkish Cypriots, Turkey disavowed the 1930 Convention on Installation and withdrew residence rights from approximately 12,000 Greeks in Istanbul, leading to their expulsion and the confiscation of their property. As a result of discrimination, expulsion and violence, the Greek Orthodox minority in Turkey, which had numbered over 100,000 in 1922, fell to 3000 by the late 1960s. The Turkish Muslim population of Western Thrace also fell considerably as a result of discrimination and the revocation of citizenship. Currently, the community numbers approximately 80,000–120,000; in other words, almost the same as in 1922. As noted by Human Rights Watch, considering a population growth of approximately 2–3 per cent, the Turkish Muslim population in Greece should have been almost three times its current size.[8]

With the constitutional breakdown and renewed ethnic violence in Cyprus, both the Greek and the Turkish Cypriot leaderships lost their already limited commitment to the 1959–1960 power-sharing formula. While the Greek Cypriots conceded at most a unitary state in which Turkish Cypriots would be accorded minority rights, the Turkish Cypriots were increasingly adamant that they secure a territorially defined solution which would permit them limited self-determination. Tensions and violence escalated following the advent of military dictatorship in Greece in 1967. This culminated in the

Greek coup in Cyprus in July 1974, which extended the Greek dictatorship to the island. The coup triggered two Turkish military interventions in the summer of 1974, which partitioned the island into two ethnically cleansed zones.

Successive rounds of negotiations since 1974 have amounted to no more than a few superficial successes and a myriad of failures. The parties, at different times and to different degrees, have rejected international proposals, refusing to alter their negotiating positions in any meaningful way. Yet the international community, embodied primarily in the United Nations (UN) Secretariat, has become increasingly precise as to what the contours of a desirable settlement should look like. This includes a bi-communal and bi-zonal federation in which the politically equal communities would share power at the centre but would be separately responsible for a large sphere of competences in the Turkish and Greek Cypriot federated states in northern and southern Cyprus respectively.

Violations, reforms, attempted solutions and pending problems in Turkey, Greece and Cyprus

The historical conception and evolution of the nation-state building project in the Eastern Mediterranean has been an underlying cause of the problems besieging minority–majority relations in the region. In Greece, Turkey and Cyprus, the prevalent and unspoken (mis)perception was that an individual could not feel a sense of belonging to a particular ethnic/religious/linguistic minority and also be a loyal citizen of his or her respective state. In the three countries, this misperception took different forms, with different effect.

Minority rights in Turkey

In Turkey, Atatürk set out to construct a new nation-state by learning from the collapse of the *ancien régime*.[9] Expansionism and national heterogeneity were viewed as two principal causes of the Ottoman disintegration. Heterogeneity was regarded as having fostered separate identities within the Empire, preventing the integration of peoples and reducing popular loyalty towards the authorities. Expansionism was blamed for the repeated wars of the Empire which led ultimately to its collapse. Atatürk thus aimed to secure the unity and loyalty of all citizens through the creation of an indivisible and homogeneous nation, whose territorial borders would not be subject to alteration through the conquest of foreign lands. In order to forge a homogenous nation in a context in which a large minority did not belong to the dominant Turkish Sunni Muslim group, Atatürk attempted to imbue the people with a sense of civic nationalism, citizenship and secularism. The 'Turk' would be a citizen of the new Republic regardless of ethnic, linguistic, cultural or religious background. Hence, no minorities, other than those mentioned in the 1923 Treaty of Lausanne, would be recognized. Indeed Article 66 of the Constitution states that 'everyone bound to the Turkish state through the bond of citizenship is a Turk'.

While theoretically Kemalism, the ideology embodied in Atatürk's reforms, endorsed an enlightened vision of civic nationalism, in practice distinct ethnic elements were incorporated into the understanding of the nation. Specific ethnic undertones in the articulation of the Turkish nation began to emerge at the time of Atatürk: For example, the population exchanges with Greece, the internal transfers of people between the Turkish west and Kurdish southeast, and the institutionalization of an education system insisting on the Turkification of all groups highlighted the distinctively ethnic features of Turkish nationalism. The combination of a theoretically civic understanding of the nation coupled with specific ethnic undertones opened the way for assimilation and discrimination. In some instances, minority ethnic and religious groups succeeded in integrating into the new Turkish nation and consequently enjoyed the same status as Turkish Sunni Muslim citizens. In other cases, an unwillingness or inability to integrate into the new environment led to serious pressures for change. These have, at times, been expressed through violent and destabilizing action, as illustrated by the civil war between Kurdish separatists and the Turkish state in the 1980s and 1990s.

When it comes to the Greek Orthodox minority, unlike other *de facto* minorities in Turkey, the Lausanne Treaty bound the Republic to recognize their rights as a minority. However, acceptance in law did not always materialize in practice. Adding to a general situation in which all minorities were regarded as untrustworthy, the Greek Orthodox community also suffered from the tense relations between Turkey and its kin-state Greece. The subsequent violations directed against the Greek minority included general human rights abuses, such as police harassment, and restrictions on the freedoms of expression and association (in other words, violations that all Turkish citizens suffered from, particularly in the aftermath of the 1980 military coup). They also included the non-implementation of the specific minority rights accorded to the three non-Muslim minorities under the Lausanne Treaty.

In terms of education rights, Greek schools faced legal and bureaucratic restrictions in the recruitment of teachers and in the approval of teaching material and curricula. In addition, the state-appointed deputy head in all minority schools was always a Muslim, with greater authority than the formal head of school. In terms of religious rights and freedoms, whereas the freedom of worship was respected, the right of the Orthodox community to manage its religious and charity foundations was seriously curtailed. The Greek Orthodox Patriarchate did have legal status, meaning that its properties could be (and were) confiscated by the state. With the closure of private religious training institutions in 1971, the state closed the Patriarchate's seminary on the island of Halki. Finally, all religious foundations remained under the supervision of the Directorate General for Foundations, which retained the power to dissolve foundations, seize properties and dismiss trustees.

While violations persist, the situation has been far from static. On the contrary, coinciding with a wider movement for reform, which has gained increasing momentum in Turkey since the turn of the century, the situation of minorities in general has improved visibly, and in particular that of the Greek Orthodox minority.

Notably since 2000, successive Turkish governments have pursued an ongoing and unprecedented process of domestic political reform. This is not to say that the reforms adopted have been either flawless or complete, or that they have all been effectively implemented and respected. Yet what appears irrefutable is that an important process of democratic change is in the making which has changed – for the better – the condition of Turkey's minorities. More specifically, in October 2001, the Turkish Grand National Assembly approved 34 constitutional amendments, most of them in the area of human rights.[10] These were followed by a set of seven harmonization packages passed between 2001 and 2003, which amended the laws in the Penal Code and the Anti-Terror Law that were used most commonly in restricting human, cultural and political rights.[11] The first two packages concentrated on the freedoms of expression and association. The third harmonization package abolished the death penalty and lifted the ban on broadcasting and education in languages other than Turkish. The fourth and fifth packages amended the Law on Political Parties, increased penalties for torture crimes expanded the freedom of the press and the freedom of association, and allowed for retrials of cases contrary to the judgments of the European Court of Human Rights. The two packages passed in July 2003 extended the freedom of speech and association; increased the *civilianization of the* (previously military-dominated) National Security Council; and extended cultural, religious and linguistic rights. A further set of constitutional amendments was passed in May 2004, covering capital punishment, freedom of expression and association, gender equality, and relations between civil society and the military.[12] This was followed by an eighth harmonization package and the adoption of a new Law on Associations and Penal Code in July and September 2004, respectively.

Among the reforms, several decisions improved the situation of the Greek Orthodox community. In 2000, a decision was taken whereby minorities would not require state permission to restore charity or religious institutions. Under the third and fourth harmonization packages, an amendment to the Law of Foundations was approved, easing the problems related to property rights. Under the sixth package, deadlines for the registration of minority foundations were relaxed and the amended Law on Public Works was extended to churches as well as to mosques. In 2004, the 1962 Secret Decree on the Secondary Committee on Minorities providing for the strict surveillance of minorities was abolished. It was replaced by the Minority Issues Assessment Board, composed of civil servants from several ministries, intended to address the problems of the non-Muslim minorities. Since 2004, children whose mothers are registered as members of a minority can also attend minority schools (previously only fathers belonging to minorities had the right to send their children to minority schools). The new Law on Associations reduced the scope for state interference in the activities of associations and legalized associations based on ethnicity or religion (previously banned). Finally, in June 2004, the Turkish Parliament adopted the Regulation on the Methods and Principles of the Boards of Non-Muslim Religious Foundations. This regulation addressed the problems relating to the election of foundation boards, which, if not held, authorized the state to confiscate property.

It is clear that Turkey's reforms constitute a momentous step forward. Yet, the reform process is still incomplete, as some laws remain inadequate or unchanged and others unimplemented. For example, while the confiscation of property is now both less likely and less frequent, the amended laws and regulations do not apply retroactively and confiscated property is not to be restituted. Conditions to apply and be recognized as a minority foundation remain restrictive. The amended Law on Foundations continues to restrict the lending and renting of foundation properties. The Patriarchate's lack of legal status has not been resolved, casting its properties permanently under the risk of confiscation. Indeed, in 2004, proceedings to confiscate some of the Patriarchate's property on the island of Büyükada were initiated. The question of reopening the seminary in Halki is pending, although in August 2003 the state undertook to reconsider its 1971 ban.

However, while many problems remain unanswered, the existence of a process of change is indisputable. Further evidence of this is the dialogue initiated in 2004 upon the request of the four main non-Muslim communities (Greek, Armenian, Jewish and Syriac) to solve outstanding problems related to their status. A final example signalling the existence of an ongoing process of change has been the establishment of a Working Group on Minority Rights and Cultural Rights mandated by the Prime Minister's Human Rights Advisory Committee. The Working Group published its first report in the autumn of 2004. This explicitly stated that the Lausanne provisions were limited and Turkey had failed to respect them fully. It suggested a complete rewriting of the constitution with the participation of civil society, the full implementation of equal citizenship for all, greater transparency and accountability of local authorities, and the full acceptance and ratification of all international and European treaties on human and minority rights. The report caused an uproar within many circles in Turkey. Yet the very fact that such a report was officially commissioned and succeeded in putting key questions relating to minority rights on the agenda proves that an unprecedented national debate is taking place in the country.

Minority rights in Greece

Unlike Turkey, Greek nationalism never espoused nor attempted to espouse a civic conception of the nation. Nor did it secularize the state as the Kemalist establishment did in Turkey. On the contrary, Greek Orthodox Christianity was hailed as a key feature of the Greek nation. Indeed, the Greek national project in the nineteenth century, and until the 1922 war in Anatolia, was inspired by the 'Megali Idea', that is, the aspiration to unify all Ottoman territories inhabited by Christian Orthodox Greeks. Until the 1990s, a Greek citizen's religion was included in his or her passport. Hence, while in Turkey minorities who did not assimilate were viewed as a threat to territorial integrity (particularly if, as in the case of the Greeks or the Armenians, their kin-state was in conflict with Turkey), in the case of Greece, minority problems stemmed from the official focus on religion. In addition, for the particular case of the Thracian Turks, the ethnic and linguistic ties with Greece's adversary, Turkey, made their full integration all the more difficult.

Nowhere was this more evident than in the Greek state's outright denial of the Turkish character of its minority. Indeed, the Lausanne Treaty emerging from the ashes of the Ottoman Empire spoke only of religious minorities, for example, the Greek Orthodox (Armenian and Jewish) minority in Turkey and the Muslim minority in Greece. It is also true that not all Muslims in Western Thrace are Turks (there are Pomaks as well as Roms). Yet it is undeniable that the Muslim minority in Greece (including Pomaks and Roms) largely defines itself as Turkish and calls for the state's recognition of its ethnic and linguistic as well as religious character. The denial of the minority's Turkish character has led to the violation of rights in itself. The state has banned and prosecuted organizations, institutions or schools defining themselves as Turkish, as well as individuals that defined the minority as Turkish. The case of the Xanthi Turkish Association – banned in 1986 due to its name – is a clear case in point. The decision to enforce the ban was upheld in the Supreme Court's ruling in 2005.

The Turkish minority of Western Thrace also suffered from other violations. As in the case of the Orthodox minority in Turkey, violations ranged from general human rights abuses such as police harassment, the expropriation of land and property, and discrimination in public employment or in the provision of services, to the non-fulfilment of the specific minority rights enshrined in law and treaties. In the field of education, Turkish schools are overcrowded, underfunded and insufficient for the number of students.[13] Greek governments, through the Ministry of Education, have exercised stringent controls over minority schools in the selection of teachers, the use of textbooks and maintenance of buildings. Teaching is of low quality and state controlled. Turks educated in Turkish universities are deemed unfit to teach, whereas graduates from the Thessaloniki Pedagogical Academy teaching in minority schools are poorly educated and have a weak command of Turkish.

In 1998, Greece abolished its infamous Article 19 of the 1955 Citizenship Law, which used ethnic origin as a reason to revoke Greek citizenship arbitrarily. Between 1955 and 1998, the article led to the deprivation of citizenship of approximately 60,000 people – most of whom were Turks – and to the presence of between 1000 and 4000 stateless persons in Greece.[14] The abolition of the article was a most welcome development. However, the abolition has not been applied retroactively. Hence, while further violations should not occur, past violations affecting 60,000 former Greek citizens are not being rectified.

Another area of minority rights violations occurred in the sphere of religious rights. Under the Lausanne Treaty, the Muslim minority was accorded the right to manage its religious affairs, including the selection of its muftis (who also act as judges in personal status and family law). However, since a 1985 government decision, codified in a 1990 law, the state appropriated the right to appoint the Muslim minority's muftis. In response, the community ignored the decision and persisted in electing its own muftis, who were prosecuted and imprisoned repeatedly. As in Turkey (*vis-à-vis* its Greek minority), another principal problem area has been that of religious foundations (the *vakfilar*). Under a 1980 law (No. 1091) and a 1991 presidential decree (No. 1), the management of the Turkish Muslim foundations has been transferred from elected committees to the state. The new law also struck at the financial holdings of the *vakfilar*. It requested official property deeds, in spite of the fact that many of these holdings date back over 500 years and are not accompanied by the necessary documentation.

Starting before Turkey, Greece also began to improve the status and condition of its own minority. Over the course of the 1990s, the Turkish Muslim minority acquired increased rights to buy, sell and repair its public property and individuals belonging to the minority acquired rights to obtain professional licences and to open restaurants and shops. In 1995 the government lifted entry restrictions along the Bulgarian border (where many Muslim citizens reside). Since the mid-1990s, authorities have engaged in a programme to improve education in minority schools and have introduced a minority quota in Greek universities. Finally, in 1994 the authorities approved a local government reform to increase efficiency and local democracy by instituting the election rather than the appointment of governors and municipal councils.

As in the case of Turkey, reforms are far from complete. Taking this last example of decentralization as evidence of the limits of the reforms, it is noteworthy that while the election of local governors was approved, the administrative boundaries of two provinces in Western Thrace were altered to dilute the Turkish presence there. The ideological break from the past in terms of the historical (mis)perception of national minorities has yet to materialize. This is highlighted further by Greece's persistent reluctance to ratify the Council of Europe's Framework Convention on National Minorities.

Inter-communal conflict and attempted solutions in Cyprus

As discussed in the preceding section, the tide of ethnic nationalism in the Eastern Mediterranean was also responsible for the eruption of inter-communal conflict in Cyprus. While there are many explanations for the emergence and consolidation of the conflict, ranging from the role of external actors to the vested interests of the local parties, the existence of ethnonationalism was the *leitmotif* underlying the problem. Drawing inspiration from the nineteenth-century Greek Megali Idea, in the early and mid twentieth century the leader of the Greek Orthodox Church in Cyprus, Archbishop Makarios, led the struggle for *enosis*. The response of Turkish and Turkish Cypriot nationalists, who abhorred the idea of assimilation into the Greek Orthodox nation, was partition.

Ethnonationalism and the articulation of mutually exclusive identities have also played a prominent role in explaining the absence of a solution to date. Ethnonationalist ideologies legitimized and bolstered bargaining positions based on legalistic and modernist conceptions of sovereignty, statehood, and military power and balance. These positions have been inimical to compromise both due to their inherent rigidity and to their inability to satisfy both parties' basic needs. Naturally, with the consolidation of the conflict, vested interests in the status quo also played a role in the continuing stalemate. Property, business interests and undiluted control over a given territory certainly served to prolong the conflict. However, ethnonationalism and vested interests were interconnected. For example, inflexible Greek Cypriot positions on the return of property have been as much about a narrative of the Turkish invasion and occupation as about property *per se*. Likewise, the Turkish Cypriot resistance to Greek Cypriot refugee return to northern Cyprus was due to both the ensuing dislocation of the Turkish Cypriots living in these areas and the fear that inter-communal intermingling could trigger renewed violence against them. Hence, interests have not only been embedded in the ethnonationaist discourse, they have strengthened and reproduced it.

Between 2001 and 2004, the then UN Secretary-General, Kofi Annan, engaged in the most dedicated attempt to date to mediate a bi-zonal and bi-communal federal solution in Cyprus, bridging the mutually exclusive bargaining positions of the principal parties. The result was the comprehensive 'Annan Plan': a detailed constitutional agreement with accompanying treaties that could have sealed a final settlement on the conflict-ridden island. The plan institutionalized a politically equal relationship between the Greek Cypriot majority and Turkish Cypriot minority with attached external guarantees. Five versions of the plan were presented between November 2002 and March 2004. In what follows, attention will be focused on the fifth and final version.

Constitutionally, the plan adopted several aspects of the Swiss and Belgian federal constitutions, providing for a loose common state at the centre and two constituent states in northern and southern Cyprus, governed respectively by the Turkish Cypriot and Greek Cypriot communities. Most powers were to be attributed to the constituent states, which would coordinate policies in their spheres of competence (including present common positions at the EU-level). The common state level would be responsible for foreign relations, monetary policy, federal finance, and common state citizenship and immigration. Common state institutions would be marked by effective political equality between the parties. In the executive, there would be a presidential council comprising six Greek Cypriots and three Turkish Cypriots, within which there would be a rotating presidency between members from the two communities. The presidential council would strive to reach decisions by consensus but could otherwise take decisions by majority vote, provided that there was effective Turkish Cypriot participation. The common state parliament was to be composed of two houses and decisions would require the approval of both chambers, including one quarter of senators from each constituent state. The lower house would be elected on the basis of constituent state citizenship, provided that the Turkish Cypriot constituent state held at least one quarter of the seats. The upper house would be composed of an equal number of Greek and Turkish Cypriots. Constituent state elections would be based on permanent residency.

The constitutional aspect providing for a loose common state was counterbalanced by territorial proposals which provided for a reduction of the northern Turkish Cypriot zone from the current 37 per cent to approximately 28.5 per cent of the land. Territorial readjustments would, in turn, allow the majority of Greek Cypriot displaced persons to return to their properties under Greek Cypriot rule. The remaining Greek Cypriot displaced persons who wished to return to their properties in the north would have the right to reinstatement under specified conditions, rules and limitations.

In terms of military security, the Greek and Turkish military contingents would be reduced progressively over time, with the ultimate objective of complete demilitarization. A UN peacekeeping force, empowered by a new mandate, would monitor the implementation of the agreement. The UN would also supervise the transfer of territory from the Turkish Cypriot to the Greek Cypriot constituent states. The 1959 Treaty of Guarantee would remain in force but would be amended so as to allow the three guarantors (Greece, Turkey and the UK) to protect the constitutional status and territorial integrity not only of the common state but also of the two constituent states. The UN plan stipulated further that Cyprus would not put its territory at the disposal of international military operations without the consent of both constituent states as well as of both Greece and Turkey until the accession of Turkey to the EU (after which the consent of the two kin-states would no longer be necessary).

On 24 April 2004, Greek Cypriots and Turkish Cypriots voted on the Annan Plan. The referendum results pointed to an overwhelming Turkish Cypriot acceptance (65 per cent) and Greek Cypriot rejection (76 per cent). The results generated widespread disappointment among many Greek and Turkish Cypriots alike but was met with a sigh of relief by those who either overtly or otherwise had rejected the plan. Many outsiders – and EU leaders in particular – expressed their surprise and dismay at the results.

In the post-referendum period, three broad options have emerged concerning the future of minority–majority relations on the island. The first and best option is that of reunification some time in the future on the basis of the Annan Plan. Thanks both to its level of detail and to its tightly interrelated compromise arrangements, the plan (with, at most, minor modifications) represents the only feasible reunification solution that could be conceivably agreed upon by all parties.

A second option in the (likely) event that a second referendum would either not take place or fail again is that the Turkish Cypriots would, ultimately, agree to a solution that is more in line with perceived Greek Cypriot interests. This would see a relatively centralized federal state in which majority decision-making (read Greek Cypriot) would prevail and most Greek Cypriots would be able to return to northern Cyprus, thus diluting the bi-zonal aspect of a federal solution. Such a solution would also see the faster and more extensive withdrawal of Turkish troops and settlers, stronger international guarantees and a weaker (or absent) Turkish role in security arrangements on the island. Such a solution could materialize with a strengthening of the Greek Cypriot bargaining position and a weakening of that of Turkey and the Turkish Cypriots that would compromise the most basic of red lines that have guided Turkish and Turkish Cypriot policy over the last half century. It could occur if, as Turkey's EU accession negotiations proceed, EU actors (including the Republic of Cyprus) exert heavy-handed pressure on Turkey and Turkish authorities become willing to 'sacrifice' Cyprus for their EU accession. To date, this remains an unlikely scenario.

A third option, in the event of a lasting 'no-solution' outcome, is the gradual drift of the Turkish Cypriots in northern Cyprus towards economic normalization (what is commonly referred to in northern Cyprus as the 'Taiwan model') and, ultimately, recognized statehood. The viability of the status quo in northern Cyprus depends largely on the approach taken by the international community. Under the existing circumstances of political and economic isolation, the status quo could evolve into an increasing Turkification of northern Cyprus (through the emigration of Turkish Cypriots to Western Europe and immigration of Turks to the island). If the international community and the EU (including the Greek Cypriots) reach the conclusion that such a scenario would not be in their interests, decisive action may be taken to lift the isolation of the north (for example, through the lifting of trade, political, social and cultural restrictions, and embargoes). This was indeed called for by the UN Secretary-General in his report published in the aftermath of the April 2004 referendum.[15] The first steps in this direction are being taken, with the EU setting aside €259 million for the Turkish Cypriots, debating the possibility for direct Turkish Cypriot exports to EU markets, as well as facilitating intra-island trade. Yet, to date, steps towards normalization remain extremely limited, due to the blocking power of the Greek Cypriot government in the EU.

Which trends will prevail in Cyprus will be determined by the complex interactions between domestic and regional dynamics, cast within the wider framework of European integration. It is indeed to these domestic, regional and European causes that the following section will turn, in an attempt to explain the ongoing evolutions of minority–majority relations in the Eastern Mediterranean.

The Europeanization of Greece, Cyprus and Turkey

The impact of relations with and integration into the EU on domestic and regional dynamics has been significant in the evolution of minority–majority relations in the Eastern Mediterranean. This influence has taken a variety of forms and has occurred in different ways according to the evolving relationships of Greece, Turkey and Cyprus with the EU.

In the case of Greece, the mechanisms of Europeanization did not take place through conditionality, either prior to or after accession. Greece joined the EU in 1981, despite its shortcomings in the fields of democracy and minority rights, and the EU's political conditionality mechanisms were still largely absent in the 1970s and early 1980s. Indeed, it was not until the 1993 Copenhagen European Council that the 'Copenhagen criteria' were developed and applied to the EU's subsequent rounds of enlargement. Nor did EU institutions exert direct pressure on Greece in the field of minority rights post-accession. Although the 1993 Copenhagen criteria inspired Article 6 of the Amsterdam Treaty, which calls upon member states to respect human rights, fundamental freedoms, democracy and the rule of law, the article omits any reference to minority rights, which are included instead in the Copenhagen criteria for accession.[16] Both due to the absence of a clear legal definition of minority rights and because of the wide variation in minority rights protection within the EU, the institutions of the latter have kept quiet when it comes to member states' minorities post-accession. In addition, in the specific case of Greece, under the Lausanne Treaty, the state had already recognized its Turkish Muslim minority and the problem has lain largely in ensuring respect for those legal obligations.

This is not to say that the EU has not played a role in the evolution of minority–majority relations in Greece. On the contrary, EU membership represented a key external determinant of the gradual improvement in the status and condition of Greece's minorities. The first mechanism of change occurred through Greece's adoption of EU political recommendations as well as legally binding EU regulations and decisions. These, while not tailored directly to minority rights, have impacted positively on Greece's Muslim/Turkish minority. For example, Greece's membership of the European Convention on Human Rights (under the Council of Europe but nonetheless a condition of EU membership), its abolition of Article 19 of the Citizenship Law (in view of the Treaty of Amsterdam's provisions on non-discrimination) its first timid steps towards greater decentralization and its lifting of the restriction zone along the Bulgarian border were all, partly, the result of EU legal and political pressure. All have, indirectly, affected Greece's minorities.

Yet perhaps the most pivotal mechanism of EU-induced change was the gradual and progressive Greek socialization into European norms, values and standards. EU membership induced the country to modernize over the decades. With modernization came the gradual and ongoing rebalancing of delicate equilibria within the country, from civil–military relations to relations between church and state. These ongoing processes of change clearly affected Greece's Muslim/Turkish minority. Another EU-induced mechanism of social change has been the state and society's increased sense of security within the EU. Since 1981, EC/EU membership imbued Greece gradually with a sense of security, which enabled policy-makers increasingly (and particularly the Pan-Hellenic Socialist Movement, PASOK the governing party throughout the 1980s and 1990s) to rationally reassess the country's security interests. A principal and ongoing reassessment has been *vis-à-vis* Greece's relationship with Turkey. As discussed below, this had important positive repercussions in terms of the state's relations with its Turkish minority.

Turning to Cyprus, the re-evaluation of Greek Cypriot–Turkish Cypriot relations could have taken place through EU policies of conditionality. The Greek Cypriot Republic of Cyprus applied for EU membership in 1990 and its accession process began after a positive Commission Opinion in 1993. Cyprus' accession, alongside that of the Central and Eastern European countries, was subject to an unprecedented (although far from perfect) degree of EU political conditionality. However, when it came to the Cyprus conflict, EU actors attempted initially to maintain pressure on both parties. The 1993 Commission Opinion retained an aura of vagueness. On the one hand, it implied that accession would require a settlement of the conflict (hence, exerting pressure on the Greek Cypriots who had applied to enter). On the other hand, it did not exclude that membership could occur despite the ongoing partition of the island (if the lack of a solution was attributable to Turkish Cypriot intransigence). However, as the accession process took shape over the course of the decade, conditionality on the Republic of Cyprus was lifted progressively, until the divided island joined the EU on 1 May 2004.[17]

The lifting of conditionality on Cyprus had a dual effect: it induced the more moderate forces in Cyprus to be more active in seeking a solution prior to accession, but contributed also to a hardening of the positions of the least flexible forces on the island. Given the deadlines inherent in the EU accession timetable, those in favour of an early solution were the supporters of the Annan Plan.

Beginning with the Greek Cypriots, it is important to note that the decision to apply for and to pursue EU membership was linked to the aim of strengthening the Greek Cypriot bargaining position in negotiations. Accession would bolster the status of the Republic, increase Greek Cypriot leverage on Turkey and support a solution more in line with perceived Greek Cypriot interests. Consequently, the EU accession process made moderate actors like former President Glafcos Clerides more open to compromise in 2002–2003 than he had been when he was first elected in 1993. This was not least because the EU accession process imbued Greek Cypriot society with an increased sense of security, raising the readiness of moderate forces to make new concessions (for example, on security or constitutional questions). In this respect, lifting conditionality on the Greek Cypriot side may have had a positive influence on the positions of the former Greek Cypriot leadership.

However, the same cannot be said of the ensuing Papadopoulous administration, elected in 2003. Having secured EU membership through the lifting of EU conditionality, Tassos Papadopoulous felt unconstrained in his flat rejection of the Annan Plan in April 2004. The President was well aware of the stronger Greek Cypriot bargaining position post-accession and felt he could use this in future negotiations to secure a more favourable agreement. These views seemed to be shared by the majority of the population, who rejected the plan in the referendum.

Turning to the Turkish Cypriots, EU conditionality appeared to have its strongest negative effects up until 2001, by raising the inflexibility of the nationalist camp solidly in power in the north since 1974. Although accession for the Turkish Cypriots was conditional on a solution, the benefits offered by membership were not valued enough by the authorities for them to make the necessary concessions. Indeed, to the most nationalist of forces, EU accession for the whole island was viewed as a threat to Turkish Cypriot security interests. Nationalists saw the *de facto* accession of the Greek Cypriots alone as a blessing in disguise for securing partition. In turn, their negotiating positions hardened over the course of the 1990s. However, the mounting pressure on the veteran Turkish Cypriot leader (and key figure in the nationalist camp) Rauf Denktaş in 2002–2003 and the ensuing change of leadership in the 2003 legislative elections in northern Cyprus shows that the lure of EU accession did generate important incentives among the Turkish Cypriot population. Aware that gains from membership could be accessed only through a solution, both the new moderate Prime Minister (since 2005 President) Mehmet Ali Talat and the majority of the Turkish Cypriot population voted in favour of the Annan Plan in April 2004.

It is far more difficult to detect whether other, more diffuse, mechanisms of EU-induced social and political change have also been at work in Cyprus. It may well be that the assiduous contact between EU officials and the former Greek Cypriot leadership (in power consistently throughout the accession process and up until 2003) had a social learning effect upon these elites. This, in addition to other factors, may explain in part their increased willingness to compromise. Yet, when it came to the broader population on both sides as well as the Turkish Cypriot elites (both moderate and nationalist), there was insufficient exposure to EU institutions and actors for the latter to have had an impact through socialization and social learning.

Finally, Turkey's Europeanization also played a pivotal role in explaining the process of domestic reform and foreign policy shifts in the country.[18] In this case, while imperfect and, at times, vaguely defined, the EU certainly exerted political conditionality. This ranged from human, cultural and minority rights to foreign policy issues such as that of Cyprus. Like other candidates, Turkey received annual Commission Progress Reports, which reviewed the policy developments pertinent to the compliance with EU criteria. Turkey also received two Accession Partnership documents, pinpointing reform priorities. In direct response to these documents, Turkey adopted a National Programme (in March 2001, and revised in July 2003) that set out the extent and means by which Turkey intended to address EU priorities. Most of the changes in the constitutional and legal harmonization packages discussed above reflect changes set out in the National Programmes. According to Turkey's Negotiating Framework agreed in October 2005, EU conditionality and monitoring are intended to continue in the period ahead.

The existence of conditionality does not exclude more endogenous and less coercive processes of domestic change in Turkey. Indeed, there is evidence that Turkey's current reform process is not merely the result of Turkey's acceptance of political conditions 'for the sake of' the EU. Even if the Turkish establishment long hailed EU membership as the culmination of Atatürk's modernization project, up until the turn of the century Turkey continued to defy EU political recommendations. It viewed these as too risky or, indeed, threatening to the country's national security. Certainly, the prospect of EU accession since the December 1999 Helsinki European Council played a crucial role in changing domestic balances in Turkey; it both raised the value of the 'EU carrot' as well as the political willingness to pass delicate reforms in view of the expectation to be enveloped in the European security community. Yet when Turkish Prime Minister Erdoğan referred to the Copenhagen criteria as the 'Ankara criteria', to be adopted irrespective of whether Turkey ultimately joined the EU, a more endogenous process of change can be seen to be at work.

However, as in the case of Cyprus, and indeed more so due to the longer-term prospect of Turkey's EU accession, it is doubtful that this more endogenous process of change has taken place through rising contact with EU actors. Up until the beginning of accession negotiations in October 2005, Turkey's accession process had not entailed sufficiently dense and widespread contacts between Turkish actors with the EU institutional framework. However, this is set to change over the course of negotiations. To date, though, it is unlikely that existing contacts have generated, in and of themselves, a process of social learning in Turkey. After the opening of six chapters in the accession negotiations with the EU in October 2005 and the successful closure of one in June of the following year, negotiations stalled in June 2007 due to continued disagreement over Cyprus. The EU has since refused to close further chapters on the grounds of Turkey's intransigence in the recognition of Cyprus. As the sections below will examine, Turkey's reform process, like the changing politics in Greece and Cyprus, appears to be the product of domestic and regional changes which have interacted with incentives at the EU level.

Changing regional and domestic politics in the Eastern Mediterranean

The gradually improving status of the Greek and Turkish minorities in Turkey and Greece respectively is linked directly with the gradual and consolidating rapprochement between these two countries. As mentioned above, historically, the condition of minorities was at its best during the years of Greek–Turkish friendship in the 1930s–1950s. This was the only period in which Greek authorities, not feeling threatened by Turkey, referred to the Muslim minority as Turkish. As relations have begun to improve again since 1999, a similar positive link between foreign and domestic policy developments seems to be developing.

The seeds of rapprochement were sown during the spring of 1999. Greek Foreign Minister Papandreou felt increasingly the need to engage in constructive dialogue with Turkey, following the period of rising brinkmanship in 1996–1999. The 1999 earthquakes in Turkey and Greece provided the trigger for a major policy shift, with groundbreaking visits of Foreign Ministers Ismail Cem and George Papandreou to one another's countries. Rapprochement then filtered through the system, through a set of bilateral agreements on 'low politics' issues. The official rapprochement also led to a surge in business and civil society contacts as well as to steadily rising bilateral trade. Greece and Turkey have not yet resolved any of their long-standing disputes in the Aegean and Cyprus. However, on the Aegean, the two have engaged in negotiations on the continental shelf since 2003. The policy of rapprochement persisted – albeit in a more low-key manner – following the change of government in Athens with the election of Costas Karamanlis' New Democracy Party in March 2004. Indeed Greek–Turkish relations were not a matter of dispute during the 2003–2004 election campaign. Both PASOK and New Democracy pledged to persist and intensify the rapprochement with Turkey and to support Turkey's EU accession.

As Greek–Turkish relations have improved, their respective minorities have reaped important benefits and are expected to continue to do so. For example, an important problem in the sphere of education was the non-implementation of the 1968 Protocol on the Exchange of Textbooks. This was due in large part to the lack of inter-state communication between the two countries. As ties between Greece and Turkey continue to strengthen, it is expected that several of these blocked reciprocal initiatives will be resolved.

Moreover, over time, rapprochement could diminish state mistrust of minorities. The fear that the Greek or Turkish minorities could fuel secessionism has underpinned the two states' mistrust of, and subsequent discrimination against, them. This is also expected to change as inter-state trust rises. In this respect, the visit by Prime Minister Tayyıp Erdoğan to Western Thrace in May 2004 was an important event. In his address to the Turkish community there, the Turkish Premier's declaration that the minority's loyalty should be exclusively towards the Greek state served as a major confidence building measure between the two countries. In turn, this is expected to have positive effects on the Thracian Turkish minority, viewed with decreasing mistrust by the establishment. Similarly, the Greek Orthodox Patriarchate's staunch support for Turkey's EU accession has also been appreciated in Ankara and has resonated positively in terms of Turkey's minority policy towards the Greek community.

Beyond these regional developments, specific domestic changes have also played key roles in explaining minority–majority relations in Greece and Turkey. In Greece, the consolidation of Greek democracy allowed key actors such as former Foreign Minister Papandreou to seize the opportunity to shift Greek policy towards Turkey, which in turn had an impact on the Turkish minority. While the country was certainly more ready for the shift in 2000 than it had been two decades earlier, the specific role of key personalities such as Papandreou cannot be underestimated.

In Turkey, the process of Europeanization has proven a powerful anchor of domestic change, change which covered both minority-related issues and issues of foreign policy towards Cyprus. However, the hypothesis of a straight-forward causal relationship between externally demanded conditions that are accepted domestically through the adoption of policy reforms misses much of the complexity at play.[19] More plausible is a far more subtle argument about the mechanisms of domestic change in Turkey. Change occurred and is occurring, not simply because it is imposed from the outside, but because it interacts with domestic developments on the inside.

In discussing the realignment of domestic politics in Turkey, a key feature has been the rising power of the AK Party (AKP) since the 2002 elections. The AKP government's commitment to political reforms and EU accession has important interest and ideology-related explanations. Beginning with interests, reform and EU accession are viewed as the most effective means for the AKP to raise its legitimacy and shed its Islamist past *vis-à-vis* the secular establishment in Turkey. Furthermore, democratic reform and EU accession are considered the best guarantee for the AKP's political survival. The AKP's predecessors (which were far more Islamist in nature) were successively banned by the Constitutional Court for allegedly threatening the secular nature of the Republic. A commitment to reform and EU accession is also part of the AKP's political ideology. The AKP refuses to define itself as an 'Islamic' party but calls instead for greater religious freedoms. In order to carry a consistent political message, it advocates personal freedoms in other spheres as well, including the cultural and linguistic domains.

Ongoing change within the Turkish military – considered the bastion of the Kemalist system and of its nationalist project – has been equally important. Since 2002, Turkey's military either did not oppose or tacitly accepted both the change of policy towards Cyprus and the ongoing reform process (including the reforms that redefined its very role). Underlying this attitude was the self-reassessment of the military's role in Turkish politics. Despite evident (although adamantly denied) differences of opinion within the Turkish Armed Forces, important personalities (most notably Chief of General Staff Hilmi Özkök) have come to the conclusion that the military's interference in politics failed to deliver stability to the country. There is, therefore, an increasing willingness within the military to 'give politics a chance'. This does not necessarily entail an agreement with the substance of the reforms. Rather, it has meant an increased willingness to desist from interference and to leave politics to politicians.

Domestic changes in Cyprus have also been key determinants of recent events on the island. The sections above recounted how the Turkish Cypriot public increasingly appreciated the appeal of EU accession and turned against the policies of its historical leadership. However, to understand the timing and form of these developments, other domestic causes of change cannot be underestimated. The steady deterioration of the Turkish Cypriot economy since 1999 (due to the repercussions of the IMF programme in Turkey in 1999 and the 2001 financial crisis) and the growing awareness that economic ills and isolation would lead to their disappearance as a well-defined community in northern Cyprus acted as key drivers of domestic change. In addition, the increasing Turkish Cypriot awareness of growing dependence on Turkey, and the realization that they were not a self-governing entity but were controlled largely by Ankara, also acted to mobilize the public. In other words, the Turkish Cypriot public and the former opposition forces increasingly came to view their self-determination and communal security as dependent on reunification and EU membership. The Annan Plan gave both moderate leaders and the public alike an acceptable specific formula through which this could take place.

Equally important were domestic causes of the Greek Cypriot 'no'. Some analysts have pointed to the feeling of insecurity prevalent amongst the public, arguing that the continued presence of Turkey in the plan's security arrangements failed to assuage Greek Cypriot fears *vis-à-vis* its neighbour. In a conflict context, a feeling of insecurity is entirely unsurprising. Yet the fear of taking a step into the unknown was probably equally high on both sides of the green line. Turkish Cypriots probably feared the renewed domination of Greek Cypriots as much as Greek Cypriots feared Turkey's persistent grip on the island. The accompanying explanation of the degree of Greek Cypriot risk aversion is their relatively more comfortable situation. In sharp contrast to the Turkish Cypriots, the Greek Cypriots have enjoyed a rising standard of living since 1974 and their political and economic status is expected to improve further as a result of EU accession. However, this is not to say that the Greek Cypriot majority opposed reunification. The point was rather that, persuaded by their leadership, the Greek Cypriot public felt that a better deal was possible and thus worth waiting for.

Concluding remarks

Minority–majority relations in the Greece–Turkey–Cyprus triangle have been transformed in important, positive ways in recent years. Underlying these improvements has been the complex interactions between key changes at the domestic, regional and EU levels.

In Greece, the gradual socialization into EU norms and practices led to key reforms, improving the legal and practical status of its Turkish/Muslim minority. In addition, specific personalities, aided by the overall maturing of Greek democracy, allowed the country to embark on an unprecedented rapprochement with Turkey. This in turn proved, and continues to prove, key to the increased respect for minority rights in both countries. The Greek–Turkish rapprochement was also a positive force militating in favour of Cyprus' reunification.

Also in Turkey, the EU has been a key anchor supporting democratization and modernization, in this case through the conditionality embedded in the accession process. Ongoing reforms have improved the status of its internal minorities as well as contributed to key foreign policy shifts, first and foremost *vis-à-vis* Cyprus. These EU-inspired processes of change are not the result of a simple linear relationship based on EU conditionality. It is also doubtful that change is taking place simply through an externally inspired process of socialization. Instead, what appears to be in the making is a process of domestic change driven largely by endogenous factors but where the precise form and timing of reforms is intricately linked to Turkey's accession process. Increasingly, Turkish actors talk about the desirability of reforming and redefining Kemalism or about the need to adopt the Copenhagen (or Ankara) criteria for Turkey's own sake rather than for that of the EU. Such a process of endogenous change is explained primarily by the ongoing development trajectory of the Turkish nation-state. Yet, at this particular juncture, Turkey's development path is being affected and supported by the EU accession course in a pivotal way, giving this general process of modernization and democratization an important Europeanized twist.

Hence, in both Greece and Turkey, minority–majority relations have been improving and much of this change has been determined by the process of Europeanization and its interaction with endogenous domestic and regional determinants. Yet insofar as endogenous variables represent the key drivers of change (or lack thereof), it follows that the extent of change will remain limited so long as the parties retain a fundamentally unchanged vision of their states and nations. In this respect, the consolidating state-to-state friendship could reinforce these domestically determined ceilings. For example, when, in 2005, the Greek Supreme Court reaffirmed the banning of the Xanthi Turkish Association, unlike in previous years, the event went largely unnoticed by Turkish officials and the media. The absence of a Turkish outcry may well be a by-product of the rapprochement, as Turkey chooses increasingly to step aside when it comes to its neighbours' internal affairs. However, it may also be that Turkey, with its own minority concerns, is not displeased when EU member Greece acts in defiance of political criteria which the EU professes only theoretically. Turkish authorities might see it as an opportunity to store up political ammunition with which to fend off what they might deem to be excessive EU interference in their minority policies.

The same sobering conclusion applies in Cyprus. On the island, the EU accession process was key in triggering the fundamental overhaul of Turkish Cypriot politics. However, in this case also, Europeanization can only be credited in part for the extent of positive change, or rather it can be credited only in conjunction with other domestic and regional changes. The rising economic ills of the Turkish Cypriots and their growing dependence on Turkey led increasingly to a sense of frustration amongst the public against the status quo policy of its historical leadership. In politically mobilizing this frustration, the moderate elites in the north, emboldened by Turkey's EU accession course and by the shifting foreign policy under the AKP government, succeeded in delivering a resounding Turkish Cypriot 'yes' to reunification and EU accession.

Yet the referendum failed to deliver reunification. Perhaps if the Annan Plan had assured greater security guarantees to the Greek Cypriot public, the result would have been different. Perhaps the problem was simply one of timing. If a referendum had taken place in 2002, when former Greek Cypriot President Clerides was still in office (but Turkish Cypriot President Denktaş had rejected the UN plan), would the Greek Cypriots have voted differently? Perhaps. However, a more sombre explanation cannot be excluded either. It may well be that the Greek Cypriot public, comfortable in its current situation, simply is not willing to shift from the status quo, in which it governs its internationally recognized state alone (albeit on half the island). Irrespective of the gains yielded in terms of territory, property and security, perhaps the larger community is just unwilling, after decades of separation, to go the extra mile and engage in genuine power-sharing with the smaller Turkish Cypriot community. Perhaps, if the Turkish Cypriots had felt equally comfortable with the status quo, reunification would not have been their best option either.

No conclusive answer can be provided to these questions. Suffice it to say that in Cyprus, as in other ethnopolitical conflicts in the European neighbourhood, from Serbia-Montenegro to Moldova and Transdniestria, a new trend could be in the making. This trend would see the previously metropolitan state slowly giving up on the idea of reintegrating its *de facto* seceded minority (as a collectivity on a defined territory, rather than as individual citizens). This becomes all the more true when the larger community, having accommodated to the loss of land (and the refugee exodus that often comes with it), adjusts to its new *modus vivendi*. It projects itself into a European future that more often than not does not envisage a place for the *de facto* seceded minority.

What the current developments in Cyprus, Greece and Turkey show is that the future of minority–majority relations, whether positive or negative, will continue to be determined in large part by internal actors and factors. The EU dimension certainly adds important incentives (or disincentives). However, the role of the latter is determined to a great extent by the precise fashion in which it interacts with ongoing domestic and regional trends. In Greece and Turkey it has led to important positive changes. However, the pace and limits of these changes continue to be set by the domestic evolution of these two countries, as well as by relations between them. In Cyprus, despite the positive momentum that the EU accession of Greece, Cyprus and Turkey may bring to bear, the reunification or otherwise of the island will hinge primarily on the interests, desires and fears, and thus on the perceptions and misperceptions, of its two communities.

Notes

1. T. Risse, M.G. Cowles and J.A. Caporaso (eds), *Transforming Europe: Europeanization and Domestic Change* (Ithaca: Cornell University Press, 2001); K. Featherstone and C. Radaelli (eds), *The Politics of Europeanization* (Oxford: Oxford University Press, 2003).
2. T. Borzel and T. Risse, 'When Europe Hits Home: Europeanization and Domestic Change', *European Integration Online Papers* 4(15) (2000); J. Olsen, *The Many Faces of Europeanization*, Arena Working Papers WP01/2, http://www.arena.uio.no/publications/wp02_2.htm (last accessed 16/05/2008). (2001).
3. K. Smith, *The Making of EU Foreign Policy: The Case of Eastern Europe* (London: Macmillan, 1999); H. Grabbe, 'How Does Europeanization Affect CEE Governance? Conditionality, Diffusion and Diversity', *Journal of European Public Policy* 8(6) (2001): 1013–31; N. Tocci, 'Europeanization in Turkey: Trigger or Anchor for Reform?', *South European Politics and Society* 10(1) (2005): 73–83.
4. P. Ioakimides, 'The Europeanization of Greece: An Overall Assessment', in K. Featherstone and G. Kazamias (eds), *Europeanization and the Southern Periphery* (London: Frank Cass, 2001), 73–94; and Featherstone, 'Cyprus and the Onset of Europeanization Strategic Usage, Structural Transformation and Institutional Adaptation', in *ibid.*, 141–64.
5. M. Albert, S. Stetter and T. Diez (2004, Mar) "The European Union and Border Conflicts – Theoretical and Conceptual Explorations", Paper presented at

the annual meeting of the International Studies Association, Le Centre Sheraton Hotel, Montreal, Quebec, Canada Online. Available at http://www.allacademic.com/meta/p73584_index.html (last accessed 16/05/2008).

6. D. Pentzopoulos, *The Balkans Exchange of Minorities and Its Impact on Greece*, 2nd edn (London: Hurst, 2002).

7. This is not to say that minority discrimination did not exist during this period. The Turkish 1942 Varlık Vergisi law, imposing a wealth tax on property with extra zeal on non-Muslim minorities, was a clear case of minority discrimination.

8. Human Rights Watch, *The Turks of Western Thrace*, Reports 11(1) (Human Rights Watch, 1999).

9. N. Tocci, *21st Century Kemalism: Redefining Turkey–EU Relations in the Post-Helsinki Era'* CEPS Working Document No.170 (Brussels: CEPS, 2001).

10. Law No. 4709 Türkiye Cumhuriyeti Anayasasının Bazı Maddelerinin Değistirilmesi Hakkında Kanun (Law on the Amendment of Certain Provisions of Constitution of the Republic of Turkey), 3 October 2001. Published in Official Gazette No. 24556, 17 October 2001.

11. These reform packages, called a variation of 'Çeşitli (bazı) Kanunlarda Değişiklik Yapılmasına İlişkin (dair) Kanun' (Law on the Amendment of Various Laws), had the following numbers and were adopted by the parliament on the following dates: Law No. 4744 on 6 February 2002; Law No. 4748 on 26 March 2002; Law No. 4771 on 3 August 2002; Law No. 4778 on 2 January 2003; Law No. 4793 on 23 January 2003; Law No. 4928 on 19 June and 15 July 2003; and Law No. 4963 on 30 July 2003.

12. The May 2004 package provided for amendments to Articles 10, 15, 17, 30, 38, 87, 90, 131, 143 and 160 of the Constitution.

13. There are 230 primary schools, two junior schools and only two high schools for a population of over 120,000.

14. Human Rights Watch, *The Turks*, *supra* note 8.

15. UN Secretary General, *Report of the Secretary General on his Mission of Good Offices in Cyprus*, 28 May 2004. S/2004/437.

16. B. de Witte, 'Politics Versus Law in the EU's Approach to Ethnic Minorities', in J. Zielonka (ed.), *Europe Unbound* (London: Routledge, 2002), 137–60.

17. N. Tocci, *EU Accession Dynamics and Conflict Resolution: Catalyzing Peace or Consolidating Partition in Cyprus* (Aldershot: Ashgate, 2004).

18. Since the rise to power of the AKP government, Turkey has shifted its stance towards the Cyprus conflict, accepting a solution in 2004 based on the Annan Plan, which provided for reunification, a considerable territorial retreat and the scaling down of military presence.

19. Tocci, 'Europeanization in Turkey', *supra* note 3.

11
The Effective Protection of Minorities in the Wider Europe: Counterbalancing the Security Track

Katherine Nobbs

What is clear from preceding chapters is that much of Western thinking on minority rights over the last decade and a half has been dominated by the perception that it was a dramatic breakdown in minority–majority relations that provoked the wave of violence that spread across much of Central and Eastern Europe in the 1990s. Ethnic tensions are commonly regarded as having been at the heart of conflicts in Kosovo, Bosnia and Herzegovina, Croatia, the Former Yugoslav Republic of Macedonia,[1] Georgia, Azerbaijan, Moldova and Chechnya. Consequently, regional organizations have formulated their approach to minority rights around the central notion that the management, resolution and, ideally, the prevention of ethnic conflicts is best (or least controversially) addressed through the diffusion of ethnic tension via the protection of minority rights.

What is also apparent, however, is that the current focus on security is coupled with an entrenched suspicion on the part of Western governments that the empowerment of minorities poses an inherently destabilizing threat to the territorial integrity and national security of the state. Government action in the field of minority rights is thus regarded as a balancing act between, on the one hand, the preservation of regional security through the general strengthening of the individual rights of persons belonging to minorities and, on the other, the preservation of national security via the limitation of group rights accorded to minorities within their borders; in other words, an artificial dichotomy is established between the protection of the rights of minorities and the preservation of the territorial integrity and national security of states.

To illustrate this premise, recall briefly some of the arguments made in relation to the four main regional institutions within Europe: the Organization for Security and Cooperation in Europe (OSCE), the North Atlantic Treaty Organization (NATO), the European Union (EU) and the Council of Europe (CoE). The goal of regional stability is clearly dominant within security-minded organizations such as NATO and the OSCE.[2] Although

Drzewicki is keen to stress that an over-simplification of the mandate of the OSCE High Commissioner on National Minorities (HCNM) as 'an instrument of conflict prevention' belies its commitment to the third 'human dimension basket',[3] it is argued that the approach remains one of conflict prevention using, *inter alia*, the protection of minority rights and not of the advancement of minority rights as a normative good *per se*.

Kymlicka's discussion of the OSCE's varying approach towards autonomy claims offers evidential support for this argument. By his analysis, whether or not the organization promotes or discourages territorial settlements is contingent on the level of threat presented by the minority group in question; those groups that have seized power extra-constitutionally are supported by the OSCE (for example, those favouring autonomy for Crimea in Ukraine, South Ossetia in Georgia, or Kosovo in Serbia), while those which do not present an immediate threat are counselled to abandon their autonomy claims (for example, the Hungarians in Slovakia).[4] Thus, while not disregarding the important work undertaken by the OSCE in the field of international standard setting,[5] its record of erratic interventions lends weight to the argument that it privileges regional stability over the subsidiary goal of the development of a uniform policy on the regional protection of minority rights.

While adherence to the so-called 'security track'[6] of minority rights protection is arguably to be expected within regional security organizations, what is perhaps more surprising is that it has permeated the institutional infrastructure of the EU, the mandate of which includes almost everything *but* security,[7] and has even seeped into the thinking of the Council of Europe, the traditional preserve of human rights. In the case of the EU, for example, Wolff and Rodt demonstrate very effectively its increasing activity in regional conflict management and prevention through the dual mechanisms of its Common Foreign and Security Policy and, more tellingly, through its Enlargement Policy via the Stabilization and Association Process in the Western Balkans. While it would again be anticipated that security policy would privilege stability, the dominance of the security approach within enlargement policy – which provided a ripe opportunity for the development of a parallel 'legal rights' track – is indicative of the depth to which the security track has become embedded within the Western European mindset.

That said, some progress was evident in the signing of the Reform Treaty in Lisbon in December 2007, which took the historic step of incorporating minority rights within the founding values of the EU[8] and in establishing 'membership of a national minority' as one of the prohibited grounds of discrimination.[9] As noted by Toggenburg, however, this provision was not supported by a sound competence base: specific reference to minorities is absent from Article 13 TEC, the so-called 'enabling' provision which requires states to take action to combat discrimination based on 'sex, racial or ethnic origin, religion or belief, disability, age or sexual orientation'. Although the reference to ethnic origin could perhaps be interpreted expansively in light of the inclusion of minority rights within the founding values, it remains unlikely that it will form the basis for the extension of collective rights to minority groups.

In the case of the CoE, although its groundbreaking Framework Convention on the Protection of National Minorities (FCNM) undoubtedly constituted a significant first step towards the development of a regional framework for the long-term protection of minority rights, its provisions were nevertheless framed as individual rights and not in terms of the recognition, protection and promotion of collective rights and freedoms.[10] The privileging of state rights over collective (and even individual) minority rights is again evident, not only in the wide margin of appreciation accorded to states by the Advisory Committee to the FCNM in their implementation of the Convention and, notably, in their interpretation of the term 'national minority', but in the fact that the Committee was accorded only advisory powers in the first place.

Thus, the institutions which together develop, implement and monitor the European framework of minority rights protection can be seen, not only to have privileged the stated goal of regional security, but by extension to have actively supported Western states in their prioritization of territorial integrity at the expense of the extension of collective rights to national minorities. It is argued that the dominance of state rights over the rights of minorities is at the root of many of the current problems relating to the protection of minorities in Europe, notably: the issue of 'double standards' within the EU; the lack of legal recourse in the event of state violation of minority rights; and the pre-eminence of weaker cultural rights over stronger rights to regional and territorial autonomy, to be discussed presently. In fact, to adopt Kymlicka's argument is to take the thesis one step further: the predominance of the security track may have the diametrically opposite effect of actually exacerbating state intransigence and incentivizing minority violence.[11]

Regional minority rights mechanisms and their respective limitations

Although the European framework for the protection of minority rights is comparatively sophisticated when contrasted with other regional systems,[12] its limitations remain significant nonetheless. A superficial survey of the core minority rights mechanisms across Europe turns up the following: the inclusion of minority rights within the EU accession criteria (the principle of 'conditionality'); the development by the CoE of a number of international instruments on minority rights, notably the FCNM and the European Charter for Regional and Minority Languages (ECRML); and, finally, the creation of the innovative office of the OSCE High Commissioner for National Minorities (HCNM).

The European Union and the problem of 'double standards'

A central problem identified in preceding chapters is the failure on the part of the EU to incorporate minority rights within its *acquis communautaire*, that is, within the bedrock of EU hard law. Although the Reform Treaty took some tentative first steps in that direction, only the negative duty of the state to prohibit discrimination was accorded legal weight; the requirement for positive state action contained no specific reference to minorities. Furthermore, the failure of the Treaty's predecessor, the European Constitution, is a sore reminder that signature is no guarantee of ratification.

Where minority rights have come to play a part in the framework of the EU is in the field of conditionality, that is, the criteria to which candidate states must adhere (in theory) prior to gaining membership.[13] However, while the EU has made ratification of the FCNM a condition of accession, it has failed to enforce those same standards in relation to its existing member states. To date, Belgium, France, Greece and Luxembourg – 4 of the so-called 'old' EU members – have failed to ratify the FCNM; 13 remain outside the ECRML, including established member states such as Belgium, France, Greece, Ireland, Italy and Portugal. These apparent double standards have inevitably called into question the legitimacy of making adherence to minority rights standards a condition of accession.

Perhaps unsurprisingly, this attitude on the part of the EU has led to charges of hypocrisy against existing member states which are seen to be insisting on the enforcement of standards to which they themselves do not adhere. Yet ratification itself is no panacea; often, it is coupled with provisos that limit the applicability of the treaty provisions. In the case of the FCNM, for example, Denmark, Germany and the Netherlands all included declarations designed to limit the benefits of the Charter to domestic groups of their own designation. Similarly, in the case of the ECRML, the UK failed to extend official recognition to the Cornish language. These derogations are indicative of a selective approach to minority rights that sits uncomfortably alongside declarations of full-scale, long-term commitment. If states are accorded such wide discretion, we must acknowledge the full extent to which we sacrifice the solidity of the resultant framework of minority rights.

Clearly, this is not to suggest a universal, all-or-nothing framework. The consensus politics of the European Union necessitates that its institutions be flexible in allowing states a margin of appreciation in their implementation of specific provisions. Nevertheless, the current two-tiered system, in which EU accession and candidate states are made to toe the minority rights line while established members meander back and forth across it, will prove increasingly difficult to sustain. With the accession to the EU of countries such as Hungary and Cyprus, which have large minority populations and problematic minority–majority relations, these issues have been internalized; they are no longer questions to be addressed solely via EU external policy-making but have been subsumed within Union borders. As such, their relative importance on the EU policy agenda can only increase.

The Council of Europe: hard or soft on minority rights?

Hofmann also identified the ongoing problem of the legal entrenchment of minority rights, but this time in the context of the CoE and the OSCE. He identifies three levels of 'law': the hard jurisprudence of the European Court of Human Rights (ECtHR), based on the hard law of the European Convention on Human Rights (ECHR) and the latter's Article 14 prohibition of discrimination on the grounds of association with a national minority; the soft law opinions and recommendations adopted by advisory bodies charged with monitoring implementation of the FCNM and the ECRML (themselves hard law); and the quasi-soft law of the recommendations and opinions of independent experts commissioned by the OSCE HCNM, although the latter cannot rightly be said to constitute 'law' proper.[14] However, in spite of this promising structural framework, the ECtHR has failed to capitalize on opportunities ripe for the advancement of minority rights and has consistently held back from an expansive interpretation of the ECHR's anti-discrimination provisions, the decision in the *Gorzelik* case providing a telling example.

Furthermore, while the soft law of the advisory bodies of the FCNM and the ECRML are undoubtedly important both in the context of the development of standards and in the gradual socialization of states parties to the norms contained within those instruments, it is clear that they are not capable of providing the minorities they seek to protect with an effective mechanism of legal recourse in the event of state persecution. It has been argued that the current balance between the protection of the rights of persons belonging to minorities and the protection of states' rights to territorial integrity and security sees the scales tipped very clearly in favour of the latter. This comparative weighting ignores the fact that it can be (and often is) states themselves that engage in the persecution of minorities; take, for example, the treatment of ethnic Albanians in Kosovo by the Serbian-dominated government of the Federal Republic of Yugoslavia or Russian heavy-handedness in Chechnya. In cases such as these, advisory opinions and soft law decisions provide no genuine protection to the individuals and groups of individuals who need them; the rights of minorities are violated by their very guarantor, and there is no higher authority to which they can have recourse.

Regional autonomy or the protection of culture?
The 'Article 1 – Article 27' debate

A more deeply rooted problem, and one that is undoubtedly harder to address, concerns the very nature of European minority rights. To recall,

Kymlicka develops a spectrum for assessing the content of minority rights norms: at the stronger end he places rights resembling Article 1 of the International Covenant on Civil and Political Rights, which guarantees all peoples the right to self-determination; at the weaker end he sets those rights more akin to Article 27 of the same treaty, which guarantees cultural rights to members of minority groups. By his analysis, the norms contained within the FCNM/OSCE Recommendations are reinforced Article 27-type rights aimed at the protection of minority language, education funding or effective political representation, and not weakened Article 1-type rights such as territorial and political autonomy arrangements,[15] an emphasis which echoes once again the pervasiveness of state fears for their territorial integrity and security.

Such rights, Kymlicka argues, are best suited to countries which are essentially ethnically homogenous and where any remaining groups are small, dispersed and already on the road to assimilation; as examples, he cites the Czech Republic, Slovenia and Hungary. By contrast, they are an inadequate tool for addressing situations involving large territorially concentrated groups, such as those found in Kosovo, Bosnia and Herzegovina, Croatia, Macedonia, Georgia, Azerbaijan, Moldova and Chechnya, where conflict has been rooted in demands for territorial and political autonomy, or for consociational-type power-sharing arrangements at the very least.

If Kymlicka is correct in his assertions, his conclusions undermine the argument that the current minority rights regime serves as an effective tool for guaranteeing regional security through conflict prevention. For such a policy to be effective, it must address the root causes of the dispute in question, and it is unlikely that the extension of cultural rights alone will provide sufficient redress in areas where tensions between mistrustful majorities and large geographically clustered minorities are high. The Article 1-type demands of Kosovo Albanians, for example, could never have been adequately addressed through the extension of the Article 27-type rights, no matter how expansively these were interpreted in practice. The same is true of other volatile regions such as Abkhazia or Chechnya. In this sense, the very content of existing minority rights is something that will need to be addressed in the longer term. It goes without saying, of course, that no substantive revision will be possible in the foreseeable future given the current difficulty of ensuring not only implementation of, but even *subscription* to, the softer Article 27-type norms that form the basis of regional minority rights instruments today.

Counterbalancing the 'security track'

This chapter has sought to illustrate that an approach which prioritizes the normative good of regional stability over that of the advancement and legal entrenchment of a coherent system of minority rights protection not only fails to address states' jealous protection of their territorial integrity at the expense of their minorities but, in some cases, actively exacerbates the very tensions which it sought to resolve. In the first place, the security perspective privileges a negative discourse of 'problems to be fixed', 'threats to be monitored' over a positive rights-based approach which sees vulnerable groups in need of international protection from discrimination or persecution. The formalization of negative perceptions within official policy-making can only stigmatize further an already beleaguered group. In addition, it can have the directly counterproductive effect of exacerbating tension by piquing state fears of disloyalty and secessionism, and incentivizing the use of violence by minority groups: if the state is anxious that minority groups will use the rights granted to them to threaten its territorial integrity, it might invent or exaggerate rumours of kin-state manipulation or of minority disloyalty as justification for its refusal to extend those rights; furthermore, state and international attention will be focused on more radical or violent minority groups while the problems of those that are not perceived as a threat to regional security will go ignored.[16]

For these reasons, it is essential that the current dominance of the security track within the European discourse on minority issues be complemented by a parallel emphasis on the development and enhancement of the legal foundations for the protection of minority rights. To that end, the final section of this chapter will focus on methods for achieving such an outcome.

The future of minority rights protection in Europe

The growing need to rebalance the dominance of security concerns within the regional framework of minority rights protection in favour of the legal entrenchment of minority rights has been acknowledged by scholars and practitioners alike, as a survey of preceding chapters will show. However, there is still much debate over how such change would best be effected. Three approaches can be identified (although the list is not exhaustive): the first is a wholesale reconceiving of minority rights within a broader approach to diversity and diversity management; a more moderate perspective advocates greater emphasis within the existing structural framework on the development of more advanced rights at the international and regional levels, such as rights to promote cultural development or the right to effective political participation; finally, a weaker incremental approach is premised on the expansion and strengthening of existing mechanisms.

Diversity management

The first of these represents a dramatic shift in minority rights thinking, not just away from a security-based approach to minority rights, but towards the very long-term goal of the replacement of the 'law of minority protection' with a more inclusive 'law of diversities' that both recognizes and facilitates cultural complexity within modern pluralist societies. It is argued that this would be achieved via the eradication of what is essentially a universalist framework of minority rights characterized by hierarchical arbitration and formal equality (and even substantive equality premised on pre-determined culturally relative norms) and its replacement with a pluralist inter-subjective dialogue in which diverse groups would negotiate and re-negotiate a dynamic consensus.

Palermo and Woelke argue, for example, that the problems of the current system stem not from the grounding of minority rights within the framework of security concerns but rather from the far more general problem of democracy premised on majority rule. The modern democratic state is necessarily conceived, organized and operated in accordance with the needs and interests of the majority; as such, minority rights are only ever 'conceded' as particularist exceptions to the democratic staples of egalitarianism and majoritarian rule.[17] Resolving this situation would require not a counterbalancing of the security track but the blanket replacement of the majoritarian values of the existing legal framework with the more inclusive values of multiculturalism. By this reading, international law would no longer be understood as a system for the promotion of universalist norms but as a technical instrument designed to facilitate an ongoing process of negotiation: majoritarian democracy would be supplanted by 'deliberative democracy'.[18]

However, it is clear that a reconceptualization of minority rights within the broader philosophy of diversity management would require a sea change in current thinking that is simply not foreseeable at the present time. As such, it is worth considering a more practical mechanism for the rebalancing of minority rights within the European regional framework; in other words, what is required is a solution that tackles the problem from within the existing framework of minority rights protection.

Strengthening the interlocking system of minority governance

The second approach addresses the current predominance of state security concerns in the European institutional framework through the strengthening and advancement of minority rights at the non-state levels of governance. Weller identifies four interlocking layers of minority rights regimes: that of international standard setting; that of regional rights protection; the sub-regional level, which includes 'special regimes' and bilateral treaties applicable only to certain states; and, finally, the individual nation-state, which enshrines international human rights and can interpret them either expansively or restrictively.[19] It is argued that these layers of protection are becoming increasingly intertwined and mutually reinforcing, each impacting upon the others to strengthen the overall framework and slowly advance the centre of gravity of minority protection along the rights spectrum, away from negative freedoms such as the prohibition of discrimination and towards positive rights to cultural development and political engagement.

In this scenario, not only is the predominance of national security concerns balanced by the removal of minority rights from the realm of exclusive state competence but, crucially, a progressive approach to standard setting at the international and regional levels can generate momentum for reconceiving the minority 'problem' within the broader philosophy of diversity management; in other words, it can help to shift the normative parameters from the goal of regional stability to the protection and, ultimately, the promotion of minority culture. In a sense, this approach can be regarded as the bottom-up, incrementalist counterpart to the top-down understanding of diversity management outlined above; while the latter advocates the initial construction of a new procedural framework within which minority rights can then be developed, the former argues that a new paradigm can emerge only through the promotion of more advanced rights within the existing interlocking infrastructure of minority governance.

However, this more moderate line would still necessitate a shift in current thinking along the Article 27–Article 1 spectrum of minority rights; as argued above, the failure of many states to subscribe even to weaker cultural rights suggests that such a development is unlikely to be forthcoming any time soon. In fact, preceding chapters have recognized that the security rationale is so deeply ingrained within the Western institutional psyche that short-term improvements to the protection of minority rights can realistically be attained only via the incremental enhancement and strengthening of mechanisms already in place. The final section of this conclusion will draw together these arguments and put forward three concrete proposals for reform.

The incremental approach

These proposals are as follows: in the first place, the EU should ensure that adherence to minority rights protection is no longer undertaken by member states on a voluntary basis but that the FCNM and the ECRML are incorporated fully into its *acquis propre*; second, the EU, the OSCE and the CoE should institutionalize the channels of communication already in existence and formalize a division of labour; finally, and crucially, the FCNM and the ECRML must be brought within the jurisdiction of the ECtHR, thereby providing national minorities with an essential mechanism of legal recourse in the event of persecution by the state. Although it is recognized that these changes would not address the deeper problems of minority–majority relations discussed above, they would nevertheless greatly strengthen and improve the existing framework of regional minority protection.

Incorporation of minority rights within the acquis communautaire of the EU

With regard to the EU, it is argued that anything less than the transformation of the current dispersed network of 'constitutional resources' – such as the Moraes Resolution that endeavours to 'slip the legal protection of minorities in via the back door', or Article 13 TEC on anti-discrimination provisions – into a comprehensive, legally binding minority rights policy will serve only to perpetuate the already pervasive perception of minority rights as a superfluity within the framework of the EU, an optional extra atop a hard base of 'real issues' such as economics and security. Tentative advances can be identified in the Reform Treaty. To recall, this document cites 'respect for human rights, including the rights of person belonging to minorities' among the founding principles of the EU[20] and accords legally binding status to the Charter of Fundamental Rights, which lists membership of a national minority as a prohibited ground for discrimination. However, these provisions – the one vague and the other framed in the negative – cannot be said to amount to a comprehensive policy on minority rights.

The extension of a positive obligation on states to protect their national minorities would not only resolve the current problem of perceived double standards but would also pave the way for deeper engagement in peripheral neighbourhood states with complex and unpredictable minority–majority relations. In that way, the EU would not only be able to address its stated goal of regional stability in more meaningful terms but would advance significantly (what will hopefully become) its founding value of the protection of the rights of persons belonging to minorities.

The inter-organizational trialogue

It is possible, however, that the current climate of the EU, in which minority rights remain intensely controversial, may not be ripe for the development by the EU of a holistic, rights-based framework of minority protection. Perhaps a more realistic project for the immediate future is the development and coordination of what Toggenburg refers to as the 'inter-organizational trialogue' between the EU, the Council of Europe and the OSCE. Although to date there has been a degree of cooperation in project funding, field missions and the regular exchange of information, a clear division of labour and the formalization of these networks would mark a significant step forward in streamlining the minority rights regime in Europe, so as to prevent excessive overlap between the institutions and to ensure maximum communication and efficiency. While the OSCE is perhaps best suited to an approach to minority rights oriented around its current policy of conflict prevention, the Council of Europe's strong background in human rights and its innovative formulation of the FCNM and ECRML makes it a natural candidate for the development and entrenchment of the as yet nascent legal rights track.

Bringing minority rights home

In order for such a division of labour to prove effective, however, it would be necessary to strengthen quite substantially the remit of the CoE. Ideally, this would be done by the incorporation of the FCNM and the ECRML within the jurisdiction of the ECtHR, for example via their annexation to the ECHR; at the very least, some mechanism should be created that goes beyond the purely advisory function of the current implementation mechanisms, and which provides individuals belonging to minorities with legal protection above and beyond that accorded to them by their home state. While it is accepted that the sensitive nature of minority rights necessitates the accordance to states of a margin of appreciation with regard to their implementation, history dictates that the states in question may not always have the best interests of their minorities at heart and, at worst, might be actively responsible for their persecution. The protection of human rights and of the rights of persons belonging to minorities is not something which can be guaranteed by state protection alone; if such rights are to be anything more than normative wish-lists, national minorities must have the possibility of recourse to an authority external to, and independent of, the state in which they reside.

Together, these reforms would go a long way towards cementing minority rights within an entrenched system of legal protection. Such a framework would act as a powerful complement to the security track, counterbalancing its dominance within the European institutional infrastructure and helping to guarantee the genuine and long-term international protection of minorities in the wider Europe.

Notes

1. Hereinafter, Macedonia.
2. It should be noted here that the potentially destabilizing counter-effects of an approach to minority rights premised on regional security actually makes the adherence by security-based organization to the 'security approach', as described above, an unwise one. This will be discussed presently.
3. K. Drzewicki, Chapter 6, at 155.
4. W. Kymlicka, Chapter 1, at 27.
5. To date, the OSCE has developed a host of non-binding standards on a range of subjects of relevance to national minorities, including: the Hague Recommendations 1996 on education rights, the Oslo Recommendations 1998 on linguistic rights, the Lund Recommendations 1999 and the Warsaw Guidelines of 19?? on the rights to effective participation, and the 2003 Guidelines on the Use of Minority Languages in the Broadcast Media.
6. Kymlicka, *supra* note 4, at 26.
7. The second pillar of the EU, its Common Foreign and Security Policy, continues to be dominated almost entirely by unanimity voting; in this area, therefore, it remains essentially an international organ and not a genuinely supranational one. As such, its powers in relation to security issues are far more limited than those relating to other areas within its jurisdiction, notably economic integration.
8. Article I-3 Treaty of Lisbon amending the Treaty on European Union and the Treaty Establishing the European Community (hereinafter, Reform Treaty), inserting Article 1a TEU.

9. Article I-8, amending Article I-6 EC, by which the Charter of Fundamental Rights is recognized as having 'the same legal value as the Treaties'.
10. See H.J. Heintze, Chapter 2, at 48.
11. Kymlicka, *supra* note 4, at 27.
12. For a comprehensive comparison of the different regional systems of minority rights protection, see M. Weller (ed.), *Universal Minority Rights: A Commentary on the Jurisprudence of International Courts and Treaty Bodies* (Oxford: Oxford University Press, 2007).
13. The Copenhagen criteria, elaborated at the meeting of the European Council in Copenhagen in 1993, list 'respect for and protection of minorities' as a condition of accession. Conclusions of the Presidency. 21–22 June.
14. R. Hofmann, Chapter 7, at 177.
15. Kymlicka, *supra* note 4, at 16–17.
16. For evidence of this, see Kymlicka's discussion on the OSCE's varying support for autonomy claims, *supra* note 4.
17. F. Palermo and J. Woelke, 'From Minority Protection to a Law of Diversity? Reflections on the Evolution of Minority Rights', *European Yearbook of Minority Issues* 3 (2003/2004) (Flensburg: European Centre for Minority Issues, 2005), 5–13.
18. T.H. Malloy, 'Towards a New Paradigm of Minority Law-Making: A Rejoinder to Palermo and Woelke's Law of Diversity', *European Yearbook of Minority Issues* 4 (2004/5) (Flensburg: European Centre for Minority Issues, 2006), 5–28, at 18. Malloy advances Palermo and Woelke's conception of diversity management through a comprehensive critique of the 'deliberative' model of democracy, the scope of which falls outside the parameters of this discussion.
19. M. Weller, 'Towards an Integrated System of Diversity Management in Europe', in J. Kühl and M. Weller (eds), *Minority Policy in Action* (Flensburg, Germany: European Centre for Minority Issues and the Department of Border Region Studies, 2005).
20. Article 1a of the Reform Treaty.

Index